English for Business

Related titles in the series

Business French
Business German
Business Italian
Commerce
English
French
Follow up French
German
Italian
Latin
Office Procedures
Russian
Spanish

Also available

Business French audio cassettes
Business French book/audio cassette pack
Business German audio cassettes
Business German book/audio cassette pack
Business Italian audio cassettes
Business Italian book/audio cassette pack
Follow up French audio cassette

English for Business

David Whitehead MA, BEd.
and
Geoffrey Whitehead BSc.(Econ.)

MADE SIMPLE
BOOKS

Made Simple
An imprint of Butterworth-Heinemann Ltd
Linacre House, Jordan Hill, Oxford OX2 8DP

Ⓡ A member of the Reed Elsevier group

OXFORD   LONDON   BOSTON
MUNICH   NEW DELHI   SINGAPORE   SYDNEY
TOKYO   TORONTO   WELLINGTON

First published 1993

British Library Cataloguing in Publication Data
Whitehead, David
   English for Business. – (Made Simple Books)
   I. Title   II. Whitehead, Geoffrey
   III. Series
   428

ISBN 0 7506 0644 4

Printed and bound in Great Britain by Clays, St Ives plc

Contents

Preface

This book provides a sound background in English as used in the business environment. It will be of most use to the following groups of students: (a) Young students with a practical, rather than literary, frame of mind who view English as a tool for communication in the everyday affairs of mankind, and wish to master these aspects of the subject, (b) more mature students taking a wide variety of business-orientated courses who are chiefly interested in mastering their specialist subjects but wish to keep their command of English ticking over, and to apply it to their specialist studies as much as possible, (c) middle management and supervisory staff who are moving up the ladder of promotion into administrative and executive fields, and who wish to revise their knowledge of English and its use in business communication, and (d) overseas students with a sound grounding in English who wish to apply their English skills in the field of business communication.

The book embodies a good deal of experience in the schools and further education fields, and contains a wealth of exercises.

In writing this book we have received much help from organizations and individuals who have made suggestions and provided artwork for use in the text. Their courtesy is acknowledged elsewhere in the book, but we should like to express our thanks for their unfailing courtesy.

All the names used in exercises are entirely imaginary, and do not relate to real firms or institutions. If we have inadvertently used a name that is in fact the registered name of a real company, or a firm, we must apologize for the coincidence.

We should particularly like to thank Doug Fox and Jacquie Shanahan of Butterworth-Heinemann for their help (and forbearance) in the course of preparation of this title.

David Whitehead
Geoffrey Whitehead

Acknowledgements

The authors acknowledge gratefully the help of the following organizations in providing illustrations, specimen letters and text material for use in this book.

Butterworth-Heinemann Ltd
Cambridge University Centre
Economist, The
Evrite Ltd
Finance and Development
Formecon Services Ltd
Her Majesty's Treasury Bulletin
Inland Revenue Department
Joynson Educational Mailings
OECD Observer
John Murray (Publishers) Ltd
Oxford University Press
Pitman Publishing Ltd
Twinlock Ltd
George Vyner Ltd
Which? Magazine

How to use this book

There are various ways in which this book can be used. It depends on who you are. Since the book assumes a reasonable knowledge of English, presumably everyone would be able to open the book anywhere and read whatever section he/she had turned to and get some benefit from it. The book is, however, really aimed at four main groups:

1 *Young people (14–17 years old)* who are not very good at English from the literary point of view, but anxious to do sufficiently well at English to take a routine business job and gradually make their way in the world. Please read Section 1 below.
2 *Young people (16–18 years old)* who have already passed a 'first' English exam, such as GCSE, but are moving over from academic studies to business studies. Please read Section 2 below.
3 *Young people (18–22 years old)* who have done well in English in their ordinary education, e.g. they have GCSE English, possibly use of English (at OA Level) and perhaps A Level English too. If such people are moving on to take professional level courses in such areas as accountancy, banking, transport, freight forwarding, marketing, insurance, etc., they should read Section 3 below.
4 *Mature students* who are working in middle management posts and wish to improve their use of English both in their everyday working lives, but also as a means of passing professional examinations in order to secure full professional qualifications. Please read Section 4 below.

Section 1 Young people 14–17 years old

Presumably you will be working in some sort of classroom and will be directed by a teacher or lecturer as to which parts of the book to study. If this is not the case, and you are using the book largely on your own, the following bits of advice may help:

(a) Chapter 1 is a useful general introduction, which is well worth reading. It tells you why English is important and how to get organized so you study well and build up a good collection of notes and pieces of work done. It has no exercises – the exercise for Chapter 1 is to get the things you need to be properly organized for your course.

(b) All the other chapters have a main subject area, which is fully explained, and with exercises to give you practice. Do these exercises – not just the ones you are told to do, but all the lot if you have time. Don't worry about who is going to mark them. You are! At the end you are going to read each exercise through and appraise it. Have you said all you could have said? Are you clear in your own mind what it was all about?

(c) After the main subject area each chapter has a number of sections such as a vocabulary section, a spelling section, etc. These are all topics that need more than a single chapter; they need repeated practice exercises. They can be taken as a separate activity unrelated to the chapter in which they appear.

(d) If you are not being guided by a teacher or lecturer, work steadily through the book and keep at it. If you find a particular difficulty with some part of the work, don't worry about it. Make a note of the pages you need to return to later and go on to the next section. As you gradually improve your vocabulary, you will find that what seemed difficult a month or so ago is now quite straightforward.

Before you come to the end of your course, or your period of self-study, get hold of copies of past exam papers and give yourself a few practice examinations, taking exactly the time allowed. Put your effort away for 24 hours and then mark it, giving yourself what you think is a fair mark. If you finish up with more than 50 per cent, and you're sure you weren't being too generous, then you will probably pass the real exam. In the meantime go over the areas in which you didn't do too well and, using the index of the book to find the right place, brush up on your knowledge of these weak points.

Section 2   Young people 16–18 years old

Those who have decided to read this section are almost certainly on business studies courses of various types. You will already have a reasonable background in the English language, and will chiefly wish to keep your English ticking over and of good quality as you move towards a career in business. The book is designed to meet your needs exactly, chiefly by building your background in vocabulary work, spelling and all the routine aspects of English as it is used practically in everyday business activities. You should take an interest in all aspects of business, including economics, finance, marketing, insurance, communications, documentation, accounts and the legal aspects of business. This will make it easier for you to read about, speak about and write about the everyday business affairs. It will help you at the end of your course in interviews for employment, and of course in the real world of employment once you get your foot in the door.

You will of course be guided by teaching/lecturing staff as you go through the book, but there are many interruptions in college life and there will be many occasions when you wish you had something to do. Be your own taskmaster on such occasions − the business world needs self-starters, not people who sit around waiting to be told what to do. The book is full of exercises that will help you in your studies. In a dead moment open the book at random and do the first exercise you come to. Get hold of past examination papers and try the questions in them. File the answers you write and read them through just before the examinations at the end of your course.

Section 3   Young people 18−22 years old embarking on professional examinations

The most desirable status for those already embarked upon business careers is full professional qualification in the profession or discipline they have selected. Most professional bodies have an entry require-ment (usually the minimum level for admission is GCSE level in about four subjects). However, the first year's study usually includes a course in Business English (or it may be called Business Communi-cation). This book has been written to cover most of the syllabuses produced by the professional bodies, so you should have no difficulty benefiting from the use of this book.

Many people study for professional examinations privately, using correspondence colleges. Others manage to find dedicated courses, i.e. courses aimed specifically at the professional body's examinations, at their local technical college or college of further education. Whether you have a lecturer or a correspondence college guiding you towards your goal or not, it is advisable to work steadily through the book, trying all the exercises − whether there is anyone to mark them or not. Appraise them yourself − that is what we have to do in real life when we write a report, send a letter or submit an opinion. The key questions are 'Have I said what I wanted to say?', 'Have I made it clear?', 'Did I leave out anything that I should have included?', 'Have I exhausted the possibilities of the question?' Sometimes students deal with one point in great detail but leave out four more that were just as important. If you only give 20 per cent of the answer, you can only get a mark of 20 per cent or less − which won't get you through the examination.

Section 4   Mature students

Many people who are well qualified technically, and in other ways, find that on promotion to lower- and middle-management posts they have to start dealing with administrative and other problems for which they need a good command of English Language. What they need is a rapid revision course in the use of English for business purposes. This book will be very helpful for such people, offering a wide range of topics and a large number of exercises that will give practice in sentence formation, paragraphing, report writing, etc. You may of course prefer to work straight through the book, revising chapter by chapter. You may prefer to use the index, looking up areas of work you have some difficulty with and turning to the examples and exercises about the particular topic. If it is your own book, don't hesitate to mark the book to remind yourself what parts you have revised, e.g. by drawing a ring in the index around the page numbers you have already revised.

Middle-management staff, however weak their academic background, should not hesitate to take student membership of an appropriate professional body and work to acquire full professional qualifications. Institutes frequently have links with technical colleges, university departments, etc., where their courses can be studied, while they may have established correspondence courses to help student members. There is no need to hold back because your educational background is weak. Books like the *Made Simple* series are specially written to help people studying on their own. This book, for example will help you pass the English or Business Communication part of almost any first-year professional level course. Within about 4 years almost everyone who has experience in an industry can acquire the necessary qualifications to work towards a leading position both in his/her firm and in the industry. After that it is a question of taking opportunities as they arise to broaden experience and enlarge your understanding of the profession and its problems.

1
An introduction to business English

1.1 The importance of English in business

When Julius Caesar invaded Britain in 55 BC there was no English. The language was introduced to the British Isles by the various Anglo-Saxon invaders who arrived in the centuries following the departure of the Romans in 410 AD. When Shakespeare was writing his plays, 1,200 years later, barely 5 million people spoke English, and those who did not included many inhabitants of the islands now called the United Kingdom. There was still a Cornish language then, and Welsh and Gaelic were more widely spoken than they are today. The change 400 years later is remarkable. Almost 1 billion people speak English, either as their natural tongue or as their main language for everyday life, and many millions more use it as the everyday language of business. Eighty per cent of the words stored in computer data banks are English words, 75 per cent of the world's correspondence is in English, and half the world's learned magazines and scientific and technical publications are in English. Other countries have adopted English words – the French have their Franglais like *le-car* and *le-snaque-barre*, the Japanese have Japlish and the Russians have Russlish.

This supremacy of English developed originally from the planting of colonies around the world by the British, and particularly in the United States of America. It was a supremacy based upon government and empire. Not many people recall today the period of almost 100 years of the Pax Brittanica, when Britain kept the peace of the world; many perhaps prefer to forget it. Its most enduring legacy today is the worldwide system of trade and business activity; for 'trade follows the flag' was for two centuries the common cry of imperialists and emigrants alike. When the British finally surrendered the mantle of imperialism, another English-speaking nation, the United States of America, was ready to take up leadership of the world. Although only about 7 per cent of Americans are now directly descended from the English, the natural tongue of all United States citizens is English. The supremacy of United States business, particularly in the years between the wars (1918–39) and directly after the Second World War, continued English as the most important language in the world, and much the most important language of business.

That other nations can leapfrog into business prominence by adopting new technologies is a commonplace of history. The French and Germans adopted Britain's industrial development and leap-frogged ahead past an iron-based economy using water power and steam into one based on electricity and a wider variety of metals.

Today the newly industrialized countries (NICs) of Asia have repeated the process into an electronic era, but they have done it using English as a business language. In countries like Singapore far-sighted leadership has particularly encouraged English as the language for high-school students, giving the country a solid basis for communication with the business world. It is a policy that has much to recommend it. Many French-speaking African countries have adopted a bilingual approach, giving equal prominence to English and the French they learned in their colonial days. By contrast, the African countries that moved into the sphere of Russian influence have lost some of their ability to make progress in economic activity as they have lost their link with the English language that the business world increasingly uses.

While the rest of the world is making progress in English, standards of English have perhaps fallen in the United Kingdom, when viewed against the business activity of the nation. Lower and middle management have serious weaknesses in their command of English. The authors of this book asked some major and growing firms for examples of their business correspondence, but received more apologies than offers of help. The replies usually included some account of the problems the firms were experiencing in getting good staff (such as technicians and sales representatives) to write good business letters. It is hoped that this book will be helpful in raising the standards of such staff.

To conclude, then, business English is an important subject in its own right. We all know that English literature has much to offer to the world. Few nations have a William Shakespeare or a Charles Dickens, or even an Agatha Christie, to offer to their fellow men. Their works are great achievements for any nation, but they pall into insignificance besides the part played by English in world production, trade and communication. In life economics is king, and everything else, literature, music, art and education, is only made possible by the business activity in the economic life of the world. It is to advance the grasp of English by young business students that we have written this book. How do we propose to set about it?

1.2   Approaching the study of business English

Mastering business English is not the work of a single day, and we all have different starting points and different backgrounds to our ability to speak and write in English. There are, however, some main threads to the subject to which we should all give some attention, and students who know they are weak in a particular aspect will naturally acknowledge this weakness and make every effort to solve their problems.

If therefore you feel a particular part of this book is fully understood by you and can be taken for granted, than skip it and go on to the next section. If you feel at the end of any section that you still need further practice in the subject area, seek similar sections in other texts, or make up your own exercises it the same style. Sometimes one can learn a great deal by inventing exercises and, having invented them, setting them aside for a week or two before coming back to them and attempting the answers. Do not worry about getting such work marked.

In business life we are constantly facing situations where we have to make up our own minds. New legislation appears and we have to read it, think about it, decide what to do to comply with the regulations and put the necessary measures in hand. We cannot have everything we do in life marked by someone. You can appraise your own efforts just as well as, and perhaps even more critically than, an overworked teacher or lecturer.

The chief 'subject areas' in the study of business English are:

- Reading and comprehension (understanding what we have read).
- Vocabulary (building our database of English words we know and can use correctly).
- Grammar and syntax (the art and science of fitting the words of a language together so as to enhance both spoken conversation and written correspondence by ensuring that the rules for that language have been correctly followed).
- Practical applications of the language in a variety of business situations, correspondence, reports, telecommunications, public-address situations, etc.
- The use of non-language aids to enhance the written words − graphics, statistics, etc.

It is easy to list such subject areas in a few lines. It is another thing to master them by patient, detailed and endless application. A few words about each may be helpful.

1.3   Reading and comprehension

We are studying business English because we wish to use English in business situations, either in our everyday business life or when we take employment at the end of an educational course. We either know already, or have some vague idea of, the business area that interests us most − the career we hope to follow. It follows that our studies will be pursued most enthusiastically, and will be of the most enduring advantage, if we relate them fairly closely to our key interests. Nowhere is this more important than in our everyday reading. The student of business English should read as much as possible about business. Do not read the sports page, or the travel and recreation pages, or even the literary section of your Sunday paper until you have read the business section.

In the business section you will find news stories, articles and commentaries that will push forward the frontiers of your knowledge of business matters. Your vocabulary will improve and so will your ability to discuss business situations knowledgeably and using the correct terminology. At the same time do not be too narrow. The actuarial student or the prospective accountant would not find enough material about these fairly narrow subjects to occupy him/her full time. One needs a wide background in economics, law, transport and distribution, politics and government to do well in any business. Become a 'journal snipper'. Cut out articles that you think will make a good read and put them in your briefcase. Get them out when you have coffee, or a 'dead' period in a lecture or class. While others are wasting their time, you will be in contact with a lively mind pursuing some enterprise or activity that widens your horizons.

The best things to read might include the following:

1   *The professional magazine of your chosen profession.* If you are a student of law, accountancy, freight forwarding or any one of 100 other important professions, there will be a magazine for you. Read it from cover to cover.
2   *The Economist.* One of the very best journals for business students to read, not only does *The Economist* cover all aspects of political and economic life in the United Kingdom and the European Community, but it gives a worldwide coverage of economic and business developments that is an endless source of interest and information. It reviews many aspects of the world we live in on a regular basis, e.g. its scientific coverage is wide, well-written and very detailed. Almost every industry is appraised from time to time, with particularly regular and detailed appraisal of financial sector developments. Regular supplements feature such industries as travel and tourism, agriculture and electronics, and its special features for students explain the nuts and bolts of economics, finance, industrial relations, ecology, etc. It offers special rates

for students and lecturers. Enquiries should be addressed to the Circulation Department, 25 Ryder St, London SW1A 1HG, or overseas students should write to the International Subscription Fulfilment Service, *The Economist*, PO Box 14, Harold Hill, Romford, RM3 8EQ, England.

3 *Freebie magazines* (ones given away to interested people and paid for by advertising) are available in some professions. You will probably know if one exists for your profession, since most of the jobs available are advertised in this type of magazine. Order your copy now. They are always on the lookout for more readers.

4 Many business English students are already fully qualified, and have served a number of years in their chosen professions. It is promotion to middle management that has pinpointed their weaknesses in English, and led them to worry about it. Such people should keep reading their own technical subject, whatever it is, because it is in that field that they have to conduct their business affairs and have to hold their own at meetings and in correspondence. Don't get out of date on your own field of expertise; on the contrary, reinforce your knowledge by reading everything you can about it.

5 Finally, keep as rounded a personality as possible by reading about politics, science, literature, art and other subjects that enable one to play a sociable part in business life. Much of the work of top management is concerned with meeting people, entertaining, etc. *The Economist* is very good at keeping one up to date on such matters, and there are other magazines one should read if possible. The American magazine *Time* gives an American view of world affairs, *National Geographic* reminds us there is a multi-ethnic world out there, and *Scientific American* keeps us in touch with both the microcosm and the macrocosm. If you don't know what those words mean look them up in a dictionary now!

1.4 Vocabulary

Many students of business English worry, quite rightly, about their vocabulary. English has 500,000 words in common use and another 500,000 specialist technical words (often called jargon) that are not in the ordinary dictionaries. This compares with an estimated 180,000 words in the German language and 100,000 words only in French. Many young people who reach lower-management level and middle-management level find that they are poor communicators because they do not know the words to use. Even worse, they don't fully understand what is being said to them.

Any middle-management role largely consists of conveying the views of top management to departments and relaying back the reactions of ordinary working people to the board. Consequently a weakness in understanding the board's views means an inadequate explanation to lower-level staff, and even if the supervisor understands the reaction of lower ranks, a poor vocabulary make it difficult to convey them to top management.

Students should start to build their vocabularies on Day 1 of their courses, and it is a procedure that should continue even after the courses are finished.

A useful birthday or Christmas present to ask for is a notebook that is indexed from A-Z. They are usually called 'address books'. If you use them to record new words as you come across them, or as they are said to you, you can build your vocabulary in a very useful way. Once the word has been recorded, use a dictionary to find out its meaning. You may find several meanings, but you will be able to sort out which one of them fits the sense in which you encountered the word.

Such a book also keeps you up to date with acronyms. We all know what UNO, WHO, or UNESCO are, but new acronyms appear every day. They are part of the jargon of the modern world. Do you know what JIT means? The JIT concept (it stands for just-in-time) is a whole philosophy in itself. It argues that businesses should arrange their affairs so that they get everything 'just-in-time'. If we need an electronic component, get Cathay Pacific to fly a supply in from Hong Kong the day before it is needed. It saves building warehouses, having storekeepers, tying up capital in components we don't want, having to pay invoices before we really need to, etc. Keep up with your acronyms! And don't disparage 'jargon'! **Jargon is the shorthand of expertise**. If a manufacturer understands JIT, and if he/she knows how to put it into practice, and can explain it to colleagues, suppliers and customers, the business will prosper. JIT lowers costs and raises the return on capital invested. On such bits of 'jargon' are prosperous economies built!

1.5   Grammar and syntax

There has been a revolution in English grammar in the twentieth century, and the 'traditional grammar' is considered obsolete, though the facts of proper English usage are enduring. The parts of speech – nouns, verbs, etc. – and the ways of stringing them together cannot change very much.

English grammar is largely a matter of sentence construction. We put sentences together to make statements that inform our readers or our audiences. It obviously must help if we have a sound background of general rules for sentence construction, and if we can unhesitatingly distinguish the various parts of sentences, and check that we have the various parts in agreement with one another. This is syntax, the art of correct sentence construction. If we say 'Laws is promulgated by central government' and don't appreciate that 'laws' is a plural noun and 'is' is a singular verb, everyone who listens to us will notice the weakness − even those who can't put their own finger on what is wrong with the sentence.

On the other hand, grammar is a vast collection of facts that cannot be studied intensively for long periods. Little and often is probably the best way to make progress. In this book there are regular sections dealing with the various aspects of grammar, with numerous examples drawn from business contexts.

1.6 Applied business English

This is the simplest part of our course, because it is all within the covers of this book. We cannot of course cover every situation where English is used, in every industry, but we have covered most of the activities and given you the chance to practise them. English is not a theoretical subject, it is a practical subject. You have to be able to write letters, postcards, telegrams, minutes, reports. You have to be able to speak lucidly in everyday business conversation in the workplace, over the telephone, over the public address system, to the television camera, etc. Practice makes perfect. 'Reading maketh a full man, conference a ready man and writing an exact man', said one philosopher. Again, don't worry about who is going to 'mark' your work. You are! No teacher or lecturer can possibly keep up with a classful of students who are all working as hard as they can. The amount you can submit for assessment has to be limited, but if you are wise, you will do every exercise in this book.

1.7 Visual aids, etc.

On an educational course you no doubt have many subjects, and all of them have coursework and projects to be completed. Many of these activities will call for the use of your business English and may be regarded as an extension of your business English course. They will need to be lightened by illustrations, tables of data, charts and diagrams. If you are studying statistics (and you should be), you will find the subject adequately covered on your statistics course. For those that might otherwise miss this useful set of skills we have included a brief chapter showing the major types of illustration that can clarify or lighten a report. By 'lighten' we do not mean 'trivialize'. It is not necessary to use a cartoon style illustration in serious reports. What we need to do is to relieve the eyes' tedium as they cross endless pages of concentrated text, by putting at least some of the material we are trying to convey into other forms: tables, diagrams, graphs, charts, etc. In this way the reader breaks off the reading to study the chart and its notes. He/she has, at the same time, the chance to reflect on what has been said, to let it go deeper into his/her brain and be fully assimilated. Then back to the main text for the next important section of the thesis.

1.8   Lever arch files

Many students find it difficult to keep their coursework, notes, etc., in good order. This is because they use ring binders for their looseleaf work rather than lever arch files (see Figure 1.1). A lever arch file gives a much better working arrangement. It is deep enough — about 6 cms — to keep all your records in the one file. It is possible to buy or make index sheets (old brown A4 envelopes are ideal for the purpose) so you keep different sections of your work separate, and you can open your records at any point you like by using the lever provided, to insert a new piece of work or extract notes or exercises you have to submit. You need a two-hole punch (very inexpensive) so that any article you see in a magazine but haven't time to read at the moment can be filed away ready for the odd 'dead' moment in class, or the coffee break. You will be much better organized with a lever arch file.

If you need one for each subject of your course keep them at home, and have one file for daily use with sub-divisions for each subject. Each night when you settle down to study you put the day's

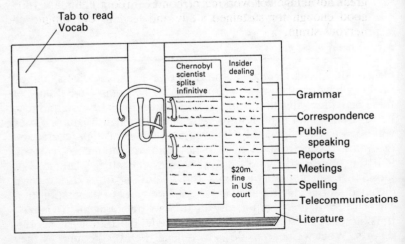

Figure 1.1   A lever arch file for business English

work into your subject files before you start, thus giving yourself a chance to reappraise your records, throwing away any obsolete or rough work and updating your permanent records.

To conclude, it takes a great deal of time to develop a full knowledge of business English, let alone a literary style of your own. Don't postpone getting down to the task. You can't do everything in the 6 weeks before an exam. Start right away to study this text and in all your written work, for whatever subject, remember that English is the handmaiden of business. Whatever you are studying, you want to be fluent in expressing yourself about it, precise in your conclusions, knowledgeable about its vocabulary and lucid in your explanations. The authors wish you every success in your studies, and trust that you will find this book some help in securing the advancement you are seeking.

1.9 Summary of Chapter 1

1 Business English is the language of the international business world. It is ordinary English, related particularly to business use.
2 Fluent business English requires us to have a wide vocabulary of general English words, and also the specialist vocabulary of the particular business activity (trade, transport, distribution, finance, insurance, law, etc.) in which we propose to specialize.
3 Progress can only be achieved by regular, steady reading and written work to acquire the knowledge, vocabulary, skill and fluency that are essential to success.
4 The essential tools include a lever arch file and a two-hole punch to punch all papers, articles, written work, etc. A desk lamp is a great advantage for working at home − room lights are rarely good enough for sustained study and lead to eye fatigue and nervous strain.

2
The parts of speech

2.1 Business communication

The whole purpose of business English, as with any language, is to communicate with our business partners at home and (provided they speak English) abroad. Language developed to assist communication, and was originally purely oral – we communicated by word of mouth. Later written language developed and written communication became very important because it enabled us to 'speak' to people who were far away. Today, thanks to the telephone, we can have long-distance oral communication as well.

Figure 2.1 shows a chart of business communication, divided into two parts – oral and written – and each of those parts is further sub-divided into two parts – communication with individuals and mass media methods of communication. The notes below Figure 2.1 explain some of the important features of the chart. Study the figure and the notes carefully now.

2.2 Importance of the parts of speech in communication

If we wish to communicate with others, we must do so with words that form coherent sentences. Although there are more than 500,000 words in the English language there are only eight different types of word. These are called the 'parts of speech'. The eight parts of speech are:

(a) Nouns, pronouns and adjectives.
(b) Verbs and adverbs.
(c) Conjunctions, prepositions and interjections.

Many students will be aware of these eight parts of speech, but it is important to be absolutely familiar with them, for they are constantly referred to in any English course and it is essential to be able to recognize them. Some brief definitions are given below, and more detailed accounts of the various types of noun, verb, etc., are given later.

Nouns: nouns are the names of persons, places or things – John, book, television set, Africa, etc.

Pronouns: words that can be used in place of nouns – he, she, it, we, they, etc.

Adjectives: words that describe nouns – *interesting* book, *clever* Peter, *frozen* Antarctica.

Verbs: these are often called 'doing' words – they tell us what the person, place or thing is doing. More strictly we should say that verbs are words that enable us to make a statement about some person, place or thing that is the subject of the sentence. In other words, they enable us to predicate (say something about a person, place or thing). Examples are run, walk, talk, discuss, etc.

Adverbs: words that describe verbs, telling us how the action is being performed. For example, run *quickly*, talk *animatedly*, stroll *slowly*. Many adverbs end in the letters 'ly'.

Conjunctions: joining words, used to link together parts of a sentence. Mary *and* John walked quickly. We could dine at the Peking Restaurant *or* at the hotel.

Prepositions: words which convey a relationship in space between one thing and another. Thus, the flowers were *in* the vase. The umpire stood *behind* the wicket.

Interjections: natural expressions inserted with some force into a sentence. Some children's comics are full of interjections, '*Oh*, I wouldn't agree there'. In comics we have, '*Wow*, Batman has saved them!'

Note that many words can be designated as nouns, verbs, etc., according to the use that is made of them in a sentence, or passage. The word 'fire' for example can be noun, a verb or an adjective, according to the use made of it. Consider the three sentences below:

1 The fire burned with an intensity undreamed of by the simple peasantry.
2 We fire indiscriminately, fearful of the hidden enemy.
3 The fire officer took control, selecting personnel to deal with particular areas of the conflagration.

In the first sentence the word 'fire' is a noun, naming something. In the second it is a verb, expressing an action of the troops. In the third it is an adjective, and is said to modify (describe or limit) the noun 'officer'.

Exercises in this book

This book contains many exercises. For convenience, the answers to the exercises are given at the end of each chapter, where they are

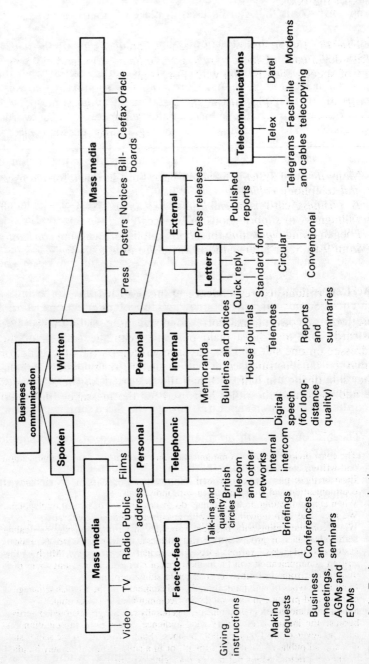

Figure 2.1 Business communication

more accessible for the reader than a separate answer section at the back of the book.

Exercise 2a In the following sentences some words are in *italics*. Write down each of these words, in columnar form, and say which part of speech each is, and why. For example:

Word	Part of speech	Reason
fire	noun	the name of something

1 Many *items* of *systems furniture* have built-in ducts for *electrical and* telephone *cables*.
2 A *business* card *is* a *small* but *permanent* reminder of *your* willingness to *supply* goods *or* services.
3 *I* began doing *typesetting* for a *book* publisher, working *constantly* from 9 to 5, or later *if* there was a *deadline* to *beat*.

2.3 Conventional correspondence − the postcard

One form of conventional correspondence used in business is the postcard. This may be a plain postcard, with the address of the addressee on one side and the message written on the other side, or it may be an illustrated card, with a picture on one side and the other side divided in half, with half the side used for the address of the addressee and the other half used for the message. Illustrated

Notes
(i)   The chart divides business communication into two parts − oral communication and written communication.
(ii) Each of these parts is then divided into two parts − mass media methods of communication and communication with individuals.
(iii) When communicating orally, we may do so face to face or over the telephone. We may deal with individuals or with groups at briefings, conferences, etc.
(iv) When communicating with business associates in writing, we may be dealing with individuals or groups within the business, or with outsiders (suppliers, customers, officials of various sorts, professional advisers, etc.). Much of this written communication will be in the form of correspondence, but some of it may be electronic in form, e.g. telex or facsimile copying.
(v)   In all these types of communication a good command of the English language is helpful, and practice in each method of communication is essential.
(vi) Mass media methods of communication generally call for professional expertise, because the impact is on a very wide audience, and a poor presentation can have an adverse effect on the whole business. Such work falls to the senior staff in a special public relations department, or in a small firm it is usually handled by the proprietor, senior partner or managing director.

cards are rarely used in business, but at least one United Kingdom firm uses postcards that show illustrations of its passenger ferries on one side.

Postcards are liable to be read by anyone, not only by postal staff anywhere along the way, but by anyone in the destination building. It is therefore inappropriate to use postcards for personal messages or anything of a confidential nature. It has been held in the English courts that to send a defamatory remark on a postcard is 'publication' of the defamatory remark, entitling the person defamed to sue for libel, since the presumption in law is that postcards are sure to be read by someone along the way.

We therefore tend to keep postcards for impersonal messages, which anyone may read, e.g. changes of address, changes of telephone number, promotional material of various sorts, notification of business visits by commercial travellers or other representatives, etc. The postcard is particularly useful in one respect: it is only a second's work to push a pin through it to fix it on a notice-board. Thus a change of address, or a change of telephone number, might be pinned on a notice-board for a month or two if we telephone or write frequently to the firm concerned. When we have fully assimilated the new information, it will be discarded in favour of more recent items.

On the promotional side, one popular use of postcards is in bulk joint mailings. Each participant in the joint mailing is allowed one card, to their own design. One side carries a description of their product and a request for literature or a demonstration of the product. The other side bears a reply-paid address to the firm's head office. Twenty or so such cards in a polythene wrapper are sent as a single postal package, making an economical mailing. Some address lists for such mailings can be enormous − 250,000 addresses are not uncommon − but the resulting flood of responses calls for a highly efficient sales department to cope with the results.

The rules for writing such correspondence are as follows:

(a)   Keep the message as a brief as possible, but make sure you include all that the addressee needs to know.

(b)   Feature the important facts − addresses, telephone numbers, etc. − in clear type, unobscured by fancy decoration.

(c)   If it is necessary to alert more than one department in a firm, either mail each department separately or feature a 'circulation list' in one corner of the card.

Figures 2.2 and 2.3 show typical business postcards, while Figure 2.4 shows a 'circulation slip'.

Exercise 2b   In each of the cases below you are asked to design a

John Stevens & Partners

Please note that we are moving to larger premises on 19 December. Our new address is

27 St James Parade,
Cambridge
CB4 1PQ

Our telephone number is unchanged

0223 635656

Figure 2.2 A 'change of address' printed postcard

We are pleased to announce that Formecon is now a **BS 5750: Part 1 Registered Firm** with BSI Quality Assurance.

As a valued customer, you are aware that we specialise in a unique range of documentation designed to ensure control within many areas of business.

We trust that we can continue to be of service and assure you that we will maintain our policy of innovation and development of both our product range and our commitment to customer service.

November 19..

Publishers for Commerce, Industry and the Professions

BS 5750

Certificate No. FM13852

FORMECON SERVICES LIMITED
Gateway, Crewe, Cheshire, CW1 1YN
Telephone: 0270 500800
Fax: 0270 500505   DX: 20163 Crewe

Figure 2.3 A promotional postcard (*courtesy of Formecon Services Ltd*)

business postcard that will meet the needs of the firm concerned. Invent such additional features as you feel are necessary.

(a) Thomas Glyn & Co of 23 Back Walk, Huddersfield, HD7 1BR announces the closure of its works for a period of 2 weeks for the annual holiday from 7 August to 21 August. An emergency telephone number is given at 0484 86 171717.

(b) Larkins PLC of Airport Road, Changi, Singapore announces

Circulation slip!	
Please circulate this change of address to all necessary departments. Tick and pass on	
Purchasing officer	
Accounts dept.	
Factory manager	
Others 1	
2	

Figure 2.4   A circulation slip

the opening of its new showrooms at 2474 Airport Complex, Changi. The company invites all interested in air-passenger and air-freight movements to visit the showrooms.

(c)   Author, who has had difficulties in the past dealing with his publishers, wishes to notify all departments at each publisher (but particularly the editorial and royalty departments) about his change of address. Design a postcard, with a circulation slip, inventing any details you require (address, telephone number, etc.).

(d)   Design a postcard for Coastal Traffic PLC promoting its shipping services to and from Norway, Denmark, Holland, Belgium and France. Mention the major ports the services visit, the types of cargo they handle (which includes roll-on, roll-off and lift-on, lift-off traffic), the company's address, telephone number and fax number; and invite customers old and new to call Ralph Bugg for a discussion of their requirements.

2.4   More about nouns

It is helpful to know the following facts about nouns.

They can be common nouns or proper nouns

A common noun is a general name, common to many things. A proper noun is a particular name, unique to one individual or thing.

Proper nouns are always given a capital letter. (*Note*: there is a popular misconception that the word 'capital letter' has something to do with capitalism. As a result, those who disapprove of capitalism often do not give capital letters to proper nouns. You will notice this on many lists of credits for films and television programmes. This is sheer ignorance really. Capital letters were used in Ancient Rome 2000 years before capitalism developed.)

Common nouns	*Proper nouns*
ship	The *Titanic*
country	Malaya
mountain	Aconcagua
book	Little Dorrit
official	Director General of Fair Trading

Exercise 2c   Rewrite the following poem, giving capital letters to all the proper nouns, and underlining all the common nouns:

columbus sailed for ferdinand and found the spanish main;
sir frances drake sailed round the world and safely home again;
montgolfier the frenchman was the first in a balloon;
But anders, lovell and borman first made rings around the moon.

walter raleigh from virginia brought us home tobacco brown;
pizarro from peru sent back pure gold to seville town;
mendana from brazil first proved elastic rubber's worth;
But armstrong and buzz aldrin brought the moon rocks back
to earth

They can be concrete nouns or abstract nouns

Concrete nouns are the names of anything that has a material form and can be perceived by the five senses of touch, sight, hearing, smell and taste. Examples are the countless items that surround us in the real world – books, cars, computers, lavender, mustard, sunrises, explosions, etc.

Abstract nouns are ideas, concepts and other immaterial notions, such as justice, fear, liberty, happiness, misery, etc.

Exercise 2d

1   Make a list of ten concrete nouns to be found in a garage and filling station, and ten more to be found in a science laboratory.

2   Think of five abstract nouns that might be experienced by a child on his/her birthday, or by a student finishing a one year 'computer programming' course.
3   In editing manuscripts it is usual to underline words that are to be printed in italic with a single straight line, and words which are to appear in bold type with a wavy line. Copy out the following three sentences and 'edit' the concrete nouns to appear in italic and the abstract nouns to appear as bold.
   (a)   The inventor revelled in the tools that made his designs, the products of his imagination, become realities.
   (b)   Those who admire courage, generosity and chivalry will not be encouraged by a close study of dictators.
   (c)   Social trends reveal that the ownership of a motor car, a television set and a refrigerator are some of the commonest ambitions of under-privileged people.

They can be collective nouns

A collective noun is one that names (in the singular) a large number of individuals. Examples are cattle, regiment, squadron, panel, jury. In business we have board (of directors), committee, tribunal, etc.

2.5   More about verbs

A verb is a word that refers to the action being carried out in a sentence. Where a verb is preceded with the word 'to', as in to type, to protest, to dispatch, to monitor, to suspect, it is said to be the infinitive of the verb. The term 'infinitive' comes from a French word meaning 'undefined'. We have not said who is 'protesting', or 'monitoring' events, so we cannot relate the verb to any particular person. If we move from the infinitive to a more precise statement 'I protest at the derogatory statement made about the Prime Minister', we now know who is protesting.

Every sentence must have a finite verb, i.e. a verb which has been changed from the infinitive to suit the subject of the sentence. Thus 'I protest' might be changed to 'he protests' or 'she protests', or 'we protest' or 'they protest'. The subject of the sentence is the noun (or pronoun) that is carrying out the action. A sentence will almost always have a subject, but on occasions the subject will be understood, as when an officer in a battle shouts 'Fire!' The subject that is understood in that case is 'You'.

Verbs have several different forms. They change form to suit the person who is performing the action, and they also change form to suit the 'tense' being used. Tense indicates the time the action is taking place (in the past, at present or in the future).

It takes quite a long time to become really familiar with all the possible changes, but if we just pause to consider the persons and number (we won't bother yet with the tenses (see p. 201) of a verb like 'to dance', we have:

First person singular		I dance
Second person singular		Thou dancest
Third person singular	(masculine)	He dances
	(feminine)	She dances
	(neuter)	It dances
First person plural		We dance
Second person plural		You dance
Third person plural	(masculine)	They dance
	(feminine)	They dance
	(neuter)	They dance

Notice that the second person singular, 'Thou dancest', is really obsolete today, though in some dialects people still say 'Where is thou going?' 'Thou' is also used when addressing God.

Person in the English language is either first person, second person or third person, and number is either singular or plural. In the *first* person we are talking about ourselves (or in the plural it is a group that includes ourselves). In the *second* person we are addressing another person directly, or a group of persons. The word 'you' is now used for the singular as well as the plural, since 'thou' is archaic. In the *third* person the individual or group is being spoken about and is neither speaking (first person) nor spoken to (second person).

Notice that the list given above is in the present tense − the dancing is taking place at the present time.

Setting out a verb in this way is called conjugating the verb. Conjugating means yoking together, or fusing together. An old joke tells of a pupil at a primary school who said, 'Please, miss, I ain't got no pencil'. 'No, Johnny', said the teacher, 'I have no pencil, thou hast no pencil, he has no pencil, she has no pencil, it has no ...' etc., going through the full conjugation. At the end the child said, 'Well, who has got all the d .... d pencils then?'

You might like to try Exercise 2e now. Giving the present tense of a verb is relatively easy. When we come to deal with other tenses, we shall find that changes occur.

Exercise 2e   Give the full present tense conjugation of the following verbs: (i) to sing, (ii) to reply, (iii) to wander, (iv) to write, (v) to be, (vi) to have, (vii) to spread, (viii) to bring, (ix) to choose, (x) to forget.

2.6   Spellings

Throughout this book there are a great many sets of spellings. One of the commonest complaints from employers these days is that school and college leavers can never spell, and it is certainly true that 'spelling' forms a much smaller part of the curriculum than it used to do in less prosperous times, when there was less to learn than there is today. The solution lies in the individual student who knows he/she is weak at spelling making a real effort to master the way in which words are built up.

In later chapters some of the commoner rules of spelling are featured, but it is a sad fact of life that there are exceptions to almost every rule. One thing that almost always helps is to split the word up into its syllables. A syllable is a basic unit of pronunciation. If we have a word of one syllable, for example cow, pig, car, we can say the whole word without interruption. Longer words may have two or more syllables. For example pub/lish and ti/ger are two syllable words. Notice that a syllable usually has one vowel sound and some consonants. These may come before the vowel, or after the vowel, or both before and after it.

Almost always the syllabification of words will help your spelling. For example:

therm/o/meter
tem/per/a/ture
en/gin/eer/ing

The sets of words in this book are nearly always business-orientated — the sort of words you will meet again and again. They are also subject-orientated — they might be about marketing, or accountancy, etc.

The perfect way to marshal sets of spellings in a textbook has not yet been discovered. In this book we have set down two sets of words side by side, with twenty words in each set arranged in groups of ten words. The idea is that two students sitting side by side can help one another by each testing the other on one set of words.

Each set of ten words is in two sets of three and one set of four. In most cases the words will be linked together, either by having a similar format, or by their meaning or relevance to one another in some sphere of business life. For example, the three words:

engine
engineer
engineering

have a similar format, and being asked to write them down by your fellow student will help print this format in your mind for future use.

By contrast, the words:

aeroplane
fuselage
mainplane

are linked together by the fact that they are all concerned with aeroplanes. The fuselage is the main body of the aircraft, while the mainplane is the main wing of the aircraft, which give the necessary lift to raise the aircraft and its passengers off the ground.

Sets of spellings make a useful exercise in an odd interval when some interruption of normal routine gives a spare moment. They may also fill a gap at the end of a lesson when there is an odd 10 minutes.

Working in pairs, test one another on these two sets of words, Student 1 asking Student 2 to spell aeroplane, aircraft, etc., and Student 2 asking Student 1 to spell aggregate cost, alternative cost, etc. It is better to write the words down rather than just spell them orally, since this creates a more enduring memory of the words written.

aviation		*economics*	
aeroplane	baggage	aggregate cost	supply
aircraft	carousel	alternative cost	demand
airline	terminal	marginal cost	surplus
fuselage	reception	fiscal	monopoly
mainplane	booking-hall	fiduciary	monopolize
tailplane	inspection	financial	monopolistic
passengers	pressurized	homogeneous	speculator
luggage	pressurization	disparate	speculative
freight	de-pressurized	equilibrium	spectrum
cargo	vacuum	disequilibrium	range

2.7   Glossary of business terms: insurance

A glossary is a collection of notes that explain the meaning of words not in common use but having a special meaning in a particular industry or activity. Since we know that students of business English may go into almost any industry, we have suggested in this book a number of 'glossaries of terms' for a number of industries. We have also set a few exercises that require you to make up further entries for the glossaries suggested. To find the meaning of the words you are asked to write a note about, you may of course use a dictionary, but if the word you are tracing is not in an ordinary dictionary, a trip to the library will find you a textbook, e.g. a textbook about insurance, which will give you an explanation of the specialist word.

Here is a glossary of five insurance terms. Learn the meaning of those words which are new to you.

Average

The word 'average' in insurance refers to a loss suffered. It is believed to come from the Arabic word *awariya*, meaning 'damaged goods'. The term 'particular average' refers to a loss suffered by a particular person, the owner of the goods damaged. However, some losses are called 'general average losses' because everyone whose goods survive must contribute to the loss suffered by others − as where someone's goods are thrown overboard to lighten a vessel to save the entire venture.

Premium

A sum of money contributed by the insured person to the pool of funds held by the insurer, from which those unfortunate enough to suffer losses can be recompensed for their loss.

Indemnity

A principle of insurance that says a person who suffers a loss will be indemnified (restored to their previous position before the loss) but not to a better position. If your old jalopy is wrecked in an accident, you cannot have a new car, but you can have enough money to buy another old jalopy.

Pirates

People who attack a ship from the sea, or from a beach (and it even includes passengers who try to take over a ship).

Paramount clause

A clause that overrides any other clause in a contract − as where an international convention has laid down the level of compensation that is payable, and anything the parties may have agreed between themselves will be inapplicable if the paramont clause says the convention is to apply.

Exercise 2f Now write a similar glossary entry for the following terms, using such reference books as you need to find the meaning of the terms: (a) subrogation, (b) inherent vice, (c) proposal form, (d) underwriter, (e) broker, (f) peril, (g) Act of God, (h) Incoterm, (i) insurable interest, (j) policy.

2.8 Oral communications project: telephone conversations

In this project two students need to work together. Each imagines he/she is going away from his/her home town for a 1-year course. You wish to let your own flat for the 1-year period and use the money to keep up your mortgage payments for the year while you are away. Draw up a detailed description of your flat (if necessary it will have to be an imaginary flat you are pretending to own). Draw up a scheme for the letting of the flat, the amount required in rent and any tax or rates required. At the same time envisage that you work for a local estate agency that manages property for landlords. Envisage all the difficulties that may arise, the likely rents that are collectable on properties, the commission you would require, what is to happen about repairs, insurance, frozen pipes in cold weather, etc.

Now one plays the role of the flat owner and makes a phone call to the agent − played by the other − to investigate the arrangements that can be made. The other is keen to act as the agent in the letting of the property, but wishes to point out the likely problems, cost, etc. Other students in the group may observe the rôle-playing and award marks out of ten for (a) clarity of the presentation, (b) ability of the agent in raising problems and making essential points, (c) courtesy and consideration in the negotiations, (d) whether or not the eventual bargain concluded was fair to both parties.

2.9 More exercises for Chapter 2

Exercise 2g Take each of the following simple sentences and decide which part of speech each word in italics is in the sentence. Write the word and its part of speech in a table, e.g. crocodiles: noun.

1 *Crocodiles* are *savage* creatures.
2 They, *and* alligators, *live* in swamps.
3 *They* swim *unobtrusively towards* their prey.
4 *Oh*, the *poor* crane, dragged below the water!
5 All *natural* things *have* their place in Nature's system.

Exercise 2h Write each of the words in the following sentence down on a separate line so that you have a column of words. Then write against each word the part of speech it is in *this* sentence, and − if you can − an explanation of its part in the sentence:

Hong Kong is a bustling and busy city; originally it was a Crown colony of the United Kingdom but it is soon to revert to a Chinese city.

Your exercise will begin:

Hong Kong − a noun (the name of a city).
is − a verb (part of the verb 'to be').

Exercise 2i   There are eight parts of speech. Write them down in a list, and against each part of speech give three examples of your own.
Your list might begin:

Noun − teacher, speedboat, whale
Pronoun − he, she, it
etc.

Exercise 2j   Design a postcard to be sent to all members of a sports club you are interested in notifying them of the date, place and time of the annual general meeting, and requesting their attendance.

2.10   Answer section

Exercise 2a

Word	Part of speech	Reason
items	noun	the name of something
systems	adjective	it modifies 'furniture'
furniture	noun	the name of something
electrical	adjective	it modifies 'cables'
and	conjunction	joins 'electrical' and 'telephone'
cables	noun	the name of something
business	adjective	it modifies card
is	verb	present tense of the verb 'to be'
small	adjective	it modifies 'reminder'
permanent	adjective	it modifies 'reminder'
your	pronoun	it replaces the card-owner's name
supply	verb	supplying goods is an action
or	conjunction	joins 'goods' and 'services'
I	pronoun	replaces the name of the speaker
typesetting	noun	typesetting is the name of an occupation

book	adjective	it modifies the noun 'publisher'
constantly	adverb	it describes how the speaker worked
if	conjunction	joining the final part of the sentence to the rest
deadline	noun	a name meaning 'target date'
beat	verb	a doing word — an action

Exercise 2b The student must appraise his/her answers from the point of view of the addressee. Does the card include all the necessary details? Is it clear and unambiguous?

Exercise 2c Capital letters required for Columbus, Ferdinand, Spanish Main, Sir Francis Drake, Montgolfier, Frenchman, Anders, Lovell, Borman, Walter Raleigh, Virginia, Pizarro, Peru, Seville Town, Mendana, Brazil, Armstrong, Buzz Aldrin

Underlining required for world, balloon, rings, moon, tobacco, gold, rubber, worth, rocks, earth.

Exercise 2d

1 and 2 Many answers are possible.
3 *Concrete nouns*: inventor, tools, designs products, realities, dictators, motor car, set, refrigerator, people. *Abstract nouns*: imagination, courage, generosity, chivalry, study, trends, ownership, ambitions.

Exercise 2e I sing, thou singest, etc. Space does not permit the full answers to be given.

Exercise 2f Answers not provided.

Exercise 2g savage: adjective; and: conjunction; live: verb; they: pronoun; unobtrusively: adverb; towards: preposition; Oh: interjection; poor: adjective; natural: adjective; have: verb.

Exercise 2h *Nouns*: Hong Kong, city, colony, United Kingdom, city. *Pronouns*: it, it. *Adjectives*: a, bustling, busy, a, Crown, the, a, Chinese. *Verbs*: is, was, is, to revert. *Adverbs*: originally, soon. *Conjunctions*: and, but. *Prepositions*: of, to. *Interjection*: oh.

Exercise 2i   Many answers are possible.

Exercise 2j   No answer given.

3
Reading for business purposes

3.1 Introduction

This book assumes that the students who buy it can read; that they have a basic literacy. This may not mean very much, for experts who investigate literacy tell us that the average adult has a vocabulary that is about the level of a 10-year-old schoolchild. It is perfectly possible to go through life with little more than the average 10-year-old's ability in reading and writing. A popular song says:

> My uncle out in Texas
> Can't even write his name,
> He signs his cheques with x's
> But they cash them just the same.

So they may, but very few captains of industry are totally illiterate and it is extremely difficult to work your way up the business ladder without the ability to read well, and to write clearly in good English. Even a weak reader can improve steadily by regular practice, and can build up a good vocabulary of general words, and a sound vocabulary of specialized words appropriate to the field of business in which he/she operates. Thus the young banker can easily acquire the 'technical' vocabulary used in banks, and the insurance clerk can quickly acquire the jargon (specialist vocabulary) of insurance.

To succeed in business it is essential to read widely, to improve your vocabulary and to assimilate the rules of punctuation so that it becomes second nature to phrase sentences correctly, whether when reading or writing. We can learn certain skills that will assist us to read business correspondence, reports and other textual material. They include scanning, skimming, rapid reading, predicting and inferring.

3.2 Scanning

Scanning is a technique used when we are trying to find a particular subject of interest to us that we believe to be included in the text we are scanning, but we have no real idea where it is. For example, if we are looking for a particular restaurant in the *Yellow Pages*, we scan the restaurant section for some sign of the favourite eating place whose name eludes us. Some formats, like *Yellow Pages*, or the table of Contents in the front of a textbook, or a glossary of terms at the back of a book, are arranged to make scanning easy. Similarly many textbooks have a 'blurb' about the book on the back cover, which helps us decide within a few seconds whether it covers the subject area we are interested in. If it manifestly does not, we put it back on the shelf in the bookshop and look for another title that does meet our requirements.

3.3 Skimming

Skimming is a technique that allows us to read a text very quickly and obtain a general idea of what it is about. After skim-reading text we know what the theme of the text is and the main idea of each paragraph.

Some of the techniques you can use to skim-read a text are listed below:

(a) Read the introductory paragraph.
(b) Read the last paragraph.
(c) Read the first and last sentences of each paragraph carefully.
(d) Read all the headings.
(e) Look at the illustrations, and any tables of data.
(f) Read words printed in special type, e.g. italics, bold, etc.
(g) Look for words that signal major points. These are words such as *primarily*, *uppermost*, *first*, *second*, etc. Other important words that act as signals are *however, next, furthermore, finally, in addition, in conclusion, nevertheless*, etc.

Skimming is not only useful as an aid to reading, it will also be useful when you are summarizing or paraphrasing other texts, since it will give you a grasp of the main ideas. You can become quite proficient at finding the main point of each paragraph quickly, an important skill in the world of business, where lengthy reports may have to be looked at quickly. At other times, such as before a meeting, certain material may have to be understood at short notice. Skimming enables you to do this.

Before a well-organized meeting the members of the committee or board concerned will usually be sent not only an agenda and the minutes of the previous meeting but also a copy of any reports to be discussed at the meeting. In this way members come to the meeting fully knowledgeable about the items on the agenda. However, some agenda items may have against them a note − 'Report to be tabled'.

This means that the report is not available yet, but copies will be placed on the table at the meeting itself. Whether this is due to inefficiency, or is unavoidable because the affair has not yet been resolved sufficiently for the report to be prepared, it calls for our skimming techniques to be used while the chairperson is making a few opening remarks. Skimming is useful, not only as a speed-reading technique, but also as an aid to understanding. You will often find it helpful to skim-read a text before reading it carefully. This will give you a general idea of what the text is trying to say and you will have prepared for it mentally by skim-reading it beforehand. You will be prepared for the points as they come up and you will already know the general 'drift' of the argument.

Exercise 3a   Skim through the passage given below about conferences and functions. Then invent a heading for the passage that tells the reader what it is about. Now read it more carefully and answer the question below the passage:

Conferences and functions are *intermittent activities*, but their success often depends upon the availability of adequate facilities. Of course many firms do hire such facilities as and when required, and hotels and conference organizers usually offer a package of facilities which includes the provision of many of the most essential items. It is still necessary to *accumulate and then safeguard* display materials, lighting fixtures, visual aids, publicity material, etc., which is likely to be of use on future occasions. This type of material should be centrally controlled so that it is available for all departments, and should preferably be in the charge of a *general handyman* with a team of strong and willing assistants. A budget should be made available which will ensure the adequacy of the equipment provided, especially such things as spare bulbs for projectors, long leads able to reach distant sources of electricity, etc. The organizer and the general handyman should get together well in advance of the actual event to *'think through'* the sequence of events and anticipate every requirement. Then facilities needed should be purchased or hired; notices should be prepared by suitable staff or *subcontracted*; fire precaution rules should be observed and any problems of security envisaged.

The failure of many conferences, and the *chaos experienced at the start*, usually reflects the inadequacy of the team made available to do the routine work. It is of little help to *second staff from other duties* to assist if they are resentful of the disturbance and uncooperative when the event takes place. There are usually some people in a department who enjoy this sort of activity. A secretary should get to know these cooperative souls, enlist their support in advance and then secure their nomination as assistants and their release from normal duties. An early meeting of those to be involved is desirable. There should be an appropriate lead from *someone of stature* in the firm to impress the importance of the event and express the management's appreciation of the co-operation of staff. Then the sequence of events should again be 'thought through', allocating special responsibilities where appropriate but *in a context of general cooperation* to achieve a smooth operation. (Courtesy of *Secretarial Practice Made Simple*.)

(i)   What is meant by the phrase 'intermittent activities'?
(ii)   On what does the success of a conference often depend?
(iii)   Explain the phrase 'accumulate and safeguard'.
(iv)   What do you understand by the phrase 'think through'?
(v)   Explain 'subcontracted'.
(vi)   What sort of things would cause 'chaos experienced at the start' of a conference?
(vii)   Explain 'second staff from other duties'.
(viii) Give your examples in any firms of 'someone of stature'.
(ix)   What are the attributes of a 'general handyman'? (In your answer explain why this is perhaps − in this situation − a better term than the non-sexist term 'handy-person'.)
(x)   What is meant by the phrase 'in a context of general cooperation?

3.4 Rapid reading

Where lengthy reports have to be read, it is often helpful to practise the techniques of 'rapid reading'. These are very similar to the techniques of skimming referred to above, but one particular aspect that is worth practising is to keep the head still and only move the eyes from side to side as the page is scanned. The normal page can be easily scanned in this way, and it does speed up reading considerably. It also concentrates the mind on the material being studied, making it all the easier to pick up those headings, words in italic or bold type, and signalling words such as however, firstly, secondly, etc. The reader is invited to practise this technique when reading this textbook, and especially any comprehension passages (passages that test your understanding), such as the one above about conferences and functions.

3.5 Predicting

If you know the topic of a lesson or lecture beforehand, you can mentally prepare for what you think you are about to hear. If the teacher or speaker gives you a brief outline of what he or she is about to say, then you should find the material you are hearing easier to absorb. As the speaker puts forward the facts, they should fall into place within the structure already outlined. You will be classifying, analysing and organizing the information as you hear it. You will be aware of how it fits into the whole.

The same process occurs, to some degree, with reading. A title or subheading is obviously the main theme of a passage. A text entitled 'Bananas' will almost certainly be about the yellow fruit we peel and eat. It possibly may be about madness, but this is unlikely. When we read any text, we make subconscious predictions about what we are about to study. Without being aware of what we are doing we mentally call up our 'bank' of knowledge of that particular subject area. If we can *consciously* develop our ability to predict what we are going to read, then we will also increase our powers of understanding. It may also help us to read faster, since we can 'skip over' some of the information we have already predicted. Furthermore, it should also help us later when writing reports ourselves to write informative titles that will help our readers in the same way. This, in turn, makes us better communicators.

3.6 Inferring meaning

When we read a text, we often come across unfamiliar words and expressions, yet we are still able to understand the main meaning of the passage. We can do this because we deduce the meanings of these words and expressions by using the context as a clue. We *infer* the meaning by making intelligent guesses, based on the clues given us by the words surrounding the word we do not know. This in fact is one of the processes by which we learn any language. We are not born with a basic vocabulary in our heads. When you are reading and you come across an unfamiliar word, you should make a conscious effort to infer its meaning. It is surprising how often you will be successful. Remember there will be many occasions when you will not have a teacher to ask or a dictionary to consult.

It is always helpful to back up the inferences you have drawn about the meaning of a particular phrase or term by later investigation. Thus at a lecture or public address it is not possible to take out a dictionary to look up a particular word used by the speaker, but it is possible to jot down a word or a phrase for later investigation. By the time you come to looking the word up you will already have inferred its meaning from the way it was used in the lecture or address, but a later investigation may develop your understanding (or even correct a wrong impression if the inference you had made proves to have been ill-founded).

To digress for a moment, there is much to be said for taking notes at lectures or at conferences, and even when watching television.

The student of politics or economics will find many occasions when a speech by a president or a prime minister, or some other politician or commentator, provides useful background knowledge that may be pertinent to his/her course. It depends on the quality of the speaker, the rapidity of his/her speech and the manner of delivery as to how good a note we can make. We may have to be satisfied with only the salient features of the speech, but if the delivery is slow and precise, or even if it is hesitant, we may be able to get it all down. This is called *verbatim*, i.e. word for word. A dull speech can at least be improved by taking a verbatim record of it, for it will at least ensure that what little material there was in the lecture we have recorded it, and it often enlivens any discussion at the end of the lecture. The speaker who is presented with a verbatim record of what he/she said can hardly deny it, and may be forced to rephrase the remarks so that they do become more meaningful. One student of the author's acquaintance floored a visiting lecturer with the comment: 'I see what you mean, but you did not say it!'

3.7 The purpose of business reading

When we read for business purposes, it is almost always a practical activity, designed to be of some use to us, either immediately in the practical affairs of mankind or for the future, in the advancement of our careers or our businesses. It has already been suggested that you become a magazine snipper – skimming through trade magazines and professional journals to find articles that may be of present or future interest. Librarians spend a great deal of time doing this sort of thing to build up a file of materials on a particular subject, which they make available to all those who at some later date become interested in the subject. Many research activities start with a literature survey in which we obtain and read all the available literature on a particular subject. Intensive reading over a period of a week or two enables us to become, if not an expert on a particular subject, at least a well-informed outsider with every prospect of success if we decide to enter the field.

Promotions and career changes

A particular situation where we need to embark on detailed reading is when we make a career change, which may be a promotion but more likely is a 'sideways move' – in other words, we change the area of our work without necessarily moving up the promotion ladder. For example, suppose we have been working in the export department of our firm, dealing with exports to the Far East, and we are switched to deal with the South American market. The first thing we must find the time to do is to 'read the files'. In the South American field we will have numerous agents, suppliers and customers, each of whom has his/her peculiar needs or interests. Some will be good payers and some bad payers. Some will always meet their deadlines and others will need constant 'chasing' to see that goods arrive as ordered and on time. We must know as much about them as possible before we start placing orders or quoting terms for supplying them. We must know all about freight charges, insurance arrangements, documentary requirements, etc., and it will all be in the files. One export clerk of the author's acquaintance had been used to quoting a certain material at £340 per ton delivered (in the UK market). On being allowed to move into the export field he quoted £340 per ton delivered, only to be told, 'We accept your offer – please deliver to Manaos' (which is 1,000 miles up the River Amazon).

New legislation

Business life is very much affected by legislation, a process by which the sovereign body of any country declares sets of rules and regulations that must be followed by the citizens of the state concerned, and also any foreigners living in, or trading with, the State concerned. In the United Kingdom it takes the form of Acts of Parliament or Regulations and Directives of the European Community. Since countless minor matters are too trivial to be dealt with by Parliament or the European Council of Ministers, they are delegated to lesser authorities who publish by-laws and regulations that must be observed.

It is essential to read and act upon all the legislation that is relevant to our particular business. In the United Kingdom an organization called Her Majesty's Stationery Office (HMSO) publishes a *Daily List*, which is a 4- or 6-page document listing all the legislation published on that day. It costs about £60 a year to receive the *Daily List* every day, and most large firms will subscribe to it and appoint someone on the staff (usually the company secretary) to scan it each day to see whether there is anything that might affect the firm. If so, copies are ordered so that all those people affected can be sent a copy of the legislation. Often a standing committee will already be in existence to handle that area of legislation (for example a health and safety committee might be in existence to deal with all matters affecting health and safety at work). In other cases an *ad hoc* committee will be set up to study the legislation and make recommendations to the Board. *Ad hoc* means 'arranged for this purpose'. For example, suppose a regulation is made about the labelling of food products and you work in the food industry. It might need an *ad hoc* committee to read the regulations and decide what your particular firm must do to comply with them.

Note that there are no rules about such legislation, although bodies such as trade associations will set up high-powered committees to advise members of the actions they should take to comply. The law requires us all to find out what we have to do and then do it. The legal rule in Latin is *ignorantia juris haud excusat* (ignorance of the law excuses no one), and if we break the regulations, very heavy fines can be imposed, while we are also open to legal action from anyone who is harmed by our failure to comply.

3.8   Comprehension exercises

Exercise 3b   Skim through the extract below and suggest a heading for the passage:

One of the arts of public relations is that of getting publicity for a business at minimum expense, and on as regular a basis as possible by press releases and 'news' items of various sorts. It is always advisable to have someone who handles PR on a continuing basis and who is alert to obtain a slot, however small, in the press, on radio or television whenever the opportunity occurs. This does not mean we need a public relations consultant full time, but we might well take advice on any major event that we are arranging. Firms who handle PR on a continuing basis look for monthly earnings of at least £100, with much larger figures where several press releases a month are involved, or a continuous monitoring of public events is required.

The person within a firm who keeps public relations under review should collect all press items and keep a scrap book of them, while a short account of each radio or television appearance should also be included. This makes it possible to review the PR field from time to time and to improve upon past efforts by more careful planning, specialist advice, careful research of trade journals, etc. Confrontations with the press should be avoided at all costs. On the contrary, everyone should be alerted to the need to cultivate good relations with journalists, editors, photographers etc. In particular, save their time by feeding them with informative, well written accounts of developments taking place, new products and projects, staffing problems, etc. This ensures sympathetic understanding when the odd difficulty arises. There is a popular misconception that the press will always distort business affairs to the disadvantage of firms. This is not always true and the press can often help a firm to keep public relations sweet (extract from *Self-employment − not Unemployment*, George Vyner Ltd, Huddersfield).

Now read it more intensively and answer the following questions:

(a) How could a public relations officer get publicity for a firm at minimum expense?

(b) Suggest five 'news items' that might bring your college or firm favourable publicity, and one news item that would bring unfavourable publicity.

(c) What would be the advantages of having a 'press officer' who was the accepted person to handle all relations with the media (press, radio and television)?

(d) Write a press release about any product with which you are familiar, as if you were the press officer for the manufacturer and wished to secure valuable 'news' mentions for it.

(e) A local journalist telephones you to tell you that a serious accident in which four people have died is reputed to have been caused by the failure of a component in the steering mechanism of one of your firm's cars. Suggest five points you might make to tone down the harmful effects his report might have on your company.

Exercise 3c   Skim through the extract below and make up a heading for the passage:

Where you can get into trouble with the Inland Revenue is if your accounts manifestly do not represent a true and fair view of the affairs of your business. The Inland Revenue has the accounts of every business in the entire nation to refer to, and is well aware what sort of profits your sort of business should be making, given its site, catchment area, number of employees, etc. If your records show that you are doing about average for your type of business in your situation then they will be happy and will not query your accounts. If they find you are reputedly earning rather less than they would have expected and appear to be one of the least profitable outlets in the UK they will want to see you and question you about your accounts.

If you can take along a set of accounts which are manifestly in apple-pie order, with every item of income recorded and every expense proved by some invoice or petty cash voucher the Inland Revenue will be quite happy. After all an average profit figure for a business is only found by calculating the figure from a host of businesses, some doing much better than average and some doing rather worse than average. You may genuinely be one of the high-cost firms with less than average profits. For a variety of reasons you may be unable to take on certain types of jobs – and consequently be unable to make as much profit as other firms without the personal difficulties you have.

The Inland Revenue meets all types — it knows that some people have to scratch about to get a living, and if there are only small profits to be made the Government's share must be small — or even nothing at all. What they can't do is let people get away with manifestly fraudulent accounts. Their solution to such problems is simple. If they cannot get a trader to admit that his/her figures are not accurate, and they feel there must be some hidden profits somewhere, they will submit an assessment which is based upon a genuine estimate of what the profits should be. This is of course subject to appeal, but if you appeal against it you can succeed only by submitting an explanation or justification for your figures which rings true to the Commissioners of Inland Revenue.

It is a salutary experience to take a day off from business, go up to London and sit in on some Bankruptcy Courts hearings. The Inland Revenue is in many cases the plaintiff, bringing an action to recover unpaid taxes. The close examination of the bankrupts concerned is not pleasant; untruths and half-truths are quickly laid bare and the manifest misery of the bankrupt will convince you how worthwhile it is to pay your fair share of taxes the moment they are due. Only those who are making profits need pay taxes, and those who *are* making them do well to pay up and look cheerful. There is a lot of misery that needs relieving, and the Government must have funds to do it. Those for whom the bell has not tolled must help those for whom fate has sounded its dismal gong (extract from *An Office in Every Home* published by Mercury Business Books.).

Now read the passage more intensively and answer the following questions:

(a)   Why is the Inland Revenue able to detect firms who might not be keeping proper financial records?
(b)   What is the best defence to a summons to the tax office to see the local tax inspector?
(c)   Why is it perfectly all right for some firms to make smaller profits than average for that industry?
(d)   If it suspects that your accounts are fraudulent, how can the Inland Revenue solve the problem?
(e)   Name at least five uses that the government would make of the taxes it collects.

3.9   A spelling rule: i before e, except after c

Many words have 'ie', and many more have 'ei', and this can be confusing. The rule 'i before e, except after c' is a useful one, but it is not foolproof. For example, the rule applies with the words grieve, achieve, thief and receive, ceiling and deceive.

It does not apply when the letters 'ei' make the sound 'a' as in sleigh, weigh, foreign, and neighbour. It also does not apply where the letters 'ei' make the sound i (as in ink) or i as in mite. For example surfeit and forfeit, or height and sleight-of-hand.

If i and e do not form a digraph (in other words a single sound) the rule does not apply. For example, we have piety and fiery, but the one who inspires the piety is called the Deity.

As Mark Twain said, the trouble with learning rules is that you turn over the page to find that there are as many exceptions to the rule as there are instances of it. (See *A Tramp Abroad* − *the Awful German Language* for a hilarious account of Mark Twain's attempts to learn German. At one point he says that he would rather decline two drinks than one German adjective.)

Here are some lists of 'ie' and 'ei' words:

Words that obey the rule:

piece	achieve	chief	grief
niece	relieve	mischief	relief
piecemeal	reprieve	priest	siege

and

receive	deceive	conceive
receiver	deceiver	conceit
receipt	deceit	conceited

Words that do not obey the rule − usually the sound is not the long 'ee' sound:

weigh	vein	heir	foreign
weight	rein	their	sovereign
sleigh	deign	heirloom	height
			sleight

Now test a fellow student on one of the sets of spelling below. Then ask him/her to test you on the other set:

Business organization		*Leisure−pleasure industry*	
sole trader	boardroom	leisure	crèche
partner	chairman	pleasure	nursery
limited	managing	measure	kindergarten
company	director		
capital	executive	session	member
equity	accountant	concession	remember
shareholder	personnel	recession	membership

department	technical	gymnast	sunbed
departmental	commercial	gymnastics	suntan
function	finance	gymnasium	tanning
functional	financial	gymkhana	sauna

3.10   More about adjectives

In Chapter 2 we defined an adjective as a word that describes a noun. Adjectives are often called 'modifiers', because they modify the noun they are describing. Thus the phrases 'a *good* friend' and 'a *poor* friend' convey quite different ideas of the friend being described. The words 'good' and 'poor' modify the impression given. Such adjectives are said to be used 'attributively' − they tell us of the qualities or attributes displayed by the noun. Thus a reliable product, an unreliable product, a proven product, a shoddy product and an aesthetic product are products displaying different attributes. In each case the adjective used modifies the noun to give a clearer account than would be provided by the noun 'product' alone.

In business English we wish to convey clear ideas, and a restrained use of well-chosen adjectives will almost always improve the statements we make about our products and services, and clarify the specifications we lay down when we order goods or services.

Some adjectives can be used for comparative purposes. The commonest type of comparison occurs when we use the three degrees known as positive, comparative and superlative.

The positive word simply states an attribute of the noun being described in a clear and positive way. For example, 'This is a good computer'. If we wish to compare this computer with another model, we can use the comparative term: 'This is a *good* computer but that is a *better* model.

If we have more than two, we can then state which, in our opinion, is the *best* computer on display. The word superlative means 'the highest degree'.

The vast majority of comparatives and superlatives are formed by adding '-er' and '-est' to the adjective, as follows:

Positive	*Comparative*	*Superlative*
large	larger	largest
tall	taller	tallest
fast	faster	fastest

With some adjectives the word may change, either a simple spelling change such as:

| thin | thinner | thinnest |
| far | farther | farthest |

or an actual change to a different root

bad	worse	worst
good	better	best
many	more	most

With most adjectives that have more than one syllable the ordinary addition of -er and -est becomes awkward. For example, we do not say:

| beautiful | beautifuller | beautifullest |

Instead we use the words 'more' and 'most':

beautiful	more beautiful	most beautiful
generous	more generous	most generous
ignorant	more ignorant	most ignorant

Exercise 3d

1   Give the comparatives and superlatives of kind, tall, fat, lovely, famous, many.
2   Copy out and complete this table:

Positive	*Comparative*	*Superlative*
white		
good		
cautious		
naïve		
curious		
sharp		
determined		
bad		
much		
little		
clear		
risky		
urgent		
ambitious		
plain		

3.11   Vocabulary: computers I

Match up the words (1–10) with the definitions (a–j). Cover the answer section until you have tried the exercise.

1	Analogue device	(a)	A small wafer of silicon on which photograph-like images have been printed to give integrated circuits of great complexity − a computer on a wafer of silicon.
2	BASIC	(b)	A modulator−demodulator, which can turn analogue (wave form) signals into digital signals, by sampling the wave pattern 8,000 times per second. The wave pattern is reconstituted at the other end, after transmission.
3	Chip	(c)	The computer's memory.
4	Winchester disks	(d)	A transmission device where the wave pattern being transmitted imitates a physical variable (such as the electric current in a telephone circuit, which imitates the human voice).
5	Modem	(e)	Unloading the contents of a memory device or file to another device such as a printer.
6	Dump	(f)	An input device consisting of a pattern of black and white lines that can be read by a light pencil or wand. Used at the point of sale and in libraries.
7	EFTPOS	(g)	A simple computer language − the Beginner's All-purpose Symbolic Instruction Code.
8	Bar code	(h)	A set of instructions in correct sequence, to tell a computer how to perform a particular task.
9	Core	(i)	Electronic Funds Transfer at the Point of Sale. A method of enabling stores to get immediate payment for goods from the bank accounts of customers.
10	Program	(j)	Hard disks for micro-computers, either single or multi platter, with a faster performance and larger capacity than the usual 'floppy-disk'.

Answers 1 = (d); 2 = (g); 3 = (a); 4 = (j); 5 = (b); 6 = (e); 7 = (i); 8 = (f); 9 = (c); 10 = (h).

3.12   A glossary of terms: computers II

The vocabulary exercise above was a glossary of terms used in the computer industry, but jumbled up to test your reading and understanding of the definitions given. From your knowledge of computers, or using such advice and help as you can get from library books, etc., write definitions for the following computer terms: (a) data validation, (b) hard copy, (c) COM, (d) integrated circuit, (e) light pen, (f) main storage, (g) mips, (h) mouse, (i) network, (j) off-line.

3.13   More comprehension exercises

Exercise 3e   Here is a passage about early English law. Read it carefully and then follow the instructions and answer the questions below:

Before the Norman Conquest in 1066 Saxon England was ruled by kings whose power was based on their acceptability to the broad democratic assembly of a tribal society. Every man could speak at the tribal gathering, though in practice a *witenagemot* (meeting of wise men) acted as a parliament. England at that time was divided into various tribal areas such as Mercia, Kent, Wessex and so on. Each tribal area had its own laws based on the original customs of the settlers in question. There were three distinct legal systems applying to different areas of England: the 'Dane law' applied in the coastal areas of northern and north-eastern England; 'Mercian law' applied around the Midlands; and the 'Wessex law' applied in the south and west of England.

The influence of 'ancient custom of the realm' is not great today, but it is still important in one or two areas of law. In particular, in the law of carriage the concept of the 'common carrier of goods' is still important. Carriage is a very ancient activity and inevitably takes the carrier over the hills and far away with our property. In such circumstances we cannot possibly know what is happening to our goods, and the ancient custom held that the carrier was liable for every loss that occurred, whether it was his fault or not. He is said to be like 'an insurer of the goods'. It is true that later the common law developed certain exceptions to this rule, called the 'common law exceptions'. These included Act of God, Act of the King's (or Queen's) enemies, fault of the consignor, fraud of the consignor and inherent vice. If a carrier proved that the loss was due to one of these causes he could escape liability.

The Norman kings gradually displaced ancient custom of the realm by a system known as 'common law'. The trouble with ancient custom was that it was not a national system of law, since it depended on the traditions and customs of tribal peoples with different ethnic backgrounds, who were now to be welded into one nation by the Norman nobility who had seized control. The process was virtually completed by AD 1189. This year became known as the 'limit of legal memory'. After that date all was clear, recorded and remembered; before that date all was vague and uncertain, because no national system of law prevailed. This period is known as 'time immemorial', a time so ancient that it is beyond memory or record. If you wish to establish that you do something by ancient custom of the realm (for example, walk along a footpath from A to B) you should really prove that your great, great, grandfathers did it before AD 1189. In practice you only need to prove that people have been doing it for as long as anyone can remember. This establishes a 'presumption of antiquity' which shifts the 'burden of proof' to the person who seeks to deny you this ancient right. It is up to this person to prove that the right was *not* exercised before AD 1189. The case of *Mercer v. Denne (1905)* illustrates the point.

Mercer v. Denne (1905). D owned part of a beach where local fishermen had for at least 70 years dried their nets. D wished to build houses on the land, but was prevented, since the presumption of antiquity could not be rebutted by proof that the right was not exercised before AD 1189.

To conclude, we may say that custom is in one sense the principal source of English law since it was the original source of common law, and gave it its broad democratic basis which is rather different from foreign, authoritarian, codes of law (extract from *Business and Commercial Law Made Simple*, Butterworth-Heinemann).

1   Suggest a title for the passage.
2   What event took place in 1066 AD?
3   What was the 'witenagemot'?
4   What did the ancient custom of the realm say about the responsibility of 'common carriers of goods'?
5   What do you think an 'Act of God' might be?
6   A carrier arrives at his destination and delivers a large crate to the person named on the label. The box proves to be empty. Which of the 'common law exceptions' might explain why the goods are missing?
7   Which year is the limit of legal memory?
8   What is meant by 'a presumption of antiquity'?
9   You, your father and your grandfather have always fished in a

lake on the edge of a village called Freewater. A rich city dweller has bought the valley and is having fences erected to keep the public out. You decide to summons him for taking away your rights. What would you have to prove to the court?
10　In England we use the 'common law'. In Europe they use an authoritarian code called the Napoleonic Code. Why do you think it is described by the adjective 'authoritarian'?

Exercise 3f　Here is a brief account of the life and ideas of Adam Smith − the founder of economics. Read it carefully and then answer the questions below the passage.

Adam Smith − the Optimist who started the 'Dismal Science'

Adam Smith was born in 1723, the son of the Comptroller of Customs at Kirkcaldy in Fife. He went to Oxford, but was dissatisfied with his course because it had nothing much to do with the things that interested him. His great treatise on *The Nature and Causes of the Wealth of Nations* was published in 1776. It was the result of 20 years' study of the industrial developments taking place around him in Britain, which was just passing through the stage known to history as the Industrial Revolution.

Adam Smith started the central economic tradition, which holds that economics attempts to understand and explain the world in which we live, but not unduly to change it. His emphasis on the natural competitive forces in the market as the thing that regulated the economy led to the idea that there were inevitable forces at work which human beings were unable to control, and should leave strictly alone.

His central doctrine was that a system of natural liberty, where free men were able to follow their inclinations, would lead to the best results for both the individual and society itself. Man's natural inclination is to increase his well-being by producing wealth. If each man is thrown on his own resources he will labour for his own enrichment, and will incidentally enrich all society. Adam Smith's book, appearing at the same time as the American colonies declared their independence, prophesied that their system of free enterprise would make them the greatest nation in the world.

The weaknesses of Smith's doctrine lay in its disregard of the distribution of wealth. He was talking about total wealth, or **aggregate wealth**. He had little hope that the distribution of wealth between manufacturers, merchants, and landlords, on the one hand, and the mass of working people, on the other, would ever be such as to benefit the ordinary people. He said, 'We have many Acts of Parliament aimed against combining to raise wages; but none against combining to lower them.' This led Smith and other economists to conclude that although wages could not fall below the point where they would keep the workers alive, they were unlikely to rise much above that point. For this reason economics was referred to as 'The Dismal Science'. It was for later economists such as John Stuart Mill to point to the distribution of wealth as a matter of fundamental importance in society.

Smith died in 1790, a man of international reputation whose central doctrine has passed into history as the doctrine of *laisser faire* (let things work themselves out). Leave men to please themselves, and they will do the best for themselves, and everyone else too. It remains a doctrine which has much to recommend it. Many politicians today believe the pendulum has swung too far away from free enterprise in recent years. They have developed 'supply-side economics' to reverse this trend. Despite this, the general belief for much of the twentieth century has been that economic affairs cannot be left entirely to free enterprise but require positive policies if prosperity and economic welfare are to be achieved for all (extract from *Economics Made Simple*, Butterworth-Heinemann).

1   What are the dates of Adam Smith?
2   Why did Smith leave Oxford and give up his course?
3   What is meant by 'the central economic tradition'?
4   What are 'inevitable forces'?
5   'The government cannot stop a slump developing, and cannot do much about rising prices in a boom.' Would you say 'slumps' and 'booms' are 'inevitable forces'?
6   What is Adam Smith's doctrine of *laisser faire*?
7   What was the chief weakness of Smith's doctrine?
8   A working man in Adam Smith's time lamented, 'We have too many children! When they come they are a great joy, but at the age of six they go to work in the factories and put their fathers out of work. There is no way we can stop them!' How was this complaint finally dealt with (in 1870 actually).
9   What is 'aggregate wealth'?
10   What do you think is meant by 'the distribution of wealth'? How is it done? (If you are not sure you can study the process in Figure 3.1.)

3.14   Answer section

Exercise 3a

(i)   Activities that only take place from time to time.
(ii)   On the availability of adequate facilities — furniture, public address equipment, etc.

(iii)   All such equipment costs money. We have to buy what we need, keep it from year to year and see it is always in good condition.

(iv)   Consider everything that might happen and provide for it, so that it all goes smoothly on the day.

(v)   When we subcontract, we get an outside person to do the work, e.g. preparing notices and signs.

(vi)   Everyone arriving at the same time and needing to be checked in, provided with everything they need and to be given directions to the correct rooms or work area.

(vii)   To second staff is to take them off their normal duties to do other things.

(viii)   The managing director, the personnel officer, the general administration officer and the factory manager, etc.

(ix)   Strength, knowledge of electricity, plumbing, electronics and a willingness to work. (There is a lot of heavy moving work to do at conferences, and it is often not appropriate work for female members of staff.)

(x)   The chief thing is that everyone must be prepared to act in an emergency to ensure the conferences goes well, and not leave things to other people. Whatever needs doing, staff must be prepared to do it.

Exercise 3b   (a) By getting mentions in the press and on radio or TV for 'news' items. (b) Many answers are possible. (c) (i) A more uniform and careful conduct of PR affairs than if *any* spokesperson could speak for the firm; (ii) a better rapport and goodwill could be built up with the local media, which know to whom they should turn; (d) and (e) many answers are possible.

Exercise 3c   (a) It has a whole nation's records available for comparison purposes. (b) A good set of records that have been properly kept. (c) By the nature of averages some firms' profits must be above and some below average. (d) They send you a big bill. If you don't want to pay it, you must prove your profits are less than they think by producing adequate records. (e) There are many possible answers.

Exercise 3d   (1) kinder, kindest; taller, tallest; fatter, fattest; lovelier, loveliest; more famous, most famous; more, most. (2) Whiter, whitest; better, best; more cautious, most cautious; more naïve, most naïve; more curious, most curious; sharper, sharpest; more determined, most determined; worse, worst; more, most; less, least; clearer, clearest; riskier, riskiest; more urgent, most urgent; more ambitious, most ambitious; plainer, plainest.

Figure 3.1 How the mixed economy works

1 To make goods and services available we need:
   (a) Land and other gifts of nature
   (b) Human labour
   (c) Capital equipment, tools, buildings, plant and machinery etc.
   These are called the factors of production. The nation's households provide them

2 The factors of production are put to work and produce goods and services

3 The goods and services belong to the organization that organized their production

4 The organizations pay the factor owners for their efforts (money payments of rent, wages, interest and profit)

Flow 1
We all contribute to the world of work and in return receive money rewards

The nation's households
take part in both flows – the flow of production and the flow of consumption

5 Now they have money to spend the nation's households start to buy goods and services from the organizations through their retail outlets

6 Except that some people save

7 And some people pay taxes

8 While the poor have to be helped with welfare payments from taxes

The welfare eddy current – taxes flow back to poor households

Parliament

Savings

Banks

9 The banks lend money to the government

10 The banks lend money to the householders

11 The banks lend money to the organizations

12 The organizations pay taxes too!

13 The government orders many things from the organizations for official contracts (arms, educational materials, health service materials etc.)

Flow 2
The households spend their money rewards on goods and services

The organizations
(firms, nationalized industries and government departments)

14 The organizations sell the goods and services to the householders. We all consume the goods, and enjoy the services. Consumption destroys production. Go back to 1 again and start a new cycle of production

Shops

Exports – money flows in

Eddy current

Foreign firms

Imports – money flows out

Note: There is a third flow of goods and services to foreign firms, paid for in foreign money, but it is exactly balanced by imports, paid for in Sterling. The balance of Payments always balances

Notes

(i) The nation's households are providing all the wealth created by the whole nation. They do it by contributing whatever factors they can supply. Some provide land, some provide capital, some provide labour and some provide enterprise and get the whole thing organized.

(ii) In return for supplying these factors they are paid their rewards in money. The landlords get rent: those who contributed capital get interest; those who contribute labour get wages; those who show enterprise get profit. However, some of this money is intercepted by the government as taxation of one sort or another – income tax, capital gains tax, corporation tax and value added tax, etc.

(iii) Now we all have money, we can spend it on a basket of goods and services to suit our particular needs. In this process we buy from the organizations the things we need – thus giving them back the money they have paid out, which they can then use to pay more factor owners in the next period.

(iv) If we don't spend all our money, we save it; but we save it with banks, who promptly lend out the money to people who want more money than they have earned. Thus the banks may help us buy houses (by granting a mortgage) or furniture (by granting a personal loan).

(v) The government is also spending a lot of money (£200,000 million in 1990). Some of it is given to those on social security; some is spent on health, education, defence, etc.

(vi) If the economy is in balance all the money paid out by the organizations returns back to the organizations so they can use it again next month.

(vii) Notice that if the organizations sell to foreigners (export trade) they can earn foreign exchange to buy goods from foreigners (import trade). These two flows should equal one another – a balance of payments.

(viii) This is made possible by the use of money. Money makes the mixed economy and the free-enterprise economy go round. It does not work so well in the centrally-planned economy, because the value of money is artificially fixed by the central planners (and there often is not very much to buy). However, that is economics, not business English.

Exercise 3e   (1) Custom as a source of English law. (2) The Norman Conquest (3) A meeting of wise men to advise the king. (4) A common carrier was liable for every loss that occurred, whether it was his fault or not. (5) An act of nature so unusual as to be only possible to someone with supernatural powers − like a thunderbolt, or a flood. (6) The most likely cause is 'fraud of the consignor'. (7) 1189 AD (8) The court will take it that the practice is very old, and has always been so. Anyone who wants to disprove it must show that it was not done in 1189 AD. (9) That fishing has been done there as long as anyone can remember. (10) Because Napoleon imposed the Code upon all the countries he conquered.

Exercise 3f   (1) 1723−90. (2) The course did not interest him. (3) The tradition that tries to see both sides of a question and understand it, but not to influence the economy by recommending action. (4) Forces that are bound to occur, and we cannot prevent or avoid the results that follow from them. (5) Yes − at least Smith thought so − it was Keynes who proposed a remedy. (6) Let business alone, to work itself out. Governments should not interfere with enterprise. (7) Entrepreneurs know how to create wealth, but they can't be relied on to share it out fairly. Some redistribution of wealth (to help the needy) is essential. (8) Compulsory education kept the children out of the factories and gave their parents a better chance. (9) Total wealth created. (10) We mean 'the way it is shared out'. It is done by rewarding the factors of production − land, labour, capital and enterprise, with a bit of help in the redistribution of income through the tax system.

4
Writing business letters

4.1 The two aspects to business letters

The writing of business letters calls for two classes of skill. First, we need to know how to lay out a business letter in acceptable form, and be thoroughly familiar with it, so that in practically every letter we write we use the standard layout. There will always be the odd letter that for some reason is non-standard, but in general we should write naturally in the well-tried, standard way, so that our correspondents will feel at ease with the letter when it arrives. The other skill is the ability to write in good English, with the letter's subject matter falling into clear paragraphs, each of which is written in lucid sentences. The ability to write in sentences, both simple sentences and more complex sentences, ensures that each part of the letter expresses a complete thought, or a group of related thoughts. This enables our correspondent to follow the points we are making, in logical steps, and to arrive at the end of the letter with a clear understanding of our point of view on the matter, or matters, that we have raised.

These two aspects require a great deal of explanation, and we shall learn the skills best if we understand the reasons behind the various practices that have been adopted over the years. We will therefore start by considering the legal aspects of business correspondence.

4.2 The legal aspects of business correspondence

Almost all business activity is contractual in nature. This means that the two people engaged in any particular transaction are undertaking certain obligations to one another and at the same time acquiring certain rights. Thus the furniture manufacturer who agrees to supply some of his/her products to a wholesaler is entering into a transaction by which he/she accepts an obligation to supply the goods specified in return for a right to receive a monetary payment called 'the price'. Where a service is to be supplied, the arrangement is just the same. For example, a security company agrees to protect premises with its security guards and specialist devices, in return for an agreed contractual fee.

Should any dispute arise, it can be settled by going to court, with the aggrieved party suing the other party. To sue someone is to summon them to court, to show why you should not have the justice you are seeking. The judge will look at the correspondence that has passed between you (including any documents such as contracts, invoices, memos, etc.) and will pronounce judgment in the matter.

It is this legal nature of correspondence that requires us to set out our correspondence in a standard form or layout. The chief points are:

- The names and addresses of both parties to the contract must be stated on all correspondence.
- All correspondence must be clearly dated.
- To assist in tracing correspondence, it is usual to give references at the top of the letter. These references will be file references to let each party know where the chain of correspondence, of which this letter forms one link, is to be found in its filing system. The references usually read:

  Your Ref. ....
  Our Ref. ....

- To make the subject matter of the letter clear, it is usual to give a subject heading at the start of the letter. In large organizations correspondence is opened by a group of middle managers, who sort it into the trays of the person most likely to deal with it. For example, a letter with the subject-heading **Overdue account of your Salisbury Depot** will at once be put into the accountant's tray, while one headed **Insurance claim – Road accident at Wembley** will probably be dealt with by the transport manager.
- To start the letter itself, we need some sort of greeting. This is called the salutation, and may be a general greeting, such as Dear Sir or Dear Madam, but may be more personal, such as Dear John or Dear Lucy.
- We then have a number of paragraphs that deal with the matter in hand. Useful points about these are given later.
- Finally we need a concluding section. This is called 'the complimentary close' or 'subscription'. It usually consists of a farewell remark, followed by a handwritten signature, supported by the typewritten name of the signatory and the position held in the company. Many people have illegible signatures and the typewritten name identifies the signatory.
- Finally, if copies are being sent to other departments, there may be a list of their names, headed CC (copies circulated.) If

enclosures are to be sent with the letter, a list of the items enclosed will be given, headed Enc.

If all these details are included, the court will have no difficulty understanding what the parties have done. Clearly we do not expect to finish up in court when we start to deal with a supplier or customer, but in case we do, the formal layout described above and illustrated in Figure 4.1 will serve as evidence (see page 52).

4.3 The layout of a business letter

Business letters may be laid out in various styles, and a large organization will usually specify a 'house style' to which all secretarial staff are required to conform. The most popular style today is the 'fully blocked' style, which is illustrated in Figure 4.1. It is the easiest layout to achieve on modern typewriters and word processors. Each line begins at the extreme left-hand margin, there being no indentation of any sort to hold up the typing of the next line of text. We thus have the full block of type down the left-hand edge of the page, which gives the style its name.

Other styles are illustrated later but it is helpful to mention here the one problem with the fully blocked style. When the letter is filed away with many other letters, all the details are given on the extreme left-hand edge, which is inconvenient when searching for a particular letter, because the file has to be fully opened before we can see the date of each letter and the references. Some people prefer therefore to use the semi-blocked style (see p. 323), in which the references and the date are brought over to the right-hand side, where they are more easily seen when filed away. A third style of letter is the indented style (see p. 143), which has a more open, pleasing appearance, and incidentally has the date, the references and also the signature on the right-hand side, where they are easily visible in a file of letters. The indented style takes slightly longer to type than the fully blocked style of Figure 4.1. Study this fully blocked letter now.

Some of the points we referred to earlier can now be explained in a little more detail.

The letterhead

One of the essential parts of any documentary evidence, whether it is a letter or a document such as an invoice, is that it should have the names and addresses of both parties to the correspondence. By having a printed letterhead, a firm ensures that the necessary details

Linacre House, Jordan Hill, Oxford OX2 8DP
Tel: (0865) 310366. Telex: 83111 BHPOXF G. Fax: (0865) 310898

17 September 19..

Our ref. MB/OJ
Your ref. CTC 31 August 19..

AIR MAIL

Inter-Gulf Textbooks Ltd
Bahrain Island
Arabian Gulf

<u>Attention of College Textbook Coordinator</u>

Dear Sirs

MADE SIMPLE TEXTBOOKS

Thank you for your enquiry about textbooks suitable for first
year students.   There are a number of titles which are
appropriate.

In the Business Studies field the titles which are most
popular include Book-keeping, Business and Enterprise Studies,
Statistics for Business, Teeline Shorthand, Information
Technology, Office Practice, Economics, Law, Business and
Commercial Law and Typing.

In languages, English, French, German, Italian, Spanish,
Russian and Latin are in great demand.

I note that you do not sell technical books so I have not
listed these titles.

We shall be delighted to supply books to you on favourable
terms, as shown in the price list attached.

Yours faithfully

Martin de la Bedoyere
Product Manager

Enc

Butterworth-Heinemann Limited, part of Reed International Books
Registered Office: 88 Kingsway, London WC2 8AB. Registered in England: 194771

Figure 4.1   A letter in fully blocked style (*courtesy of Butterworth-
Heinemann Ltd*)

about its own name, address and telephone number are recorded on every letter. Then, when the typist types in the name and address of the addressee (see 'The internal address', p. 54), the letter will contain the names and addresses of both parties to the correspondence.

Since letterheads can be used in evidence as proof of a firm's contractual activities, they present a security problem. They should not be allowed to fall into the hands of outsiders — say visiting commercial travellers. The issue of headed notepaper should be closely controlled and if some new piece of legislation or change in the letterhead details renders stocks of stationery obsolete, the surplus stock should be cut up and used as scrap, or even shredded for packing material.

The date

Dates should always be typed with the month clearly stated in words. This avoids confusion, since in the USA it is usual to specify the month first. In the United Kingdom the day is usually specified first in an all-number date. Thus 4.12.94 means 4th December 1994 in the United Kingdom, and 12th April 1994 in the USA. Many firms have now dispensed with abbreviations like 'st', 'nd', 'rd', and 'th' after the number of the day, so that the date would usually be written in the style 17 September 1994. In Figure 4.1 the year has been shown as 19.. to save dating the artwork.

The references

As mentioned above, the letterheading often includes lines reading 'Our Reference' and 'Your Reference'. Depending upon the size of the organization concerned, references may simply pinpoint particular executives and their secretaries. WSG/AL would perhaps refer to the executive W.S. Gilbert and his secretary Alison Laker. Government correspondence often pinpoints the department and file number holding the correspondence, as those who correspond with the Inland Revenue authorities will know.

Mailing instructions

The name and address of the addressee must appear at the top of the letter, as explained in the section about letterheading. As this internal address is used in the preparation of the envelope, it is usual to include two other items — the mailing instructions and the attention line. They thus become part of the inside address and are incorporated on the envelope.

As regards mailing instructions, many letters are sent by special mail services, e.g. air mail, registered post, recorded delivery, special delivery, etc. It is usual for these instructions to be typed above the internal address, in block capitals. Because the envelope is usually prepared from the internal address, the mailing instruction can then be typed on to the envelope, or if a rubber stamp is available, the instruction can be stamped boldly on the envelope. Besides drawing attention to the special instructions when the envelope is being prepared, the inclusion of the mailing instruction on the letter in this way assists subsequent enquiries about the non-arrival of a letter by pinpointing the method of dispatch. Our file copy of the letter tells us which service was used.

Attention lines

Where a letter is addressed to a particular individual within a firm, it is more expeditiously handled when mail is sorted in the addressee's mail room. The address would therefore start with the individual's name. Where this is prevented by an instruction in the addressee's letterhead requiring all letters to be addressed to the firm, it is customary to mark the letter and the envelope 'Attention of . . . .' This attention line should be underscored, and may be adapted to direct the letter to a particular department. Typical attention lines would be

Attention of Mr David Lane
Attention of J. Senior, Esq., Sales Manager
CONFIDENTIAL: Attention of the Personnel Officer

Although a firm may reserve the right to open all mail such a letter would almost certainly be put unread into the mail tray of the person required to attend to it, while the confidential letter would probably not be opened.

The internal address

The internal address serves the two purposes of (a) naming in the letter itself the other party to the correspondence, and (b) providing a guide to the secretary in the preparation of the envelope. If the internal address is correct, then the envelope prepared from it will be correct too.

The salutation and the complimentary close

The salutation is the greeting at the start of the letter, and the complimentary close is the closing remark before the signature. These two parts of the letter are related in that the degree of familiarity or formality shown in the salutation will conform with that in the complimentary close. For example, a letter beginning with a rather formal 'Dear Sir' will usually end with an equally formal 'Yours faithfully'. A letter where we are personally acquainted with the addressee might begin 'Dear Mr MacIntyre' and end with the more personal 'Yours sincerely'. When the letter begins with a very familiar 'Dear John', the secretary may not type the salutation at all, the executive writing 'Dear John' in his/her own handwriting and ending with a personal salutation such as 'Very sincerely, Alex'.

The complimentary close and the signature are sometimes referred to as 'the subscription', a word which means 'written below' (the body of the letter).

Subject headings

A subject heading has several uses. It is usually inserted just after the salutation. The subject heading assists in the distribution of mail when it is opened in the addressee's mail room. It also assists the executive to whom it is addressed by immediately disclosing the subject matter of the letter − recalling any earlier correspondence at once to his/her mind. It is also a useful reminder to a busy filing clerk, secretary or executive of the subject matter of the letter when searching through a file of correspondence.

The main body of the letter

This consists of a number of paragraphs dealing with the subject matter of the letter. The important points about the actual content of the letter are explained in Section 4.4.

The signature

After the complimentary close it is usual to leave sufficient space (five single lines) for a handwritten signature, followed by the type-written name of the person who has signed the letter, and his/her official position. Some companies like to have the name of the company included in the subscription. It often happens that executives ask their secretaries to sign letters p.p. (per pro) themselves. The actual meaning of per pro is *per procurationem*, which means 'by the action of' and implies that the person signing has the authority to sign. The following styles of signature might therefore be appropriate:

Yours sincerely

P. Green
General Manager

Yours sincerely,
THE FARM EQUIPMENT CO LTD,

P. Green.
General Manager

Yours sincerely,

Rosemary Squires,
p.p. Peter Green
General Manager

Enclosures

An 'enclosure' is a separate item from the letter that is to be sent in the same envelope. Sometimes the enclosures are kept in bulk in the post department, and it will be there that the letter is finally sealed.

It is usual to put details of the enclosures at the end of the letter. These are generally typed at the left-hand margin of the page, and may include the number of enclosures thus: Enclosures 4. Alternatively, this may be abbreviated to Encs. 4. It is possible that the enclosures will be enumerated to prevent any misunderstanding, so that the entry reads:

Enclosures: 1   price list
2   catalogue
3   order form
4   reply-paid gummed label

It is the responsibility of the person actually dispatching mail to ensure that the envelope is 'stuffed' with all the items it should contain, i.e. the letter itself and the correct number of enclosures.

Distribution

It often happens that a letter is intended to go to a number of people, either because they are all equally interested, e.g. the members of a committee, or because they must be kept informed of the contents of the letter. Usually the distribution list comes at the end of the letter, thus:

Distribution: Head of Department — Engineering
Head of Department — Sales
Head of Department — Production
Chief Accountant
Managing Director
Chairman

Where the distribution is limited to one or two people only, the abbreviation cc (copy circulated) would be used, say cc Mr Charles Smith. The addressee then knows that Mr Charles Smith has been acquainted with the contents.

Sometimes it is desirable to pass a copy to some other party without the addressee being aware of the fact. Thus if it was felt advisable to pass a copy to the legal department without letting the addressee know, a request to send a carbon copy to the legal department might be marked NOO — not on original. The top copy of the letter is removed before this is typed on to the second copy. Seeing the NOO sign, the legal department knows that, for the time being anyway, the addressee is not aware that legal action is being considered against him/her.

Continuation sheets

Letters on headed notepaper are continued on to sheets of plain bond paper. The word 'cont'd' leads on to the next page, where the page number, addressee's name, and date are typed at the top to assist in identifying a loose page, should it become separated from the body of the letter. This can be typed right across the top of the continuation page, thus:

Mr Thomas Cross   —2—   23 December 19..

4.4   The body of the letter

Although the layout of a letter is important and familiarity with the standard layout helps us to get down to work quickly and methodically, the actual letter we write is the most important activity. We have to say what we want to say as clearly and concisely as possible. If this is the first letter we have written on the matter, we want to start with the maximum impact. If it is one in a chain of letters, we want to recall to our correspondent's mind all that has gone before and update him/her by a further piece or pieces of information.

It is advisable before starting the letter to jot down the points to be made and to number them so they are in the best order. If the letter is to be dictated, it is particularly important to be well-organized, with all the bits of information you need to dictate. A secretary will not be impressed by an executive who does not know the surname of the correspondent, or his/her initials, or the address, and who hesitates over the dictation, searching for odd scraps of paper in pockets, handbags, filofaxes, etc. If dictation is to a machine, the machine has to be told everything, so that the audio-typist can get on with the letter without delay. While a secretary can perhaps look at past correspondence for missing details, the audio-typist is remote from the scene of operations and possibly in a completely different building.

Having collected your information, you are ready to start the letter.

The opening paragraph

The opening paragraph tends to be short and often continues the greeting begun in the salutation if we are on familiar terms with our correspondent. In more formal situations it outlines the subject matter of the letter, reinforcing the subject-heading. It may refer to earlier correspondence, and it always sets the tone of the letter. Thus a letter that was intended to make the strongest possible protest about the products or services supplied by the correspondent would not begin in a light-hearted way, but would start seriously and formally. By contrast, a letter acknowledging a large order and anticipating a long and fruitful course of dealings with a customer would begin pleasantly and keep a friendly tone throughout.

The main subject matter

The body of the letter would consist of one or more paragraphs, each dealing with a topic that is an element in the subject matter to be dealt with. Paragraphs should not be too long, unless the subject matter is particularly serious and can sustain the reader's interest because of its urgent nature. If a series of important points is being made, they may be listed (a), (b), (c), etc., or if they have a paragraph each, the paragraphs may be numbered. It is in this part of the letter that the writer must explain what he/she feels about the matter, and what he/she feels the next step should be. If detailed recommendations are being made, they may be listed in the final paragraph so that the correspondent can deal with them item by item.

Within this framework we may list the following points:

1 *Be brief* Everyone is busy and has dozens of things to do. A long-winded style is irritating. Get to the point straight away, or with the briefest of opening remarks if the correspondent is known to be new to the arrangements.
2 *Be positive* State the facts. If there are alternative points of view, state them in turn with equal clarity. Then, if your opinion is important, state clearly what you believe and why. Management is about decision-making. Those who endlessly sit on fences only gain splinters in inconvenient places.
3 *Write simply* There is no point in trying to show your erudition. The people who employ you probably chose you because of it. Use simple language, state plainly what you have to say, put out signposts indicating the direction of your thoughts (such as subheadings) if necessary, and come to a clear conclusion.
4 *Be courteous* Bluster is rarely effective in correspondence. You should always keep a rein on your statements even when you feel strongly about the matter in hand. To be courteous even in a serious matter adds force to your message, for your very restraint shows how seriously you view the subject.
5 Summarize the matter in the final paragraph. Generally speaking, a final paragraph that shows the way ahead (even if the best way ahead is to do nothing) leaves your correspondent with a clear guideline for the future.

4.5 Exercises: writing business letters

In each of the following exercises pretend you are working for one of the following:

(a) Your own firm, if you are employed and are studying as a day release or evening class student.
(b) If you are in full-time education, write as if you were employed by your school or college.
(c) If neither of the above categories suits you, write as if you were employed by any firm that advertises in your local or national newspaper. In all cases it is a wise precaution to head each piece of work you submit *Educational Exercise Only*.

Exercise 4a You are interested in buying a plain paper fax machine which uses ordinary photocopier paper and which offers high quality printing and long life, without fading. You have been told that a firm called Whatfax Ltd, of 21 Hill Rd, Littlemere, Dorset, DH1 2SP, offers sound advice on the full range of fax machines. Write and ask them to recommend a suitable model and quote a price, including full details of warranties, service contracts, etc.

Exercise 4b   Your firm has been asked by Balloons for Hire Ltd to sponsor one balloon for a charity balloon race from Lands End to John o'Groats. The cost is likely to be £1,250. Write expressing your sincere regret, inventing a sensible excuse, and enclosing a donation of £25 to the charity.

Exercise 4c   Your firm is planning to run a seminar, for which it is hoped 300 top executives will enrol, on the subject of 'Safety in the Ports' − with particular reference to the ports of your own country. Write a letter to be circulated to six organizations that might have a hall, dining facilities and seminar rooms suitable for this event. Ask for the fullest details, including charges, menus for lunch and dinner, accommodation for out-of-town visitors, facilities available, etc.

Exercise 4d   A firm has written to you offering to visit your premises and demonstrate their locking devices, which it says can be fitted to any type of equipment and prevent its theft. As your recent stock-taking reveals the theft of several items of office equipment and scientific equipment, you agree to a visit and give a choice of three dates in the near future. Ask for a prompt response as your calendar is rapidly filling up.

Exercise 4e   Your local chamber of commerce (see telephone directory) has expressed the view that too few firms and institutions are willing to complete its regular questionnaire on business trends and prospects. Write offering to appoint a senior member of staff to deal with this matter, and collect and collate opinions of managers in the various departments before completing it. Ask to be put on the mailing list for this project.

4.6   Punctuation

There are about ten different punctuation marks, some of which are used in more than one way. The word 'punctuation' is from the Latin word for 'point', meaning 'a stopping place'. Attitudes to punctuation have changed in the last 50 years, chiefly in response to the mechanization (and later computerization) of correspondence. It is now held that one does not need to put punctuation marks in where they add little to our understanding. Thus the abbreviations Mr and Mrs gain nothing from having a full stop to show that they are abbreviations. It is no improvement to read Mr. and Mrs. Similarly in writing addresses, 36 Hill Road is as readily understood as 36, Hill Rd. Leaving out such unnecessary punctuation marks saves a secretary's time and reduces wear and tear on both the machine and its human operator.

By contrast, the writing of no. to indicate number continues to have its abbreviation mark (a full stop). Otherwise it might be mistaken for 'no' − meaning a negative.

The purpose of punctuation

The purpose of punctuation is to advance understanding by turning what might otherwise be long and complex sentences into shorter, more manageable, phrases. The phrases are linked together by well-understood symbols − the punctuation marks. They give the reader clues about the tone and character of the written passage. Thus a question mark at the end of the sentence causes the reader to alter his/her voice to change the emphasis on the words, the inflection given to them. Without punctuation marks many sentences would be too complex to follow at a first attempt. They might have ambiguous meanings; they would lose the clarity of ideas their author had hoped for and would not convey his/her meaning accurately.

The full list of punctuation marks consists of:

(a) The three terminal punctuation marks: the full stop (.), the question mark (?) and the exclamation mark (!).
(b) The three 'pause' marks: the comma (,), the semi-colon (;) and the colon (:).
(c) The apostrophe ('), which shows possession.
(d) Quotation marks (' '), which show we are quoting from someone else's work.
(e) Inverted commas (" " or ' '), which are used when we wish to indicate direct speech interrupting a prose passage.
(f) The hyphen or dash (-), which is used to separate off a thought in a sentence. Alternatively we may use commas, or brackets ( ) to isolate the phrase, which is then said to be 'in parenthesis'.

The full stop

This is used at the end of a sentence to show that the writer has reached the end of the statement he/she is making. If the sentence contains several phrases or clauses, then the final full stop indicates the end of that sequence of statements.

Full stops are also used to indicate when a word has been abbreviated or contracted, but as has already been explained, the modern tendency is to reduce the use of full stops as abbreviation marks unless there is some risk that the abbreviation may be confusing in some way.

The question mark

A question mark is used at the end of a direct question. Thus the direct questions below require a question mark:

'Has the banker's draft arrived from Kuala Lumpur?'
'Can you tell me whether the space has been reserved for our cargo on the *Queen of the Pacific*?'

We would not use a question mark if we are using reported speech:

I asked him whether the banker's draft had arrived from Kuala Lumpur. His reply was negative.

Exclamation marks

These are used with obvious exclamations such as 'Oh!' or 'Halt!' or 'Look lively, there!' They are also used to give emphasis where a statement otherwise might not convey the writer's true meaning or feelings. For example; 'Keyserburg, the sole survivor, had been forced to eat parts of his dead comrades. Strange behaviour for an avowed vegetarian! Later he opened a restaurant in California. I'd like to eat there, I don't think!'

Weight of pause marks

An American teacher suggested:

(a)   A comma is 25 cents worth of breath.
(b)   A semi-colon is 50 cents worth of breath.
(c)   A colon is 75 cents worth of breath.
(d)   A full stop is a dollar's worth of breath.

This weighting does give some idea of the relative lengths of the pauses, in the ratio of 1, 2, 3 and 4.

The comma (,)

Commas are used within a sentence to do a variety of different jobs. They never appear at the end of a sentence, when one of the terminal punctuation marks is used to bring the sentence to a close.

The chief uses of the comma are:

(a) To separate items in a list. For example, 'The commonest business documents are invoices, credit notes, debit notes, statements and receipts'. Note that the last two items in the list are not separated by a comma but joined by the conjunction 'and'.

(b) To separate clauses in a complex sentence. For example, 'Although the new furniture became available in September, and was actually assembled in early October, it was late October before the premises were refurbished and the furniture could be installed'.

(c) To put some part of a sentence in parenthesis, to separate it off from the main sentence. For example, 'Mr Lee, the former president, expressed his delight at the progress of the society'.

The semi-colon (;)

The semi-colon is a longer pause than a comma, and is used to separate two parts of a sentence that are themselves quite complex, but at the same time closely linked to each other. For example, 'The marketing manager favoured heavy advertising expenditure and a drive to increase market share; the managing director emphasized the need for caution and careful evaluation of the reaction of competitors'.

The semi-colon may also be used when two sentences that are closely related are joined together to show the relationship. For example, 'The driver arrived two hours later than expected; the road had been swept away by the floods near Dodford'.

Note that the two parts of this sentence could have been written as short sentences (with a full stop after the word expected and a capital T for 'The'). They could not have just been separated by a comma. We need, as our American teacher would say, 50 cents worth of breath for this pause.

Finally, a semi-colon can be used to separate off the items in a list that is too complicated for commas to handle. For example, 'To extinguish these hundreds of fires we need: five heavy duty pumps capable of delivering 20,000 gallons of water per hour; five heavy goods vehicles carrying liquid nitrogen; at least ten steel screens, mounted on wheels and capable of being manoeuvred right up to the wells; 100 sets of fireproof wearing apparel for the crews to be deployed and at least three back-up teams of medical personnel'.

The colon

The colon is used in several ways. It is a lengthy pause which implies that something important will follow. For example:

(a) It may be used to introduce a list, as in the case of this list (after the words 'For example':).

(b) It may be used to stress or emphasize a point, as in 'The poor results of the group are easily explained: lack of real commitment to the project'.

(c) It may be used to separate off a clause that explains or amplifies what went before. For example, 'We believe the statement by the safety officer that he did order the evacuation of the tunnel: it is just that that order was never heard because of the failure of the telecommunication system'.

The apostrophe

The chief use of the apostrophe is to show possession, e.g. in such phrases as the government's position, the cricketer's score, the policeman's squad car. The other use is to indicate missing letters in words, e.g. hasn't, didn't, you'll, we'll, etc. Actually the two uses are closely linked, e.g. 'the government's position' is really only a shortened way of saying 'the government (its) position'.

Apostrophes cause a little confusion with some students because where the singular and the plural are being used the apostrophe can easily be misplaced. For example:

The boy's ball
The boys' ball
The child's ball
The children's ball

Where the plural word ends in s, as with 'boys', the apostrophe comes after the s, but where the plural is achieved by changing the word, as in the case of child and children, the apostrophe comes before the s in both singular and plural.

Quotation marks

Quotation marks are placed around any words quoted from someone else's work or speech. They may be single (' ') or double (" "). The rule is to place the quotation around the actual words quoted. For example, Shakespeare said, "Uneasy lies the head that wears a crown".

If a punctuation mark such as an exclamation mark refers to the words quoted, it comes inside the quotation marks, e.g. The junior member of staff was heard to mutter "Rubbish!" during the managing director's speech.

If the punctuation mark is not part of the quotation, it is placed outside the quotation marks. For example, Why are you objecting to the slogan "Long live the Republic"?

Inverted commas

Inverted commas are used when direct speech is given in a passage. Direct speech uses the actual words spoken, not modified in any way by the one reporting them. (As with quotation marks, inverted commas may be single (' ') or double (" ").) For example: The personnel officer said "We welcome applications from all members of the community whatever their ethnic origin".

Had the same sentiments been conveyed in reported speech, they might have read: The personnel officer stated that the company welcomed applications from all members of the community, irrespective of their ethnic origin. In that case no inverted commas would be required, as the actual words were not used.

It frequently happens that the inverted commas need to be opened and closed twice, as in "We are satisfied", said the managing director, "that our policies meet the requirements of the Code of Practice laid down by the Equal Opportunities Commission".

Capital letters

Strictly speaking, the use of capital letters is part of punctuation. Reference has already been made (see Section 2.4) to the popular disregard of capital letters by some misguided people. The use of capital letters is correct for all proper nouns, and we may list:

(a) Personal names – John Smith, Jane Austen, etc.
(b) The word God, Almighty and other references to the deity.
(c) Countries, counties and towns.
(d) The titles of books, plays, etc. e.g. *The Merchant of Venice*, *Great Expectations*, *The Mill on the Floss*. In books these generally appear in italics.

(e)   The word 'I'.
(f)   The names of firms and companies, e.g. Sorrell and Son, High Flow Valves Ltd, European Freightflow PLC. (It is incorrect to use small letters for plc.)
(g)   Poetry usually begins each line with a capital letter.

4.7   Exercises on punctuation

Exercise 4f   Copy out the following sentences, punctuating correctly:

1   the machinery was purchased by power tools plc for £86,000
2   singapore has become one of the most important asiatic countries said the prime minister addressing the symposium on pacific fringe trade
3   no one said the managing director can change over to export trading without studying finance of international trade and documentation of sea and air cargoes
4   where can i exchange your gift vouchers asked the customer
5   at any branch of our store and at w h smith s debenhams and waterstones bookshops replied the sales assistant

Exercise 4g   Copy out the following sentences, punctuating properly:

1   today we should have received cheques from glasgow and dumfries did they arrive asked the chief accountant
2   beware said the chief cashier of counterfeit £20 notes we know how widespread these activities are becoming
3   you say shes kind but if she be not kind to me what care i how kind she be said the downcast lover
4   they sell the pasture now to buy the horse wrote the playwright
5   complaining about his war time rations one u s soldier wrote home to fight and die for uncle sam deserves a better food than spam a worker in the canning factory wrote back to this effect to your complaint we make reply theres not much chance that you will die so eat your spam you lucky dog youre dining high upon the hog

4.8   Vocabulary: exporting

Here are ten terms used in exporting. The explanations have been jumbled. Write down the numbers 1–10 and against them write the letter that contains the correct explanation.

1	Incoterms	(a)	An abbreviation of roll-on, roll-off transport, in which goods travel to destination on their road haulage vehicle, which is ferried to the continent from the United Kingdom.
2	Bill of exchange	(b)	A sign meaning *tirage internationale routier*, carried on lorries. We could translate this as 'transport by international road-haulier'.
3	Ro-ro	(c)	A document supplying evidence that goods have been laden on board ship, in good order and condition.
4	Bill of lading	(d)	Insurance cover taken out at Lloyds of London to cover goods sent in the agreed manner in a vessel of agreed type.
5	Letter of credit	(e)	A system giving access to other firms' computers to insert data directly about cargo movements.
6	Documents against payment	(f)	A French word meaning 'note-book'. It consists of sets of documents that allow goods to pass through customs unexamined and without payment of any duty until they reach the country of destination.
7	Lloyds cover	(g)	A set of thirteen terms used in freight-forwarding which have clear international meanings, e.g. FOB means 'free on board' and DDP means 'delivered duty paid'.
8	TIR	(h)	A system of securing payment in international trade. The payment of the agreed money secures the release of the documents of title to the goods, which can then be claimed from the carrier at the port or airport, on arrival.
9	Direct trader input (DTI)	(i)	A letter from an overseas customer to an exporter declaring that funds are available for transfer to the credit of his/her account at a named bank as payment for goods ordered, so long as they meet

the requirements laid down in the letter.

10 *Carnet*   (j)   A document ordering a debtor to pay money to a creditor on a due date, on pain of loss of his/her good name. To dishonour a bill of exchange is a serious matter, and casts doubt upon the creditworthiness of the trader for all future transactions.

Answers   1 (g); 2 (j); 3 (a); 4 (c); 5 (i); 6 (h); 7 (d); 8 (b); 9 (e); 10 (f).

4.9 Spellings

Where a word ends in 'e', and we wish to extend it by adding a suffix (a syllable at the end) the rule is: if the suffix begins with a vowel, drop the 'e' and add the suffix. For example:

> leave, leaving
> grieve, grievance
> refuse, refusal

However, the rule does not apply if the end of the main word has a soft sound, such as a soft 'c' or a soft 'g'. In that case the 'e' is retained when the suffix begins with a vowel. For example:

> peace, peaceably
> manage, manageable

Even this exception does not always apply, e.g. 'forage' becomes 'foraging' and 'manage' becomes 'managing'.

If the suffix begins with a consonant, retain the 'e' and add the suffix. For example:

> resolute, resolutely
> remote, remotely
> encourage, encouragement

There are exceptions, e.g. awe, awful, and true, truly.

Now test a fellow student on one of the sets of spellings below. Then ask him/her to test you on the other set:

Statistics		*International trade*	
average	probable	consign	banker's draft

median	improbable	consignor	bill of exchange
mode	probability	consignee	irrevocable credit
arithmetic mean	trend	transaction	exchange
geometric mean	variation	order	foreign exchange
harmonic mean	random	quotation	foreigner
range	distribute	credit	contain
inter-quartile range	distribution disperse	letter of credit	container
semi-interquartile range	dispersion	documentary credit	container-ization
standard deviation		irrevocable credit	groupage

4.10   Comprehension exercise

Exercise 4h   Read the following account of the case of **People v Collins (1968) State of California**. Then answer the questions that follow the passage.

In this celebrated case a robbery was committed in the presence of a number of eyewitnesses by a couple, a Negro man and a white girl. The witnesses gave evidence that the Negro man had a beard and a moustache, and that the girl had blonde hair in a pony tail. The get-away car was declared to be partly yellow in colour. Later a couple who matched these descriptions were arrested and charged with the robbery. Their vehicle was partly yellow in colour.

At the trial a lecturer in mathematics gave evidence that the *probability* of a Negro having a beard was 1 in 10. Other probabilities were as follows:

Males having a moustache	1 in 4
Girls having blonde hair	1 in 3
Girls having pony tails	1 in 10
Cars painted partly yellow	1 in 10
An inter-racial couple driving a motor vehicle	1 in 1,000

In mathematics, the lecturer said, details like this are called events. Where two events are independent — the occurrence of one event having no possible connection with, or influence upon, the occurrence of the other — the probability that both will happen is the product of their probabilities, in other words one probability multiplied by the other. Thus if A's chance of promotion this year is reckoned to be 0.2 and the chance that the company will earn a presidential award for industry this year is put at 0.05, the chance that both events will happen this year is 0.2 × 0.5 = 0.01. This is called the *special rule of multiplication*. Therefore, the lecturer told the court, by the rules of mathematical probability the chance that all the events listed by the eyewitnesses would occur at the same time could be found by multiplying the probabilities listed above, which comes to one chance in 12 million (1 in 12,000,000).

The couple had pleaded not guilty to the charge of robbery, but the prosecutor asked the jury to convict them on the grounds of the extreme unlikelihood that there would be another such couple, there being only 1 chance in 12,000,000 that the couple were innocent. No other evidence, fingerprints at the scene, or stolen goods in their possession was presented. They were convicted.

1   In which country was the trial held?
2   Explain the word 'probability'.
3   What do we call a knowledgeable person like the lecturer in this case, called to give evidence for one side or the other in a trial?
4   Explain the special rule of multiplication in the mathematics of probability.
5   Do you think the figure of 1 in 4 for males having a moustache is an accurate probability?
6   Do you think the figure of 1 in 1,000 for an inter-racial couple in a car is accurate?
7   The population of the USA is approaching 250 million. How many couples like the couple in this case probably could be found in the USA if the statistics given were true?
8   In the USA you are only to be convicted if the case is proved 'beyond reasonable doubt'. Would you say there was any reasonable doubt in this case?

4.11   Answer section

Exercises 4a–4e   You will have to evaluate your letters for yourself. Assess in each case (a) the quality of your layout, (b) the quality and content of the letter itself.

Exercise 4f

1   The machinery was purchased by Power Tools PLC for £86,000.
2   "Singapore has become one of the most important Asiatic countries", said the Prime Minister, addressing the Symposium on 'Pacific Fringe' Trade.

3   "No one", said the managing director, "can change over to export trading without studying *Finance of International Trade* and *Documentation of Sea and Air Cargoes*".
4   "Where can I exchange your gift vouchers?", asked the customer.
5   "At any branch of our store and at W.H. Smith's, Debenham's and Waterstone's bookshops", replied the assistant.

Exercise 4g

1   "Today we should have received cheques from Glasgow and Dumfries. Did they arrive?", asked the chief accountant.
2   "Beware", said the chief cashier, "of counterfeit £20 notes. We know how widespread these activities are becoming."
3   "You say she's kind; but if she be not kind to me, what care I how kind she be?", said the downcast lover.
4   'They sell the pasture now to buy the horse', wrote the playwright.
5   Complaining about his war-time rations, one US soldier wrote home:

'To fight and die for Uncle Sam,
Deserves a better food than Spam'.

A worker in the canning factory wrote back to this effect:

'To your complaint we make reply,
There's not much chance that you will die;
So eat your Spam, you lucky dog,
You're dining high upon the hog'.

Exercise 4h

1   In the USA, in the State of California.
2   Probability is defined as the likelihood that an event will occur.
3   An expert witness.
4   The multiplication rule in probability theory says if the probability of one event happening is known and the probability of another event happening is known, then the probability that both events will occur is found by multiplying the two probabilities.
5   It probably isn't very accurate; it could only be found by taking a sample — and polls at election time tell us samples are not all that accurate.
6   No — probably it is largely guesswork.
7   About half the population would be too young to drive cars. Suppose we say 120 million are adults; at 1 in 12,000,000 there could be about ten such couples.

8   There must be some doubt, but with only ten couples spread
     around fifty states the balance of probability seems to make con-
     viction reasonable, provided we accept the individual probabilities
     as reasonably accurate.

5
Some special types
of letter

5.1 Standard form letters

Correspondence costs money, and anything we can do to reduce the time spent on it is a saving for the business. The standard form letter is such an arrangement. Suppose a business is a mail-order house, and most of its business comes from people who write in and order one or other of its products. Many orders will of course be quite straightforward and will be dispatched by return of post. However, many orders will be defective for some reason, and many of the errors will be repeated again and again. In such a situation a standard form letter is a great help. All we do is write a number of short paragraphs, one for each problem area. They are printed one after the other on a sheet of A4 paper with a box or dotted line to show which one applies in the case of any particular customer. An example is shown in Figure 5.1.

The usual thing with standard letters is to run off 100 or so on a plain paper copying machine from a master copy that is then filed. Each time one of the problems listed arises, the secretary simply takes a copy of the standard letter and completes the few details required, ticking the paragraph that applies in this particular case. An envelope is written and the letter placed in the 'mail outwards' tray.

5.2 Standard paragraphs

Many typewriters and word processors today have electronic memories that can store a large number of standard paragraphs. This means that the machine will type out a whole paragraph on a simple keyed instruction. The executive dealing with a defective request might write on the request 1, 17, 19. The typist will insert a sheet of paper in the machine and type in the internal address. Then, when the typist presses the 01 keys, the typewriter will type Standard Paragraph 1 from its memory. The secretary types 17, and the machine will produce paragraph 17, and the same procedure

The 'Troy was in England' Society
Gogmagog Ring
Cambridge
England
CB4 1PQ
(0223) 11100

Our Ref: . . . .
Date: . . . .

Museum Admission Tickets

Dear . . . .
Thank you for your letter enquiring about admission tickets. We cannot deal with your request for the reason ticked below.

1   You failed to state which date you intend to visit us. Please send us this information, referring to the reference no. given above. . . . .

2   We are fully booked on the date you request. Your cheque is returned herewith. . . . .

3   We are fully booked on the date you request, but can offer you tickets for . . . . or . . . . Please inform us if either of these dates will do. A telephone call will ensure a reservation. . . . .

4   We regret we cannot issue tickets except on 'Cash with order' terms. Please send a cheque or postal orders for £ . . . . when we shall be happy to comply with your request. . . . .

5   Your cheque cannot be presented because . . . . It is returned herewith. Would you please rectify the error and return it in the enclosed FREEPOST envelope. . . . .

Yours faithfully,

R. Thomas
Secretary

Figure 5.1   A standard form letter

produces paragraph 19. The result is a standard letter that looks as if it is an ordinary letter to which the executive has paid personal attention.

The selection of standard paragraphs in Figure 5.2 has been kindly supplied by George Vyner Ltd, the publishers of *Simplex Account Books*. The typewriter has room for 100 standard paragraphs in its memory.

Exercise 5a   Draw up a standard form letter for use when returning cheques to customers. The following faults are the most likely to occur, and should be given a line or paragraph on the letter. Ask them in the opening paragraph to return the cheque once the correction has been made. Common faults:

1   They forget to date the cheque.
2   The cheque has been dated, but with last year's date.
3   They forget to sign the cheque.
4   The word 'pounds' is left out of the written part of the cheque, e.g. it reads 'Pay one hundred and twenty 59'.
5   The amount in words and the amount in figures are not the same.
6   They have altered the cheque, but the alteration has not been initialled.
7   The cheque is postdated but you cannot accept a postdated cheque.

Exercise 5b   Draw up a standard form letter to be used by a fashion warehouse dealing with customers by mail order. The chief items to be mentioned in the order are as follows:

(a)   They forgot to send the payment and you only deal on CWO (cash with order) terms.
(b)   The cheque sent had some defect. Leave a space so you can tell them what is wrong with the cheque.
(c)   The colour they requested is out of stock. You are sending the nearest to it.
(d)   They forgot to send payment for the postage and packing. Ask them to send this at once, and leave a space to say how much.
(e)   The goods were too large for the postal service and will be coming by rail on . . . (leave space for date). Will the customer please arrange to be in on that date.

1   Thank you for your letter enquiring about *Simplex Account Books*. We enclose a brochure giving full details and a current price list.

2   Thank you for your letter enquiring about our free sets of material for use in United Kingdom schools. I enclose a 'Teacher's Set' of materials and if you let me know, either by telephone or letter, how many students you will be teaching this year, I will send you enough material for each student to try our practice exercise.

3   Thank you for your letter. We understand that, as you are commencing your own small business, you wish to take advantage of our special offer of *Simplex Account Books*. I enclose details of this offer and if you complete the form and return it, we will dispatch your books by return of post.

4   We thank you for your letter dated ... and as requested have pleasure in enclosing herewith an application for membership of the Simplex Club. This entitles you to free advice on any book-keeping problems you meet when using our *Simplex Account Books*.

5   We thank you for your letter dated ... and have pleasure in enclosing herewith our special notes in connection with the final accounts of partnerships.

6   We thank you for your letter dated ... and have pleasure in enclosing herewith our special notes in connection with the final accounts of a limited company.

7   We are also enclosing an application form for membership of the Simplex Club and leaflet/order forms about our two publications. *Simplified Book-keeping for Small Businesses* and *Self-Employment, Not Unemployment*, in which you may be interested.

8   Finally I wish you every success in your new venture and trust that you will be a Simplex user for many years to come. For your future convenience the *Simplex D Account Book* now includes a priced re-order form which appears between weekly pages 47 and 48.

9   If we can be of any further assistance to you please do not hesitate to let us know.

10 Yours faithfully,

Brian Senior
General Manager
GEORGE VYNER (DISTRIBUTORS) LTD
PO Box 1, Holmfirth, Huddersfield, HD7 2PR
(0484) 685221

Figure 5.2   A selection of standard paragraphs (*courtesy of George Vyner Ltd, Huddersfield*)

5.3   Quick-reply letters

A quick-reply letter is used by many types of administrative offices, e.g. central government departments and local authorities. They are constantly faced with the need to open a file on businesses of various sorts for control purposes. One of the many bodies of this sort is the Inland Revenue Department. Figure 5.3 shows the IR form 41G, which is included in its booklet '*Starting in Business*'. Many people who have been employees, and therefore appear in the UK tax records as employees, paying tax under the PAYE (pay as you earn) scheme, leave to become self-employed. This leads to a change in their tax records. It often means a refund of tax, which benefits the new business, because businesses sometimes take a little while to become profitable, and while they are not making profits, they cannot be charged tax. To make the change, and get their business file opened with the Inland Revenue, the quick-reply letter shown in Figure 5.3 must be completed.

Note that the chief feature of a quick-reply letter is that the page is divided in half by a centre line. Short, detailed questions are listed on the left-hand side, with space for a quick reply on the right-hand side. The design of such a form is usually a cooperative effort, the rough draft being passed around various people so that nothing is overlooked. When completed by the addressee, and returned, the file for the new business can be started up and will be kept as a current file for all the years that the business continues to run. It becomes a very detailed record of the business's tax affairs, and the various tax inspectors can see at a glance the profits made, the promptness of payments, the good times and the bad times, etc.

Such forms should be reviewed from time to time to see that they still meet the needs of the department, and a named individual will usually be charged with the duty of collecting and collating points that arise during the lifetime of the form. Then when it comes up for review, account can be taken of any defects that have come to the department's attention.

Exercise 5c   You are appointed by a student body to supervise the money available in a charitable fund to relieve the distress of students who for some reason are not properly funded. Draw up a quick-reply letter to be completed by all students who seek help from the charity, asking such questions as you think would be necessary to establish that the applicant is in fact a student, and what his/her true financial position is. In the letter make it clear that there is a limit of £100 for any grant in any one term.

Exercise 5d   Devise a quick-reply letter to be completed by all

ENQUIRIES	REPLIES
1. In what name is the business carried on, if not in your own name?	1.
2. (a) What is the business address if different from your private address?	2. (a)
(b) What is your private address?	(b)
3. What is the nature of the business?	3.
4. When did you start in this business?	4.
5. If you took over an existing business, from whom did you acquire it?	5.
6. Have you any partners? If so, please give their names and private addresses.	6.
7. To what date do you propose to make up your business accounts? If they are to be prepared by an accountant, please give his name and address.	7.
8. If you are not already operating PAYE as an employer, have you any employees earning—	8.
(a) more than £34.00 a week	(a)
(b) more than £1 a week who have other employment?	(b)
9. If in addition to running your business you are in paid employment, or are continuing an existing business, please give particulars.	9.
10. (a) If your have left employment, please state the name and address of your employer and the date you left. If you still have the leaving certificate form P45 handed to you by your last employer, please attach it.	10. (a)
(b) If you have discontinued another business please state the nature and address of that business and the date it ceased.	(b)
11. If you have previously made a tax return, please state—	11.
(a) the name of the Tax Office to which you made it.	(a)
(b) the reference number in that office.	(b)
(c) if the office was Centre 1, enter your National Insurance number in the box provided.	(c)

(If you are a married woman the answers to question 11 should relate to your husband. If you cannot give these particulars, state the name and address of your husband's employer or his business address).

Full Name... Date............... 19 ....
(In BLOCK letters)

If you are a woman state whether single, married, widowed, separated or divorced; if married give your husband's Christian or other Forenames

....

41G

Figure 5.3 A quick reply letter for notifying commencement of a business. (*courtesy of the Inland Revenue Department*)

tenants in a block of flats about the uses to be made of a surplus of £20,000 in the maintenance funds to which they have all contributed. Various proposals have been suggested, including a refund *pro rata*, a reduction in next year's charges, and three or four improvements that could be adopted. Use your imagination as to what these might be. Remember that the completed form should have all the details you need to know about the tenants, as well as their views on the matters under discussion.

5.4 Circulars

A circular is a letter or leaflet to be distributed among a circle of interested people, such as potential customers. It will often be in letter form but may be in leaflet form. This means that it will not have any address of the sender (other than a 'published by . . .' line, usually at the foot of the page). Nor will it have an addressee's address, since it is for general distribution. This kind of circular is used, for example, at election times by political parties. They are pushed through our letterboxes in the hope we will find the contents of interest, and will be influenced to vote for the policies proposed.

For business purposes circulars usually take the form of open letters, addressed to all and sundry. Such a circular, written to accompany catalogues and price lists is shown in Figure 5.4.

The essential feature of a circular is that it should have maximum impact − conveying the information required in a crisp, businesslike, lively style rather than in a formal way. Such letters stand a great chance of being considered 'junk-mail', especially if the number of addressees is large. One company the authors frequently deal with has lists of up to 300,000 addresses. A circular sent out to such a vast number of addressees must find many who are just not interested in the client's product. The circular is 'filed in the waste paper basket'. A good response rate from such a mailing might be 1 per cent, which would be 3000 responses.

By contrast, if we reduce the mailing list to those more likely to be interested, the costs will be less and the response rate will be better. The difficulty is that a mailing house finds it less profitable to keep such specialized lists for the few people that require them. We may therefore find it necessary to build up our own mailing list, or find a specialist list seller with a list in the field we are trying to approach. There are such firms about. Formecon Services Ltd is one. Another is Profords Associates, 56 Earl Howe Road, Holmer Green, High Wycombe, Bucks, HP15 6QT, which has over 500 specialist lists.

Another such firm in the educational field provided the circular shown in Figure 5.4 about one of their services. The following points about circulars may be studied from this illustration:

March 19..

Publishers for Commerce, Industry and the Professions

FORMECON SERVICES LIMITED
Gateway, Crewe, Cheshire, CW1 1YN

Telephone	●	**0270 500 800 (Customer Sales)**
	●	**0270 500 000 (Administration)**
Telefax No.	●	0270 500 505
Doc. Exch.	●	DX 20163 Crewe

Dear Sirs

EXPORT DOCUMENTATION - TO REACH THE DESTINATION!

In today's international business world it's more important
than ever to make sure that your export procedures are carried
out correctly and efficiently.

To achieve this, you need documentation which is simpler to
complete, guarantees the provision of all necessary
information and instructions, and is presented in an
internationally recognisable format.

The Formecon range of International Documentation fulfils
these requirements. The superior quality of our products also
promises you the benefit of a competent, professional image
being presented by your organisation to your contacts and
customers throughout the world.

We have pleasure in enclosing <u>eight new catalogues of Export
Documentation</u>. In addition to a full range of shipping
documentation published to the latest approved format,
including a complete set of 13 Incoterm forms, there are
products for internal use to help you to control and maintain
your export business.

Our documentation is designed for easy completion by hand or
typewriter, but if you are considering computerisation of your
export procedures, our Formfill Export Software will enable
you to make a smooth transition to automatic production of all
shipping documents - please see Catalogue No 18.

Why leave things to chance? You **know** that one small error,
ommission or misunderstanding can have disastrous and far-
reaching implications - for that shipment and for future
business.

Get the paperwork right first time, get the goods delivered on
time and <u>get paid on time</u> - Formecon products are designed to
help you achieve that, every time.

Yours sincerely

Wm J Thompson
Wm J Thompson
Managing Director

Registered in England No. 1049487
Directors
Wm. J. Thompson; P. B. Frayling; A. B. Perkins
Member of
The Law Services Association; The North Staffs.
Chamber of Commerce and Industry; The Institute of Export
BSI Quality Assurance BS 5750: Part 1 (Registered No. FM 13852)

Figure 5.4   A circular for a direct mailing (*courtesy of Formecon Services
Ltd*)

1 There need be no inside address – it wastes space and the circular is going to a wide variety of addresses.
2 The message delivered to the recipient is clear – even strident.
3 Clear instructions are given about how to respond to the circular.
4 The use of variable type can give variety to the circular and emphasize points about a product or a service that make it different from those offered by competitors.
5 The use of boxes to display the main features and build in contractual points draws them to the attention of the addressee. For example, the box labelled POSTING warns the addressee that the postal delivery is slow (up to 7 days). The important thing about such mailings is the cheapness of the mailing. Speed is really irrelevant because the head of department is going to take some time to place an order anyway, and arrange finance, etc. Prices, mailing dates, discount for prompt payment, etc are all featured in the display.

Exercise 5e Write circulars for each of the following situations:

1 Imagine you work for the publisher of this textbook and wish to send a direct-mail shot to all schools and colleges, drawing it to the attention of the teacher/lecturer i/c business English. Tell them about the book, give all the details and offer inspection copies to those interested. Design an application form for an inspection copy, to appear in a tear-off section at the bottom of the circular.
2 Draw up a circular to go to the chief administration officer of all large companies in an area, announcing a display of office furniture and equipment at a local venue. There are 320 manufacturers and wholesalers taking stands. Tell them you are enclosing two free admission tickets and further free tickets may be obtained by applying by telephone, letter or fax. Point out that the ticket details should be completed before arrival to avoid delay in entering the exhibition, and that children under the age of 14 are not admitted.
3 Imagine you work for a charitable institution whose particular interest is to preserve links with prisoners in countries with oppressive regimes. Draw up a circular to be sent to all student unions at major educational establishments. You want to obtain the names and addresses of students willing to write on a regular basis to a particular, named prisoner. You also hope that the students will organize some event to raise funds for this work, or makes some sort of donation from union funds.
4 You work for a credit-card company. You want to increase your market share by persuading present card-holders who have records of absolute reliability to increase their commitment to your card

and give up other cards that you suspect they have. To this end you are introducing a 'goldcard', which can be taken in place of your present card and have added to it the credit limit of any card they decide to surrender. As an inducement for them to transfer, you will, on proof of surrender of the other card, cancel 5 per cent of the debt outstanding on the card surrendered. Your goldcard bears an interest rate 2 per cent below the APR of your present card, as a further inducement. Write a circular to be sent to all the specially selected card-holders whose credit rating is deemed to be high enough.

5.5   Sentences

When we communicate in English, we speak or write in sentences. Sentences can be simple, or intricate, but the essential feature of a sentence is that it expresses a complete thought. Some thoughts can be expressed so succinctly that they only need one word:

'Halt!'

The sentry could amplify his thought with a few more words:

'Halt, or I fire!'

This is a compound sentence. It has two equally important parts. The consequences of not obeying the first part might bring on the second − with fatal consequences.

Subjects and predicates

There must be two elements in a sentence, a subject and a predicate. The subject is a person, or thing, to speak or write about. The predicate is a statement made about the subject. In the following simple sentences the subject has been written in italics and the rest of the sentence is the predicate. Strictly speaking, the subject of the sentence, since it is the name of a person, place or thing, must be a noun (or perhaps a pronoun), but for convenience in these sentences any adjectives describing the noun have been included as part of the subject.

(a)   *The managing director* telephoned the factory manager.
(b)   *The returned dining suite* had been damaged in transit.
(c)   '*The Right Honourable Member* is being misled by his own party's propaganda.'
(d)   *Time* flies.

JOYNSON EDUCATIONAL MAILINGS

Correspondence to: PO Box 6, Abingdon, Oxon OX13 6EL.

Deliveries to: Unit 5, Wootton Business Park, Besselsleigh Road, Wootton, Abingdon Oxon.

Telephone: (0865) 736361 *Fax:* (0865) 326244

There are 3 million 16-plus students in just 4500 FE Colleges and Schools. Now you can get DIRECT to heads of English.

NEW ..... and very low cost
SHARED MAILINGS to the HEAD OF ENGLISH DEPARTMENT in FE
Colleges and Schools with 16-plus students ..... Mailed DIRECT to the
SUBJECT HEAD.

For the first time you can now obtain the effectiveness of a solus
mailing to the HEAD OF ENGLISH in 4500 Colleges of FE and Schools
with 16-plus students, PLUS get the big savings you expect from a JEM
Shared Mailing. No longer need you rely on the intelligence, or the
goodwill, or the good luck, of secretaries or postroom staff in getting
your leaflet into the hands of the appropriate subject head. JEM will
mail your literature DIRECT to the Head of English, at less than one-
third of the cost of going solus. (Even cheaper if you send payment
with order!)

**To book, just ring, write or fax, then deliver your material to us 2
days before the required mailing date.**

Shared mailing to HEAD OF ENGLISH departments in 4500 Colleges/Schools

TO BE MAILED:	**PRICE LIST PER 4500 TOTAL:**	**15% DISCOUNT**
June 26th 199 • September 25th199ⁱ (material to JEM 2 days before required mailing date)	1st insert ....£299 Subsequent ....£59 Weight surcharge over 15gr. £12 per gr. VAT is additional.	if sending payment with order (remember to add the VAT!) otherwise JEM will invoice you after mailing for payment in 30 days.
SIZE LIMIT: A4	**POSTING:** All mailings sent Mailsort 3 on dates shown . . . allow maximum 7 days for delivery.	

NB

*This mailing covers only 4000 Secondary Schools having 16–18 year
olds. If you wish to mail the 2000 Secondary Schools otherwise
missed (ie. 11–16) then we can do this at pro rata rates. Just ring,
write, fax or photocopy this and tick box*

☐ **YES** — *add 2000 schools!*

Figure 5.5 A circular for a direct mailing with more pronounced
salesmanship features (*courtesy of Joynson Educational Mailings*)

If a speaker only mentions a subject — say 'The managing director' — he/she has not spoken a sentence. One instinctively wants to say 'Well — what about him?' or 'Well — what about her?'

The alert student might ask 'How can a single word be a sentence?' A single word cannot be both a subject and a predicate. The answer is that, in some situations, the subject of a sentence is understood. Both the sentry and the person or persons approaching him know who is meant to halt when the sentry shouts 'Halt!' it could be expressed as '*You who are approaching me* (understood) halt!'

Similarly suppose we hear a cry of 'Help!' We know the subject of that sentence is '*Someone — anyone* (understood) help!'

Types of sentence

It helps our general command of English to know the four main types of sentences. They are:

Statements or declarative sentences, which make a statement about the subject. For example:

> 'We specialize in airfreight forwarding'.
> 'This factory makes television sets'.

The most famous declarative sentence is the one that begins:

> 'We hold these truths to be self-evident, that all men are created equal . . .'

It is of course the first sentence of the American Declaration of Independence.

Interrogative sentences   These ask questions:
'Can you deliver the prototype by the end of February?'
'Is the advertisement legal, decent, honest and truthful?'

You can remember the name of this type of sentence by calling to mind the many chilling films and TV dramas you have seen where people have been subjected to interrogation.

Imperative sentences   These give commands that must be obeyed. They include many one word sentences where the subject is understood.

> 'Go'.
> 'Run'.
> 'Fire'.
> 'Report to the Head Teacher'.
> 'Switch off the machine'.

Exclamatory sentences   These express strong feelings:

'That's crazy!'
'Impossible!'
'Certainly not!'
'Heaven forbid!'

In business life the vast majority of the sentences we use are either statements or interrogative sentences. We may occasionally utter imperatives, and the odd bout of strong feelings may be given vent to on such occasions as a disciplinary enquiry or when wage negotiations are taking place. Calm statements clearly expressed and lucidly explained are often the most appropriate in business communication.

The structure of sentences

Another way of classifying sentences is to group them according to their structure. We have already met two of the four groups, which are:

(a) Simple sentences.
(b) Compound sentences.
(c) Complex sentences.
(d) Compound−complex sentences.

Simple sentences are those with a subject and a predicate, as described and illustrated earlier in this section.

Compound sentences are sentences that have two or more main parts called clauses. The two parts are independent of one another, and of equal importance. For example, 'A telephone transmits the wave pattern of a person's speech, but a modem measures the wave and transmits it as a series of measurements in digital form'.

Note that the two parts of the sentence could be delivered separately and make complete sense. One sentence would tell us what a telephone does. The other would tell us what a modem does. (For those readers who are not familiar with a modem it is a device that measures the wave pattern of speech 8,000 times in a second, and transmits the measurements to another modem, which reconstitutes the wave pattern so the message can be understood on the telephone at the receiving end. The word 'modem' is short for 'modulator−demodulator'.)

Complex sentences have one main clause and one or more subordinate clauses. For example:

(a) 'The standard container is 20 feet long and 8 feet square, which is a convenient unit−load for heavy duty cranes'.
(b) 'Misrepresentation is a dishonourable practice, for it strikes

at the root of contractual arrangements, which depend upon good faith between the contracting parties'.

Compound—complex sentences are sentences that have two equal main clauses, either or both of which may have subordinate clauses. For example:

(a)   'Despite the industrial dislocation, the factory delivered its full complement of components to the assembly plant and was able to secure repeat orders from its valued customer, whose production was not interrupted'.

(b)   'Surgeons are essentially members of a skilled team of medical staff, each of whom plays some valuable part, but the surgeons' skills are the chief element in the success of most operations, calling for decision-making of a high order'.

Exercise 5f   Consider each of the following sentences and decide whether it is a simple sentence, a compound sentence, a complex sentence or a compound—complex sentence:

1   Our office has a fax machine.
2   A fax machine transmits facsimile copies of documents over the telephone network to destinations remote from its owner's office.
3   The early fax copiers had to have a separate telephone line but the latest versions can connect to the ordinary telephone circuit.
4   Such a machine saves expense.
5   This type of machine can decide automatically whether an incoming call is a voice call or a document, and can switch between the two.
6   The best fax copies are obtained over glass fibre cables, which have less interference, but fax machines will work on ordinary telephone circuits, giving copies good enough for most ordinary purposes.
7   An A4 page of text can be transmitted worldwide in 17 seconds.

Exercise 5g   Copy out from Exercise 5f any sentence you decided was a compound sentence and underline the two main clauses.

Exercise 5h   Copy out from Exercise 5f any sentence you decided was a complex sentence. Put a continuous line under the main clause and a dotted line under the subordinate clause, or clauses.

5.6 Varying sentence structure

Business correspondence must always be clear, but a succession of short simple sentences can be dull to read, while the endless interruptions that 'full stops' impose on the reader can be very frustrating. We must therefore vary the types of sentence that we use so as to give the reader a free and less interrupted path through our text or manuscript. This means in fact that the majority of the sentences we write will be complex sentences, having one main clause and one or two minor clauses. We shall occasionally use compound sentences and even compound–complex sentences. The latter, however, can be confusing, and they may even confuse the writer. Remembering that many of these who read our material (unsophisticated users of consumer goods, for example) may not be very good readers, we should avoid very long sentences.

Consider the sentences in the following passage:

Accountants are busy people. They deal with the financial aspects of business. They control cash. They control cheques. They require budgets for future expenditure. Some managers dislike accountants. They hate budgeting ahead. They order goods without thinking. The firm will always pay. It has to. Accountants dislike unplanned expenditure. It forces them to borrow. Interest rates may be high. High interest rates mean lower profits. They could mean bankruptcy.

You can see how disjointedly the passage reads. It will flow much better if we use suitable conjunctions to join some of the sentences together. It may be necessary to rephrase them slightly, but our sense of what the passage is trying to say will help us to make good connections in most cases. Some examples are:

(a) The first two sentences can be joined by the word 'who'. 'Accountants are busy people who deal with the financial aspects of business.'

A rather similar word is 'which'. This is used when people are not involved, and the passage is about 'things' – inanimate objects. For example, 'The teacher picked up the books which the publisher's representative had left for her'. 'That' could have been used instead of 'which'.

(b) The next two sentences can simply be joined with the word 'and'. 'They control cash and cheques.'

(c) We then come to a sentence which should really be left as a simple sentence because it does not flow on to the next lot of sentences. The subject matter has changed and we are on to a different topic – the dislike some people have of accountants.

(d)   The next three sentences can be made into a single complex
      sentence — but first notice this little problem. Suppose we run
      the first two sentences together, to read 'Some managers dislike
      accountants because they hate budgeting ahead'. Can you see
      what the problem is. The pronoun 'they' muddles the meaning
      of the sentence. We don't know if it refers to the accountants
      or the managers who dislike them. The meaning is ambiguous
      (which means it can be taken two ways).

      A better way to join up these sentences is to change them
      slightly. For example, 'Some managers, who hate budgeting
      ahead, dislike accountants. Such people often order goods
      without thinking, relying on the firm to meet its obligations to
      pay for them'. We can then continue, 'Accountants dislike
      unplanned expenditure, which requires them to borrow, perhaps
      at a time when interest rates are high. High interest rates mean
      lower profits and could lead to bankruptcy'.

Exercise 5i   Improve this passage by consolidating the simple sentences, where appropriate, into compound, complex or compound—
complex sentences:

Book-keeping is an involved subject. It starts at 'dawn on day
one' of a new business. Every business deal is called a transaction.
Some transactions are cash transactions. With a cash transaction
you pay at once. Other transactions are credit transactions. With
a credit transaction the debtor has time to pay. Sometimes the
time allowed is 30 days. Some big firms take 90 days' credit. This
is unfair. They are using their suppliers' money for their own
purposes. As soon as we start a business, transactions begin. We
must record them in our books. Small payments are recorded in a
petty cash book. Larger payments are made by cheque. They go
in the main cash book. If cash is not paid at once, the customer
becomes a debtor. A debtor is a person who owes us money.
Many suppliers are not paid at once. They become creditors. A
creditor is a person to whom we owe money.

Exercise 5j   Improve this passage by consolidating the simple sentences, where appropriate, into compound, complex or compound—
complex sentences:

What is the purpose of filing? It is to keep papers together. It is to
build up a collection of information. A collection of information is
called a file. It may be contained in a file cover. The file covers
may be contained in a filing folder. This folder may have a title-

holder. The title-holder will be made of clear plastic. Many folders are hung up in a frame. This is called suspension filing. We can look down on these files. This enables us to see the titles of the subjects filed. The files are vertical. This is called vertical filing. Another system is lateral filing. Lateral means 'side'. We look at the files sideways on. They are hung up like clothes in a wardrobe. The labels stick out sideways. Even computers can run a filing system. The data are grouped together in separate files. We can call any file up to look at it. It shows on the VDU screen. We can read it. We can copy it. We can update it. We can delete bits. We can dump the whole lot. This is electronic filing.

5.7 A treasury of words

In business, as in all other areas of life, good communication is helped by a good vocabulary. We need to know the correct words to use to give exact expression to the ideas we have to convey. Often we hesitate in our writing because we know what we want to say, but the exact word eludes us. A dictionary is no help, for that only gives us the meanings of words. We want the opposite. We need the word that expresses the meaning we have in mind. In this situation we turn to a thesaurus. The first and most famous thesaurus was compiled by Peter Mark Roget, a London physician of French extraction. It is called *Roget's Thesaurus*.

The word 'thesaurus' means 'treasury', and *Roget's Thesaurus* is a treasury of words and phrases. You can buy a copy in any good bookshop. It has sold millions of copies since it first appeared in 1852. Of course it has had to be constantly updated because new words are appearing all the time and have to be added to the treasure so painstakingly collected by Roget (it took him 50 years). Every student should have a copy.

How do you use a thesaurus

The starting point is your own idea. You know what you want to say, but you can't think of the exact word. Suppose you want to say that a customer is in danger of 'going broke', but the exact word to use in place of this slang expression eludes you. The back half of the thesaurus (over 600 pages of it) is an index of words. You look up any word and it gives you a number of synonyms, i.e. words of the same meaning. When we look up 'broke' it only has two synonyms:

penniless   836.10
bankrupt   840.11

Now we have to choose the nearest synonym to the idea we have in mind, so it seems that in our case − in the business situation − the better one to pick is 'bankrupt'. The index tells us that this is dealt with in section 840.11.

We now turn to the front of the book and find 840.11. The front of the book is a collection of guide words, and the 840th word is, so the index says, the best guide word for us. When we turn to it we find that this guide word is **NONPAYMENT**. There are thirteen groups of words collected under this guide word and we are told to look at the eleventh group (840.11). When we do so we find the following list of words: 'insolvent, bankrupt, broke (slang), busted (slang US) ruined, failed, on the rocks, destitute, gazetted, in the gazette'.

It depends on what meaning we had in mind, and what we were trying to say, but probably the word 'insolvent' is the word we were looking for. An insolvent person is one who has no liquid resources available, and therefore cannot pay his/her debts. A liquid resource in business is a cash resource. A person who is insolvent is not quite the same as a bankrupt, but is in grave danger of becoming one. A bankrupt is a person against whom a court has made a bankruptcy order, because he/she has committed 'an act of bankruptcy'. The commonest act of bankruptcy is to fail to pay a debt that is due for payment.

To conclude, then, a thesaurus offers us a whole collection of words that are close to the meaning we are trying to convey. With any luck at all, we shall find the exact word we need in the first group we are advised to study, but, if we don't, we try the other synonyms to see if they can help us.

If you have a thesaurus of your own, use it to do the following exercises. If you don't have a thesaurus make arrangements to get one (they make excellent birthday presents, etc.). They will last you a lifetime, will always be useful, will solve many problems and will broaden your vocabulary to your enduring advantage.

Exercise 5k   Use your thesaurus to find the best word in the following situations:

1   You are reporting on the behaviour of a branch manager in the retail trade. You want to say that he is bad-mannered when dealing with customers. Find a better word.
2   You want to say that in your opinion your supervisor is too ingratiating with senior management and therefore does not represent the shopfloor's view. Find a better word than 'ingratiating'.
3   An accident in the car park has knocked over a lamp-post and you want to send a memo to the maintenance department for it to be checked for safety. The only word you can think of is

'insulate', but to ask them to insulate it doesn't seem quite right. Find the best word.

4   You are writing a memo recommending management to set up a committee to gather information in a certain subject area, to throw a bit more light on it. It is a security matter. Find a better word than 'information'.

5   You want to say that a proposal to join up with a rival firm would be opposed to the best interests of your company. Find a stronger word than 'opposed'

Exercise 51   Use your thesaurus to find better words than the following slang expressions: 1 shindy; 2 brass-hat; 3 sticky situation; 4 jade; 5 scoop; 6 squawk; 7 bone up; 8 quisling; 9 square deal; 10 grubstake.

5.8   More spellings: words ending in 'y'

When a word ends in 'y' and we wish to extend it, either by making a singular word into a plural or by adding a further syllable to the word, there are a few rules.

If the 'y' is preceded by a consonant, we make the plural by changing the 'y' into 'i' and adding 'es':

baby, babies
lady, ladies
enemy, enemies

Similarly to add a syllable we change the 'y' to an 'i' and add the suffix, but this rule does not apply if the suffix itself begins with 'i'. So we have:

lazy, laziest
hazy, haziest
handy, handiest
beauty, beautiful
plenty, plentiful

but

carry, carrying
marry, marrying

With the suffix 'ness' the 'y' does not change to 'i':

shy, shyness
dry, dryness

If the word ends in 'y' but a vowel precedes it, the 'y' does not change to 'i':

alloy, alloys
donkey, donkeys
monkey, monkeys
money, moneys

It is true that some dictionaries are now showing monies as the plural of the word money, an example of how endless mistakes by, one authority puts it, 'endless generations of clerks' can make a wrong spelling 'acceptable'.

Other examples are:

boy, boys
buy, buys
say, saying
play, playing

but exceptions do occur:

day, daily
lay, laid

pay, paid

Now test a fellow-student on the first set of spellings below and then ask him/her to test you on the second set.

Statistics		*International trade*	
vary	table	import	agent
variable	tabulate	export	agency
variables	tabulation	transport	principal
discrete	pictogram	visible trade	bilateral trade
discretion	diagram	invisible trade	multilateral trade
continuous	histogram	capital movements	tariff
population	graph	merchant	invoice
sample	scattergraph	merchandise	bill of lading
sampling frame	break-even chart	consignment	air waybill
representative	Gantt chart	consignee	consular invoice

5.9 A glossary of terms: premises

Every business needs premises from which to operate, and has to take on responsibilities and duties to do with the premises it occupies. In the glossary that follows the ten words or phrases listed have explanations written against them, but these have become mixed up. Write down the numbers 1–10 and against them write the letter ((a), (b) etc.) that is the correct explanation for each of them. The answers are given at the end of this section.

1	Premises	(a)	The liability of the occupier of premises to all who use them, whether as employees, visitors or even trespassers, that they shall not suffer harm or injury.
2	Change of use	(b)	The name of the business, bearing the proprietor's name or names, which must be exhibited on all premises so that those dealing with the business know where to deliver legal documents, goods, etc.
3	Defective premises	(c)	Property used for business purposes.
4	Planning permission	(d)	One of the two types of landed property, where the owner holds the land, free of any claim upon it, for his/her own use, and for the benefit of his/her heirs and successors.
5	Freehold	(e)	The other type of landed property, where the occupier has a right to use the property for a term of years (or fractions of a year, such as a month or week) by virtue of a lease granted by the landlord.
6	Business name	(f)	Premises that are liable to cause harm to people using them because of poor construction, poor repairs, unsuitable materials, or any other defect.
7	Occupier's liability	(g)	A term in a lease that requires the tenant not to do a particular thing, e.g. sub-let the property to a third party, and thus restricts his/her enjoyment of the full rights of an owner of property.
8	Registered land	(h)	When a property that has been used for one purpose is proposed to be used for another, planning permission must be asked for, because the new use may be unsuitable for that area, e.g. it may cause noise, fumes, smells, an increase in traffic, etc.
9	Leasehold	(i)	Land whose position and description has been registered with the Land Registry,

together with details of its ownership, and any charges on it (such as mortgages). Registration makes the land easier to transfer to a new owner.

10   Restrictive   (j)   Permission to use premises for a particular
     covenant   purpose, because the use appears to be
                              unobjectionable, and allowed under the
                              planning regulations.

Solutions   1 (c); 2 (h); 3 (f); 4 (j); 5 (d); 6 (b); 7 (a); 8 (i); 9 (e); 10 (g).

Exercise 5m   The following words or phrases are also to do with business premises. Write a glossary of terms about them, using such sources as are available to you, dictionaries, encyclopaedias, etc.: 1   rateable value; 2 estate agent; 3 commercial property; 4   overheads;   5   deeds;   6   hereditaments;   7   mortgage; 8   searches; 9 sub-tenant; 10 trespasser.

5.10   Dictating correspondence

At the very topmost level in firms and companies a top executive has a personal secretary (or even a personal assistant − a slightly more prestigious title) who will take dictation and produce impeccable correspondence for signature and subsequent mailing. The ability of such a secretary to take dictation accurately and at high speed will make the dictation session the favourite way of dealing with correspondence. However, it will not be the only method used, and accordingly a preliminary word about other methods is desirable. They may be listed as follows:

(a)   Brief verbal instructions.
(b)   Outline notes.
(c)   Manuscript draft.
(d)   Recorded dictation.
(e)   Direct dictation.

Brief verbal instructions

Many letters call for perfectly routine replies, and are repeated endlessly as a succession of correspondents writes in with the same request or query. The executive usually disposes of these by handing them over to the secretary at the start of the dictation session, giving a few verbal instructions if a particular point has to be emphasized in a particular letter. The secretary should note down these points, with the name of the addressee to whom each point refers. He/she should then take the group of letters and place them face down on the desk close by, so that by the end of the dictation session all the letters to be answered will be available in the correct order.

Provided the secretary has the necessary linguistic skill and can compose suitable replies this type of correspondence presents few problems and is very economical of the time of both parties.

Outline notes

Sometimes an executive will draw up outline notes on a particular matter and leave it to the secretary to compose the actual letter — or perhaps a first draft. This is a more time-consuming method as far as the executive is concerned, but it may assist him/her in thinking out the salient points of the matter in hand. The outline notes can be changed and altered until the chief features are in the best order. The executive does not have to waste the secretary's time as would be the case if this rearrangement process took place in a dictation session. The secretary then uses his/her linguistic skills to produce a first draft, or perhaps a final letter based upon the outline. In this activity the secretary will be greatly helped by knowledge of the firm and its general policy, and by his/her understanding of the executive's personal preferences in language. Sometimes a secretary will write letters that mirror so cleverly the executive's own choice of words that it will be difficult to decide who did write the letter should any query on it arise later.

Manuscript draft

The word manuscript means 'written by hand'. Where an executive writes out letters in longhand, he/she does of course waste a tremendous amount of time. Normally this would only be done with particularly difficult letters or reports. For example, a report of a technical nature, full of mathematical formulae, might be very difficult to dictate and require such precision of language that it would be difficult to hit the best words and phrases at a first attempt. Another situation where a secretary might be given a great many letters in manuscript form is where secretarial services are shared among a number of executives. This frequently happens in colleges and universities where the ratio of secretarial staff to executive staff is low. A lecturer who wants to clear his/her in-tray might write out letters at convenient times and leave the bundle in the secretary's tray to be typed when time permitted.

One difficulty with manuscript drafts is the writer's handwriting.

A secretary should appeal to the executive to write all the letters 'in a big round hand', like W.S. Gilbert's ruler of the Queen's Navy. Another difficulty is that many rising middle management staff may be less literate than their secretaries, and the manuscript consequently might be less well presented than a dictated letter.

Recorded dictation

Recorded dictation has only developed in the last 20 years, but it has to be accepted by almost every secretary that some part of his/ her work will be transmitted in this way. In particular, the refined hand-dictators coming into use in the mid-nineties are so reliable and convenient that every top executive will find this time-saving method of use. Although the top secretary, rather naturally, is reluctant to see vital shorthand skills bypassed by the dictation machine, it is a fact that such a top secretary is more capable of using the dictation machine than other staff. Audio-typing requires a real grasp of spelling, punctuation, sentence structure, etc., which many audio-typists do not have. The top secretary has no such difficulties and can therefore produce top-quality work however the subject matter of the letters is imparted.

Using the dictation machine

There are many types of dictation machine. Whichever type is in use, the chief points about its use may be listed as follows:

(a) You must introduce yourself by stating your name and department. This facilitates the return of your typed correspondence.

(b) You must give the details of the work required, particularly the number of copies required, and some indication of the length of the letter. This will assist the typist to select the right size paper to start with, and to judge what layout to adopt. Since delay inevitably occurs in multi-bank dictation systems, which enable many people to use the dictation machines, you should state the date you wish to appear on the letter. You should specify the enclosures to accompany it, and the references of both the addressee and your own department.

(c) You should speak in a clear, deliberate voice, in phrases of about six words, using the recommended 'letter analogy' alphabet for spelling out names and addresses or specialized technical words.

(d) You should use the recommended method for paragraphing and punctuation, as laid down in the in-house training sessions.

(e) With multi-bank systems an endless succession of dictation overloads one typist and prevents the even distribution of work, which is the chief advantage of the system. Normally the dictation of one long report or five short letters is a suitable package of work. By disconnecting, and, after a short pause, reconnecting, the dictator gives the supervisor a chance to allocate work among the staff.

Direct dictation

Sometimes an executive dictates to the typist as he/she is typing. The resulting end-product is immediately available, but the system is less satisfactory than most other systems. Unless the typist is absolutely excellent he/she will cause delays with the odd error – which interrupts the flow of dictation and wastes executive time. Some executives find it almost impossible to dictate while the typewriter is clattering away, and the system is therefore most appropriate for correspondence that has to be dispatched immediately.

The dictation session

When a dictation session is taking place, the executive and the secretary must work together to clear whatever backlog of correspondence has accumulated in the executive's in-tray. It is essential for both parties to adopt a businesslike approach, which will reduce the length of the session as much as possible without overlooking any item or postponing it to a later date. This approach requires that both parties make preparation for the session beforehand and thus ensure an immediate start on the work, concentrated activity during the session and a prompt conclusion.

Although these days many executives are female and an increasing number of male secretaries are leaving the training colleges, the following passages have regarded the secretary as female and the executive as male, to save excessive use of the his/her style.

Executive preparation

A secretary should try, for her own convenience as well as for his, to organize her executive to be ready to start at once when he calls her in for a dictation session. It is a great waste of the secretary's time if he proceeds to search the drawers of his desk or turn out his pockets to find odd scraps of information which he needs. If he is not the most organized of people she should tactfully suggest he prepares for his dictation session in the following ways:

(a) It is a good idea to keep a special **tear-off memo pad**, preferably with a distinctive cover, in his briefcase or even in his wallet if it is a slim pad. This will be available at all times for the quick pencil jotting − 'Write to Lever & Johnson re insurance updating'. This will ensure that matters of importance are not forgotten, and get the whole day's work cleared up in one session.

(b) He should keep files and correspondence that are due to be answered by him perhaps in a **desk organizer** of the sort illustrated in Figure 5.6. This enables him to pass over the letters as he deals with them, and saves dictating names and addresses, reference numbers, etc.

(c) Before the dictation session, he should make notes of the points he wishes to deal with in each letter, minute, memorandum, etc., and also how many copies he requires and who is to receive them. Sometimes an extra note is dictated to the secretary to be added to the other copies − but not to go on the original. The signal 'NOO' item ('not-on-original') will alert her to the need to ensure that only the copy receives this extra note. Some copies are 'blind' − that is, they are not allowed to show particular parts of a letter for security reasons. For example, the despatch manager's copy need not necessarily include the contract price. At the point where a copy is to be 'blinded' the typist will turn up a few lines and insert a sheet of plain paper between the carbon and the copy, so that the plain paper receives the impression and not the copy.

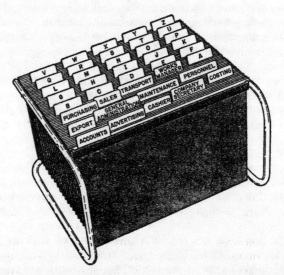

Figure 5.6   A desk organizer (*courtesy of Twinlock Ltd*)

If the letter is so intricate that dictation is not really appropriate, he should write the manuscript letter before calling in his secretary − or at least make a note to warn his secretary that he has a difficult manuscript letter to write, which she will be given later that day.

(d) He should prepare the room for the secretary so that she can sit comfortably in a good light, have a firm surface to work on if she prefers this, and have the best chance of hearing what is said by being seated face to face.

Preparation in the ways described will ensure that the actual dictation session proceeds at a good pace, suffers a minimum of interruption since it will be concluded with reasonable speed, and is sufficiently well organized to be a pleasurable contact between executive and secretary. A secretary who finds that she is forced to waste precious time with a disorganized and rambling dictation session must take steps to see that her executive's efficiency is increased.

Secretarial preparation

The secretary must be in a state of continuous preparation for dictation, since she may be called upon at any time, but particularly at those times of the day when she knows it is customary to deal with correspondence. The tools of the trade are shorthand notebooks with stiff covers, and pens, or pencils with fairly soft leads. Experienced secretaries usually develop their own ways of noting down alterations to the text and instructions for dealing with the letter, so that they rarely bother to draw margins or divide the page down the middle as suggested in many theory books. The shorthand pad should be readily available, with a rubber band encircling the pages already used. This can be used also to hold the pen or pencils on to the pad, so that one quick hand movement will pick up the whole collection when the secretary is called in for a dictation session.

Pencils should be soft, but not too soft, and it is good to have a couple of spares available. The inconvenience caused if a pencil is dropped and the point broken can interrupt the dictator's flow of words. If the notebook and pencils are always kept in the same place, they can be picked up quickly whenever they are required. It is always advisable to take them with you when called into the executive's office, even if dictation is not anticipated, since it gives you somewhere to write down notes of any instructions you are being given.

The dictation session is the ideal time to take up with the executive any queries or difficulties you have. It is also a good moment to discuss the diary, and any possible changes he may have made − perhaps in his private diary overnight. Part of your preparation should include a quick note of any such queries. At the end of the session you can turn to the appropriate place in the pad, raise the matters you have noted there and put down a note about any instructions he issues about dealing with them.

Other requirements are a spare pad if you are getting near the end of your current pad, and a manilla folder for correspondence. This folder is useful to contain all the letters and other slips of paper he gives you in the course of the dictation session.

The art of taking dictation

When a secretary is called for dictation, she should go in immediately. However tempting it is to finish the task in hand, it is more cost-effective to go at once. The executive is more highly paid than his secretary, and if he is kept waiting the time that is being wasted is more valuable. Enter briskly and take up your usual position. This should be facing him, preferably with a flat surface to work on and room to rest your elbows. As soon as you are seated, open your dictation book at the next clean page and write the date, and, if necessary, the initials of the executive, on the *bottom* line of the pad. This will help you find the correct place at a later date, should it be necessary, by simply flicking over the pages of the pad at the bottom. To open the pad easily, a thin elastic band of a suitable size is put round the used part of the pad, so that it can be opened at once to the next clean page. If you write shorthand notes with your right hand, you should raise the edge of the notebook page with your left hand and get a grip on the paper. As the letter proceeds, you gradually move the page upwards so that the line you are writing on is always at roughly the same position on the pad. When you get to the bottom of the page, a quick flip will turn the page over and you are away on the top line of the next page.

Letters succeed one another fairly rapidly and it is important to give a clear indication of where one ends and another begins. Therefore at the end of letter draw a clear horizontal line across the page.

Executives vary in their voices, speeds and mannerisms. Some speak distinctly and slowly, others speak poorly and too fast. Some dictate every piece of punctuation, others show by the expression in their voices when they expect punctuation to be inserted. The secretary must make the best of her executive. If he is slow and hesitant, she should use the odd seconds to write in longhand any outlines that she feels may be difficult to recall later. If he is dictating well and within your capacity, keep up with him, and if you miss a word, ask him about it at the end of the letter while he can still recall what he said. If he forgets your limitations and speaks at 250 wpm, you must stop him. To go at that pace when you are limited to 120 wpm means he might as well be talking to himself.

As each piece of correspondence is dealt with, the executive should either hand it to his secretary or place it face downwards on the table beside him. This gives a neat pile of correspondence, which will be in the same order as the letters on the secretary's pad. It may then be necessary to indicate to the secretary any letters that are particularly urgent, so that she does them first and presents them for signature in time to catch the first available post.

It is quite usual in a busy office for dictation to be interrupted by telephone and intercom calls. The executive cannot fail to lose concentration at such times and may repeat himself or use similar phrases, which he would have avoided if uninterrupted. It is useful to point these out, or to develop a working relationship that permits you to tidy up any such matters that become apparent during the transcription of the dictated material. For example, the executive who refers to a 'pleasant occasion' and then to a 'pleasant chat' will usually not mind his secretary changing the wording to an 'interesting chat'.

If the executive changes a paragraph of a letter — perhaps after hearing it read back — the page must be marked with a quick code — an asterisk or perhaps a number — which is then repeated at the end of the letter where the corrected paragraph has been taken down.

The alert secretary will soon invent her own short forms peculiar to the firm for which she works. Thus a secretary in a chemical works required frequently to write about cyclohexane will soon develop a short form which she knows refers to that word.

The student of business English will see from the description just given that there is much to be said for developing real facility with the English language. Both those who aspire to top secretarial work and those who seek executive status in one of the important walks of life need a sound knowledge of business English if they are to provide the clear, concise yet comprehensive correspondence that deals adequately with all the problems that arise in business life.

5.11   Answer section

Exercises 5a–5e   Lack of space prevents us supplying answers. You should appraise your own efforts carefully, making sure nothing has been omitted from the letter you have written.

Exercise 5f   1   A simple sentence; 2   complex; 3   compound; 4   simple; 5   compound; 6   compound–complex; 7   simple.

Exercise 5g   Sentences 3 and 5.

Exercise 5h   Sentence 2.

Exercises 5i and 5j   You must appraise your own work.

Exercise 5k   1 impolite (or discourteous); 2 obsequious (or servile); 3 isolate; 4 intelligence; 5 contrary.

Exercise 5l   1 commotion (or disturbance); 2 officer; 3 predicament; 4 wanton; 5 it seems 'scoop' has no synonym; 6 own up; (7) study; (8) traitor; (9) fairmindedness; (10) financial backing.

Exercise 5m   Appraise your own work.

6
Writing in paragraphs

6.1 The importance of paragraphs

Whenever we write, whether it is in correspondence, in reports or in literary passages of any sort, we should write in paragraphs. A paragraph is a collection of several sentences dealing with one idea. It would be possible to have a paragraph that only had a single sentence in it − perhaps for dramatic effect. Charles Reade, a Victorian author whose gripping novels have enthralled generations of students, has one passage in which two travellers are besieged in an inn in Italy by a band of robbers. They are crouched behind barricades made of their beds and mattresses, waiting to be attacked. We then get the following few lines.

'Look out, Gerard.'
'Ay. What will they do next?'
'We shall soon know.'
'Shall I wait for you, or cut down the first that opens the door?'
'Wait for me, lest we strike the same and waste a blow. Alas! we cannot afford that.'
Dead silence.
Sudden came into the room a thing that made them start and their hearts quiver.
And what was it? A moonbeam!

What actually happens is that, as the moonbeam reaches the doorpost, they see a hand creeping through a secret hatch in the doorpost to unlock their door. Dennis shoots with his crossbow to fix the hand to the doorpost, and with a swift sword blow Gerard severs it from the arm. Life in the Middle Ages was described by one philosopher as 'nasty, brutish, mean and short'. If you want a good read, try Charles Reade's *The Cloister and the Hearth*.

It is not likely that many of our letters or reports will give an opportunity for a single-sentence paragraph. More likely a paragraph will have two or three sentences, which together deal fully with the idea we wish to convey to the correspondent or committee we are addressing. The importance of paragraphs may be explained as follows:

- They break the information in a long letter or report down into shorter sections.
- They make it easier for the reader to follow the subject matter and to understand each stage as it is developed.
- They enable the writer, e.g. the author of the report, to organize his/her ideas, getting them into correct sequence. This logical order will assist the reader. A disjointed report will be incoherent and will tend to lower the author in the reader's estimation.

6.2   The nature of a paragraph

A paragraph consists of a key sentence and a number of other sentences lending it support. Very often the key sentence will come first, and the other sentences will provide extra facts, information or evidence to elaborate upon the idea conveyed in the key sentence. If the idea that is the subject of a paragraph is at all controversial, the supporting sentences may look at it from various angles and give the points for and against it − the *pros* and *cons*.

Consider the following paragraph. You are trying to decide what is the key sentence:

> The tribunal's view was that the young person had been improperly dismissed and was entitled to compensation. First, there had been no warning about the view that would be taken of such conduct, and a person of that age could not be expected to know the seriousness of the offence. Second, summary dismissal was only permissible for offences where theft or utterly disgraceful conduct had occurred. Thirdly, the young person had been given no opportunity to explain his conduct. A refusal to apologize at once was not a good excuse for dismissal − given a little time the young man might have seen that he had been hasty and that an apology was due. Finally, there had been a clear breach of natural justice. The managing director to whom the remark was addressed had been accuser, judge, jury and executioner all at the same time. No one should be a judge in his/her own case.

It is clear that the first sentence is the key sentence. It tells us what the paragraph is all about. The other sentences outline why the tribunal reached this decision.

There are many occasions in business life when this sort of problem might arise. There has to be a proper procedure for dismissal and the procedure must take into account the two rules of 'natural justice'. These are:

(a)   No one may be a judge in his own case.
(b)   We must always hear both sides.

A useful third rule is that we should not reach hurried conclusions. We often hear complaints about the law's delay, but to be too quick with any trial is also a defect. Everyone is entitled to the 'due process of law'.

On the point about the sequence of ideas in a paragraph. Consider the following group of sentences. They all come from the same paragraph, but the sequence has been disturbed. Work out the correct sequence. The answer is given at the end of this section.

1   They will arrive at 2 pm and will be touring the entire building.
2   Petra Angellis will stand in for Mr Hicks during the tour of their division.
3   All staff should be ready to respond to any questions put to them.
4   Tomorrow the managing director and the finance director will be visiting the department.
5   There will be a break for the touring party, for coffee at 3.15 in the canteen.
6   The visit will end with a question and answer session at 4.30 pm in the long laboratory.
7   Although you are free to air any grievances at the 4.30 meeting, I hope staff will make some attempt to speak positively about their work.
8   All personnel are required to be in attendance from 2 pm onwards, except John Hicks, who has a vital appointment elsewhere.
9   Some people will have to stand as the seating is limited in the laboratory.
10   May I thank you in advance for your cooperation on this important occasion.

Answer   The original order was 4, 1, 8, 2, 3, 5, 6, 9, 7, 10.

6.3   Building a paragraph

Many students find it difficult to write robust paragraphs. We need to plan a paragraph so that it is a complete and comprehensive account of the idea outlined in the key sentence. It should be forceful, vigorous, concrete and clear. It does not improve a paragraph simply to pad it out with wordy, meaningless phrases. Each sentence must add something useful to the key sentence. If the key sentence is to be at the end, then each sentence must be a step in that direction. A good plan goes like this.

(a)   *Write the key sentence*
This sentence should be a clear statement of your thoughts about the matter in hand. Ideally it should be a distillation of your thoughts about the matter. Many great writers have left us their key sentences as **aphorisms**, which are short, pithy maxims that have moved into everyday speech. For example:

'No people do so much harm as those who go about doing good'.
'Property has its duties, as well as its rights'.
'Never look back, for if you did how could you bear to go away'.
'A journey to China begins with a single step'.

Even Chairman Mao left a whole book full of his *Thoughts*.

(b)   *Consider how to reinforce the key sentence*
You might try:

(i)   Illustrating it − with a few 'for instances' or examples.
(ii)   Amplifying it − taking each part of it and showing more fully what it really means. Concrete examples always help. The term here is the opposite of 'abstract'. Concrete examples bring out what the phrase means here and now, in the practical affairs of mankind.
(iii) We can draw comparisons perhaps. What shall we gain by one line of policy, and what shall we lose if we adopt an alternative programme. 'Compare' and 'contrast' are two related approaches − to contrast our key idea with another key idea may strengthen the reader's understanding.
(iv)   Use analogies. In an analogy we liken the idea we have to another idea that is a parallel case. A celebrated analogy was given by a Saxon wise man listening to St Augustine. He said, 'A man's life is like a sparrow flying in from the darkness at one end of a great hall and then flying out again at the other end after a brief interval, never to be seen again'. Sometimes an analogy clarifies an idea.

6.4   Connectors and paragraphs

Connectors are words or phrases that show the reader how one sentence connects with another sentence. They are like signposts, indicating to the reader the direction in which the author's thoughts are tending to go. Without these signposts some readers might become confused and might not be able to see the trend in the writer's reasoning.

A connector is not quite the same thing as a conjunction, which is a word that can actually join two sentences together. However, some conjunctions can act as connectors because they do show the way forward. Examples are 'and', 'so', 'like', 'yet', 'but' and 'or'.

For example, 'The man seems to be an honest enough employee, yet there is one pattern in his behaviour that is unusual'. The word 'yet' suggests to the reader that we must be cautious – it isn't absolutely certain that the man is honest. What was the next sentence in the report? It was the fact that the man always worked late in the office, staying until everyone else had gone home. There could be several reasons why he did this, and his behaviour might be perfectly innocent. Still the connector has hung out a sign to the reader showing the direction of the security officer's thoughts.

Many statements, e.g. those made by witnesses in police investigations, are time-related. They describe a sequence of events, and the connectors tying the statement together can be time-related too. Thus 'first', 'next', 'then', 'after that', 'subsequently' and 'finally' would keep the time sequence clear from start to finish, and the reader would be in no doubt of the witness's understanding of the events.

Many connectors cannot join sentences together, i.e. they are not conjunctions, but they begin the next sentence to show its relation to the previous sentence. The connectors 'so', 'therefore', 'hence', 'as a result', 'accordingly', and 'that is why' all show that the next sentence is going to convey an idea that is the result of something said in the previous sentence. Of these only 'so' is really a conjunction, and all the rest would be connecting words or phrases that started a new sentence. For example:

> Unscrupulous customers will order goods even though they have not paid for goods supplied on an earlier occasion. Consequently we must establish a credit control system that limits the value of goods to be supplied to anyone.

The word 'Consequently' shows the link between the two sentences.

Sometimes a second sentence contrasts with a statement made in the first sentence. For example, 'The team physio had no formal medical qualification. He had a natural understanding of the skeleton and could manipulate a dislocated shoulder or finger back into place to the instant relief of the injured player'. We could use 'yet', or 'nevertheless' or 'however' or 'on the other hand' at the start of the second sentence to show that a contrasting statement to the first one was about to be made.

A further example would be, 'The prospectors hugged each other to see the bright yellow gold in the rock they had discovered. Yet all is not gold that glisters'. The word 'Yet' is a connector that tells us the prospectors were due to be disappointed.

6.5   Exercises on paragraphs

Exercise 6a   Use your imagination to write a paragraph of at least four sentences on each of the topics below:

(i)   A witness's account of an accident in which a police car, pursuing a joyrider, was in collision with a delivery vehicle at a road junction.

(ii)   A description by a mountaineer of his discovery of a body frozen into the ice in an Alpine valley.

(iii)   An explanation of how to do a percentage sum on an electronic calculator.

Exercise 6b   Use your imagination to write a paragraph of at least five sentences on any two of the topics below.

(i)   The importance of climate in the successful operation of any agricultural activity.

(ii)   The economic environment of a village shop.

(iii)   The advantage of heavy goods vehicles in distribution activities.

(iv)   Cassette music.

Exercise 6c   Rearrange these jumbled sentences into the best order and write them out as a paragraph. The correct sequence is given at the end of this chapter, but you may start by knowing that number 1 is in fact the first sentence.

1   The speaker's subject was entitled 'Was Troy in England?'

2   For example, he talks of 'a wine dark sea', but the Mediterranean sea is almost always blue.

3   Thirdly, the story as told by Homer is an epic poem.

4   He advanced many ideas to justify his belief that it may very well have been.

5   Second, most of the towns named in Homer were not to be found in any part of the Mediterranean under those names, yet towns with those names, or very similar, do exist in Northern Europe.

6   Each year they still give a prize to the bard who delivers the best epic poem.

7   First, Homer's account of the siege of Troy contains many things that simply do not fit the Mediterranean scene.

8   The one country in the world famous for its epic poems is Ancient Britain, though its descendants have now been pushed into one corner of the country and are called the Welsh.

9   Another piece of evidence is that in the United Kingdom precious metals are still measured in Troy ounces.

6.6 Advertising copy

Chapter 5 was about special types of business letter. Advertising copy is a special type of writing for business purposes, though with larger firms it may be an activity that is carried out by a specialist advertising agency. Here we will consider the more simple type of advertisement, for which usually an agency would not be employed.

Classified advertisements

A classified advertisement is a small newspaper or magazine advertisement written to appeal to a particular class of reader. Such advertisements are grouped together under a class heading, e.g. 'Items for sale', 'Rented accommodation', or even 'Lonely Hearts', hence the name 'classified advertisements'. Charges vary, but 20 pence per word to 80 pence per word (depending upon circulation) is about the usual charge. The advertiser must include a name and address, or perhaps a telephone number. Those who do not wish to reveal either of these pieces of information may use a box number supplied by the journal used, for which an extra charge is made. Responses to the box number may be collected from the journal's offices. Students could study their local press or their favourite magazine for examples of this type of advertisement. Two examples are given below:

- South Cambridgeshire: Detached family home with large private garden to let April–November. Moderate terms. References required. Leyside Homes 0223 07125.
- Young attractive lady, 25, embarking on Himalayan adventure trip requires three companions either sex. Support of £3,000 approx. each essential for successful trip. Plans fluid except for departure date (August 1). Write to Box 1745, ASAP.

Abbreviations are frequently used in such advertisement. ASAP is of course 'as soon as possible.'

Exercise 6d   Write a classified advertisement for your firm, which rents out holiday cottages at various seaside resorts. Offer a brochure to interested parties and give your address and telephone number.

Exercise 6e   Write a classified advertisement for the 'Lost and Found' column of your local press about an item you have lost that has little value to any finder but is of great importance to you. Offer a reasonable reward.

Exercise 6f Write a classified advertisement to appear in an American magazine in which you offer to exchange your home with someone in America for a 6-week period in the summer. Give full details of your house, facilities, etc.

Display advertisements

Display advertisements are larger than classified advertisements and more expensive. As the name implies, they are usually set off from other advertisements by being surrounded by a box. They may include not only written material (called 'copy') but illustrations and application forms, according to the type of advertisement. An example of a display advertisement appears in Figure 6.1.

Obviously the layout of a display advertisement is important, and so is the writing of the actual copy. It is important to make a list of all the points that need to be made in the advertisement and ensure that they are all included. If you are given the task of working out a first rough draft, think the whole thing through from start to finish. We could list these points:

Figure 6.1 A display advertisement

(a)   Who are you trying to reach with the advertisement?
(b)   What message do you want to convey?
(c)   What vital facts must be included?
(d)   How is the interested customer to respond to the advertisement?
(e)   Is an application form to be included? The design of an application form is an important task in itself.
(f)   Do we need an illustration of any sort?

When you have done your best with the rough draft, it is always advisable to circulate it to three or four others for their comments and approval. If this is not done and anything proves to be wrong with the copy, the full force of the blame will fall upon you. If several others are consulted, not only will most of the errors be picked up but the eventual blame (if there is any) will be shared.

It is common to test the response rate achieved by the advertisement by putting in some coded part of the address. Thus, where an advertisement is to appear in the London *Daily Telegraph* we might include in our address the code (Dept. LDT). As responses arrive, a member of staff will be deputed to keep a record on the five-barred gate system to reveal what responses were received from each advertisement. See Figure 6.2.

Daily Telegraph (DT)
卌 卌
卌 卌
卌 卌
III

Daily Mirror (DM)
卌 卌
卌 卌
IIII

Sunday Express (SE)
卌 卌 卌 卌
卌 卌 卌 III
卌 卌
卌 卌
卌 卌

Woman's Own (WO)
卌 卌
卌

Saga Magazine (SM)
卌 卌 卌 卌
卌 卌 卌 卌
卌 卌 卌 卌
卌 卌 卌 卌
卌 卌 II

Cosmopolitan (C)
卌 卌
卌 卌
卌 卌
卌 卌
II

Figure 6.2   Checking response rates

6.7   Exercises on advertising copy

Exercise 6g   Make a collection of display advertisements from your local press and any popular or specialist magazines you take. Try to obtain at least two about (a) jobs on offer, (b) holidays on offer, (c) transport or travel, (d) products of use in the office, (e) products of use at home. Also try to collect (f) two with illustrations, and (g) two with application forms.

Exercise 6h   Design a display advertisement for one of the following:

(i)   A product or service offered by your own firm or company.
(ii)   To advertise the college course you are at present pursuing as if enrolments for next year were being actively pursued by the head of department. Give entry requirements, an outline of the course and full details about how to apply.
(iii)   An advertisement aimed at collecting funds for a good cause, announcing one or more fund-raising events and soliciting subscriptions generally.
(iv)   An advertisement about holiday work on offer to students prepared to assist in caring for and amusing handicapped children going on a 'sailing adventure' holiday sponsored by a national charity, such as the television channels organize from time to time. Give details of the qualities that would be most helpful in an applicant, and an application form on which they may apply if they are interested.

6.8   More spellings: some rules about plurals

Regular nouns simply add 's' to the singular to form the plural:

shoe, shoes
boy, boys
pencil, pencils

If the singular ends in 'o', add 'es' to get the plural:

echo, echoes
tomato, tomatoes
potato, potatoes
Negro, Negroes

However there are some exceptions:

solo, solos
piano, pianos
Eskimo, Eskimos

Now ask a colleague to test you on one of these sets of spellings, and in return test him/her on the other set:

Parliamentary affairs		*Word processing*	
Parliament	debate	electronic	buffer memory
Lords	discussion	automatic	standard letter
Commons	deliberation	reprographic	standard paragraph
Cabinet	election	tabulation	display
prime minister	candidate	centring	salutation
chancellor	ballot paper	underscoring	complimentary close
privy councillor	legislation	visual display unit	search facility
prerogative	proposal	monitor	impression control
appointment	amendment	keyboard	mandatory instructions
honour	committee	printout	justified margins

6.9 More about punctuation

Exercise 6i Here are four sentences that have punctuation errors and possibly spelling errors as well. Write down in the format shown below what is wrong with each sentence. There may be more than one error in a sentence. Suggested format: 'In sentence (a) the apostrophe after the word years' is wrong because .... etc.'

(a) This years' World Development Report recommends that allocations of financial aid be linked to a countries' efforts to alleviate its own poverty.
(b) The data focuses on national accounts; international transactions and other indicator's of development.
(c) She said, "I see no reason why the feminine role in the family need be diminished by participation in a career activity!"
(d) The term 'full punctuation' may be contrasted with 'open punctuation,' where punctuation mark's are reduced to a minimum. For example NIC is widely used in plaice of N.I.C. for 'national insurance contributions.'

6.10 Answer section

Exercises 6a and 6b You will have to appraise your own efforts.

Exercise 6c   The correct sequence is 1; 4; 7; 2; 5; 3; 8; 6; 9.

Exercises 6d, e, f, g and h   You will have to appraise your own efforts.

Exercise 6i

(a)   'year's', 'country's'.
(b)   'focus' (data is plural); a comma is needed after accounts, not a semi-colon; the word 'indicators' is a plural — no apostrophe required as it does not show possession.
(c)   An exclamation mark is not really required — the sentence is a statement, not an exclamation.
(d)   The quote after 'open punctuation' should be to the left of the comma. No apostrophe is required on 'marks', and a 'plaice' is a type of fish. It should read 'place'. The final quotation mark should come before the full stop.

7
Face-to-face communication

7.1 The importance of face-to-face communication

There are countless situations where face-to-face communication is necessary in business. At the very lowest level we are all working away in an environment where the success of our activities depends upon cooperation and mutual support and understanding. The newcomer must be able to learn the job in the first place, a process called 'induction'. When we induct a new employee, we must give instructions in a clear, calm way. We must bring out the importance of the work, the possible hazards and the quickest and best way to do things. We must give the newcomer an opportunity to ask questions, and to practise what is required. Few people can do even a simple operation correctly at the first attempt.

At a higher level there will always be times when sections of a workforce, or possibly the entire staff, have to be briefed on a new situation. It may be the launch of a new product, or of a new method of working. It may be the take-over of the firm by another company, or the securing of an important contract. It may be a special event, such as a Royal visit or an annual general meeting of the company. Whatever the event, there will be someone who needs to act as spokesperson and to use his/her skills of face-to-face communication. Nothing is more testing. Presidents and prime ministers have lost elections because of a single poor performance on television. Managing directors have been voted off their boards, trade union leaders have been deposed, generals and field-marshals have been retired, and all for the want of a little preparation and instruction in face-to-face communication.

Good communicators are made, not born. Of course there are odd individuals who are gifted speakers, able to rise instantly to their feet and hold forth in a lucid and interesting way on any and every subject. They are not very numerous, though. The Irish (a nation noted for their ready way with words) say that those who have kissed the Blarney Stone will ever after 'have a cajoling tongue and the art of flattery'. Not many of us can travel to Blarney Castle near Cork, and kiss the Blarney Stone. When it comes to face-to-

face speech we have to learn how to do it, and hope that eventually
we will do it well.

7.2   Principles of face-to-face communication

The first principle of face-to-face communication is detailed preparation beforehand. You must know all you should know about the
subject on which you are to address the individual, group or mass
meeting. Assemble your facts, check all the relevant details, arrange
them in the correct order for coherent presentation and make notes
of any important points.

Now think carefully about the actual presentation. There are
often certain courtesies you must observe. These include welcoming
the audience and thanking them for their attendance − if that is
appropriate for the occasion. There will perhaps be a need to
introduce some of the people present. Make sure you have their
names right, and if they have titles or offices that should be mentioned,
be quite sure you know all the facts. If you intend to use some sort
of visual aid, make sure it is available. Check that any working parts
are in order, it is visible and conveniently placed, etc. Think the
whole thing through and envisage the worst that can happen.

If you are delivering a report or making a speech that has to be in
a precise form − for example, because it is being delivered to the
press as a 'press report' after you have delivered the speech, make
sure you get your copy clearly typed in a big print size so you can
read it easily. These days any copy-shop on every street has a photocopier that will double the size of any document copied on it. If you
don't see too well, spend a little money on enlarging your copy so
you can read it easily.

If you are so familiar with your subject that you can speak 'off the
cuff', then at least make up a set of cards with all the salient
features so that you keep the thread of your argument going as you
originally intended. Better still, buy some sheets of cartridge paper
and make your 'salient features' into a flip chart, which can be hung
up at the start of your talk and serve as an outline for both yourself
and your audience. This is a particularly good idea if the speech you
have to give is one you deliver regularly, e.g. to every new batch of
employees. Preparation only needs to consist of getting down the
flip chart, turning over the pages to remind yourself all about it, and
making the arrangements so it can be displayed easily, e.g. on an
easel or some similar device.

The actual delivery should be brisk and businesslike. A slow or
hesitant speaker soon becomes a bore, and a manifestly disorganized
person who loses the thread of his story or whose visual aid or
apparatus is defective in some way makes the audience restless and
ill at ease.

It is often necessary to allow time for questions or discussion at the end of a talk. Finally, there may be further courtesies to be gone through to ensure that the event is rounded off in a pleasant and decorous way.

7.3   Giving instructions

When giving instructions, you have a number of aspects to consider. The chief ones are:

(a) The circumstances surrounding the need to give instruction. These include the age and sophistication of those being instructed.
(b) The nature of the instructions to be given.
(c) The need for practice or recapitulation.

The circumstances

Unless instructions are to be given to an individual or a very small group, we must be sure we are able to secure the attention of those being instructed, and that they can all hear us and see us. If it is in the open air, we must ask them to gather round, and give them a chance to do so before beginning. Wait for reasonable silence — perfect silence can rarely be achieved. Getting on with the message to be delivered compels the odd murmurer to pay attention. Speak up, or when speech is unlikely to be heard by the large group being addressed, either use a loud-hailer or some form of public address system.

Young people, new employees or recruits need to have instructions given in a more simple way than mature people. Spell out what has to be done clearly, and, if necessary, go over it more than once.

The nature of the instruction

Obviously there is a huge range of instructions, but the speaker needs to know what has to be said and to say the items in correct sequence. The best thing to do is to make a list of the points, and, if possible, have them written on a blackboard or other notice-board. This gives a focus of attention and keeps both speaker and audience on the thread of the discussion.

Go through them point by point, and don't be embarrassed by the fact that the group can read them for themselves. It may be that some cannot read, but in any case your one-word headings will not convey the full instruction you are intending to give. Take each point and amplify it, seizing any opportunity to warn of hazards or emphasizing the simplicity of the operation. If it is appropriate, invite questions on each point, so that any difficulties are cleared out of the way at once.

At the same time don't delay too long – press on to the next section if time-wasting questions are being asked.

The need for practice and recapitulation

Remember that if the instruction is to do with a practical activity, it is almost certain many of the group will not understand the procedure first time. A wall chart or diagram, which can be referred to again and again after instruction is over, may be a desirable feature of your talk. It is almost always, even with the simplest instructions, desirable to recapitulate the points made, so that those under instruction have a second or third chance to follow the procedure.

A final chance to ask questions will clear up any further points. It may also reveal one or two in the group who are hopelessly at sea, and cannot really follow the instructions at all. This does not mean they are totally incapable of doing the work – they may in fact prove to be ideal. One of the authors of this book was once asked by an employer, 'Have you a really dull pupil you can recommend for a routine job'. Upon inquiry it became clear that a very weak and slow learner, while taking a long time to learn a particular task, was likely, once it had been mastered, to go on doing it for a long time. Any change of employment would force him to learn something else and lose him wages, since the job could earn quite good money once the output was at a reasonable level. The employer lost a little at first with the need to train a slow learner, but gained in the end because the labour turnover in the job was almost non-existent.

7.4   Exercises on giving instructions

Exercise 7a   Choose five locations not too far from your present college, school or home (if you are studying on your own). Now choose one person to instruct the group in how to reach the place chosen, starting from the school, college, etc.

Exercise 7b   Each person chooses any place, such as a shop, place of entertainment, scenic spot, etc. Work out a set of instructions how to get there, and list the chief points of interest. Deliver this as a set of instructions to your group. The group should appraise your efforts.

Exercise 7c Think of some activity with which you are familiar, such as baking bread, making a meal, repairing a flat tyre on a bicycle, etc. Deliver this as a set of instructions to other members of the group. The group should appraise your efforts.

7.5 Making requests

Giving instructions is a relatively simple form of face-to-face communication, because those instructed usually have some interest in performing the activity. It may be essential for them to carry out the instructions because it is part of their job, or it will ensure that they enjoy the activity, or make progress in their career, etc. It is not quite so easy to make requests, because people are under no compulsion to accede to a request and have to be persuaded by the force of the argument presented to them.

The main points here are as follows:

- Have it clear in your mind what it is you are asking people to do.
- Clarify in your own mind why it is desirable that they should do what you are asking. It may be that you can advance compelling reasons for their cooperation, perhaps for business reasons but possibly for humanitarian or ecological reasons.
- Make sure that the means for cooperation are provided, if that is possible, e.g. collecting boxes if you are asking them to support a charity, or forms to complete if you are asking them to apply for membership of some body.
- To leave a lasting impression, it is often best to set out the points you have made again in a typewritten summary, or possibly a leaflet. This not only serves to remind them of the request you are making but enables them to take something tangible away to discuss with other people who were unable to be present, e.g. wives, or husbands, or colleagues. Such a summary is also useful to put in the pigeonholes of members of staff not present at the meeting, or the in-trays of executives in other departments.

Exercise 7d Prepare a short speech to be made at a staff meeting in which you ask colleagues to agree to the donation of a trivial sum, say 5p. per week, to a charity in which you are interested. The management has agreed to extract the money from pay packets as a computerized payroll deduction, paying it over in a lump sum once a month to the charity, so long as at least fifty employees agree to the scheme. Deliver the speech to your class or group, and listen to their appraisals of your effectiveness.

Exercise 7e   As a contribution to the local community (the area being fairly isolated), the firm has agreed to the use of its main meeting hall for (a) disco evenings on Saturdays and (b) youth club meetings on Tuesdays. Volunteers are required to take charge of the premises on these occasions, although a caretaker and paid officials will be present to conduct the actual activities. The role is 'low-profile' supervision to meet insurance and police key-holder requirements, between the hours of 6 pm and 10.30 pm. Prepare a speech requesting help so that a rota of staff can be drawn up. Deliver the speech to your class and listen to their appraisal of your efforts.

Exercise 7f   Prepare a speech requesting members of staff to give blood once every 6 months, in view of the shortages being experienced by the local hospital. Arrangements are being made for a visit every 6 months from the local blood-transfusion centre, so that employees may give blood on the premises by taking a short break at some time during the day. Deliver your speech to the class or study group, and listen to their appraisal of your efforts.

7.6   Talk-ins and quality circles

Talk-ins and quality circles are rather similar in that both consist of small meetings, usually departmental meetings or smaller 'cost-centre' meetings. The talk-in is a general meeting in which all those present are free to speak their minds on any matter that they consider important. It might be introduced by a manager or supervisor of some sort, giving an official view of one or two problems or developments. This would be followed by the views of other leading people, and then a free-for-all session would be open to anyone else wishing to join the discussion. Obviously the chairperson has the chance to influence the choice of speakers, but this does not necessarily militate against the person with strong views. It is commonly held that it is desirable to let those who wish to let off steam do so. This relieves to some extent whatever frustration they are feeling, and allows more temperate members of staff to think through the points raised and perhaps rebut them in a later contribution to the debate.

The chairperson or some 'minuting-secretary' will make a note of really useful points made by contributors, with a view to action being taken on the matters raised. It may even be considered desirable to appoint a small sub-committee of the most interested people to pursue a particular matter further, and report back either to a similar meeting at a later date or through the 'house journal', if one is available. Such a committee is called an *ad hoc* committee, meaning one 'arranged for this purpose'. More permanent committees are called 'standing committees', which continue year after year, e.g. a 'safety committee'.

Quality circles are a new development, originating in Japan, but now spreading throughout the world. They consist of small meetings grouped around cost-centres in factories and offices, whose aim is to discuss methods of working and to improve where possible both the quality of the product and its 'value for money', and therefore its competitiveness in the marketplace. The essence of the quality circle is to increase the participation of the ordinary employee in the management process. The shopfloor worker is much closer to the point of production than the management, and may notice things of which top management could never become aware. The quality of materials, the use of glues, paints, securing brackets and a host of minor items, may in fact be a source of dissatisfaction not only to employees but to customers and end-users. Problems may be brought to the group's attention as a result of customer complaints, minor accidents on the production line, excessive scrap, failure of components to pass quality control checks, etc. Bringing them back to the quality circle, or raising them with the quality circle if the fault is found by a shopfloor worker, allows the mistakes or errors to be rectified, or traced to some outside source (such as a subcontractor) with whom representations about the fault can be made.

Quality circles are not *ad hoc* committees. They meet regularly, usually fortnightly, and there must be follow-up action to implement the ideas brought up by group members if confidence is to be maintained. If an idea cannot be adopted, at least the reasons for its rejection must be fully explained, together with some expression of management's appreciation of the idea.

The leader of the quality circle (often a person at supervisor level) may be given training in the organizational aspects of group activities − in particular how to stimulate discussion of problems and how to listen to the views of others in a receptive way, rather than with a closed mind. Any sarcasm or destructive appraisal of a group member's contribution is undesirable, in an atmosphere where all are trying to make constructive suggestions. The group leader's aim is to encourage responsibility for quality, smooth systems of work and wholehearted cooperation with the production process.

Exercise 7g Hold a classroom talk-in, with one of the leading personalities in the class acting as chairperson, to discuss the general organization of the class and its effectiveness as an educational institution. Keep the discussion impersonal rather than personal, and positive and practical rather than negative and theoretical.

At the end of the discussion choose a new chairperson and appraise (a) the conduct of the talk-in by the first chairperson and

(b) the speeches of the participants. Who made the best speeches and why?

Exercise 7h   Imagine you are a member of a quality circle in one of the following situations. Draw up a list of ways in which the quality of your goods or service could be improved or made more competitive, so as to ensure increased market share and increased job security:

(a)   A manufacturer of motor vehicles.
(b)   A manufacturer of kitchen cabinets.
(c)   A 'painter and decorator's' business.
(d)   A private school.
(e)   An old people's home in the private sector.
(f)   A National Health Service hospital.
(g)   A landscape gardener's business.
(h)   A hairdresser's salon.

7.7   More spellings: plurals and possessive pronouns

When a word ends with 's', there is a great temptation to put an apostrophe either before or after the 's'. One often sees notices outside shops or public houses with this mistake, e.g. 'Fresh cake's', or 'Home-brewed ale's'.

There are two uses for apostrophes. One is to show that a letter or letters has been left out − in other words, a contraction (a shortening of the word or phrase used). For example:

They're = they are
I'm   = I am
we'll   = we shall or we will

The other is to show possession, e.g. 'This is Peter's calculator'. You could regard a possession as just one more type of contraction. The word 'Peter's' really means: 'This is Peter his calculator.'

To return to cakes and ales, neither of these is a contraction or a possessive. Cakes is simply the plural of cake and ales is the plural of ale. Just because a word ends in 's' does not mean it wants an apostrophe.

There are four rules about possessives:

(a) *Don't confuse contractions with possessive pronouns*
For example, it's (is short for it is)
                    its (is a possessive pronoun)
                    It's getting late.
                    The dog wags its tail.

they're (is short for 'they are')
their (is a possessive pronoun)
They're going to the airport any minute.
They have their air tickets.

(b) *Don't use apostrophes for possessive or relative pronouns that happen to end in 's'*
   his, hers, its, ours, yours, theirs, whose.
No apostrophes with any of these

(c) *If you want to show that something belongs to a person (or persons) whose name does not end in 's', then we do need an apostrophe before the 's' in the singular, or after the 's' in the plural:*

(i)   Before the prince's visit could begin, his helicopter had to negotiate a difficult landing.
(ii) Before the princes' visit to the factory, they called at the local hospital.

(d) *If the noun does end in 's', you need an apostrophe after the 's' but without any final 's' in the plural:*

(i)   The waitress's uniform is provided by the hotel.
(ii) The waitresses' uniforms are provided by the hotel.

Now here are two more groups of spellings. Test a fellow student on the first set, and ask him/her to reciprocate by testing you on the second set.

Law		*Marketing*	
contract	common law	market	sale
contractual	statute law	market trader	saleable
party	custom	market maker	saleability
representation	equity	marketable	inform
misrepresentation	equitable	marketability	information
puff	fair-play	market overt	informative
innocent	municipal	advertise	agent
negligent	international	advertisement	representative
fraudulent	private	persuasive	traveller
corrupt	personal	persuasion	factor

Note: Market overt is a legal term which means 'open market'. If you buy a thing in market overt you are deemed to buy honestly. If you buy in other circumstances, e.g. from a stranger in a public house, you may not be deemed to buy honestly, but perhaps to have 'received' stolen goods.

7.8   Briefings

A briefing is a face-to-face meeting between one person who has
information to convey and a group of people who need to know the
information for one purpose or another. For example, in wartime,
where rumours abound and everyone needs to know the current
situation on the various battlefronts, it is usual to hold a briefing
meeting at a set time – say noon each day. At the appointed time a
high-ranking official will appear to give an account of the current
state of affairs and to answer such questions as are put to him/her.

Similarly actual operations may be begun by briefing all those
who need to know about them. For example, aircrews are called to
a briefing-room to be told of the next target to be attacked, the line
of flight selected as being the least hazardous, the diversionary raids
to be carried out to confuse the enemy, etc.

The police frequently hold briefing meetings for the press where
there is widespread interest in a particular case. They may also use
it as a means of collecting further evidence by giving the press, for
example, photo-fit pictures to reproduce in their next editions.

The word 'brief' means short, and a briefing is not intended to be
a lengthy account of events. Usually the statement read out is quite
short – a digest of the facts as they are known and an account of the
lines of enquiry that are being followed. The term is of course
closely linked to the 'brief' solicitors prepare for counsel who have
been selected to represent their clients. A 'brief' is a short account
of the client's predicament, telling what happened and giving the
client's point of view of the matter. The barrister studies the brief
before going into court, and as the case unfolds is able to rebut the
allegations made against the client and explain the client's view of
the matter.

In giving a briefing therefore the following points are important:

- Keep the account of events brief and factual without expressing
  opinions (which can be misrepresented).
- Assist the press (or other audience) by giving interesting headline
  cases where this is possible without breaching security. A particularly successful project, a piece of shrewd detective work, or
  an act of great personal bravery makes a briefing more interesting
  and lively.
- Be prepared to deal with questions by having a good background
  knowledge of the situation; but remember the limits beyond
  which it would be unwise to go.
- Think ahead to envisage the sort of awkward questions that
  might come up, and decide how you will answer them.

Exercise 7i   Draw up a short statement to brief the press on each of
the following events:

(a) The Declaration of Independence, 1776, by which the American colonies broke away from the United Kingdom and formed the United States of America.
(b) The storming of the Bastille on 14 July 1789, at the beginning of the French Revolution.
(c) The assassination of President Kennedy at Dallas.

Exercise 7j Draw up a briefing statement to announce your company's take-over of a rival firm in the same industry. Give details of the arrangements made about:

(a) The agreed price.
(b) The closure of one set of premises and the transfer of both businesses to a single work-site.
(c) The arrangements made for staff − some redundancies are inevitable but it is hoped to achieve them by voluntary, rather than compulsory, redundancies.

Exercise 7k Draw up a briefing statement about the development of a new product. Tell the press what it is, how it has been developed, what the market is likely to be and what influence you expect it will have on the expansion of your firm, its profitability and the likely job opportunities that will result.

7.9 Comprehension exercises

The following extract is from the publication *Economic Briefing*, and is dated May 1991. *Economic Briefing* is published by HM Treasury, whose courtesy in allowing the use of this extract, and the one which follows, is acknowledged.

The Bank of England

All countries have central banks. In the United States it is the Federal Reserve Bank (sometimes called the Fed). In Germany it is the Bundesbank. In France it is the Banque de France. In the UK it is the Bank of England.

What does the central bank do? Essentially, it has three functions. The first is to advise on and execute monetary policy − that is, policies aimed at safeguarding the value of money in the economy. The second is to ensure the soundness of the nation's financial system, including direct supervision of banks and other participants in City financial markets. The third is to promote the efficiency and competitiveness of the financial system, particularly in the field of domestic and international payment systems, and systems for settling securities transactions, so that the City of London can serve industry and commerce at home and maintain its place as the world's leading financial centre.

To achieve these aims the Bank acts as banker to the government and as banker to the commercial banks. All the government's revenues and expenditures go through accounts that it holds at the Bank of England, and the clearing banks ultimately settle their transactions through their own accounts at the Bank. The Bank is also responsible for arranging the government's borrowing and holding the government's foreign currency and gold reserves. And it has a statutory responsibility for the supervision of all banks operating in the United Kingdom.

The Bank of England was founded in 1694 by a Scottish entrepreneur called William Paterson. He set it up in order to help the government fund the Nine Years' War against the French, which had begun five years before. In return, the Bank was given a Charter of Incorporation, which was very rare in those days when almost all business was done by partnerships. It also began to undertake a substantial private banking business, including the issue of bank notes.

For many years, the Bank of England carried out many of the functions of an ordinary bank, as well as being the government's banker. By the mid-nineteenth century, however, when it acquired a monopoly on the issue of bank notes in England and Wales, it was withdrawing from commercial banking and concentrating on its role as central banker. Nowadays, it is mainly just employees and pensioners of the Bank itself who have accounts there.

After over 250 years as a privately owned bank, the Bank of England was brought into state ownership in 1946. This did not involve any change in its function, since it had for many years acted as a public institution with public functions.

The Bank is run by a Court of Directors, all of whom are appointed by the Queen. Most are non-executive directors, drawn from the City and industry; up to four may be full time executives of the Bank. The Chairman, who is also in day-to-day charge of the Bank, is the Governor. The present Governor, who has been in office since 1982, is the Rt. Hon. Robin Leigh-Pemberton. (By long custom, the Governor of the Bank of England is appointed a Privy Councillor, with the title 'Rt. Hon.', but, most unusually for someone so eminent in public service, does not receive a knighthood.)

Exercise 71   Read the extract carefully and then answer the following questions.

1   What is the name of the American central bank?
2   What is the name of the German central bank?
3   What is 'monetary policy?'
4   Who started the Bank of England?
5   What year did the Nine Years' War start?
6   When did the Bank of England get a monopoly of the note issue in England and Wales?
7   When was the Bank of England nationalized?
8   Who runs the Bank of England?
9   What is the difference between a non-executive director and a full-time executive of the Bank, serving on the Court?
10 Who was the Governor of the Bank of England at the time this article was written?

Now read the second extract.

The Bank and the government

Most of the Bank's day-to-day operations are carried out quite independently of the government. It's role is quite distinct from that of the Treasury. In general terms, the Treasury, under the Chancellor of the Exchequer, is responsible for setting the overall framework of economic and monetary policy, while the Bank is responsible for seeing that those policies are carried out in the City's financial markets. Obviously the two need to coordinate their activities very closely, and the Treasury frequently looks to the Bank for advice on monetary and market matters.

In the main, government expenditure is financed by revenues raised from taxation and other sources. All such receipts are paid into the Bank, which in turn arranges for the government's expenditure commitments to be met.

From day to day, the flows of government revenue and expenditure are large and unpredictable. It is rare for the government's spending and receipts to balance exactly on any day. An important part of the Bank's function therefore is to balance these short term fluctuations in government finances.

It does this partly from its own resources but mainly by short term borrowing from and lending to City institutions known as discount houses, who in turn deal with the banks and other financial institutions. This is done by buying and selling commercial bills of exchange and Treasury Bills. These are both types of short term debt, repayable within typically three or six months, and which may be traded on the money markets many times during their life. This influence over the amount of money made available to the banking system enables the Bank to influence short term interest rates.

The Bank also has to carry out regular operations in the foreign exchange markets. This is because a good many of the government's transactions are with overseas governments, suppliers or customers and are hence denominated in foreign currency. This also involves responsibility for managing the government's £20 billion gold and foreign exchange reserves.

The Bank is thus a very significant participant in both the domestic money markets and the foreign exchange markets. This means it is able to influence interest rates domestically and, in certain circumstances, to carry out operations in the foreign exchange markets to smooth fluctuations in the level of sterling. This in turn enables it to use its market operations to put into effect the government's policies for interest rates and the exchange rate, which are the major elements of monetary policy. The Bank and the Treasury therefore keep in constant and close touch to ensure that they act together for the benefit of the financial system.

Quite separately from the management of short-term fluctuations in the flow of its finances, however, the government also issues longer-term debt, known as 'gilt-edged stock'. This helps to finance the difference between government revenue and expenditure. These stocks involve borrowing over anything from five to forty years, paying interest twice a year. They are bought and sold by a wide range of investors, who include individuals and institutions like pension funds and insurance companies. In years when the government's expenditure exceeds its revenue, new issues will be made to increase the outstanding stock of lending. But in years when revenue exceeds expenditure – like 1988–89 and 1989–90 – some of these stocks can be repaid early. Again, it is the responsibility of the Bank of England to arrange and manage this programme of borrowing.

Exercise 7m   Answer the following questions about the extract:

1   What is the function of the Treasury?
2   What is the function of the Bank of England?
3   How is Government expenditure financed?
4   Who handles the Government's money when it is received, and when it is used to pay the Government's bills?
5   Suppose the Government is short of money one day. How is the shortage made up?
6   How much money is there in the gold and foreign exchange reserves?
7   Suppose the bank influences interest rates on the domestic money market to raise the rates being charged. What effect do you think that will have on business?

8 Suppose the pound is weak on the foreign exchange market. What could the Bank of England do to strengthen the pound?
9 What is 'gilt-edged stock'?
10 Explain the term 'revenue exceeds expenditure'. If revenue exceeds expenditure what will the Bank of England do to use up the money available?

7.10 More about adverbs

We have already seen (Section 2.2) that adverbs are words that describe verbs, telling us more about the action that is being performed. In this situation they are said to be 'adjuncts' to the verb, adding something more to our understanding. Consider the four sentences below:

> John worked swiftly.
> John worked steadily.
> John worked enthusiastically.
> John worked desultorily.

The four adverbs change our understanding of the way John worked, and are often called 'adverbs of manner', because they describe the manner of John's performance. They are useful adjuncts to the basic sentence. Even so they are only **optional** extras. The sentence 'John worked' is a complete sentence by itself, but of course it doesn't convey as much information as any of the other sentences.

Sometimes a sentence is not complete without an adverb, and the adverb is said to be **obligatory**, rather than optional. In this case the adverb may be not a single word, but an **adverbial phrase**. For example, consider the sentence 'The lecturer's rostrum stood on a high platform'. The sentence 'The lecturer's rostrum stood' is incomplete, and we are obliged to continue it if it is to make sense. The phrase that describes the verb 'stood' is 'on a high platform' and is therefore an adverbial phrase.

We can also have a type of adverb called an **adverb particle**. The word 'particle' is used to mean a minor part of speech. Thus the word 'in' is sometimes used as an adverb particle, although more commonly it is a preposition. For example, consider the sentence 'At this moment the Prime Minister hurried in'. The word 'in' is an adverb particle which completes the verb 'hurried'.

In our writing the use of adverbs, whether they are adverbs of manner, adverbial phrases or adverb particles, improves the quality of our written work and makes the passages we write more interesting and more informative.

Kinds of adverb

Simple adverbs can be divided into a number of types. They are:

(a)   *Adverbs of time* − answering the question 'when?'

> She will arrive *soon*.
> The machines will come *tomorrow*.

(b)   *Adverbs of place* − answering the question 'where?'

> The advertisements appeared *everywhere*.
> The stored messages were transmitted *throughout the network*.

(c)   *Adverbs of manner* − answering the question 'how?'

> It worked *perfectly*.
> It failed *miserably*.

(d)   *Adverbs of degree* − answering the question 'to what extent?'

> The investor was *extremely* rich.
> The model was *quite*, *quite* beautiful.

Comparison of adverbs

Just as adjectives can have their positive, comparative and superlative forms, so can adverbs. Generally speaking an adverb that has only one syllable takes 'er for the comparative and 'est for the superlative:

fast	faster	fastest
late	later	latest
soon	sooner	soonest

Adverbs with more than one syllable usually take 'more' and 'most':

quickly	more quickly	most quickly
efficiently	more efficiently	most efficiently

A few adverbs are compared by changing the stem of the word:

well	better	best
much	more	most
little	less	least

If the comparison is negative, we use 'less' and 'least':

sweetly	less sweetly	least sweetly
pleasantly	less pleasantly	least pleasantly
rapidly	less rapidly	least rapidly

Exercise 7n

1 Copy out the ten following sentences and underline the adverbs and adverbial phrases.

  (a) The shareholder spoke animatedly against the take-over proposal.
  (b) The answering machine responded instantaneously to the ringing tone.
  (c) The managing director came in, followed by the personnel officer.
  (d) The trespasser had tied himself to the jib of the crane.
  (e) 'Eat up', said the nurse to the patient.
  (f) 'I've found three errors already', said the editor to the typesetter.
  (g) The machine was calculating the results electronically, and throwing them up on to the screen.
  (h) I advise very earnestly that you do not pursue this legal action.
  (i) At noon the meeting broke up.
  (j) The keyboard operator performed the complex calculation effortlessly.

2 Copy out the following sentences and then underline the adverbs and adverbial phrases. Write in brackets at the end of the sentence the verb that the adverb modifies:

  (a) He played bridge professionally.
  (b) The guide to the reserve had formerly hunted wild animals.
  (c) The outcome of the research was very unsettling.
  (d) Some Druids are known to have spoken Latin and Greek fluently.
  (e) At this point the senior detective went out.
  (f) The prototype lay in its cradle, partially complete.
  (g) The induction of the new members of staff proceeded smoothly.
  (h) Go away!
  (i) Suddenly, up she goes!
  (j) The scientific procedure alone had the key to the problem.

7.12   Answer section

Exercises 7a–7k   See notes about appraisal in text, or appraise yourself.

Exercise 7l   (1) The Federal Reserve Bank. (2) The Bundesbank. (3) Policy aimed at safeguarding the value of money in a society. (4) William Paterson. (5) 1689 AD. (6) In the mid-nineteenth century (the actual year was 1844). (7) 1946. (8) The Court of Directors. (9) A non-executive director is not employed by the Bank, but is a knowledgeable outsider from some other industry or profession. (10) The Rt Hon. Robin Leigh-Pemberton.

Exercise 7m   (1) To set the overall framework of economic and monetary policy. (2) To implement the policy in the financial markets, by its influence in the City of London. (3) By revenues raised from taxation and other sources. (4) The Bank of England collects the sums received and uses them to pay the government's bills. (5) Partly from the Bank's own resources, but chiefly by borrowing from the discount houses. (6) £20 billion, i.e. £20,000 million. (7) It will make borrowing more expensive and discourage entrepreneurial activity. (8) It would buy pounds, to keep the price up, using the foreign exchange in the official reserves. (9) Long-term government stock (promising to repay the money borrowed in 5–40 years). (10) Revenue is tax money coming in. Expenditure is money going out. If revenue exceeds expenditure, the Bank of England will use the surplus to reduce the National Debt. (It actually does this by buying the stock back on the Stock Exchange from someone trying to sell it, and cancelling it.)

Exercise 7n   (1) You should have underlined:

(a) (i) animatedly; (ii) against the takeover proposal; (b) (i) instantaneously, (ii) to the ringing tone; (c) (i) in, (ii) followed by the personnel officer; (d) to the jib of the crane; (e) up; (f) already; (g) (i) electronically, (ii) up on to the screen; (h) very earnestly; (i) (i) at noon, (ii) up; (j) effortlessly.

Exercise 7n   (2) You should have underlined as shown in italics, with the verbs in brackets at the end of the sentences as shown:

(a) *professionally* (played); (b) *formerly* (had hunted); (c) *very* (was unsettling); (d) *to have spoken Latin and Greek fluently* (are known); (e) *out* (went); (f) (i) *in its cradle*, (ii) *partially complete* (lay); (9) *smoothly* (proceeded); (h) *away* (go); (i) *suddenly*, *up* (goes); (j) *alone* (had).

8

Communication about marketing

8.1 The marketing sequence

Correspondence about marketing covers a number of activities and procedures. It is helpful to list them, and then discuss the items in the list in detail, to build a full picture of the marketing procedure. A full list would include the following matters:

(a) Voluntary offers.
(b) Inquiries.
(c) Responses to inquiries.
(d) Estimates and quotations.
(e) Standard terms and conditions and credit control.
(f) Orders by telephone.
(g) Orders by fax.
(h) Traditional orders.
(i) The acknowledgement of orders.
(j) The acceptance of orders.
(k) The fulfilment of orders.
(l) Complaints.
(m) Conciliatory responses.
(n) The rejection of complaints.

While this list does not include all possible matters that might require correspondence, the reader will see that it is still a very long list and there is much to consider. Before we begin a detailed study, we must set the scene.

The whole point is that any form of marketing is a contractual matter, and we must have some idea of what happens in the making of a contract.

8.2 The nature of a contract

A contract is a voluntary agreement between (usually) two parties whereby each party agrees to do something for the other party, and to stand by that bargain as promised, according to the law. Since the agreement is to be legally binding, either party may sue the other party if he/she is dissatisfied with the outcome. The word 'sue' means 'to summon into court and require the other party to appear and explain why the plaintiff should not have the justice he/she seeks'. Failure to appear means that the court will hear what the plaintiff has to say, and pronounce judgement on the matter.

In order to prove that a contract does exist three things must be proved:

(a) *Offer*   There must have been a clear offer, made by one party to the other (but sometimes an offer is made to the world at large, and the court will regard this as a clear offer to anyone who acts on it, e.g. by responding to an advertisement in a magazine or newspaper).

(b) *Acceptance*   There has to be a clear acceptance of the offer, either by word of mouth, or in writing or by a course of action. See (c) below.

(c) *Valuable consideration*   There has to be some 'valuable consideration' given to make the bargain complete. This may be in money form, as when we purchase a computer and pay the price − £300. It may be in some other form, as where a garage proprietor takes a secondhand car in return for a trailer, or where two antiquarian book dealers exchange one 'first edition' for another. The courts are willing to consider all situations. For example:

(i) The Countryside Bus Co. drives a bus up a village high street and stops it at the bus stop. That is an offer.

(ii) Three people get on. That is 'acceptance of the offer'.

(iii) One shows his season ticket, and two others pay the fare into town. That is the valuable consideration. Not a word has been said, but the actions taken are enough to make three binding contracts with the Countryside Bus Co.

In considering the correspondence we shall be studying in this chapter bear in mind all the time that you are dealing with contractual matters. Be careful what you write! Don't say 'We accept your offer' unless you really mean that you are prepared to be legally bound by the arrangement. The importance of what is being said will become clear as we look at each stage in the marketing process.

8.3   Voluntary offers

A voluntary offer is an invitation to a possible customer to do business with you. It may be made to another business person, to a member of the general public, or to the world at large. We all have to start somewhere, and a circular letter to businesses in a particular area may be the best way. We might take the local *Yellow Pages* telephone directory and write to all the garages in the area, or all the head teachers of local schools, etc. It depends what goods or services we are offering.

Such a circular has already been featured in Figure 5.4 (see p. 80). Figure 8.1 shows a slightly more formal circular. It is brief and to the point, since it refers to an illustrated brochure that gives full details about the product. Therefore the letter need not do more than make the formal 'offer' to open the negotiations, which may lead to a contract.

8.4   Exercises on voluntary offers

Exercise 8a   You work for the firm of Pollock & Warner, 1027 Hill St, Weybridge, Bristol, BS27 4PQ. Write a circular to go to all local plumbers in the Bristol area offering your range of plumbing products at special introductory discount rates. Refer to a catalogue you are enclosing and invite responses by telephone, fax or letter in the manner described on page 47 in the catalogue.

Exercise 8b   You work for the Bank of Commerce and Agriculture, 2756 Lombard St, London, E1 1PQ. Write a circular to go to all small businesses in the area inviting them to request an interview with your Small Business Adviser. Refer to your comprehensive range of business services outlined in the attached brochure and refer especially to your favourable rates of interest on loans below £5,000.

Exercise 8c   You work for HFI (Health for Industry), which specializes in providing in-factory facilities for employees of major firms. Draft a circular to go to all the large firms in your county inviting expressions of interest in a 'Health Review Programme'. This will be a detailed analysis of the facilities that could be provided. As a gesture of goodwill the offer includes a free health check for all Board Members at a nationally known clinic in the capital city.

8.5   Letters of inquiry and telephone and fax inquiries

Not all negotiations start in the seller's marketing department. The

On-line Timer Ltd, Sussex House, Norfolk St,
Drakesville, NM5 3ST

Abtel Manufacturing Co.,
Acorn Trading Estate,
Yorkway Street,
Sheffield,   3 February 19..
DG5 7TY   Our Ref RTB/JG

Dear Sirs,

<u>Flexible Working Hours</u>

We hope you will find the enclosed brochure about
our new 'On-line Timer for flexible working hours' of
interest. We are the sole supplier in the United Kingdom
of this unique system manufactured in Singapore by one
of the leading electronics manufacturers. We know that
you are at present discussing the installation of a
'flexible working hours' system and hope very much that
you will permit us to demonstrate our system for you.

Full instructions for making contact with our local
agents are given in the brochure, or you may prefer to
call me at this office to discuss arrangements.

Yours faithfully

R.T. Benson
Managing Director

Enc. On-line Timer brochure

Figure 8.1   A 'voluntary offer'

buyer is also active in seeking his/her requirements. Traditionally a
letter of inquiry has been used to elicit information about products,
services, terms and conditions of sale, etc., but in these days there is
much to be said for short-circuiting the inquiry process by using the
telephone or the fax machine. It costs the average firm between £3
and £5 to write a letter – and many letters of inquiry prove abortive.
The firm written to may not have the product concerned, or may not

have the plant capacity to manufacture an item. A telephone inquiry clarifies the position in a few seconds and costs very little. It also enables you to find an actual person who deals with the type of inquiry you are making, so that if, at the end of the call, you do wish to write to the firm or to place an order, you have an actual name to write to. A typical conversation might go like this:

Telephonist: 57203. Good morning.
Caller: Is that Smith & Dunbar?
T : Yes − how may I help you?
C : I wish to speak to someone about the purchase of prefabricated platform units. Could you put me through to someone who would know about such things.
T : Yes, I think the best person would be our estimator Tom Price. Ringing for you!
C : Thank you.
TP: Price speaking.
C : My name is Peter Standish. I'm an educational supplier. We've had an enquiry about prefabricated platform units for temporary staging in halls, gymnasiums etc. I wondered if you could supply such items.
TP: Yes, we do have a range of standard units, and, if necessary, we could custom-build to your detailed specifications.
C : Oh, that sounds very helpful! Could you let me have a brochure and price list so that I can begin to work out what we would require. Just one other thing! It so happens that this order is an export order from Zimbabwe. Could you pack and ship direct to our instructions.
TP: Well − that would be no problem. The thing is would we be paid by you or by the Zimbabwean importer?
C : Oh, we would pay you against a shipped bill of lading backed by an insurance policy. Our customer is the Zimbabwean Government, so they are absolutely reliable, but we deal with them. We wouldn't expect you to deal direct.
TP: Oh, that's fine then. And thank you for approaching us. Now, let me have your name and address and I'll send you all the details by first-class post today.

Clearly this sorts out a major procurement problem in a few minutes and at a cost of only about 70 p. Each firm has made a valuable link, not just for this occasion but perhaps for many years to come.
Remember the rules for good use of the telephone:

(a) Speak clearly and identify yourself at once: 'Price speaking'.
(b) Be interested in the person at the other end. The order that may result could keep the factory going for a year.

(c)   Have a pencil and paper handy to jot down any details − in particular get the caller's name and address.
(d)   Never be smart, sarcastic or even witty at the caller's expense. You have no idea who it is or how important he/she might be. One young man in a third-world country was so courteous and helpful that the caller said 'May I know your name?' On giving it, the caller said 'I used to know someone of that name'. 'It may have been my father', said the young man. 'How is he?', asked the caller. 'I am afraid, Sir, he's been in prison for eight years. I'm not sure why − but it is very sad.' 'This is the President speaking' said the caller. 'Tell your mother he'll be home tomorrow' And he was!

The exercises below call for two people, one of whom pretends to be making an inquiry about a product and the other is responding to the inquiry. Draw up on a sheet of A4 paper the points you might need to raise with the other party, according to which side you elect to take. There are three questions to choose from. Then draw lots to pick who is to play the parts and (using a mock telephone set if one is available) practise your telephone manner in front of your fellow students. The class should be allowed time to appraise the efforts of those chosen. The 'call' should not last longer than 4 minutes.

Exercise 8d

(i)   You are inquiring about the possibility that Morris & Co. could provide you with a motor vehicle accessory − a windscreen wiper − made to a fairly close specification. The requirement is for 500 of the items per day (Monday−Saturday) delivered to the assembly plant each day at the time specified in a daily fax message. This is for a JIT (just in time) factory. Full specifications will be provided and there is a 6 week time gap before deliveries start to enable M & Co to set up a production line, etc.
(ii) Replying for Morris & Co., you are very keen to get the order, but there is a snag. You usually manufacture such items much more quickly than 500 a day − more like 2,000 a day. You will probably therefore do it by batch production, producing a lot and storing them until they are required. (You don't have to tell them that.) You want to know how you will get paid. You also want to price them high enough to cover the daily delivery costs. You can't give a price until you've seen the estimate. You can't set up a production line unless they will specify a minimum supply period − say at least 120 days.

Exercise 8e

(i)   You want a pure white horse for a circus. You know that
       Albino Stud PLC specializes in the breeding of white horses.
       You can't pay more than £2,000, and you want a young horse
       with a reasonably long working lifetime ahead of him/her.
       Have they any young animals that might be suitable? Could
       you travel down to see them?
(ii)   As the owner of Albino Stud PLC, you know you have three
       colts that might do, and one filly. You have reservations about
       circuses. You will want to see not only the owner but also the
       trainer. The price is on the low side anyway.

Exercise 8f

(i)   You run a magazine called *Parents and Kids*. You want someone
       to be educational editor to arrange a number of items for a
       small section of the magazine each month. The age range for
       this section is 7–11, and it is to be educational not just enter-
       taining. You believe an author who has written a lot of books
       at a rather higher level but who has experience in this age
       range might be willing to take it on.
(ii)   As the author being approached you are a bit hesitant. You
       need to see the magazine. You need to know what the rate of
       pay is and how tight the deadlines will be. You do have a lot of
       ideas for that age range, but quite a lot of them would need
       illustrations and you are no artist. Would back-up with artwork
       be provided?

Inquiries with fax

A fax machine is a device that transmits A4 pages of information
over the telephone network to the destination address. It takes only
a few seconds to transmit such a page, and the cost is quite minor,
probably less than the cost of having a letter typed. The beauty of
the system is the speed of transmission, right into the office of the
firm or company to whom you are making the inquiry. It enables
you to include a detailed specification in written or typewritten
form, and even a diagram or illustration can be transmitted.

A fax message needs to be laid out in a satisfactory way, giving all
the information that will enable it to reach the correct person or
department. While it is useful to use an ordinary letterhead it must
have the Fax No. of the addressee. The machine will print on the
copy sent the time, day and date of despatch.

A typical letter of inquiry is shown in Figure 8.2.

Thomas Bushill & Sons, 2755 Camside, Cambridge, CB4 1PQ

Formecon Services Ltd,
Gateway
Crewe   Tel: (0223) 397059
Cheshire   Fax: (0223) 397060
CW1 1YN   30 April 19. .
Fax No. 0270 500 000
Time sent   13.50 Wednesday 30.4.19. .

Dear Sirs,

<u>Incoterms 90</u>

  Would you please advise me whether you supply
sets of documents for use in international trade carried
out under Incoterms 90. We intend to specify Incoterms
90 CIF in all negotiations with overseas customers. Any
assistance you can give us in setting up such
arrangements will be helpful.
  A reply by post enclosing full details of your
services re Incoterms 90 would be appreciated.
Yours faithfully

Thomas Bushill
Managing Director

Figure 8.2   A faxed letter of inquiry

Exercise 8g   Draw up a faxed letter of inquiry to Croner Publications
Ltd, Croner House, London Road, Kingston upon Thames, Surrey,
KT2 6SR, Fax No. 091–547–2737, asking them to send you by post
full details of their handbooks for businesses. Refer in particular to
their *Reference Book for the Self-employed and Smaller Businesses*
and their *Reference Book for Exporters*.

Exercise 8h   Draw up a faxed letter of inquiry to R. Milton and
Sons Ltd of 1284 Camside, Cambridge, CB4 1PQ, asking for details
of their range of office sundries, which you are proposing to stock in
your new stationery outlet. Ask for their terms of sale, and minimum
order sizes. Mention that you hope to trade on terms which give you
2 months credit.

8.6   Responses to inquiries

When we respond to an inquiry, we shall of course be as helpful as
we can, because that is the way to make friends and get business. At
the same time it is no good getting business if the person you deal
with does not eventually pay for the goods or services you supply.
Therefore it is essential to convey the impression that you are a
reputable firm that can be relied upon absolutely to perform your
part of the bargain, but equally you expect that your potential
customer will be honourable and will pay according to the agreed
terms and conditions of sale you have established for your business.
A full explanation of this is given later (see Section 8.8). The point
is that, in your very first response to the inquiry, you enclose a set of
these 'conditions of trading' and ask them to confirm when placing
their first order that they have received the conditions and find them
acceptable. This will not lose you the order from a genuine customer,
because a genuine customer expects to deal with someone who is
legally advised and works within a set of standard trading conditions. If
it does lose you an order, that is probably an order you would not
have been paid for anyway – so all you have lost is a bad debt.

Figure 8.3 shows a letter responding to a faxed letter of inquiry
asking the firm concerned for details of their Teachers' Record
Books. Study this letter now and then try the questions below.

Exercise 8i   Referring to the letter of inquiry mentioned in Exercise
8(g) above, write a response to this letter as it might have been
written by Croner Publications Ltd. Mention that the *Reference
Book for Exporters* is described on p. 16 of the brochure you
enclose, and the *Reference Book for the Self-employed and Smaller
Businesses* is featured on p. 2.

Exercise 8j   Referring to Exercise 8(h) above, write a reply to the
enquiry, enclosing a catalogue of office supplies as requested but
drawing their attention to the fact that you do not supply new
customers on credit terms unless the firm concerned can supply you
with very good references from other trade suppliers. Tell them,
however, that you will be prepared to supply them against a bill of
exchange drawn at 60 days' notice so long as the bill is accepted by
them before delivery of the goods. Tell them that if they are not
familiar with the bill of exchange procedure their bank will advise
them.

THE VYNER GROUP

INTERNATIONAL DISTRIBUTORS   ⟨ SIMPLEX ⟩   **RECORD & ACCOUNT SYSTEMS**

GEORGE VYNER LTD
Regd. No. 580231 England

GEORGE VYNER (DISTRIBUTORS) **LTD**
Regd. No. 929814 England

P.O. BOX No. 1
HOLMFIRTH
HUDDERSFIELD HD7 2RP

Our ref: BS/AB

Your ref:

TEL. No. HOLMFIRTH (0484) 685221
CABLES VYNER HUDDERSFIELD

Fax. No. (0484) 688538

The Headteacher,   2nd April 19..
Hatch End High School,
Headstone Lane,
Harrow,
Middlesex.
HA3 6NR

Dear Sir,

We thank you for your recent enquiry concerning the Simplex Teachers Series of Record Books. From the range, three books would be suitable for your school. They are:

<u>Simplex T2 - Subject Teachers Record Book</u>

<u>Simplex T5 - Subject Teachers Lesson Preparation Book</u>

<u>Simplex T3 - Head of Departments Book</u>

A detailed description of these books is given in our current brochure, a copy of which we enclose, together with a price list.

As a matter of interest we are the publishers of the Simplex range of Account Books which are used extensively throughout the country by small businesses and the self employed and it occurs to us that your Business Studies teacher may be interested in our Simplex Training Exercise for the book-keeping section of the Business Studies course.

The Simplex Training Exercise covers a four week period and not only do we provide the Exercise but we also provide an answer section and sets of loose pages of the Simplex D Account Book and the Simplex VAT Record Book on which it can be worked. For information and reference purposes I am enclosing one set of the training material and look forward to receiving your observations. We make no charge for these training materials to United Kingdom schools.

If, after considering our brochure, you would like to have inspection copies of T2, T3 and T5, or if you wish to order the free training exercise (state no. of students on Business Studies courses) we shall be happy to send them by return of post.

Yours sincerely,
GEORGE VYNER LTD.,

B. Senior,
Managing Director.

SIMPLEX BRAND PRODUCTS ARE DISTRIBUTED AND COPYRIGHT THROUGHOUT THE WORLD

Figure 8.3   A response to an inquiry (*courtesy of George Vyner Ltd*)

8.7   Estimates and quotations

In many businesses a bargain cannot be struck until a good deal of preliminary work has been done and the costs have been estimated. For example, many construction projects are extremely complicated, requiring the prefabrication of many parts or components. Many printing and packaging jobs depend upon preliminary typesetting and artwork, and the size of the print run will affect the price. If 1,000 copies only are required, the unit cost will be higher than if 100,000 copies are to be printed, because the initial costs can be spread over a much larger output.

In such cases the customer's inquiry must be followed up by clear specifications, which will form the basis of a costing exercise by the supplier. The customer will then be sent either an estimate or a quotation. There is a distinction between the two, since an estimate is an approximate price that can be revised later if the work proves to be more expensive or difficult than anticipated, and a quotation is a rather more formal offer to do the work at an agreed price, and as such it is capable of being immediately accepted, to make a binding contract between the parties. Even so, in inflationary times it is not unknown to include a special clause in a quotation that permits the quoted price to be increased if the costs rise through no fault of the supplier. For example, raw material prices may rise, and wages may be raised as a result of some national negotiation that is quite outside the supplier's sphere of influence.

From the point of view of correspondence on such matters it is important to emphasize the legal impact of the letters written. An estimate is not an offer, but the mere supply of information. If the customer thinks the estimate is fair, it is for the customer to place an order (an offer to buy) which the supplier will then accept. With a quotation, it is the supplier who is offering to supply on the terms stated in the quotation, and the customer can accept this offer and make a binding contract by his/her acceptance. Figure 8.4 shows a typical estimate.

Exercise 8k   Draw up an estimate for Mrs T. Large of 2752 Hill St, Mopham, Lincs, LN7 TD, for the overhaul and refurbishing of her kitchen area. Invent such details as you like and nominate a charge (less than £4,000) for doing the work. Ask for a 20 per cent deposit and written confirmation that the estimate is acceptable to her. Use your own name and address.

Exercise 8l   Draw up a formal quotation for Loamside Contractors PLC of 1274 Quarry Rd, Brickhill, Beds, BD32 5LS, for the marking out of their lorry-park and car-park areas, to their specifications, at a total cost of £2,200. Also charge for the installation of lighting to their specifications, at a further total cost of £3,500. Specify that, as agreed, payment is to be made by noon of the seventh day after completion of the work, by a credit transfer into your bank account, details of which you have already supplied. In addition, specify that acceptance of the quotation should be made within 14 days of the date shown on the quotation.

Mrs A. Peterson,
2145 Mutley Ave,
Grays,
Essex,
RM16 1PQ

Peter Greenfingers and Co. Ltd,
2142 Woodview Road,
Grays,
Essex.
RM16 4YR

25 April, 19..

Dear Mrs Peterson,

Estimate for Landscaping project

To removing old fences and disposal thereof, earthmoving and drainage work as required by your specifications, patio and footpath construction, turfing of embankments and lawns and supply and planting of trees, shrubs and rose bushes .... £2,250.

If this estimate is satisfactory will you please write a letter stating that you wish the work to go ahead, and send with it your cheque for £450 being a 20% deposit to enable us to purchase materials, etc.

If this estimate is not accepted within 7 days, we reserve the right to increase the price should materials increase through no fault of our own.

We feel sure that we can transform your front garden adding considerably to the value of your property, and hope to hear from you right away so that we can put the work in hand.

Yours sincerely,

P. Greenfingers
Managing Director

Figure 8.4 An estimate for a landscaping project

Exercise 8m Draw up a formal quotation for the supply of goods to Homeware PLC of 2912 Long Lane, Sheffield, S36 6FH, on a regular basis − forty sink units Type X at £19.50 per unit and eighty kitchen cabinets at £15.80 per unit to be supplied on the 15th day of every month until countermanded by them. Goods to be invoiced monthly and paid for within 30 days of invoice date. The prices are subject to revision annually on 1 January each year. Acceptance of the quotation to take place within 14 days of the date on the document.

8.8   Standard terms and conditions

Every set of standard terms and conditions is different from all others, because it has to suit the particular needs and requirements of the business it is intended to serve. Very often a trader will take legal advice about drawing up a set of trading conditions, since a good background knowledge of contract law is necessary. The word 'conditions' is important. A condition of a contract is a term in the contract which is so important that if the term is not observed, the failure to do so counts as 'breach of contract' and entitles the disappointed party to sue for breach of contract. Many organizations use a set of standard terms and conditions drawn up by a trade association. Such an organization has plenty of funds to employ the finest lawyers in the land, and can also negotiate with the Director General of Fair Trading, who will usually want to vet the set of conditions to see if they comply with the Unfair Contract Terms Act 1977. Good examples of such standard conditions are the Road Haulage Association's Conditions of Carriage and British Rail's Conditions of Carriage. The sets of conditions drawn up by the major credit-card companies, such as Barclaycard and Access, are readily available, and students who want to study the layout of such documents should ask for copies at their local banks.

When drawing up a set 'in-house', it is best to number the terms – in the following way;

1   In this set of conditions of trading the term 'Trader' means .... (here we give the name of the firm issuing the set of conditions) and the term 'customer' means any person, firm or company to whom the trader supplies goods or services of any sort.
2   It is a condition of the contract that no valid contract exists until we have formally accepted a written offer from the customer by a written acceptance. Until that moment the arrangements shall be deemed to be negotiations only.
3, 4 etc. Covering all the types of arrangement made as to supply, delivery, terms of payment, etc.

Exercise 8n   Here is a term from a set of standard conditions dealing with credit cards:

9   If the card is lost, stolen or mis-used by someone who obtained it without your consent you will be liable for the first £100 of any

loss to the bank. If it is mis-used with your consent you will be liable for *all* losses suffered as a result of the misuse. You will not be liable for losses to the bank which take place after you have told the bank of the theft, etc. provided you confirm any oral message in writing within 7 days.

(a) Give your opinion of the term above that mentions £100.
(b) What is your opinion of the clause referring to *all* losses?

Exercise 8o Your company sends goods to customers on sale or return. The following problems arise:

(a) Some customers say goods have not been received, although you feel fairly sure they have arrived.
(b) When goods are returned, the packaging is often incomplete and goods suffer damage on the return journey. The packaging costs £5.
(c) Some customers return goods that have obviously been worn.
(d) Some customers return goods that have been washed.

Draw up a set of 'conditions of trading' to cover these points.

Exercise 8p Your company collects goods from various factories for delivery to depots some distance away. At the point of collection the following problems arise:

(a) Some firms have no loading facilities to lift goods on to delivery vehicles, although this is the duty of the consignor.
(b) Where the vehicle itself has a crane, such firms frequently bribe the driver to load the vehicle using his crane, but it carries some risks. You wish to avoid these risks and to make a charge for the loading if you are forced to do it.
(c) Some firms try to reduce the price for the carriage of the goods by getting the driver to accept a lesser payment than the agreed contract price. You wish to stop this practice.
(d) Some goods are improperly packed and suffer damage as a result, for which you are held responsible. You wish to avoid claims of this sort.

Draw up a set of conditions covering these points.

8.9 Credit control

While new customers are essential to every business, especially a business that is trying to grow, there is no point in starting to deal with a risky business, e.g. one that has already established a reputation as a poor payer, with unrealiable or inefficient management procedures. The following points are worth listing in this respect:

(a)　It is not usual to deal with a complete stranger on credit terms — in other words, on terms where he/she can have the goods and services now, and need not pay until later.

(b)　If they are asking for such terms, it would not be usual to accept without good references from reliable people.

Credit reference agencies specialize in collecting information on such matters, and will, for a relatively modest fee, report anything they know. For example, they verify the trading title of firms and companies, their registered addresses, etc. They check records at Company House and report, for example, on whether a company is borrowing so widely that it appears to have cash-flow problems. They also check the financial records of company directors, partners, etc., and the County Court judgments against debtor firms.

Other goods references come from trade creditors in the same trade as yourself. Don't just accept a letter of recommendation, actually phone the firm or company concerned and ask if the letter is genuine and whether they have any reservations at all about the potential customer. Banks will often give an opinion but they are usually of the 'believed to be good for their ordinary business transactions' variety, which means very little. The firm's accountants or auditors (if they have any) may be better.

(c)　The usual first step is to ask for cash-on-delivery (COD) or payment by pro-forma invoice. This means you send them an invoice showing the value of the goods and if they pay the invoice, you dispatch the goods. This means they have to trust you — which is always better than you trusting them, because you know *you* are reliable, so they are not at risk.

(d)　If you do agree to give them credit terms, set a credit limit that is reasonable — say twice the value of their first order — and don't let any future order exceed it. Some firms place one or two small orders and pay promptly, but then send a massive order for which they do not intend to pay.

(e)　You have specified a credit period — say 30 days from invoice date. If you don't get the money by that date, phone them and ask why. Insist on payment according to the agreed terms. If they don't pay on time but still place further orders, don't send the goods. Put them on a pro-forma basis and ensure that the first invoice you send includes all the outstanding amounts.

(f)　Finally, when you have tried (i) a phone call and (ii) a letter requesting payment, and still have no response, ask your solicitor to write and demand payment within 7 days on pain of legal action. Most solicitors have a system for chasing bad debts that goes through a set procedure. Early on in this procedure legal action is commenced and a writ is served. Suing for payment does not mean we expect to go to court. What we intend to do is to put the debtor under pressure. The threat of court action, if pursued to the end, would lead to the court ruling that an act of bankruptcy (non-payment of a debt) had occurred. Under this threat the debtor pays up. People usually pay the creditor who is worrying them the most.

The full chain of correspondence on credit matters is therefore:

(a)   Pre-contract negotiations about the supply of goods or services and the method of payment.
(b)   A request for references (and perhaps, simultaneously, inquiries via a credit reference agency).
(c)   The setting of a credit limit and its monitoring whenever a further order is received.
(d)   A telephone request for payment of an overdue account.
(e)   A formal written request for payment, coupled with notification that the customer will be reduced to pro-forma invoice terms for future orders.
(f)   A solicitor's letter, followed by the commencement of legal action.

Now try the following exercise related to credit control.

Exercise 8q

1   Write a letter to T. Wall & Sons, 22 Long Line, Maidstone, Kent, ME2 5PQ telling them that, while in principle you do not supply goods on credit to customers in their first year of trading, you will in fact do so for orders in excess of £50, up to a limit of £500. Make it clear that your terms of trade are 'cash net, 30 days after invoice date', but a discount of 5 per cent can be taken if invoices are settled within 15 days. End the letter in a suitably courteous way.
2   Write a letter to M. Kimber & Sons, 2475 Hadrian's Way, Newcastle on Tyne NE3 7ST, requesting payment of the balance outstanding on their account £520.75. Point out that the payment is already 2 weeks overdue, and if the bill is not paid within 7 days you will commence legal action. Point out also that if they lose their credit status by failing to comply with this request, even if the matter is finally resolved, you will be forced to deal with any future orders on a pro-forma basis.

3   Write to your solicitors, Hewitson, Lamb and Partners, of 2 The Abbey Close, Ely, CB6 9AH, asking them to make a formal request for payment to A.J. White of 2159 Rippleway Rd, Sawston, Cambs CB5 2EH, in the sum of £426.32 (as per copy invoice, which you enclose). If payment is not forthcoming in 7 days, will they please institute proceedings against the debtor.

4   Write a letter to a customer who has a good record for placing orders over a 2-year period but who claims that his present position paying on pro-forma terms is inconvenient. He wishes to be allowed to pay on 'open account' terms, paying 30 days after a monthly statement has been received. State your willingness to agree to this, but only for a 1-year trial period. Further add that the credit limit you can allow is only £1,500 (because on one occasion he did place an order for goods worth £5,000). Don't say so, but while you were happy to supply him when he was paying the £5,000 in advance, you would not be quite so happy to give him credit for such a large amount. Make it clear also that, while you value his custom greatly, if he does not abide by the terms of payment, no further goods will be supplied on open account, and he would have to revert to pro-forma trading.

8.10   The acknowledgment of orders

Where an order can be fulfilled immediately from stock, and the arrangements with the customer are known to be sound, it should be filled at once, and invoiced and dispatched the same day. Nothing pleases a customer more than to get goods by return of post, or within a very short time span. Most carriers can offer guaranteed delivery within 3 days in the United Kingdom. If the order is CWO (cash with order) or on pro-forma terms (in other words they pay before you dispatch the goods) and payment has already been made, or on 'open account' terms (in other words they are allowed to trade on credit, with your agreed terms of trade), send the order off with as little delay as possible.

Where an order is not of the type that can be fulfilled at once, e.g. because you have to manufacture the product to their specifications, then an acknowledgment of the order is called for. Note that an acknowledgment is not an acceptance of the order and the words 'We accept your order' should not be used. This is because such orders are usually quite complex, and the order may be expressed in a way that is not acceptable. We need a little time to check that the order complies in all respects with the pre-contract negotiations. For example, it may refer to different specifications, or prices, or delivery dates, and we do not wish to accept an order that is in any way incorrect. Therefore a typical acknowledgment, often in the form of a pre-printed card with spaces left to fill in certain details, might be as shown in Figure 8.5.

The essential point is that an acknowledgment does not make a binding contract. It is a holding exercise, which gives time for the order to be checked carefully to ensure it is a valid order expressed in agreed terms. After verification, a formal letter of acceptance will make the binding contract between the parties, and the necessary production, packing and dispatch operations will go ahead.

8.11 The fulfilment of orders

We can only touch briefly on the train of events that leads to the fulfilment of complex orders such as export orders. There may be many technical aspects of the production process to be done

```
┌─────────────────────────────────────────────────────────┐
│                        T. Knight & Co.,                  │
│                        2754 Hill Rise,                   │
│                        Newtown,                          │
│  To                    Essex,                            │
│  ................      SS16 2DT                          │
│  ................                                        │
│  ................      Date ...................          │
│  ................      Your Ref ...............          │
│                        Our Ref ................          │
│  Dear ...........                                        │
│                                                          │
│                 Acknowledgement of Order                 │
│                                                          │
│  We acknowledge receipt of your order dated...........   │
│  which is receiving attention. You will be hearing from  │
│  us very shortly. In case of any difficulty please ask for, │
│  or write to, the person handling the order, whose name  │
│  is ...................................................  │
│                                                          │
│  For the Sales Manager:                                  │
│                                                          │
│                                                          │
│  ..................                                      │
│  Order Clerk                                             │
└─────────────────────────────────────────────────────────┘
```

Figure 8.5 Acknowledgement of an order

and checked at every stage, such as fabrication, assembly and packing. There are also many aspects of documentation to be arranged. Many countries will not accept and pay for goods if they have not been authorized as essential imports. Invoices have to be certified by consuls as being authorized imports (consular invoices). The shipment of cargoes has to be made on bills of lading, which effectively become the documents of title to the goods while they are on the high seas. Purchase of the bill of lading is purchase of the goods. There will usually be an insurance policy associated with the cargo − if the cargo is lost the buyer of the bill of lading can claim on the policy. Finally, there may be situations where the eventual importer will not pay for the goods until they arrive − and possibly not for 6 months after arrival. Some way of ensuring payment is made has to be devised. All these procedures take time to arrange and require much correspondence by air mail, fax, etc.

This is as far as we can go in the discussion of marketing matters. It is clear that business English is necessary at every stage of the marketing process. One of the best organizations to help the trader through the maze of regulations on both home and overseas trade is Formecon Services Ltd. As the name implies, they supply all the forms required in a very economical way, with a complete range of both manual and electronic systems. Their order form is given in Figure 8.6. It is a good example of an order form that can be sent out by the *seller*, e.g. to accompany a catalogue or information pack, for return either by post or fax. The seller thus ensures that the buyer gives all the details required, knows exactly how to pay, etc. A new order form, which incorporates the latest price list, is sent out with every fulfilled order, so that the customer always has an up-to-date order form to use when placing a further order.

As an example of electronic software to complete export documentation, we may refer to Formecon's 'Formfill' software.

Formfill − an electronic form filler

Imagine an export consignment in which we need twenty copies of an invoice, three bills of lading, and forty other assorted documents. Imagine also that if even one letter overlaps into another box on the master document, it will cause trouble (because in the masking process that letter will be sure to be masked off on some form). We clearly need to be careful in typing our master. Fortunately help is available with a computerized system called Formfill. Schools and colleges with computer facilities might like to consider ordering the package from Formecon, whose address is given in Figure 8.6. It does the following things:

● Streamlines exporting to every country in the world.

FORMECON

Publishers for Commerce, Industry and the Professions

FORMECON SERVICES LIMITED
Gateway, Crewe, Cheshire, CW1 1YN

Telephone: 0270-500 800
Fax: 0270-500 505

Please detach along perforation

FORMECON ORDER FORM

1992

Date of Order   /   /19

Customer Name & Address (for invoice)	Delivery Address (if different)
BLOCK CAPITALS	BLOCK CAPITALS
Postcode	Postcode

Order No./Ref.	
Order to be marked for attention of	
Telephone No.	
Fax No.	

Please ✓
Sole Trader/Proprietor ☐ Partnership ☐
Private Ltd. Co. ☐ Public Co. ☐ Reg. Charity ☐
Government Organisation ☐ Not in business ☐
Other (state)________ ☐

Type of Business ________ Number of Employees ____

Item	Product Ref.	PRODUCT DESCRIPTION	UNIT PRICE £	UNIT PRICE p	IN UNITS PER	ORDER QUANTITY	TOTAL PRICE £	TOTAL PRICE p
1								
2								
3								
4								
5								
6								
7								
8								
9								
10								
11								
12								
13								
14								
15								
16								
17								
18								
19								
20								

1. Please send goods on 30 days credit ☐
2. Payment enclosed with order ☐
3. Payment by Access ☐ Visa ☐

Please tick as applicable

Card No. ____ Expiry Date   /

DISCOUNT 5% Discount for Cash with Order	GOODS VALUE	
	DEDUCT %	
HANDLING & DELIVERY (Min. £1.50p – Max. £75)	NET VALUE	
	ADD 10 %	
VAT @ Standard Rate	DELIVERED VALUE	
	ADD %	
	ORDER TOTAL	

A VAT invoice *(receipted if payment with order)* will be sent with goods

Cardholder's address (if different)

Postcode

Comments/Remarks

(Order not valid unless signed)

Signature

Thank you for your custom – please post to Formecon Services Limited or fax (No. overleaf)

Figure 8.6 A seller-generated order form (*courtesy of Formecon Services Ltd*)

- Enables you to complete export/shipping documents very simply by computer.
- Contains all the latest design forms.
- Shortlists the forms appropriate to the particular country of destination, which it knows from its memory of stored data.
- Lets you select which documents to complete, just one or more, per shipment.
- Displays on the screen each form in 'live' format as you call them up for completion.
- Allows you to choose, in any order, which boxes to complete.
- Each box 'zooms-in' to full size for entry of your particular data.
- Has a 'help' facility to give you an explanation of the information required in every box.
- Means you only complete each different box heading once. When one box, say the exporter's name and address, has been completed on one form, the software repeats the data on every form where required, reducing keyboard time and improving accuracy.
- Automatically completes the shipment forms selected, through your computer printer (including multipart sets).

The simplicity of this system is marvellous. For example, the exporter's name and address appear on every form. The whole form appears on the screen, but by means of a 'mouse', an electronic cursor device, we can call up any particular box to appear by itself. This removes the form from the screen and replaces it with the 'exporter' box. We type in the exporter's name and address, check it carefully, and, when we are satisfied, return it to its place on the screen. It shrinks down to a tiny size, much too small to read, while we call up the next box we wish to complete. From now on every form we print will have the exporter's name and address on it, full size, without any work from us, and when all the forms are printed, the whole electronic master document will be filed away in the computer's memory.

The databank on which the Formfill system depends is able to store in its memory every detail of every country's export requirements, and can be kept up to date by update disks, which are fed into the computer to delete changed items and insert the revised information.

8.12   More spellings: rules about doubling consonants

Where a word ends in a consonant and we wish to extend the word by adding a further syllable, the general rule is to double the final consonant:

(a)   If the final consonant is preceded by a single vowel, thus:

hit	hitting
pat	patting
drop	dropping
run	running

but where there is a double vowel, or two vowels, we do not double the final consonant:

wait	waiting
droop	drooping
scout	scouting
roam	roaming
foil	foiling

(b)   If a word of more than one syllable has the accent on the last syllable, we double the final consonant:

omit	omitting
remit	remittance
confer	conferred
occur	occurred

but where the emphasis shifts from the second syllable to the first syllable, we do not double the last consonant:

confer	conference

We also do not double the final consonant if there are already two consonants at the end of the word. For example:

part	parting
hurt	hurting
help	helpless

Now ask a fellow student to test you on the first list of spellings below, and then reciprocate by testing him/her on the second set.

Accountancy			*Personnel*
double entry	creditor	core work	wages
debit	creditworthy	contract work	salaries
credit	accredited	casual work	reumuneration
debt	ledger	industrial	discrimination
debtor	journal	commercial	racial discrimination
indebtedness	day book	professional	sexual discrimination

account	audit	recruit	interview
accounting	auditor	recruitment	interviewer
accountancy	auditing	employment	interviewee
accountant	actuary	employer	interviewed

8.13　A glossary of terms

Here is another collection of important terms used in business. They all relate in some way to the control of business activity. Unfortunately the appropriate definitions have become separated from the terms they describe. Write down the ten terms listed, then write against each one the definition that seems to you to relate to it. So your answers might read, 1　Controlled capitalism ... (c), if you think that definition (c) correctly explains the term 'controlled capitalism'.

	Term		*Definition*
1	Controlled capitalism	(a)	Costs that have to be borne by the general public instead of private industry because there are insufficient controls over industry, which is consequently able to dispose of waste products into the atmosphere or by dumping on land, or at sea.
2	Zoning regulations	(b)	An organized complaint against some malpractice, e.g. by environmentalists against an extension of nuclear power. Such protests are often made in the lobby of the House of Commons − hence the name.
3	Social costs	(c)	A situation where a reasonable degree of control is exercised by the sovereign power over business activity in what is fundamentally a free-enterprise system.
4	Monitoring procedures	(d)	A requirement laid down in the Consumer Protection Act 1987, which holds that it is an offence to supply goods that are not reasonably safe, or which contain defective substances or infringe regulations about that type of product.
5	Misleading price indications	(e)	Any procedure laid down to check the operations of activities that require a high standard of performance, and ensure that they meet

the required standards envisaged by the planning authorities when they permitted the project to go ahead.

6 Monopoly

(f) A fine imposed on a director or other official of a company that persists in contravening a regulation despite conviction in the courts for the offence. The fine is imposed every day that the company continues the malpractice.

7 Monopolies and Mergers Commission

(g) A situation where at least 25 per cent of the total national output of a particular good or service is produced by one firm. Thus there are only three firms in the United Kingdom detergent industry, so this is a monopoly situation.

8 Lobby

(h) Regulations that are part of the Planning Regulations and designate certain areas as industrial, residential or agricultural, so that reasonable control of developments is achieved. Applications to site factories, depots, etc., in the wrong zones will be rejected.

9 Daily default fine

(i) A commission charged with investigating any situation suspected of being a monopoly, or in the case of mergers of creating a new firm that will be a monopoly, the commission will report whether there is anything in the conduct of the company that is against the public interest.

10 General safety requirement

(j) An offence created in the Consumer Protection Act 1987. Anyone who misleads the public about the price of any article, e.g. with hidden charges not revealed until after a contract is signed, is liable under the Act to a fine, etc.

Answers 1 (c); 2 (h); 3 (a); 4 (e); 5 (j); 6 (g); 7 (i); 8 (b); 9 (f); 10 (d).

8.14   Answer section

Exercise 8n   (a) The £100 is rather high. Most credit cards make the innocent cardholder liable for only the first £25. (b) This clause would be deemed fair in law. If you allow someone to misuse your card, you are conspiring to defraud the bank, and that leaves you liable for every loss that occurs − not to mention criminal charges that may be brought against you.

Note: It is impossible to give 'answers' to the many exercises that require letters in this chapter.

9
English and business meetings

9.1 The nature of business meetings

There are many types of business meeting. Some are formal meetings, e.g. those required by statute under the Companies Acts 1985–9. Examples are the Annual General Meeting (AGM) and, more rarely, an Extraordinary General Meeting (EGM). Other formal meetings include board meetings and committee meetings.

Board meetings are usually held monthly. The board of directors meets under its chairman (or perhaps we should say chairperson) to discuss the major affairs of the company, and plan its future development. There will usually be present, with the chairman, the managing director and a number of full-time executive directors, including the marketing director, the production director (factory manager), the chief accountant and the personnel director. Finally, there will usually be a number of part-time non-executive directors. The term 'non-executive' implies that they play no part in the actual operations of the company but are present to give advice to the board on matters within their field of expertise. Thus there might be a banker, a lawyer, or a technical expert to do with the company's activities. Very often one of the non-executive directors will act as deputy chairperson, should the chairperson be absent for any reason.

The company secretary is present, and is responsible for drawing up the minutes of the meeting, but it is possible that a minuting secretary will also be present to take detailed records of what is said. Figure 9.1 shows a typical board of directors.

Committee meetings, although at a lower level than board meetings, are still very important and may be required by statute. Thus, under the Health and Safety at Work Act 1974, large organizations must set up joint safety committees, with representatives of both management and staff, to consider all matters affecting the safety of staff. Such committees would hold formal meetings and be conducted in the way described in this chapter.

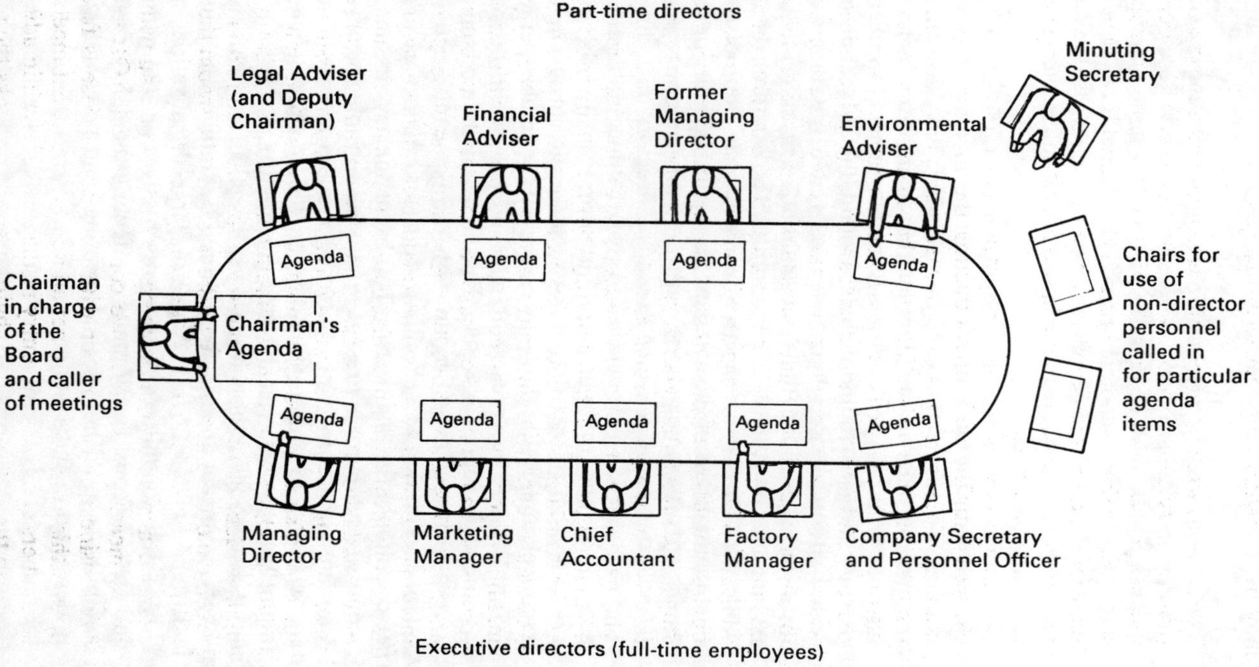

Part-time directors

Minuting Secretary

Chairs for use of non-director personnel called in for particular agenda items

Legal Adviser (and Deputy Chairman)

Financial Adviser

Former Managing Director

Environmental Adviser

Chairman in charge of the Board and caller of meetings

Chairman's Agenda

Managing Director

Marketing Manager

Chief Accountant

Factory Manager

Company Secretary and Personnel Officer

Executive directors (full-time employees)

Figure 9.1 A board of directors

9.2 General principles of business meetings

We may list the following general principles:

(a) The secretary will be responsible for calling meetings in consultation with the chairperson. The term 'secretary' here does not mean a person with secretarial skills, but a senior member of staff (usually the company secretary). In a club or society the secretary is an elected representative of the members who has undertaken to assume the often onerous duties of organizing the club's activities.

(b) The chairperson is the most important person at the meeting, charged with the duty of conducting the meeting in a proper manner. To ensure that only one person speaks at a time, all remarks must be made 'through the chair'. This means that anyone invited to speak addresses his/her remarks to the chairperson, and not to individuals around the table, since this would invite a direct response and reduce the meeting to disorderly squabbles. While any speaker is addressing the chair, no one else may speak. This prevents Mr B talking to Mrs C while Mr A is addressing the chair. If such a sub-discussion begins, the chairperson will say 'Through the chair, please' to stop it. The minuting secretary, for example, cannot possibly take down two speeches at once.

(c) The basis of the meeting is the 'agenda', drawn up beforehand by the secretary after consultation with the chairperson. There are certain items that form the framework of the agenda. These are explained later in more detail, but we may just mention one or two. An agenda always begins with 'apologies for absence' to let members know who is not able to be present and why. This is followed by the 'minutes of the previous meeting'. In theory these are read out, but to save time, especially if the minutes have been circulated to members beforehand, someone will move that 'the minutes be taken as read'. If this is agreed, we pass on to 'matters arising', i.e. 'matters arising from the minutes'. For example, members might ask whether the family of a member of staff whose death in an accident had been reported at the last meeting had been taken care of. A short report of the action taken would then be given.

We are now on to the items on the agenda dealing with the present meeting, and finally we come to an item AOB − any other business. Any member with a matter to raise is free to do so at this point. We then get an item 'date of next meeting', so members can make the entry in their diaries well in advance and keep the date free. The chairperson then thanks the members for their attendance and declares the meeting closed.

9.3   The agenda

The agenda is the detailed schedule of matters to be discussed at a business meeting. It will be drawn up by the secretary in consultation with the chairperson, who wields considerable influence over the items to be included in the agenda. Usually any person may ask for an item to be included on the agenda, but the request should be made well before the agenda is due to be prepared, and the inclusion of an item may be subject to the chairperson's veto. Items not included on the agenda proper may still be raised by an aggrieved member under 'any other business.'

The agenda will be circulated to the members with a covering letter – the 'notice of meeting' – which tells people the date, time and venue (the place where the meeting will be held). The minutes of the previous meeting will also be included unless these have been circulated earlier. A typical agenda might read as follows. Items 4,5 and 6 have been included by the chairperson. Items 7 and 8 have been requested by other members:

1   Apologies for absence: Peter Jones.
2   Minutes of the previous meeting.
3   Matters arising.
4   The new legislation: health and safety.
5   The 'Health and Safety Policy' statement.
6   Crawling boards: pavilion roof.
7   The town's fun run (15 July).
8   Asbestos danger – the old sheds.
9   Any other business.
10   Date of next meeting.

A typical 'notice of meeting' is shown in Figure 9.2.

The chairperson's agenda

The chairperson is usually provided with a special agenda, which has more space on it than the agenda circulated to ordinary members of the committee. It will have room for brief notes about each items on the agenda to remind the chairperson of the salient points about the matter concerned. For example, take the note about 'Health and Safety Policy' statement in the agenda given earlier. The chairperson will probably introduce the item by referring to his notes on the chairperson's agenda, explaining the legal requirement in the Health and Safety at Work Act 1974 to draw up such a policy and publish a statement about it. He/she might then call on Mr Brown, the chairman of a small sub-committee that has been drafting policy on the matter, for a progress report. During Mr Brown's report the chairperson

Factory Manager's Office
Leyside Depot
Our Ref HSC TD/ab
4 March 19..

To all members,
Health and Safety Committee

Notice of Meeting

Date   20 March 19..
Time   11.00 hours
Venue   Boardroom, Head Office
         22 Kilby Street

Dear . . . .
    May I draw to your attention the meeting to be
held as shown above. Please arrange with your section
supervisor to be freed from duty on the date given until
15.00 hours. The meeting should conclude by 13.00
hours, and members will lunch at the Head Office
canteen between that time and 14.00 hours, before
returning to their respective workplaces. If for any
reason you are unable to attend please send your
apology, in writing, to me at the Leyside Depot. If
possible your supervisor should provide a substitute to
whom these papers should be passed.
    I look forward to seeing you on 20 March at Kilby
Street.
Yours sincerely

Mary Dant
Secretary

Enclosures:
Agenda
Minutes of meeting on 20 January 19..

Figure 9.2   A 'Notice of Meeting'

might make notes about some of the areas that appear to be giving
trouble. He/she would then lead a discussion about these matters
after Mr Brown has concluded his statement. Finally the chairperson

might record 'actions to be taken', e.g. a problem might need to be taken up to a higher level – a full board meeting – for a ruling on the matter. It might be necessary to take legal advice, and this would be done before the next meeting.

The chairperson's agenda would also be useful in preparing the minutes of the meeting, even though a minuting secretary has been taking a full record. The minutes are always agreed with the chairperson, since it is easy in drawing up the minutes for a secretary to put a slightly different view from the chairperson's of the matters being recorded. The minutes have to be signed by the chairperson when all those at the next meeting agree that the minutes do give a true record of the earlier meeting, and if there is any feeling that this is not the case, the chairperson may not be willing to sign.

Exercise 9a Draw up an imaginary agenda for the annual general meeting of the Happy Traveller's Dining-out Club. The purpose of the club is to provide car-owners with a series of meeting places where they can enjoy a good meal and pleasant company. As this is the AGM, include in the agenda an annual report on the club's activities by the secretary and a financial report by the treasurer. Resolutions have been proposed to pay an honorarium to (a) the secretary, (b) the treasurer and (c) the outings organizer, who has done most of the work in finding suitable venues and making most of the arrangements.

Exercise 9b Write an imaginary speech for the secretary of the club mentioned in Exercise 9(a) above about the year's activities. Mention one or two amusing things that have happened, and remember to thank those who have contributed to the enjoyment of others – not least those who, by avoiding alcoholic drink, have ensured the safe return of all club members.

Exercise 9c Draw up an imaginary agenda for a meeting of the personnel committee of a big company. The chief items on the agenda concern the annual reappraisal of staff, which has to be carried out by departmental managers shortly, and the revision of induction procedures, for which a small *ad hoc* committee is to be appointed. Staff representatives have asked to discuss three special points – disciplinary treatment of T. Holmes, V. Johnson and M. Salmon. These are quite separate cases.

9.4 Business meetings: a glossary of terms

The glossary of terms below to do with business meetings has become jumbled. Pair up the words or phrases labelled 1−10 with the explanations labelled (a)−(j). The correct sequence is given at the end of the section.

1 Quorum

(a) A body of rules established at the very start of an organization or committee structure, by which the body comes into existence and is governed throughout its lifetime.

2 Resolution

(b) It means that the committee, having given a good opportunity for the discussion of a particular agenda item (and the argument not getting anywhere), should move on to the next item of business.

3 Constitution

(c) The minimum numbers of members who must be present if a meeting is to carry on valid proceedings.

4 Point of order

(d) The break-up of a meeting that has not concluded its business, but is unable to continue because time is short and perhaps other duties call. The meeting will be resumed at a later date.

5 *Ex officio*

(e) A formal decision carried (or perhaps rejected) at a meeting. It has to be proposed, seconded and voted upon, and usually a simple majority makes it an effective decision of the committee.

6 Posponed *sine die*

(f) A Latin term that is applied to a member of a committee who is entitled to be present because of his/her official capacity, rather than because he/she has been chosen as a representative of some group or department.

7 Adjournment

(g) A method of breaking into a discussion which appears to be developing in a way that breaches the constitution of the committee or the rules of conduct established over the years. The chairperson must at once rule whether the point raised is correct, and if it is must follow the rule of conduct.

8 'that the motion be now put'

(h) A Latin term which means 'without date'. The matter will be postponed indefinitely.

9 'that the

(i) A way of bringing the discussion of a

| motion lie on the table' | | motion to an end, by putting the motion to a vote. |
| 10 'move next business' | (j) | A motion having been discussed fairly fully and agreement on it being unlikely, it is not voted on but is left to be discussed another time if anyone cares to bring it up again as a future agenda item. |

Answer   The correct sequence is 1 (c); 2 (e); 3 (a); 4 (g); 5 (f); 6 (h); 7 (d); 8 (i); 9 (j); 10 (b).

9.5   Acquiring skills for business meetings

'Meetings skills' may seem to be a very minor part of a business English course, but since most business activities call for some sort of committee work, there is much to be said for acquiring these skills. The best way to do so is to volunteer for service on any committee that comes up and take an active part in its activities. Many students, for example, hesitate to join committees at the start of their courses, being still uncertain how much study they are going to have to do. It is therefore usually fairly easy to get chosen for a committee whose activity interests you, and besides acquiring the skills needed, you meet a wider range of people than your own particular study group. Such contacts can prove invaluable later. The following sub-sections cover most of the skills required.

Active listening

Active listening implies that you are paying real attention to what is being said, and thinking about it carefully within the context of the agenda heading that is being discussed. Are the speaker's points valid, and is he/she right? It helps to make a note of what the points are, so that you can refer to them if you decide to speak yourself. You may want to support the speaker or to rebut the points he/she has made.

The active listener develops a sensitivity to the speaker's voice, which, by a variation of tone or pace, may convey a subtle commentary on the words actually being said. You should notice the structure of the speech that is being made – its introductory remarks, its arrival at the main point or points, its development of the argument and its summary of the speaker's views before the speech is concluded. You are listening to it critically – so as to appraise it. You may find that you agree with it, or you may deplore the speaker's proposals, but the active listener knows what has been said and has formed a view of it by the end of the speech. This is better than letting it wash passively over you.

Speaking in public

There are three main types of public speaking. They are (a) the formal speech, (b) the report and (c) a contribution to a discussion.

The *formal speech* should be carefully researched, well-planned, and as brief as the circumstances allow considering the subject matter to be conveyed. It should be rehearsed.

The *report* is usually more straightforward, since it is the outcome of a period of effort and investigation, which means the subject matter is familiar to you as speaker. You should begin by saying what the investigation was about and why it was undertaken. The actual course of the study should then be described and the conclusions or recommendations should be clearly stated.

A *contribution to a discussion* is less formal, and more impromptu. It should be kept as short as possible, and should concentrate on one or two points only. A long, detailed reappraisal of the opinions of all the earlier speakers is seldom effective in a discussion. An oft-quoted piece of advice to those who speak in discussion groups is 'stand up, speak up and shut up'. Some points to remember are the following:

1 Adopt an appropriate style for the audience concerned.
2 Use formal English (in other words, avoid slang expressions).
3 Avoid jargon, but if you must use it, at least explain it for the benefit of the uninitiated.
4 Avoid acronyms – not everyone knows what they mean. A speaker who constantly refers to JIT will have most of his audience mystified. A few may know it means 'just in time', but some of them may not know what that means. (It is a production system that gets raw materials, components and packaging to the point where they are to be used just in time for the production staff to use them.)
5 Speak clearly, varying the tone of your voice. Those who speak in a monotone end by sounding monotonous, which the dictionary defines as 'wearying by sameness'.
6 Speak up. Some people will tell you that a person who speaks quietly commands attention, but it is not always so. You have decided to make a speech – at least let them hear it.
7 The manner of delivery is important. Hurried speech gives an impression of nervousness. A measured pace is best, neither too slow nor too fast. Pauses at judiciously chosen moments emphasize the importance of particular statements.

8   Humour is always helpful, and a frequently told story usually goes over better than an unrehearsed one – so long as the audience have not heard it before.
9   What to do with one's eyes is important. If you look vaguely into the remote distance, the audience may feel your subject has little to do with them. On the other hand, if you eyeball a single individual for too long, he/she may become embarrassed. The better plan is to look at individuals all the time, especially those showing the greatest interest, but only for a short moment each.

9.6   The minutes of a meeting

The minutes are the formal record of a meeting, constituting the authorized version of what has been discussed and agreed at the meeting. In order to draw up a set of minutes, it is best to appoint a minuting secretary, who will take down the most important remarks made by the various speakers. He/she may of course produce a complete verbatim report, but more usually the notes made will be a summary of the various contributions. The minuting secretary must therefore be able to listen intelligently to the discussion, and follow each contribution, making a mental summary of it and jotting down notes in sufficient detail for later consideration.

Many speakers give **oral indications** of important points coming up in their speeches. It may be only a change of tone or pace in their speech. Sometimes a significant gesture will be used to emphasise a point, stabbing with a forefinger to make the essential impact. Some words such as 'firstly', 'secondly' 'furthermore' and 'moreover' are known as **discourse markers**, because they help the audience to pick up important points. A minuting secretary will make a note of the points that follow such discourse markers.

Where a minuting secretary is not appointed or is unable to attend, the chairperson will nominate a suitable member of the committee to make notes for the minutes.

Language and tone of the minutes

Minutes should be in formal language and restrained in tone. Colourful use of language should be avoided. For example, we would not refer to 'a violent discussion', but use restraint and say that 'a lively debate followed'. The summary of any speeches should be impartial, and the actual wording used should be vetted by the chairperson so that any possibility of offence is avoided. Since the minutes are to be published and circulated in the chairperson's name, this is only fair to the chairperson. Minutes might, in very rare circumstances, be the subject of legal action, or be used in evidence in a court of law, and as such should be taken seriously.

At the end of the meeting the minuting secretary will transcribe the notes made in an established format, which is illustrated in Figure 9.3. Note that items in the minutes are given a number that relates to the year's proceedings, so that a cross-reference to a particular item in earlier minutes is easily made. The reference 44/93 refers to the forty-fourth item in the year 1993.

The draft minutes will then be submitted to the chairperson for approval, before being duplicated and circulated to members before the next meeting. It is usual, as shown in Figure 9.3, to use appropriate headings and sub-headings; to give capital letters to all official names, such as Chairperson, Secretary, Personnel Officer, etc. The signature space at the end of the minutes is not signed by the chairperson until the next meeting, when the members will discuss the minutes and will be asked to agree that the minutes are a correct record of the earlier meeting. If this is agreed, the chairperson will sign and the minutes then become part of the formal record of the committee, which may be quoted or referred to in any future deliberations on the matters recorded.

<u>Personnel Committee Meeting − Brymer Electrical Ltd</u>

Minutes of a meeting held at 2.15 pm Wednesday 5 March 19..
   in The Board Room, Longstaff House.

Members present: Mrs P. Brymer (Chairperson)
                     Mr T. Robertson (Secretary and
                     Personnel Officer)
                     Mr R. Jones (Training Officer)
                     Mrs M. Lomax (Office
                     Representative)
                     Mrs H. Longstaffe (Officer
                     Supervisor)
                     Mr T. Arkwright (Factory Manager)
                     Mr T. Roper (Shop Steward)
                     Miss M. Newcastle (Minuting
                     Secretary)
                     Messrs. T. Morris, D. Gooch and R.
                     Walker (Factory Representatives)

Apologies for absence Mr T. Draper (Transport Manager) was absent due to ill health.

Figure 9.3 The minutes of a Personnel Committee meeting

Figure 9.3   Continued.

41/93 *Minutes of previous meeting*
The minutes of the previous meeting were taken as read, adopted as a true record and signed by Mrs P. Brymer (Chairperson).

42/93 *Matters arising*
Mr R. Jones (Training Officer) reported that, after discussions with Thurrock Technical College, a special 'in college' day-release course for apprentices had now been agreed, which would give a major qualification over a 3-year period in electrical and electronic assembly. It was felt that this would, in time, resolve the shortage of skilled workers in the main assembly plant.

43/93 *Annual staff review*
Mr T. Robertson drew the attention of members to the annual staff review, which was to take place in the week commencing Monday 24 March. Heads of Sections would be presented with folders outlining the careers to date of subordinates, which would be made available to the members of staff 30 minutes before the interview. These folders would then form the basis of a discussion with the member of staff. Recommendations for promotion, merit rises, etc., would then be considered by the Personnel Department. Members were asked to make themselves available if required to consider any dispute that might arise.

44/93 *Racial bias in employment*
Mr T. Arkwright reported on a policy document distributed by the Race Relations Board requiring managements to review the statistical facts associated with racial bias in their organizations. The figures required were designed to discover whether recruitment in the various departments was 'fair' to ethnic groups within society today. It was felt, *prima facie*, that the organization was at some fault in these matters, but it was essential to discover the facts. He asked for a small *ad hoc* committee to be set up to discover the true position. He was prepared to chair such a sub-committee. Mr T. Roper and Mrs H. Longstaffe agreeing to be part of this investigation, they were proposed, seconded and unanimously elected to the Racial Bias Investigation Committee, and it was agreed that this should be an agenda item at the next meeting of the main Committee.

45/93 *Unfair dismissal − Peter Roach*
Mr Robertson reported on the case of Peter Roach, whose
dismissal for theft had been held to be unfair by the
Industrial Tribunal. It was conceded that the theft had
occurred, but dismissal of a handicapped person who had
no previous experience of employment and its
temptations was held to be too severe a punishment. Mr
Roach had been offered the choice of re-employment with
a reprimand as the appropriate punishment, or a lump
sum payment of £500. He had chosen to be reinstated.
Management therefore hoped that he would be welcomed
back without prejudice and given every opportunity to
make good in the company. Mr Robertson expressed his
own regrets that he had applied the rules about
dismissal without fully taking account of the employee's
difficult employment background.

46/93 *Any other business*
D. Gooch, a factory representative, referred to the
unsatisfactory state of the first aid service in the factory,
and in particular the recent accident for which no
member of the qualified first aid staff had been available.
The Personnel Officer agreed that he would raise this at
the Health and Safety Committee, of which he was a
member, and asked Mr Gooch to let him have a written
account of the whole incident.

There being no other business the meeting adjourned
at 4.12 pm.

Date of next meeting
Wednesday 2nd April 19. . in the Board Room, Longstaffe
House.

These minutes are agreed to be a true record of the
meeting on 5 March 19. .
Chairperson 2 April 19. .   . . .

Exercise 9d Make a collection of minutes of meetings you have
attended, or which other people are prepared to make available to
you. Study the format used and familiarize yourself with it.

Exercise 9e Using the following agenda as a basis, draw up a set of
minutes, inventing such names and events as you feel are appropriate:

HEALTH & SAFETY COMMITTEE, XYZ LTD
Meeting at the Recreation Annexe,
Long Road
11 am Tues., 4 September 19..

1 Members present.
2 Letters of apology.
3 Minutes of the previous meeting.
4 Matters arising.
5 Car park accident, 27 August 19..
6 First aid panel: training course.
7 Hazardous chemicals: storage
8 Disciplinary proceedings – smoking in plastics store.
9 Presentation of departmental safety awards
10 Any other business.

Exercise 9f Using the following agenda as a basis, draw up a set of minutes for the annual general meeting of the M.J. White Ltd Social Club, inventing such names and events as seem to be appropriate.

M.J. WHITE LTD SOCIAL CLUB
Annual General Meeting for the year April 19..–March 19..
Held at the Recreation Centre, 7.00 pm, 29 March 19..

1 Members present. (A list will be circulated. Please add your name to it as it is passed around.)
2 Letters of apology.
3 Minutes of the previous AGM, held on 30 March 19..
4 Matters arising.
5 Secretary's report on the year's proceedings.
6 Treasurer's report (a set of accounts will be distributed at the meeting).
7 Welfare report (the Welfare Committee deals with all cases of hardship, bereavements, etc.)
8 The Easter outing. The secretary will report on the plans made.
9 Open forum for discussion. The committee hopes members will feel free to speak their minds on past (and possible future) events.
10 Any other business.

9.7 More comprehension exercises

'Let us now praise famous men', says Ecclesiasticus XLIV. In the world of business there have been many famous men, and the two descriptions of famous men in this section are taken from a companion volume, *Economics Made Simple*. Read the passages and answer the questions below them.

Thomas Robert Malthus (1766–1834) and the Malthusian doctrine

Thomas Malthus was the son of a country squire, who became a parson for a short while after leaving university where he read mathematics and philosophy. The climate of thought at the time, when the French Revolution had not yet turned ugly and revengeful, was optimistic. Progress was in the air; it was an Age of Reason. Tom Paine's book of that name was just about to appear, and the development and perfection of a better society, with better men to live in it, was optimistically forecast. Malthus was sceptical, and when the mood in France changed, he pondered on the forces acting against the improvement of mankind. He decided that population pressure was the chief cause of poverty, and his *Essay on Population* described, without real evidence of any kind, the 'inevitable' nature of the forces at work.

Briefly, the *Essay on Population* held that population tended to increase in geometrical ratio, e.g. 2–4–8–16–32–64 etc., with world population doubling every twenty-five years. By contrast, land was limited in area and could only be improved by heavy capital investment. The likely improvement in food supplies was at best an arithmetic progression, e.g. 2–4–6–8–10–12. The difference between the two ratios made poverty inevitable unless the passion between the sexes could be controlled. Why, then, had mankind survived thus far? Because natural checks were exerted to redress the balance between population and food supply. These checks were of two sorts. Self-restraint, displayed chiefly by the rich and prosperous, was used to reduce the size of families for fear of poverty or decline in the social scale. Marriage was postponed until later in life, and the size of families was limited voluntarily to maintain the standard of living of the family.

For the poor, with no motive for reducing sexual appetite, nature had devised positive checks. Infant mortality, infanticide, diseases, epidemics, plagues, unwholesome foods, dangerous occupations and even famine which 'with one mighty blow, levels the population with the food of the world'.

His theories were at once seized upon and expounded by the leaders of society of his time. The spokesmen of the poor reviled the essay and its author, but were powerless to defeat arguments which fitted so well with the established political and economic framework of the times. Why pay higher wages when the only result would be an increase in sexual appetite and a new generation to eat the parents down to the poverty level again? Why envisage safer working conditions, better housing, and better sanitation when these checks and balances were but a natural device to prevent famine from stalking the land? Well might William Cobbett, the radical writer, say 'Parson! I have during my life detested many men; but never anyone as much as you'.

Although respectable opinion took up his arguments, and Malthus himself was much listened to throughout his lifetime, the world has escaped until now the dire calamities be foretold. The opening up of the American prairies, the Ukraine, Australia, New Zealand and Argentina proved capable of supporting mankind for a century or two. Whether Malthus might yet be proved right is a different matter. There are politicians today who call themselves Neo-Malthusians who believe that recent huge increases in world population are about to prove Malthus right, and quote recent famines in Africa and elsewhere as evidence in favour of their beliefs.

Exercise 9g

1   The French Revolution began in 1789. How old was Malthus at that time?
2   What did those who believed in the 'Age of Reason' think had now become possible?
3   How did the mood in France change shortly after the revolution began?
4   What did Malthus say was the main force acting against the improvement of mankind?
5   How did the rich reduce population pressure?
6   What was their chief reason for doing so?
7   How was population pressure from the poor resolved?
8   Which of nature's measures is the most powerful?
9   Malthus's ideas led to the workhouse system, in which the poor were forced to go to the workhouse, and men and women were segregated. How would this implement Malthus's ideas?
10 Why did the Malthusians oppose housing policies, safety in factories, sanitation schemes, etc., which we regard as very desirable today?
11 How did William Cobbett refer to Malthus?
12 What is Neo-Malthusianism today?

John Stuart Mill and 'the Utilitarian Society'

John Stuart Mill (1806–73) was a boy genius whose father, James Mill, was a follower of Jeremy Bentham, the practical philosopher of the Industrial Revolution. His father took personal care of the boy's education from an early age. He began to learn Greek when he was only three, and Latin shortly after. At the age of 12 his studies included philosophy, political economy and logic. By the age of 16 he had founded the Utilitarian Society, whose members supported Jeremy Bentham's political theory of 'utility'. This theory held that the standard by which we must judge all the actions of men, institutions and Governments was the yardstick of human happiness. The action that promoted the well-being and happiness of the greatest number of people was the right one. It is an idea that still commands widespread respect.

Mill did not overthrow the ideas of Adam Smith, Ricardo or Malthus. He moved their ideas on a short step in a more optimistic direction. He agreed with them that production of wealth was a bitter process, subject to harsh, inexorable laws like competition. 'But', he says in his *Principles of Political Economy*, 'it is not so with the Distribution of Wealth. That is a matter of human institution solely. The things once there, mankind, individually or collectively, can do with them as they like.'

And, no doubt, what mankind did with the wealth they had created was to be judged from the standpoint of the greatest good to the greatest number. It was an idea that shook a sleeping world awake, and led eventually to the type of managed prosperity which has been such a feature of the second half of the twentieth century.

Mill defined economics as 'the practical science of the production and distribution of wealth'. Not only must man produce wealth, he must distribute it more reasonably. Too great a believer in the advantages of competition to advocate Government intervention himself, Mill sowed the seeds of State interference on many 'exceptional' grounds. One of these was that he thought the State should introduce compulsory education; another was that the State should compel factory owners to obey the legislation Parliament had enacted even though it raised costs. He died in 1873, during Gladstone's great Parliament of 1868–74, when a burst of legislative activity on education, public health, electoral law, control of corruption and control of monopolies was passing through the British Parliament.

Exercise 9h

1 Explain the words 'genius', 'philosopher' and 'logic'
2 Who was Jeremy Bentham?
3 What did the theory of 'utility' advocate as a correct approach by governments and institutions to the problems of the day.
4 Why was the production of wealth 'a bitter process' in those days?
5 What did Mill recommend should be done with the wealth that had been created?
6 How did Mill define economics?

7   Why is the state the best organization for introducing compulsory education?
8   How old was Mill when he died?
9   Did he live to see any of his ideas being put into practice?
10 How important are education, public health, electoral law, control of corruption and control of monopolies today?
11 Whose ideas had widest acceptance and implementation in the end, those of Mill or those of Malthus?
12 If you were asked to say, in a nutshell, the essence of Mill's ideas, what would you say?

9.8   More about punctuation: end punctuation marks

Today punctuation, especially in business letters, tends to be simple and straightforward. We do not usually write long and complex sentences, such as might be found in doctoral theses at university level. Consequently we need less signposts to help the reader follow the direction of our thoughts. If a punctuation mark is necessary to clarify the text, we use it. If the text can be perfectly well understood without it, we omit the punctuation mark. The real test is 'Does this punctuation mark clarify the author's statements, and promote the reader's understanding'. If it does, we use the punctuation mark.

Full stops

The three end punctuation marks are the full stop, the question mark and the exclamation mark. They all indicate that the sentence has come to an end – a full stop. The word 'period' is often used to mean 'full stop', especially in the United States.

Question marks

These come at the end of sentences that ask a question; in other words, interrogative sentences. They may be used within a sentence in certain circumstances, e.g. when a sentence contains several questions: 'Will he contribute capital? or ideas? or experience? or will he be an albatross around our necks?'

In business letters we often ask courtesy questions, which are not direct questions but only imply that any business that can be put our way would be deemed a favour. It is usual to leave out the question mark in such cases, e.g. 'May we hope for an early response to this information package'.

Exclamation marks

Exclamation marks should be reserved for strong exclamations, and even then only one is needed. Do not use two or three. Leave that to the illustrated comic books. A damsel in distress may say: 'Saved!' An outraged headmaster at a Parent-Teacher Association may exclaim 'Heaven forbid!' But a sense of genuine relief does not need an exclamation mark if the tension of the situation has passed: 'Well, we have survived'.

Exercise 9i   Insert the correct end punctuation marks in the following sentences:

1 We wish you every success in your new enterprise
2 Can we assist you in any way
3 Our service is free Absolutely free
4 Well done Well done indeed
5 Thank you for your kind inquiry May we hope for an order by return
6 HM Customs will not tolerate late payment Why should they It is their money you have collected from your customers
7 If the document is in electronic form in someone's computer system, it is still a document if it can be called up on to a VDU screen
8 'Can the document be recalled' 'It seems so, my Lord'
9 'Then arrange a demonstration of it at some premises where I can see it Seeing is believing, is it not'
10 I declare that the document is binding under the Carriage of Goods by Sea and Air Act The defendant will pay the contractual charge And the costs

9.9   More spellings

Ask a fellow student to test you on the first set of spellings below. Then reciprocate by testing him/her on the second set.

Business documentation		*Personnel*	
invoice	letter of credit	person	induct
statement	documentary credit	personal	induction
credit note	irrevocable credit	personnel	training
debit note	consignment note	labour	application
advice note	air waybill	staff	appointment
petty cash voucher	sea waybill	human resources	rejection

bill of lading	combined transport document	skill	dismiss
bill of exchange	standard shipping note	skilled	dismissal
bill of sale	documentary collection form	unskilled	redundant
letter of hypothecation	phyto-sanitary certificate	skilful	redundancy

9.10   Answer section

Exercises 9a–9f   Appraise your own efforts.

Exercise 9g   1   23 years; 2   That a better society on earth was now possible; 3   The reign of terror started, with the guillotine being used to kill off the aristocrats; 4   The growth of population; 5   By postponing marriage and exercising sexual restraint; 6   Fear of decline in the social scale; 7   By natural checks, disease, malnutrition and famine; 8   Famine; 9   If the sexes are segregated, they will not have children; 10   They thought that these measures would act against nature's balance and only make the problems worse; 11   'Parson, I have in my lifetime detested many men; but never anyone as much as you'; 12   It is a body of people who believe that the world is seriously overpopulated and Malthus may yet be proved right.

Exercise 9h   1   Genius, a gifted person of high intelligence; philosopher, a person of great wisdom whose life is guided by high principles; logic, the science of reasoning which resolves problems by thought; 2   The founder of the Utilitarian Theory; 3   It holds that the actions of men, women and governments should be judged by the yardstick of the human happiness they provide; 4   Because production was free of controls about working hours, safe systems of work, methods of payment, etc.; 5   Mill held wealth should be shared more fairly; 6   As 'the practical science of the production and distribution of wealth'; 7   Because education is non-profit-making, so ordinary entrepreneurs will not provide it; 8   67 years; 9   Yes – compulsory education, public health, the Factory Acts, etc.; 10   They are all extremely important; 11   The ideas of Mill were most widely adopted; 12   However bad competition may be in the production process, it doesn't have to affect how we share up the wealth we have created. That can be done according to our ideas of reasonableness, and with a view to creating as much happiness as possible.

Exercise 9i   1   Full stop at end; 2   Question mark at end; 3   Exclamation mark after 'free' in both cases; 4   Exclamation mark after 'done' and after 'indeed'; 5   Full stops after inquiry and after 'return'; 6   Full stop after 'payment', question mark after 'they', full stop after 'customers'; 7   Full stop after 'screen'; 8   Question mark after 'recalled', full stop after 'Lord'; 9   Full stop after the second 'it', question mark after 'not'; 10   Full stops after 'Act' and 'charge', exclamation mark after 'costs.

10
Writing a summary

10.1 Nature of a summary

A summary is a brief statement that gives the important facts of a situation but dispenses with needless details to convey the essential points only. Another word for a summary is a précis. The vast majority of summaries in business life are drawn up from longer reports, pieces of legislation, etc., with the intention of improving the awareness of the target audience without bothering them with excessive detail. If we can acquaint the vast mass of the staff with the background picture, we can leave those who eventually are charged with the responsibility of implementing the legislation or report to deal with the detailed requirements.

Summaries are used in business life for the following.

Briefing sessions

For example, a new Act of Parliament may impose certain duties upon managements. People queue up outside Her Majesty's Stationery Office on the day of publication to purchase the Act – it may cost as much as £15. It is then handed over to the most likely person (depending on the subject matter) to prepare a summary of the Act's requirements. This will be used to brief the board of directors, who will take steps to implement it. This usually means appointing an *ad hoc* committee to draw up plans, cost the procedures, and make proposals about them.

Policy statements

Most businesses operate by a series of policies that let everyone know, in every field, how to deal with matters that arise. These policy requirements may be imposed from outside – by law, by trade associations, etc. Thus we have to have a Safety at Work policy, and a Race Relations policy and an Equal Opportunities policy. Other policy statements are developed 'in-house' to cover situations that may develop. Thus there are policies on redundancy, on dismissal of staff, on absence from work and many other matters. A policy is a summary of a firm's position on some matter.

Manuals of procedure

Many tasks are of a technical or organizational nature, and to ensure correct procedures it is usual to draw up 'manuals of procedure'. These are revised from time to time, e.g. as products change, and are useful for retraining staff as they earn promotions or switch jobs. The first task for the new incumbent of any post is to read the manual of procedures. This is better than trying to pick the brains of the previous occupant of the post — who will perhaps have gone elsewhere, or may even have died. Manuals (or summaries) of procedure ensure continuity of method.

10.2   Telex messages and cables

These message systems are summaries of a sort, since they depend upon sending a brief message containing enough detail to start action on a particular matter. They are available locally in many countries, but their chief use is in international trade and in the activities of multi-national companies.

Much of the telex traffic and cable traffic is totally routine — lists of engine numbers for exported vehicles, notification of the movements of staff posted overseas, clarification of orders, dates of delivery, types of insurance cover required, etc. On the other hand, emergencies arise at any time. Consider the following facts.

On 27 July 19.. at 4.30 am an amateur radio enthusiast (a radio ham) in Manila picks up on SOS message that an oil tanker is in difficulties in the South China Sea. Although air searches are instituted at once, there is no sign of the vessel, but daylight reveals a massive oil slick at a point 200 km west of Manila. The Philippine government makes a general enquiry to all oil companies in the Philippines and finds that a tanker, *The Tempaso Gulf*, was in the area. Attempts to call this vessel produce no response, and it is decided to alert the head office of its company, Tempaso Oil of Houston.

What should such a message say? A possible answer might be:

Tempaso Oil Houston. Radio report at 4.30 am 27 July stop Oil tanker in South China Sea in difficulties stop Possibly your Tempaso Gulf stop Please check radio links with Tempaso Gulf and advise stop Oil slick sighted stop Marine Superintendent Manila.

Exercise 10   Telex messages and cables

1   Send a telex to deal with the following matter:

Peter Brand was about to set off by air to Sydney, Australia, to become the manager of the Newcastle (New South Wales) branch of Heavy Lifts Ltd, as a replacement for Alec Walters, who was due for home leave. On the way to the airport he was the innocent victim of a robbery that went wrong at a service station. His car was hijacked and he was shot. He is now in intensive care in North Middlesex Hospital. It is necessary to cancel Alec Walters' home leave until a replacement can be found. This will take 2 weeks. Meanwhile tell Alec to resume control of the Newcastle branch and to await faxes on the Newcastle Marine Ltd contracts, which were due to be renegotiated by Peter Brand. Tell him he will have to handle the renegotiation after reading the material, which will be faxed shortly. Final point – we have just heard that Peter is stable, but seriously ill. The telex number is 895410 HEAVL1 A.

2   Send a cable to deal with the following matter:

George Haji Inc. of 5212 Dock St, Dar es Salaam, has sent a letter of credit confirming the availability of £20,000 at the Bank of Tanzania for the supply and delivery of machinery that has already been the subject of negotiation. However, the agreed price was £120,000, not £20,000. The difference may be only a slip of the keyboard in the typing of the letter of credit, but you cannot go ahead until the matter is sorted out. You want confirmation that the funds made available by the Bank do correspond with the original agreed price. One other point is that while the letter of credit mentions CIF terms under Incoterms 90 the company has not specified whether it wants the 'all risks' cover (Institute cargo clauses 'A') or some lesser cover. This point needs clarifying.

3   Send a telex to deal with the following matter:

Your firm exports high value power-station equipment to countries around the world. You have received a telex from the owners of the *Southern Cross*, a vessel carrying some cargo for you, that a fire on board has damaged some cargo, and caused other cargo to be jettisoned (thrown into the sea), and that the vessel's owners are about to exercise a lien on all the good arrived cargo to claim general average contribution. In such an accident the owners of cargo saved by the jettison of other cargo thrown overboard to save the entire venture have to contribute to the losses of those whose cargo is lost. Until the compensation is paid (or guaranteed by an insurance company), the captain can refuse to allow cargo to leave the ship.

You want to telex your agent in Cape Town to ask him to meet the vessel, preferably in the company of the local Lloyds agent, to find out (a) whether your cargo is safe and (b) if it is safe, whether it can be released against a general average bond issued by the Lloyds agent, since the cargo is insured at Lloyds. (A bond is a promise to pay a sum of money.) If the cargo is lost, you want to know so that you can expedite a replacement cargo, but you also want your agent to collect evidence for the claim on Lloyds for the lost goods.

10.3 Making a summary

When making a summary we have to exercise two skills:

(a) We have to extract *relevant* information from the passage or document that has to be summarized.
(b) We then have to express that information concisely in fluent, correct English.

Relevant information

In an examination we may have to keep within certain rules laid down by the examiner. For example, we usually have to keep within a certain number of words, and any breach of this limit may be penalized. We may be asked to extract information relating to a particular part of the subject matter. If we extract irrelevant matter not required by the examiner, we may lose marks.

In real life the situation is rather different. We shall know what real-life problem is facing us, and shall therefore be able to judge what is relevant or irrelevant. The task of drawing up a summary, e.g. of an Act of Parliament, will have been imposed upon us by some higher authority — the managing director or the chairman of the board. He/she may have laid down clear guidelines, but more often the instructions we are given may be much more sketchy. 'Find out what it says and give us a summary by Friday. In particular what do we need to do to implement the legislation.'

We have to detect the main points of the passage, whatever they are. Read the passage paragraph by paragraph and pick out the key sentence in each (see Section 6.2 to remind yourself of this important part of a paragraph). Copy out the key sentences, or make a note of the chief point of the paragraph in your own words. As you read the passage paragraph by paragraph, build up a list of key points as the basis of your summary. If a paragraph is clearly not relevant, leave it out, or just make a note: Para. 2. N/A (N/A is short for 'not applicable').

Decide what is the best order for your points in the summary. It depends upon the passage. For example, an account of an accident will probably be dominated by the sequence of events, and the points may fall into a natural pattern. With other passages, e.g. many reports, the final section of the report usually consists of clear 'recommendations', which are perhaps what your audience (the Board of Directors) will really want to know about. Therefore your summary may only deal very briefly with the events that led up to the conclusions, and will largely consist of the recommendations made, and what these mean in terms of action to implement the report in your particular firm or company.

Writing the summary

You are now ready to write your first draft of the summary. It should be written in correct sentences, making the points you have listed simply and clearly, in the sequence you consider most appropriate. So far as possible you should avoid using words and phrases that appear in the original document. Where this is impossible it should at least be the case that what was originally said should manifestly have passed through your own head and be largely expressed in your own words. For example, where an Act of Parliament refers to the introduction of a 'Test of Reasonableness' when contracts are being drawn up, you could hardly prepare a summary of the Act without using those words. That is the chief point of the Act – to give the courts some measure they can use to test whether a clause in a contract is fair or not. You will need to feature that test in your summary, and explain what Parliament has prescribed. By using 'connectors' (see Section 6.4) you can link your points together to lead your audience along the path you are seeking to make clear. You can give emphasis to those points you believe to be the most important by using such connectors as 'chiefly' or 'the main requirement' etc.

The first draft should now be checked for the following:

(a) *Its length*. If there is a word limit, count the words.
(b) *Its accuracy*. Does it express the key facts of the original passage correctly? Is anything omitted or given the wrong weight and emphasis?
(c) *Its quality*. Is any of it awkwardly expressed? Is it correctly punctuated and are there any mis-spellings?

If your summary is too long, go through it and see whether there is anything of a non-essential nature that might easily be left out. If so, delete it. See also whether any of the essential items could have been expressed more succinctly. Sometimes unnecessary adjectives and adverbs, which add to the descriptiveness of the summary without really being necessary to the contents, have been included. Deletion of these may bring your summary down to the correct length.

It is now time to write or type out your summary in its final form. Write neatly, or type accurately, checking for errors of any sort. Finally, read it through carefully to ensure it is as polished a piece of work as possible.

10.4 Exercises on summaries

Before we come to the exercises below, we should consider one or two other points about summaries.

First, in real life it is sometimes impossible to summarize a document. If you have an Act of Parliament, or a set of guidance notes that have been drawn up by a government department, you will often find it is almost impossible to summarize them. What you can do is leave bits out, but that is not really helpful. The thing is that such documents have been written and rewritten to such an extent by some of the finest minds in the country that they have been reduced to the bare essentials anyway, and almost every word is necessary. If you are called upon in real life to summarize this type of material, it is always a good idea to emphasize at the start of your summary that it has been extremely difficult to summarize the material.

Second, in real life, wherever possible, when asked to summarize a report, try to get a lead or hint from the person asking for the summary what particular angle or aspect of the report interests him/ her. To have an idea of what is really wanted by the person commissioning the summary will sharpen your attack upon the subject matter you have to read.

You should now try some of the exercises given below.

Exercise 10b Summarize the passage below, reducing it to about 150 words.

The demand for transport

To some extent all economies are free enterprise economies, for it is in the nature of mankind to find personal solutions to the problems of demand and supply. When we feel a need for some particular good, or service, we seek out someone who can supply it, and offer him an inducement to do so. Economists have therefore divided elementary economic studies into the studies of demand and supply. When a person wants something sufficiently to be prepared to pay for it − that is to say, he will offer an inducement to any supplier prepared to supply it − he is said to 'demand' the good. Payment is most often arranged in 'cash': some officially sponsored form of 'legal tender' such as pounds or dollars. The demand for a good, or service, is therefore that quantity of the good or service for which people are prepared to pay at a certain price.

Many goods are demanded 'directly', that is to say they are wanted for the satisfaction they yield. The demand for fish and chips arises directly from the hunger of consumers for that particular combination of foods. The demand for houses arises directly from the need for shelter.

There is another kind of demand which is indirect rather than direct. Here the object demanded is not demanded for itself alone, but only as a means to provide other desirable goods and services. The demand for sewing machines is great, and continuing, but no one actually 'wants' sewing machines. You cannot eat them, drink them or wear them. We want them because they are producer goods; they help us produce clothing and furnishings which are directly beneficial in our everyday life, bringing warmth, comfort and privacy. The demand for sewing machines is a 'derived demand', derived from our need for clothing, curtains etc.

The demand for transport is this type of demand, an indirect demand. It stems from mankind's need for goods and services of every type. We demand the transport of Japanese video recorders because we demand the entertainment they provide. Our demand for a taxi to the dentist derives from the demand for his services. Transport facilities are 'producer goods'; goods which have a part to play in the production process. Their particular function is to bridge the geographical gaps between producers and consumers (courtesy of *Transport & Distribution*, Longman Publishing Ltd).

Exercise 10c Summarize the passage below, reducing it to about 200 words:

The services of accountants

Taxation is a system adopted by governments to finance their activities. These days, especially in Britain, government agencies perform such a wide variety of activities that enormous sums have to be collected to finance the nation's defence, education, social security and medical services. Whether or not you personally support such programmes, you have to keep within a framework of taxation laws which are imposed by the government and will be enforced against you if you infringe them. This body of rules is being constantly changed and revised, from year to year. Penalties for breaches of the tax laws can be severe, but are usually reduced where full and frank admissions of misconduct are made. The best rule is to keep accurate and honest records, and thus pay your fair contribution to the needs of the nation. Genuine grievances can usually be aired through trade associations, or your Member of Parliament.

Whilst accepting the statutory requirement to keep honest records and pay your fair contribution to the nation's finances, it should be stated that the courts have held that the taxpayer is entitled to take any legal means to avoid paying tax. If the Chancellor imposes a heavy tax on tobacco, I am free to avoid it by giving up smoking. If he taxes certain business activities, it is quite permissible for me to change my arrangements so that I can legally avoid the tax. It is for the Chancellor to devise a tax system which is free of loopholes. What you, as a businessman, may not do is to avoid taxation by illegal means, such as making fraudulent declarations.

The accountant, by virtue of his knowledge of the tax laws and his understanding of the cases already heard in court may be able to ensure that you do not pay more tax than you really need to pay. This can save his fee many times over.

At certain times in the development of firms it is essential to have the help of an accountant. There is no objection to writing to two or three firms and explaining the position you are in at present, outlining the services you are likely to require and asking them to submit a proposal for advice for the future − say an initial two or three years, subject to review. A reliable firm will probably ask to visit you and look at your books − emphasizing the confidentiality of such a procedure. This is the only real way they can tell what help you need and appraise your present position. Fees are usually based on the charging-out of work done by different members of staff at rates appropriate to their skills and experience. Thus the annual charges might include a large proportion of low-paid time by junior members of staff with a one hour review by a senior partner every few months. Accountancy is a hand-holding exercise most of the time − with real expertise available on occasions, such as when finance is required, or some danger signal is triggered. Many accountancy firms are members of the Institute of Management Consultants and can provide some-one with expertise in almost every field of management (courtesy of *Self-employment not Unemployment*, George Vyner Ltd).

Exercise 10d Summarize the passage below, reducing it to about 250 words:

The human relations movement

The human relations movement sees the behaviour of any individual in employment as one aspect of the individual's behaviour in society generally. A person behaves cooperatively in a working situation if he is at ease with himself in all his social activities. The movement holds that even the most careful scientific appraisal of operations and procedures will be useless if the individuals who are to perform the operations are distrustful, uncooperative and unmotivated. One rather illiterate young lady described her situation more graphically than she intended when she told her personnel officer that she felt 'Like a clog in a big machine'. People resent being treated like cogs in a machine, and management must therefore get its human relations as right as its procedures and mechanical lay-outs, if it is to achieve the full benefits from scientific management.

All employees bring to their employment situation a basic personality, made up of three elements: temperament, behaviour patterns learned as a child and the background culture passed on by his/her parents. Temperament is largely inherited, but our understanding of the complexity of genetics these days leads us to believe that it is not necessarily just a matter of 'like father, like son'. It is just as likely to be 'like grandfather, like son' or even 'like great-grandmother, like son'. This inherited temperament is in any case modified by environment. Childhood circumstances may permit or inhibit the full development of inherited temperament, while child-rearing patterns of behaviour and cultural influences may suppress some inclinations and develop others which meet with parental or social approval. The employee therefore displays a basic personality which motivates all his/her behaviour. He/she reacts to the work situation in a way that reflects past experiences, and these reactions will be unique, for every individual is different. The employee's reactions will be such as to satisfy his/her needs. These may be listed as primary needs, such as food, clothing, shelter, rest and recreation, and secondary needs, like companionship, self-esteem, respect of others and self-realization. In advanced societies such as our own, primary needs are satisfied very easily by even the most routine employments, and a good deal of companionship follows. The really crucial aspects for the success of a business are the more sophisticated needs: self-esteem, the respect of others and self-realization. The last of these refers to the total development of the individual: his/her attainment of the very best levels of achievement possible.

The significance of these needs for management is that their frustration can cause enormous disruption of business activity. The worker who is unable to realize his own ambitions in the productive process will frustrate the best laid plans of scientific management. He must be treated like an individual and his problems and attitudes analysed. The good manager displays empathy, not sympathy. Empathy is the ability to 'feel with' the employee, and see the situation in the way that the employee sees it. If the manager is mature enough to see the situation from the employee's point of view he is more likely to be able to devise a policy that will ensure cooperation and acceptance by the employee of the system of work as one of which he approves. The human relations movement in management therefore seeks to replace 'reason' (the motivation behind scientific management) by 'self-realization'. Every employee should feel that he/she is as interested as anyone in the production process, for through it lies the achievement of his/her self-esteem, the esteem of others and even the total realization of his/her own natural capacities. This restores work to its natural place as an activity giving mental and spiritual satisfaction, rather than a tedious monotony of time to be endured (courtesy of *Secretarial Practice Made Simple*).

10.5 Telephone messages

The telephone is the most ubiquitous of communication devices. That means you find them everywhere. We have already mentioned some of the more important rules of answering the telephone (see Section 8.5). A few more useful rules follow.

Never let a telephone ring − answer it at once. It isn't just the goodwill of the person at the other end of the line, or the order he/she might be prepared to place. A ringing telephone uses up line-time and raises capital costs. If every ringing telephone was answered at once, it would cut the numbers of cables, etc., required by about one-third. It is a matter of national importance to answer the telephone promptly.

It will often be the case when you answer a telephone that the person called is not available. This is particularly likely to be the case in the early morning and after normal working hours, because the exchange lines are switched through to someone who is likely still to be on the premises. If you are known to be an early arriver or a late leaver you may find you are the person who gets the calls. This places the responsibility on you to take messages and see they reach the correct destination.

In taking such a message, these are the main points to know:

(a) Who is the caller trying to reach? In what department does he/she work?
(b) Who is making the call? For what company does he/she work?

What is the telephone no. and extension no. of the caller?
(c)   What is the exact nature of the query?
(d)   Suppose the person called is not available, is there anyone else who can handle the query to the caller's knowledge?
(e)   How urgent is the query? There are often messages that need attention as soon as possible. For example, urgent medical requirements may miss flights because of some minor defect in documentation, or cargoes may miss sailing times when there is not another ship to that part of the world for several weeks. Give a message an appropriate degree of priority so that your firm or company does not lose a customer or suffer financial loss.

Many firms use pre-printed telephone message pads, which consist of about 50 forms ruled up as shown in Figure 10.1. You can buy these at most stationers, relatively inexpensively, or some firms have them drawn up specially to suit their own business needs and ask a local printer to run them off for them. If the paper is a distinctive colour − say a bright pink or yellow − they will attract attention when left on a recipient's desk, with a suitable paperweight to anchor them to the desk-top. Note that the last line 'Message taken by ...' enables the person called to contact you if there is any query about the message.

Exercise 10e   Write out a suitable telephone message (in the form shown by Figure 10.1) for the following messages left on an answering machine overnight.

1   This is Peter Lake of Shane Tempelford, calling Mike Roselaar in Exports Department. It is 10.30 pm. I've just heard that the SS *Ruritania* sank in the Gulf over the weekend. It was due to carry our cargo to Bahrain on its next journey. Can you check out the possible replacement vessels and make alternative arrangements, preferably at the same price. We don't want any delay, as time on the Bahrain contract is getting critical. Please let me know what progress you make. Thanks.
2   This is Mary Rose, from Design. At present I'm in Stockholm. Sandra Leach has my phone number. Please ask her to find out the answers to the following queries. (a) We have a possible order for 10,000 garments in the 'Spring 602' design but only if we can deliver by 8 February. Is this possible? (b) Can the price of Summer 501 be reduced by 10 per cent if the order is for 5,000 garments? (c) Has she any news about the accessories from Taiwan? If not, will she fax them right away asking for a prompt account of the current situation and requesting air freight at earliest possible date. Thanks.

```
         Telephone  Message  Form

                         Date.............
                         Time.............

    Caller's name...............................
    Address...........................................
    Telephone No. .............. Ext. No. .........

    Message for...................................

    Message: ...........................................

    ......................................................

    ......................................................

    ......................................................

    ......................................................

    ......................................................

              Message taken by.....................
```

Figure 10.1 A useful telephone message pad

3 My name is Grace Carmichael of 23 Fife St, Edentown, EH5
   1 DT. My phone number is 1234 27565. I would like a copy of
   your catalogue and current price list with a view to the purchase
   of some of your lines. Also could you advise me of your terms
   and conditions of sale. I look forward to hearing from you. As
   the matter is urgent, first class post would be appreciated.
4 This is Alec Holmes of 22 Ridgeway, The Chalk Hills, Folke-
   stone, Kent, FE7 2DP. Mike Thomas promised me some literature and an application form for insurance cover for employer's
   liability. It hasn't arrived and I'm not covered. Could Mike
   phone me to confirm that you will hold me covered while the
   policy is being sorted out. I'll fill up the application as soon as it
   arrives. My phone number is 2174 326596. Thanks.

10.6 Memos and memo-sets

A memorandum, or 'memo' for short, is an informal written communication used within an organization to convey information,
request advice, give instructions, etc. It passes between head office
and departments or branches, or from individual to individual within
departments. It is usually short, and deals with a specific point of
detail, though longer memos are sometimes circulated as part of the
procedure before a discussion of general policy. A memo is more
permanent than a verbal message, and more effective, since it is less
likely to be forgotten. It is often typed on specially printed memo

paper, and different colours are sometimes used to pinpoint memos from the more important members of staff.

A particularly effective type of memo-set is the three-part NCR (no carbon required) memo-set. Here the sender addresses the memo to its recipient and sends him/her two copies, retaining one copy for himself. The recipient writes a reply, which duplicates on to the lower copy. He/she then returns one copy and retains the other. Both parties thus have a copy of the original message and the reply. Such a memo-set ensures that memos are not forgotten. It will be obvious to the sender that no reply has yet been received, since the original will not be matched up with a second copy returned from the recipient. A particularly happily named memo set of this type is the ping-pong memo set, sold by Evrite Ltd of Cradley Heath, Warley, West Midlands. The name derives from the fact that the copies are bounced to and fro like (and let us hope just as quickly as) the proverbial ping-pong ball. Such a memo-set is illustrated in Figure 10.2.

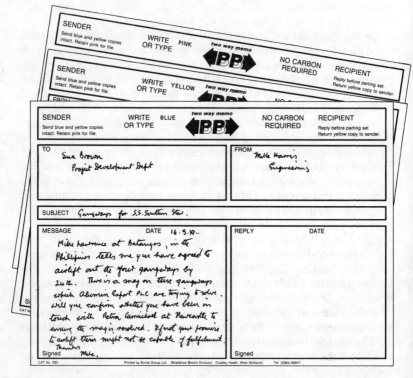

Figure 10.2   A ping-pong memo-set (*courtesy of Evrite Ltd, Cradley Heath, W. Midlands*)

One further point about memos today is that where a firm has invested heavily in networks of computers, it is possible to replace the ordinary memo by **e-mail memos**. E-mail refers to electronic mail. Any memo keyed in at any terminal can instantly be received at the destination terminal (or if the terminal is busy, it can be queued for delivery as soon as possible). Microsoft, the largest software company in the world, claims that its executives receive on average 100 memos a day, 'ranging from detailed product–strategy briefings to rude remarks'. One hopes they have time to answer them all, but certainly such a statement brings out the wide use made of memos.

Exercise 10f Rule up a few memo forms in the style shown in Figure 10.2 and enter the following items on them:

1 Memo from Carole Chalmers in Finance Department to Peter Blaker in Special Projects, dated 13 Sept 19.. Just a reminder that the budget for his department is now overdue, and is holding up the preparation of the Master Budget. Will he please phone when he arrives back from Singapore to tell Carole what the problem is (if any). The master budget is supposed to be presented to the Board on the 18th, so it is vital his part of it becomes available as soon as possible.
2 Memo on 14 June 19.. from the Managing Director, Bill Clark, to the Personnel Officer, Sandra Carmichael. While up in Aberdeen earlier this week, Bill was approached by Tim Stevens, an extremely good site engineer, who is being made redundant on 31st. We were proposing to head-hunt someone for the site engineer's job in Doha, but as Tim is quite willing to serve in the Gulf, we could save a lot of money by giving him the job. Will she watch out for his CV, which is coming by recorded delivery, and fax it through to Doha with his personal recommendation. If Doha gives the OK, will she please write to Tim Stevens right away so he knows he need not look elsewhere.
3 Memo from Mrs Coker, Canteen Manageress, to Buying Department, dated 20 October 19.. She is very dissatisfied with the quality of the meat being supplied to the canteen by the approved supplier Bestmeats (Camside) Ltd. She has raised the matter with the delivery man several times and also expressed her dissatisfaction in writing on delivery notes. Will the Buying Department please raise the matter officially with the firm, and threaten to find an alternative supplier. Please may she have a copy of the letter for her file.

10.7 More spellings

Here are two further groups of spellings. Ask a fellow student to test you on the first set and then reciprocate by testing him/her on the second set.

Transport		*Freight forwarding*	
motor	charter	terms	groupage
motive	charterparty	terminology	cabotage
motive power	charterer	Incoterms 90	break-bulk
truck	tramp	gantry	pirate
truckload	liner	container crane	piracy
articulated vehicle	conference	straddle carrier	privateer
berth	conveyor	freight	load
roll-on, roll-off	pipe-line	freighter	discharge
lift on, lift-off	flume	air freight	delay
conventional	escalator	freightliner	demurrage

10.8 Making notes

There are many business situations in which we need to make notes. Quite apart from the formal occasions when notes are made, e.g. by the minuting secretary at a meeting, it is helpful to take personal notes at meetings, seminars, conferences, etc. We often need to extract information from handbooks, reference books, Acts of Parliament, etc. Students take notes from their main textbooks in order to reduce the volume of reading to manageable form for revision purposes, and to simplify the material, and extract the essential elements from it. Alas this activity does not cease when we leave college, but continues for our working lifetimes!

The basic rules of note-taking are as follows:

- Notes should be as brief as possible.
- They should concentrate on the main ideas.
- Details should only be noted if they are essential supportive material.
- Subheadings should be used and numbering is usually helpful.
- At lectures and seminars you should listen actively − to follow the speaker's discourse − and then make brief notes of the essential points made.
- Watch for clues from the speaker's delivery − a change of pace, tone or volume. A change of inflection (the way the voice rises

and falls in a sentence) may help you to follow the speaker's argument.

- When taking notes from books, the reading of the passage is important, and hence the selection of the key words and sentences.
- Connectors − words such as 'therefore', 'consequently', 'however', 'but' − will show the direction of the writer's thoughts on the matter.

An example of notes gleaned from the study of a reference book on export procedures might look something like this:

1 The seller has to be told by the foreign buyer what terms he/she wants to use. Suppose CIF is specified.
2 The price is to cover cost, insurance and freight to the foreign post.
3 With CIF the basic insurance is Institute Cargo clauses (C). If the buyer wants a fuller cover, he must ask for it in advance.
4 The exporter must pack the goods and deliver them to the ship.
5 As the goods cross the ship's rail, the risk passes to the buyer (and so does the insurance policy to give the buyer cover).
6 Unloading at the destination port and transport to final destination is for the buyer to arrange at his/her own expense.
7 If the foreign buyer should reject the goods, it is a breach of contract. If he/she finds some flimsy excuse, it can mean a serious loss. To guard against this, the seller can take out 'seller's interest' insurance.
8 Don't tell the buyer this − it may encourage him/her to reject the goods if only the insurance company will suffer.

Exercise 10g   Make notes on the following passages: The first comes by courtesy of *Secretarial Practice Made Simple*:

The objectives of the overseas visit

A visit must have positive objectives if the considerable expense involved is to be justified. The preparatory work for an overseas visit should be particularly rigorous since the expense is greater and the event rarer than a visit to an inland market area, depot or plant. This preparation must be based on a careful review of performance in the area selected for a visit, an analysis of the operating and trading results and an examination of the strengths and weaknesses. This may lead us to the conclusion that the chief object of the visit is to build upon the strong position already established, or perhaps to cure the weaknesses revealed. It may include a comparison of the present organization with an 'ideal' structure envisaged for that particular market.

Reviews of the type referred to have to be based upon evidence, and reports on the current situation may have to be called for well in advance. Planning must therefore start early, and a clear warning of the proposed visit will usually tighten up arrangements in a very desirable way at the start.

If the intention of the visit is to develop new markets and there is no earlier base to work from, it requires the most careful market research prior to the event. It may be advisable to employ a specialist market research agency, perhaps with government support. The *Export Handbook*, issued free by the British Overseas Trade Board, gives details of such assistance.

It is usually helpful to estimate the costs of the visit and the benefits to be derived from it. This will quantify the visit in financial terms and may lead to more rigorous action to increase the benefits or cut the costs.

The conclusion of this review is to draw up a list of precise objectives which are capable of being achieved, so that the progress of the visit can be assessed while it is actually taking place, and at the end some comparison between objectives and actual achievements becomes possible.

The second passage is by courtesy of *Economics Made Simple*:

A policy for controlling monopolies

Throughout the nineteenth century monopolies were regarded quite rightly with great suspicion, for the early capitalists did not hesitate to abuse their monopoly positions. A continuing battle was fought for Parliamentary control of the railway companies, for example. This control was finally achieved by the Railway and Canal Traffic Act of 1888. The climate of public opinion at that time was firmly against amalgamations, yet by 1911 the Russell Rea Report was saying that amalgamations were inevitable and even desirable. There is a conflict here between the achievement of economies of scale and the protection of the consumer from exploitation. As the Russell Rea Report said, there is no sense in complaining until a proposed change actually does have an adverse effect on consumers. The time to complain is when some adverse result actually does follow from a change in organization − the change of policy may prove to be beneficial rather than harmful.

A further illustration, this time of oligopoly, is the case of the British cement ring. Traditionally it has been assumed that this ring of cement manufacturers was against the public interest. An investigation in 1946 showed that in fact the Ring had been careful not to exploit its monopoly position; it had achieved only a 10 per cent return on capital invested and this was about fair for this type of industrial enterprise.

By contrast, the restrictive practices to be found in many fields of industry and commerce have been held to be undesirable.

In 1948 a Monopolies and Restrictive Practices Commission was set up to enquire into the manufacturing conditions of a wide range of commodities. Later, the 1956 Restrictive Trade Practices Act split the control of restrictive practices away from the control of monopolies and set up a Restrictive Practices Court to investigate them. A Restrictive Practices Registrar was appointed to register such practices and bring before the Court any which seemed to be against the public interest. The reader should note that a restrictive practice is an arrangement made between suppliers not to compete with one another in some way. For example, where a dozen firms tender for a public contract and all submit the same tender it is clear there is collusion between them to keep up the price of projects at the expense of the public.

Of about 2,500 practices registered in the early years of the Registrar's activities over three-fifths were voluntarily abandoned by firms before a trial could be held rather than face the expense of a court hearing.

The third passage is also by courtesy of *Economics Made Simple*:

A policy for population?

Population has given man concern since time immemorial. Primitive men practise infanticide so that only the strongest children are reared. The Eskimos used to practise polyandry (one wife and many husbands) because so many girls were killed off in infancy. Darwin found the inhabitants of Tierra del Fuego eating their grandparents when times were hard: it had a double effect on the food situation, reducing demand and increasing supply.

Mention has already been made of the Malthusian Doctrine, which held that population was likely to rise beyond the ability of agriculture to supply food. Although the severity of the problem was much reduced by the opening up of new countries like the USA, Australia, New Zealand and Argentina, present-day calculations seem to indicate that Malthus may yet be proved right. Some population statistics bearing on this situation are given in Table 10.1

The phrase 'Gigabirth Nightmare' has been coined to describe the serious trends in world population. Table 10.2 illustrates the same figures by comparing the speeds with which a gigabirth increase has taken place.

The staggering increase predicted for 1980–2000 (twice as large an increase in 20 years as was produced in the period from the dawn of history to 1830) gives some idea of the problems to be faced. Already in parts of Africa nomadic people, whose whole

Table 10.1   Estimated world
population, 1650–2000

Year	Population (millions)
1650	450
1830	1000
1930	2000
1960	3000
1980	4000
2000	6250

Table 10.2   World population trends

Population ('000m)	Reached by AD	Number of years needed to produce an increase of one thousand million inhabitants
1	1830	From the dawn of life, say 100,000 years
2	1930	100
3	1960	30
4	1980	20
5	1990	10
6	2000	10

economy for hundreds of years has depended on their ability to graze large areas of land in times of drought, are finding barbed-wire fences across their ancient migration routes. More settled people need the land for intensive farming, and the disputes and battles that result are not pleasant. Thirsty cattle cannot wait.

These predictions, sometimes called **Neo-Malthusianism**, have revived interest in Malthus's arguments. The development of more intensive agricultural methods and some form of population control can probably postpone a crisis for some years in the advanced countries, but in the less developed nations population pressures are likely to become insurmountable. These countries do not have the capital to establish intensive agriculture, or to keep both population and the standard of living rising. The natural aspirations of such people cannot be realized in the slum shanty towns on the outskirts of great cities. The overwhelming advance of population requires national and international policies to be devised.

In 1949 a Royal Commission on Population reported in favour

of stabilizing Britain's population, and appointing a body to review the problems of population and national policies affected by it. For years little was done, but the aim now seems to have been largely achieved through the improved methods of birth control available and the free availability of abortion. If this trend continues, the almost universal demand for increased living standards becomes much easier to manage, and the imbalance of population less severe. The imbalance in the population is centred on the changing proportion of working and non-working people. While successive bulges in the birth rate mean a high proportion of young people, each of whom tends on average to stay at school longer, the increasing longevity associated with medical developments results in a larger number of retired people. As both these groups have to be supported by the declining proportion of people actually at work, the burden on these becomes greater.

10.9   Figures of speech 1: similes

A figure of speech is an expression used in conversation or in written English that enriches the language by conveying an idea in a brighter, more interesting and more informative way. There are a number of figures of speech, including similes, metaphors, euphemisms, personifications, antitheses, hyperbole and litotes. These figures of speech can often enhance our writing if we know how to use them, and add variety, interest and subtlety to our essays and reports. Although business English is rarely considered fine literature, for its value does not often lie in the beauty of its form or its emotional effect, it can still be enhanced by the use of figures of speech.

Similes are expressions in which an idea is conveyed by likening something to something else – an animal, or a machine, or some other inanimate object that displays a particular characteristic. They take the form 'as . . . as a . . .' There are countless examples. Here are a few. As you read them, make sure you understand the characteristic referred to. A question mark in brackets pinpoints one or two of the less obvious ones. You might like to look up the word you are not sure of in your dictionary.

as agile as a monkey	as blind as a bat
as brave as a lion	as bright as a lark
as cunning as a fox	as fat as a pig
as bitter as gall (?)	as bold as brass
as clean as a new pin	as clear as crystal
as cold as charity	as dead as a doornail
as deaf as a post	as hungry as a hunter
as obstinate as a mule	as old as Methuselah (?)

as patient as Job (?)   as poor as a church mouse
as sharp as a needle   as smooth as clockwork
as sober as a judge   as thick as thieves
as wise as Solomon   as rich as Croesus (?)

10.10   Answers section

No answers are provided for the exercises in this chapter. Please appraise your own efforts.

11
The tenses of verbs

11.1 What is a tense?

Tense is the form taken by a verb to show when the action is taking place. It is actually a corruption of the Latin word *tempus* (time). For example, the simple present tense tells us the action is taking place now. The simple past tense tells us the action took place at some time in the past, while the simple future tense tells us it will take place at some time in the future. We can follow this best if we take a verb like the verb 'to sing'. For convenience we will take all the persons, both singular and plural. In the present tense we have:

	Simple present tense
First person singular	I sing
Second person singular	Thou singest
Third person singular	He sings
There are three cases, male,	She sings
female and neuter)	It sings
First person plural	We sing
Second person plural	You sing
Third person plural	They sing

Looking at these we are all quite happy except that we know that in English the word 'Thou' is now obsolete except in some country dialects, and we use the plural 'You sing' even when we are talking to only a single person.

When we change to past tense the root, or stem of the verb changes. 'I sing' turns to 'I sang':

Simple past tense
I sang
Thou sangest
He sang
She sang
It sang
We sang

You sang
They sang

Again, 'Thou sangest' is obsolete, and today we would say 'You sang' for the second person singular.

When it comes to the future tense we need an auxillary verb, which is a verb that is helpful to other verbs because it helps them change tense. The verbs we use are 'will' and 'shall', and they do cause a bit of confusion. This is referred to later. For the present all we need to know is that 'shall' is used with the first person (both singular and plural) and 'will' is used with the second and third persons. So we have:

Simple future tense
I shall sing
Thou wilt sing
He will sing
She will sing
It will sing
We shall sing
You will sing
They will sing

Again, 'Thou wilt sing' is obsolete.

To develop familiarity with these changes it is helpful to go through the simple present, past and future tenses of some common verbs. Try these exercises now.

Exercise 11a   Give the present tense, past tense and future tenses of the verb 'to work':

Present	*Past*	*Future*
I work	I worked	I shall work
etc.	etc.	etc.

Exercise 11b   Give the present, past and future tenses of the verb 'to dance':

Present	*Past*	*Future*
I dance	I danced	I shall dance
etc.	etc.	etc.

Exercise 11c   Give the present, past and future tense of the verb 'to drive':

Present	*Past*	*Future*
I drive	I drove	I shall drive
etc.	etc.	etc.

If you would like to try a few more here is a list of further verbs:

(a) to correspond   (b) to signal
(c) to distribute   (d) to object
(e) to manufacture   (f) to telephone

11.2   The use of simple tenses

There are, we shall see, twelve tenses that we really need to know, but if we just deal with the three simple tenses first, it is helpful to know when each is used.

The simple present tense

This is used to express something that is happening at the present time:

He works in London.
She studies English.
They appear nightly at the Playhouse Theatre.

The present tense is also used to express truths. For example:

Easter is the first real festival of the Christian year.
Patriotism is the love of one's country.
Mathematics is the Queen of the Sciences.

A further use is to express habitual actions:

The Trial Balance is always taken out on the last day of the month.
The security vehicle collects cash daily at noon.

The simple past tense

This is used to show that something happened at some time in the past, and is no longer happening at the present time:

He visited Japan last month.
They placed the order last Spring.

The past tense of every verb except the verb 'to be' has only one form, which ends in 'ed'. The verb 'to be' has two forms, 'was' and 'were':

I was at the hospital.
We were at the hospital.

To get the past tense of all other verbs, we obey the following rules:

(a)   Add the letter 'd' to all verbs ending in 'e', e.g. 'assemble' becomes 'assembled' and 'dabble' becomes 'dabbled'.
(b)   Add the letters 'ed' to all verbs that do not end in 'e', e.g. 'play' becomes 'played' and 'kick' becomes 'kicked'.
(c)   If the verb ends with a vowel followed by a consonant, the consonant is doubled. Thus 'stop' becomes stopped and 'rap' becomes 'rapped'. If the verb is of two syllables, and the second syllable is stressed, we double the last letter. Thus 'occur' becomes 'occurred', but 'offer' (where the stress is on the first syllable) becomes 'offered'.
(d)   If the verb ends in the letter 'y' the 'y' becomes 'i' before the 'ed' is added. Thus 'try' becomes 'tried' and 'occupy' becomes 'occupied'.

The simple future tense

There are several ways of referring to the future but the most common is by the use of 'shall' or 'will'.

As explained earlier, we use 'shall' plus the 'root' word of the verb in the first person singular and first person plural. We use 'will' plus the 'root' word of the verb in the second and third persons, both singular and plural. Thus the future tense of 'to arrive' might be used as follows:

I shall arrive at noon tomorrow.
She will arrive at 6 pm.
They will arrive at the weekend.

Exercise 11d   Copy out each of the following sentences and underline the verb in each case. Then write in brackets at the end of the sentence what tense the verb is in.

1   He will call you on his return.
2   The cuckoo sings in May.
3   The consignment left yesterday.

4 HM Customs impounded the contraband items.
5 The corn will ripen in late July.
6 The document is available.
7 The typesetter worked all night to complete the job.
8 We shall visit you frequently.
9 The security firm delivered the crate overnight.
10 It will arrive too late for manufacture.

Exercise 11e Copy out these sentences, underline the verbs in each case and write at the end of the sentence what tense the verb is in:

1 They mail the colleges every 2 weeks.
2 We shall expect payment on the due date.
3 He calls, but never receives an order.
4 It exploded harmlessly in the quarry.
5 The bank collected payment in Lagos.
6 You will receive the goods on the 27th.
7 Honesty is essential in business transactions.
8 Stop that man!
9 I shall negotiate the deal personally.
10 He undertook the dangerous mission without hesitation.

11.3 A chart of tenses

There are a number of tenses in the English language, and to study them fully is more than we require for a business English course. The chart shown in Figure 11.1 shows the main tenses and explains how to form them. Study it carefully now and then try the exercises below.

11.4 Exercises on tenses

Exercise 11f Write down the numbers 1−5 on a sheet of paper. Against these numbers write (a) the verbs from the five sentences below and (b) in brackets, the tense that has been used.

1 You were working here at the time of the robbery.
2 I have completed the assignment.
3 You had been advocating expansion of the company.
4 I shall have completed my research by July.
5 She will be delighting us all with her witty conversation.

(A verb changes tense to show when an action takes place, or took place, or will take place)

	Past	Present	Future
Simple tenses			
Uses	**Simple past tense** For things that happened in the past but are no longer true at the present time	**Simple present tense** (a) Things true at the present time (b) General truths (c) Habitual actions	**Simple future tense** For actions that will take place in the future
How formed	Use the past participle	Use the root word of the verb	(a) Use *shall* in the first person plus the 'root' word (b) Use *will* in the second and third persons plus the 'root' word
Examples	*He worked at the factory*	(a) *He works at the factory* (b) *Spring comes after Winter* (c) *She drives to work each day*	*I shall work at the factory eventually* *You will operate this machine*
Continuous tenses			
Uses	**Past continuous tense** To show that something happened in the past, and went on for some time	**Present continuous tense** To show that something is happening now and has been going on for some time	**Future continuous tense** To show that something will happen in the future, and will continue for some time
How formed	Past tense of the verb *to be* plus the present participle	Present tense of the verb *to be* and the present participle	Use *shall* or *will* plus *be* plus the present participle
Examples	*He was working here before the accident*	*I am calling about our product* *They are waiting*	*She will be appearing at the theatre in January*

Perfect tenses	Past perfect tense	Present perfect tense	Future perfect tense
Uses	When discussing a past action and referring to an even earlier event. This earlier event was past even in the past	The action has been completed but still has some effect at the present time	Used to refer to an action that will be completed at some time in the future
How formed	Use the past tense of *to have* plus the past participle of the verb	Use the present tense of *to have* plus the past participle of the verb	Use the future tense of *to have* plus the past participle of the verb
Examples	*They had visited me earlier that month*	*I have typed the letter* *He has investigated the crime*	*I shall have completed my inquiries by then*

Perfect continuous tenses	Past perfect continuous tense	Present perfect continuous tense	Future perfect continuous tense
Uses	Used when referring to two past events, one earlier than the other, but continuing until the time the second event took place	A recent action has been continuing up to the present time	Used when an action will have been completed at some future time, after continuing for a considerable period
How formed	Past tense of *to have* plus *been* plus the present participle of the verb	Present tense of *to have* plus *been* plus the present participle of the verb	Future tense of *to have* plus *been* plus the present participle of the verb
Examples	*You had been complaining for several months before treatment was arranged*	*I have been typing this report for three hours*	*You will have been advertising for three months before replies can arrive by surface mail*

Figure 11.1 A chart to show the tenses of verbs

Exercise 11g   Write down the numbers 1−5 and against them write (a) the verbs from the following sentences and (b) in brackets, the tense that has been used:

1   I am calling with reference to your insurance claim on my company.
2   I shall have manufactured most of the items by that time.
3   You had been supplying us with excellent components until this deterioration in the final painting of the items.
4   The deceased worked at our factory until his death.
5   The managing director will be investigating the matter.

11.5   Comprehension exercises

The following extracts have been reprinted from the *OECD Observer*, the magazine of the Organization for Economic Cooperation and Development. Read each passage carefully and then do the exercises below them.

Matching supply and demand in education

An education authority which has apparently matched the supply of school places to the number of pupils cannot sit back. Even when *enrolments* are apparently stable demands are changing in other ways. *Curriculum content*, pedagogical methods, and educational technology are all *dynamic factors*, never more so than at present.

New curricula, with their emphasis on technology and 'hands-on' experience, pose questions about the provision, maintenance and accommodation of equipment. When computers first came into schools they were put into computer rooms where often they were treated to an especially clean and air-conditioned environment, and were kept safe behind especially secure doors. Now the time may not be far away when all schools will have as many *computers* as desks. The evidence so far is that a pupil working at a computer requires more space than one working with books at a desk. But computers are getting smaller and it is by no means clear that this situation will continue. Hitherto the presence of computers and printers has implied the presence of many metres of cables. Even if one cannot predict with certainty how much cabling will be required in future it is at least possible to limit the pressure for costly adaptations by leaving open the possibility for cabling every workplace.

Vocational education is the sector where the variety of equipment which schools require to prepare their pupils adequately is growing most dramatically. Many vocational schools possess what amounts to a *museum* of 19th- and 20th-century tools and equipment. All too few are adequately provided with the up-to-date machinery that industry is using. And how can one teach a practical course (painting motor vehicles, for example) without equipment and *ventilation* comparable with that found in the industry. This is expensive and raises health and safety issues. Perhaps more students should do their practical work on industrial premises, and more use should be made of simulators. Where full-scale production equipment is available in an educational institution ways must be found for it to be used more intensively and it should be used for industrial production.

New teaching styles present even more *difficult issues* for planners and designers. In spite of some differences of emphasis, most schools in OECD countries were built on the supposition that pupils would be taught in groups of fixed size (whether 25 or 30 or even 40) and in a certain way. Classroom size and layout reflect teaching method, and although one no longer sees tiers of desks bolted to the floor and facing the master's rostrum, there is still a certain uniformity in classroom design. This broadly reflects a past homogeneity in pedagogical practice which is showing signs of breaking down. More and more pupils spend time working in small groups, or doing individual project work; teachers more frequently work in small teams with their colleagues, teaching smaller classes.

Designing schools which can accommodate these and other changes without losing the advantages of the traditional approach is the challenge facing school designers today. The involvement of teachers in the briefing of the architect is an important step in ensuring that the solution adopted is workable and does not create new constraints of its own. Architects who try to impose their view on teachers without consulting them will be unsuccessful. Experiments with 'open plan' schools in the 1960s and 1970s, where teachers had not been brought in to the briefing and design process, failed.

Information technology, moreover, opens up possibilities which until a few years ago were only dreams. A teacher can talk to, be seen by, and correct the work of pupils who are ten, or one hundred, or *one thousand miles away*. The potential for the exchange of information between schools in different countries is dramatic, but there are implications too for small, remote schools, which can be *networked* to larger establishments. Instead of closing the village school it may be enough to install a micro-computer, a modem and a satellite dish. *Severely handicapped children*, who are unable to go to ordinary schools, may be able to join in classes from their own homes.

The essence of the challenge lies not in change itself, but in the rate of change. Many large companies in the 1960s invested with what appeared to be considerable foresight in powerful mainframe computers housed in massive hangars. The lucky ones had a few years use out of these monsters, the *unlucky* saw their project become obsolete before it was even completed. OECD public education systems are in an analogous position. They have to make decisions about their hardware − their buildings and equipment − without any certainty that they will not be overtaken by events.

Exercise llh

1   What are 'enrolments'?
2   What does the author mean when he says that 'curriculum content, pedagogical methods and educational technology are all 'dynamic factors'?
3   Suggest a word that means the opposite of 'dynamic'.
4   What is 'curriculum content'?
5   What are the implications for an educational authority of a decision to give a school as many computers as it has desks?
6   What is 'vocational education'?
7   Why are the present schools teaching vocational education compared with 'museums'.
8   We cannot teach car spraying in schools because of a 'ventilation problem'. How does the author suggest this problem could be overcome?
9   What change in teaching methods is presenting educational authorities with 'difficult issues'?
10   What is 'information technology'?
11   How could a teacher talk to, be seen by and correct the work of a pupil 'one thousand miles away'?
12   What is a 'network', and what could it mean for a village school?
13   What does the author suggest could be done for severely handicapped pupils?
14   Explain the phrase 'the unlucky saw their computer project become obsolete before it was even completed'.
15   Why does the 'rate of change' in educational technology make life difficult for education authorities.

Now read the following extract from the *OECD Observer* and do the exercise below it.

Swapping debt for nature
by
Michel Potier

Debt affects environmental protection in a range of ways, all restricting the ability of *Third World* countries to manage their natural assets in a way that promotes sustainable development. The same is true of fluctuations and *downtrends in commodity prices*, especially when coupled with lower inflows of foreign capital and growing debt service.

The rising cost of oil imports has forced some African countries into intensive *forest clearance* to meet household needs. But the consequences have been particularly serious in Latin America, on account of the *scale of its indebtedness*. In order to *service their debt*, Latin American countries have made impressive efforts to find new products to export – raw materials, foodstuffs and resource-intensive manufactures – thereby accentuating the pressure on their natural resources and on the environment as a whole.

Against this background, considerable thought has been given to ways and means of combining Less Developed Country (LDC) debt reduction and environmental protection.

A debt-for-nature swap is an arrangement by which an indebted developing country undertakes, in exchange for cancellation of a portion of its foreign debt, to establish local currency funds to be used to finance a conservation programme.

The mechanism brings a *number of partners* together: the debtor government, the creditor, and a non-governmental organization (NGO), often international, concerned with the environment. The NGO will act as intermediary between creditor and debtor, the debtor's central bank, and an agency on the spot (generally an NGO as well), which will receive the proceeds of the debt conversion and implement the conservation programme.

The first stage is to establish the terms of the debt conversion. The debtor government, the central bank and the local agency have to agree on the exchange rate for converting dollar-denominated debt to local currency; the percentage of face value at which to redeem the loan; the types of financial instruments to be issued and the conservation programme to be set in hand.

Next, the *money to acquire the discounted debt* must be found. Creditor banks are generally reluctant to make outright donations; funds are generally secured from private donors or bilateral aid agencies.

Last, acquiring debt titles requires an experienced agent to enter into a formal exchange agreement with the creditor bank, which will transfer custody of the title to the debtor country's central bank. The central bank then converts the title into cash, local currency bonds or some other instrument to fund the agreed conservation work. The funds or instruments are then held by the local agencies, private or public, responsible for setting the programme in hand.

The mechanism is advantageous for all the participants:

- for the debtor country it is an opportunity to buy back part of its debt and raise funds for conservation without ceding any part of its sovereignty, since the debt-for-nature swap (unlike conventional debt-equity swaps) does not result in a foreign stake in a local corporation,
- for the creditor bank it is a means of relinquishing claims that may well be irrecoverable,
- for the NGOs it generates additional funding for conservation work.

Exercise 11i

1   What is a 'Third World' country?
2   How does a 'downtrend in commodity prices', e.g. tea, coffee, and timber prices, affect a Third-World country.
3   What did the rise in oil prices do to the forests of Africa?
4   Why was Latin America most seriously affected by the rise in oil prices.
5   What does the author mean by 'servicing their debts'.
6   What is a 'debt-for-nature' swap?
7   What three parties come together to improve the environment in a 'debt-for-nature' swap?
8   Suppose a country is in debt for £10 million, and there is not much chance of it ever paying the debt. What figure would you say was 'fair' to offer the banker in cash to cancel the debt?
9   Where would the money to settle the debt come from?
10   What would the government of the developing country have to do as its part of the bargain once the debt was cancelled.

11.6   Sentence errors: agreement between subject and verb

A great many errors can creep into our sentences, and need practice to eliminate them. One of the commonest errors concerns the subject of the sentence and its verb. The basic rule is that *the verb must agree with its subject in number*. There are only two numbers that matter, one (called in English 'singular') and more than one (called in English 'plural'). If the noun is singular, and denotes one only – as with man, woman, computer, etc. – then the verb must also be singular.

In the following five sentences which of them has a verb that does not agree with its subject in number?

(a)   The telephone rings.
(b)   The manager answers the telephone.
(c)   The caller are making an inquiry.
(d)   The parts are ready for the customer.
(e)   They is collected by the security firm.

Clearly (c) is wrong, because a singular noun 'caller' has been given a plural verb 'are'. It should be 'is'. Similarly (e) is wrong, because it has a plural pronoun 'They', which is the subject of the sentence, but the verb 'is' is singular. 'They' stands for 'the parts' and the plural noun (or pronoun) needs a plural verb 'are'. So the sentence should read 'They are collected by the security firm'.

These examples are obvious enough, but it does get more difficult if there is a single noun that is enlarged to refer to several other items, usually by a phrase introduced by the preposition 'of'. For example, which of these is correct?

(a)   A programme of events has been drawn up.
(b)   A programme of events have been drawn up.

The rule is that the verb must agree with the subject of the sentence, which is the word 'programme' (and is singular). The number of the noun introduced in the phrase beginning with 'of' does not affect the verb. So (a) is correct − 'A programme of events has been drawn up'.

Exercise 11j Copy out these sentences, using the correct verb in each case from those given in brackets.

1   One of the orders (cost, costs) more for materials than the other.
2   The price of the components (is, are) exorbitant.
3   Taiwan firms (export, exports) electronic equipment.
4   British vessels of P and O Line (sail, sails) regularly to Australia.
5   The largest of America's transport aeroplanes (is, are) the Skylifter.

Exercise 11k Copy out these sentences, using the correct verb in each case from those given in brackets.

1   One of the students (fetch, fetches) the meals from a communal canteen.
2   The elements of cost (is, are) to be reduced by 10 per cent.

3   Budgets from only two departments in the whole organization (were, was) deemed to be excessive by the budget officer.
4   The most extensive of the proposals (is, are) the Rebuild Group's design.
5   A glossary of useful terms (have, has) been drawn up by the accountant.

Where two subjects are joined by 'and' the verb is plural

For example, 'Taiwan and Singapore (exports, export) electronic equipment' ('export' is correct). 'Here (comes, come) the Prime Minister and the Foreign Secretary' ('come' is correct). 'Where (is, are) the screw and washer for the assembly?' ('are' is correct).

Where a single subject is followed by a prepositional phrase beginning with 'with', 'along with', 'together with' or 'as well as'

The verb agrees with the single subject.

For example:

(a)   The pianist's busband, as well as the entire audience, was anxious for the concert to begin.
(b)   The marketing manager, together with the personnel officer and the factory manager, was delayed by the bomb alert'.

Even though the sentence just quoted is grammatically correct, it still sounds awkward and even pedantic. It is much better when we get an awkward expression like this to rephrase it so that the plural verb can be used. Thus, we could rephrase it to read: 'The marketing manager, the personnel officer and the factory manager were delayed by the bomb alert.'

Where two subjects are joined together by 'either ... or', 'neither ... nor', 'not only ... but also' or just plain 'or', usually the verb agrees with the noun closest to it.

For example:

(a)   The partners or the accountant supervises the work.
(b)   The accountant or the directors prepare the report for the Annual General Meeting.

Sometimes a sentence has a separate clause introduced by a pronoun such as who, that or which. In that case the verb in the clause must agree with its subject (the pronoun) and we have to look to the noun that that pronoun replaces to find out whether it is singular or plural. Thus, 'The 747 is one of the largest passenger planes that (has, have) ever been designed'. The subject of the verb 'is' is 'the 747', which is singular. The subject of the verb '(has, have) been designed' is the pronoun 'that', and this pronoun refers to the word 'planes', which is plural. The verb must therefore be plural and the corrected sentence reads 'that have ever been designed'. The word 'planes' in this case is called the 'antecedent' of the pronoun 'that'.

Exercise 11l   Copy out these sentences, using the correct verb:

1   One of the auditors (express, expresses) reservations about the accounts.
2   The staff and the Board (support, supports) you fully in your campaign.
3   Where (is, are) the plaintiff and the defendant.
4   Neither Jane nor her brothers (have arrived, has arrived) at the lecture theatre.
5   The engineer, along with the gang of pipelayers, (were waiting, was waiting) for transport to the site.

Exercise 11m   Copy out these sentences, using the correct verb.

1   Either the accounts department or the costing staff (is responsible, are responsible).
2   Inflation of prices (is, are) the biggest threat to growth in any economy.
3   The ambulance and the police car (arrives, arrive) at the same time.
4   Safety at work and safe arrival at work (is, are) the twin problems facing the safety officer in freight forwarding.
5   There (goes, go) the Japanese and Taiwanese delegates.

Exercise 11n   Copy out these sentences, choosing the correct verb from those in brackets:

1   The rat is one of those animals that frequently (features, feature) in scientific experiments.
2   The tanker is one of those vehicles that (moves, move) out to the right before turning left.
3   Accountancy is one of these professions that (calls, call) for meticulous attention to detail.

4 Personnel work and public relations work (is, are) of interest to graduates in English.
5 Economics is one of those disciplines which (calls, call) for cheerful confidence when faced with the unpredictable.

11.7 Problems with 'shall' and 'will'

Reference was made earlier to the fact that 'shall' and 'will' present problems to students. The reason is that there are two uses for these words, one of which is already familiar to us − their use to form the future tense. Remember that 'shall' is used for the first person (both singular and plural) and 'will' is used for the second and third persons (both singular and plural).

The second use for these words is to convey personal determination on someone's part. What happens is that the roles are reversed when personal determination is shown, and 'will' is used with the first person (both singular and plural), while 'shall' is used for the second and third persons.

Thus if a person says 'I will ensure that the deadline is met', the commitment to make certain that the work is done is stronger than if the word 'shall' had been used. Similarly, 'We will be making an approach to purchase your company' is stronger than 'We shall be making an approach to purchase your company'.

When 'shall' is used in reference to the second and third persons, it indicates a promise or a command:

(a) Cinderella shall go to the ball.
(b) They shall answer for it in the High Court.
(c) You shall give evidence against him, for you know it is your duty.

Exercise 11o Copy out these sentences, choosing the correct verb in each case:

1 I (shall, will) arrange for the class to visit the atomic power station.
2 I (shall, will) do it, whatever the expense.
3 He (shall, will) be in attendance as promised.
4 He (shall, will) appear, make no mistake, for the law requires it.
5 They (shall, will) visit both Oxford and Cambridge during their visit to the United kingdom.

Exercise 11p Copy out the following sentences, choosing the correct verb in each case:

1   She (shall, will) take the test as arranged.
2   We (shall, will) purchase the company, I assure you, however much it costs.
3   They (shall, will) send you the goods on a consignment basis; that is, you need only pay after selling them to a third party.
4   They (shall, will) pay, even if I have to seek satisfaction through the courts.
5   You (shall, will) receive a pro-forma invoice, which, on payment, will release the goods to you.

11.8   More spellings

Ask a fellow student to test you on the first set of words. Then reciprocate by testing him/her on the other set.

Spellings: Law		*Spellings: Marketing*	
tort	sue	research	promotion
tortious	suit	development	media
trespass	suitor	intelligence	publicity
nuisance	agent	brochure	exhibit
negligence	agency	leaflet	exhibition
defamation	principal	circular	exhibitor
crime	accuse	merchant	break-even
criminal	accused	merchandise	contribution
criminality	accusation	mercantile	profit
felony	accusatorial	mechantable	profitability

11.9   Figures of speech 2: metaphors

A metaphor is a figure of speech in which we apply a name or a descriptive phrase to an object or action to which it cannot literally be applied. Thus to say 'The camel is the ship of the desert' implies not only that the camel carries most of the cargo that ever moves across a desert but also that in doing so it navigates across uncharted areas as featureless as the waters of the deep.

   Many metaphors are essentially poetic and therefore perhaps little suited to business English. We all remember such phrases as

   The moon was a ghostly galleon tossed upon cloudy seas,
   The road was a ripple of moonlight over the purple moor ...

Notice that in a metaphor we do not say that the road was like a ripple of moonlight − that would be a simile. We actually apply the name to the thing described — the moon *was* a ghostly galleon.

We might use metaphors in our business letters and reports. For example, to say that the diesel engine is the workhorse of modern agriculture gives a very clear picture of the part tractors, caterpillar tractors and combine harvesters play on our farms today.

Three possible hazards lie in the way of those who use metaphors (and other figures of speech). We may, if we try to use metaphors too frequently, mix our metaphors. Thus to say that 'the diesel engine is the workhorse of modern agriculture and enables it to steam into the harbour of prosperity' is to mix our metaphors (and drown a great many figurative horses).

The second hazard is the cliché. A cliché is a trite, hackneyed or stereotyped expression that has become stale and tedious from over-use. Some dog-lovers may not agree, but the statement that 'the dog is man's best friend' has become a cliché — those who deliver letters have been heard to doubt it, and take out insurance against possible attacks.

The third hazard is that once we embark upon a descriptive phrase or two in our reports, we may be unable to stop, and stretch both the reader's imagination and his/her credulity to breaking point. For example, the following passage illustrates what is called the *overwrought* figure of speech:

The computer is a genie of the modern world. This genie has been let out of some oriental bottle in Japan or Hong Kong to work untold miracles for us, but in doing so he has opened a Pandora's box of evils. Where is the advantage of the infinite wealth our genie can create for us if he makes us all unemployed and even unemployable; for old dogs cannot learn new tricks, especially such slick tricks as these. We can jump through hoops, but not as fast as the genie, who constantly tantalizes us with his demoniacal powers.

Our figure of speech, like the genie it describes, has taken us over and is dominating our text of its own volition.

11.10   Answer section

Exercises 11a–11c   Mark yourselves.

Exercise 11d   1   will call (simple future — sf); 2   sings (simple present — spr); 3   left (simple past — sp); 4   impounded (sp); 5   will ripen (sf); 6   is (spr); 7   worked (sp); 8   shall visit (sf); 9   delivered (sp); 10   will arrive (sf).

Exercise 11e   1   mail (spr); 2   shall expect (sf); 3   calls (spr); receives (spr); 4   exploded (sp); 5   collected (sp); 6   will receive (sf); 7   is (spr); 8   stop (spr); 9   shall negotiate (sf); 10   undertook (sp).

Exercise 11f   1   were working (past continuous); 2   have completed (present perfect); 3   had been advocating (past perfect continuous); 4   shall have completed (future perfect); 5   will be delighting (future continuous).

Exercise 11g   1   am calling (present continuous); 2   shall have manufactured (future perfect); 3   had been supplying (past perfect continuous); 4   worked (simple past); 5   will be investigating (future continuous).

Exercise 11h   1   An enrolment is the act of joining a class or group. 2   The things to be taught (curriculum) the teaching (pedagogical) methods and the equipment used are all changing. 3   'Static' is the opposite of dynamic. 4   The detailed list of things to be studied during a course. 5(a)   They must allow more room per pupil; (b) they must make proper cabling provision in the layout of classrooms. 6   Education directed at future employment in particular professions and industries. 7   Because their equipment has never been updated to keep abreast of commerce and industry. 8   By making arrangements for such things to be learned in industrial premises. 9   The switch to working in smaller groups. 10   Equipment which can spread information easily from one place to another. 11   By radio and television, and the use of computerized networks. 12   A network is a system where a number of remote terminals are linked to a single host computer. It could link the village school to specialist teachers in the local city. 13   They could have a terminal in their own homes, and be educated over the computer network. 14   The progress in computerization was so rapid that before one project could be completed, it was made out of date by a newer, more powerful and more efficient system. 15   Because their plans may be overtaken by new developments.

Exercise 11i   1   A country that is still relatively undeveloped. 2   It makes it difficult to sell their basic raw materials and agricultural products except at very low prices. 3   It reduced the forests as local people cut them down for firewood. 4   It had more massive debts, and had to increase exploitation of its natural resources to pay the interest. 5   It means paying the interest on the loans and repaying the instalment of the original capital due for repayment. 6   An arrangement where foreign debt is cancelled in return for action that helps the world environment. 7   The debtor government, the creditor bank and a non-governmental organization. 8 About half, £5,000,000. Bad debts can usually be sold for about 50 per cent. 9   The non-governmental organization would collect funds for environmental purposes from anyone willing to contribute. 10   It would see that money in local currency to the same value as the funds collected would be made available in its own country to help the environment.

Exercise 11j   1   costs; 2   is; 3   export; 4   sail; 5   is.

Exercise 11k   1   fetches; 2   are; 3   were; 4   is; 5   has.

Exercise 11l   1   expresses; 2   support; 3   are; 4   have arrived; 5   was waiting.

Exercise 11m   1   are responsible; 2   is; 3   arrive; 4   are; 5   go.

Exercise 11n   1   feature; 2   move; 3   call; 4   are; 5   call.

Exercise 11o   1   shall; 2   will; 3   will; 4   shall; 5   will.

Exercise 11p   1   will; 2   will; 3   will; 4   shall; 5   will.

12
The use of the dictionary

12.1 About the dictionary

A dictionary is a book that lists in alphabetical order the words of a language, together with their meaning, pronunciation, derivation from earlier languages, etc. For the student of English who is naturally interested in words and their spelling, meaning, use, etc., a dictionary is a mine of information, which can be opened up by a small initial study of the method of presentation adopted by the editors.

In this chapter the examples used are from the *Concise Oxford Dictionary* (COD), probably the most popular student dictionary for United Kingdom and Commonwealth students. Permission to reproduce the page shown in Figure 12.1 is gratefully acknowledged, but it is hoped students will obtain a copy for their personal use, so that the full implications of this chapter can be appreciated.

Even the *Concise Oxford Dictionary* has some 50,000 entries on its 1,400 pages. A dictionary is not an encyclopaedia, and though it gives us a great deal of information, there is no attempt to deal exhaustively with a subject – only enough to make the meaning of a word and its use in everyday speech clear at the time of publication. To this end, revised editions appear from time to time, so that 'new' uses of an old word can be added and completely new words, which have come into the language recently, can be incorporated. Those who find the *Concise Oxford Dictionary* too limited for their studies might like to buy the *Shorter Oxford English Dictionary*, which is considerably longer than the COD. The fullest collection of all is the twelve-volume *Oxford English Dictionary*, with 'supplements' added from time to time.

Business studies students who eventually reach influential positions in commerce and industry might remember their student days and buy the full *Oxford English Dictionary* for reference by younger personnel working for their professional qualifications. Many firms and companies are slow to acquire such obvious aids to efficient correspondence.

12.2　What the dictionary actually tells us

In every book before it actually begins with the numbered pages
there are several pages, often numbered with roman numerals,
called the prelims (preliminaries). These pages include the title
page, the table of contents and often a foreword or preface. Then,
in the COD, comes the 'Guide to the Use of the Dictionary', which
tells us about the conventions used in preparing the dictionary.

Listing these, we have:

(a)　The headword.
(b)　Pronunciation.
(c)　Part of speech.
(d)　Inflection (the COD spelling is 'Inflexion').
(e)　Definition.
(f)　Illustrative examples.
(g)　Grammatical information.
(h)　Usage.
(i)　Phrases and idioms.
(j)　Compounds.
(k)　Derivatives.
(l)　Etymology − the development of the word.
(m)　Prefixes and suffixes.
(n)　Cross-references.
(o)　There then follows a list of the abbreviations used in the
　　　dictionary.

We must now consider each of these in turn, but as our account is
necessarily brief the reader is urged to refer, when using a dictionary,
to these preliminary pages, which are bound to cover any point of
difficulty that arises. In Section 12.3 below one or two entries from
the specimen page used in Figure 12.1 have been looked at in detail
to clarify the rather lengthy entries made in this section.

The headword

Each of the words listed in the dictionary is called a 'headword' and
is printed in bold Roman type or in bold italic type if it is a word
that has not yet become naturalized in English. The aim of the
dictionary is to enable its readers to add words to their vocabularies
by giving the meanings of every word, and illustrating the uses made
of the word in everyday modern life. Thus a brief phrase might be
included to show a popular use of a word. If a word has a more
restricted use, an indication will be given in brackets, e.g. (colloq.)
indicates that a word is in use colloquially, but would not be used in
formal correspondence or formal speech. An indication (*Law*) would
indicate that besides the explanation already given of the word in

general use it has a more restricted use in the legal profession. For example, the word 'lapse' in Figure 12.1 has a special use in law, which is explained.

In many cases where a word has two or three distinct uses, they are included with a raised 1, 2, 3 etc. above the word. In Figure 12.1 we have 'lap[1]', 'lap[2]' and 'lap[3]'. Therefore, when we look up the meaning of a word, we must skim through the various meanings to locate the meaning that is appropriate to the subject we are studying or the context in which we hope to use the word.

Variant spellings of the headword may be given in brackets before the definition, beginning with the word 'also', e.g. 'racoon (also raccoon)'. Such alternative spellings usually apply to the whole word, including any derivatives, but where an alternative spelling is given with a more limited importance, it is given in brackets at an appropriate point. A variant spelling in America is shown by the letters (US) and the American spelling.

Normally the headword is in small letters, but if a headword normally has a capital letter (as with 'Laplander' in Figure 12.1), it is given in that form.

Pronunciation

This is based on the so-called 'Received Pronunciation' used in Southern England, and a key gives the sound to be given to each particular symbol. It follows that the alert student who turns back to the key can work out the correct pronunciation of each word. The symbols used are those recommended by the International Phonetic Alphabet (IPA).

A mark ~ over a letter indicates a nasalized sound, which is not natural in English. An example is the word 'Señor'.

Stress is shown by preceding the stressed syllable by a small′, e.g. the word 'lapel' shown in Figure 12.1 is shown |lə′pel|.

Part of speech

All words are identified as noun, verb, adjective, etc., and if they are used in more than one way, a list is given and then the various uses are shown by a long dash — adj. (followed by the explanation) — n. (followed by the explanation), etc.

Inflection (Inflexion)

(Inflection is a change in a word resulting from some grammatical requirement, e.g. as nouns change from singular to plural or adjec-

slide for projection by a magic lantern etc. (see SLIDE *n.* 5b). **lantern-wheel** a lantern-shaped gearwheel; a trundle. [ME f. OF *lanterne* f. L *lanterna* f. Gk *lamptēr* torch, lamp]

lanthanide /ˈlænθənaɪd/ *n. Chem.* an element of the lanthanide series. □**lanthanide series** a series of 15 metallic elements from lanthanum to lutetium in the periodic table, having similar chemical properties; also called *rare earths* (see RARE[1]). [G *Lanthanid* (as LANTHANUM]

lanthanum /ˈlænθənəm/ *n. Chem.* a silvery metallic element of the lanthanide series which occurs naturally and is used in the manufacture of alloys. ¶ Symb.: **La**. [Gk *lanthanō* escape notice, from having remained undetected in cerium oxide]

lanugo /ləˈnjuːgəʊ/ *n.* fine soft hair, esp. that which covers the body and limbs of a human foetus. [L, = down f. *lana* wool]

lanyard /ˈlænjəd, -jɑːd/ *n.* **1** a cord hanging round the neck or looped round the shoulder, esp. of a Scout or sailor etc., to which a knife, a whistle, etc., may be attached. **2** *Naut.* a short rope or line used for securing, tightening, etc. **3** a cord attached to a breech mechanism for firing a gun. [ME f. OF *laniere*, *lasniere*: assim. to YARD[1]]

Laodicean /ˌleɪədɪˈsiːən/ *adj. & n.* —*adj.* lukewarm or half-hearted, esp. in religion or politics. —*n.* such a person. [L *Laodicea* in Asia Minor (with ref. to the early Christians there: see Rev. 3:16)]

Laotian /ˈlaʊʃən, lɑːˈʊʃən/ *n. & adj.* —*n.* **1 a** a native or national of Laos in SE Asia. **b** a person of Laotian descent. **2** the language of Laos. —*adj.* of or relating to Laos or its people or language.

lap[1] /læp/ *n.* **1 a** the front of the body from the waist to the knees of a sitting person (*sat on her lap; caught it in his lap*). **b** the clothing, esp. a skirt, covering the lap. **c** the front of a skirt held up to catch or contain something. **2** a hollow among hills. **3** a hanging flap on a garment, a saddle, etc. □**in** (or **on**) **a person's lap** as a person's responsibility. **in the lap of the gods** (of an event etc.) open to chance; beyond human control. **in the lap of luxury** in extremely luxurious surroundings. **lap-dog** a small pet dog. **lap robe** *US* a travelling-rug. □**lapful** *n.*

on a beach. **3** liquid food for dogs. **4** *sl.* **a** a weak beverage. **b** any liquor. [OE *lapian* f. Gmc]

laparoscope /ˈlæpərəskəʊp/ *n. Surgery* a fibre optic instrument inserted through the abdominal wall to give a view of the organs in the abdomen. □□ **laparoscopy** /-ˈrɒskəpɪ/ *n.* (*pl.* -ies). [Gk *lapara* flank + -SCOPE]

laparotomy /ˌlæpəˈrɒtəmɪ/ *n.* (*pl.* -ies) a surgical incision into the abdominal cavity for exploration or diagnosis. [Gk *lapara* flank + -TOMY]

lapel /ləˈpel/ *n.* the part of a coat, jacket, etc., folded back against the front round the neck opening. □□ **lapelled** *adj.* [LAP[1] + -EL]

lapicide /ˈlæpɪsaɪd/ *n.* a person who cuts or engraves on stone. [L *lapicida* irreg. f. *lapis -idis* stone: see -CIDE]

lapidary /ˈlæpɪdərɪ/ *adj. & n.* —*adj.* **1** concerned with stone or stones. **2** engraved upon stone. **3** (of writing style) dignified and concise, suitable for inscriptions. —*n.* (*pl.* -ies) a cutter, polisher, or engraver of gems. [ME f. L *lapidarius* f. *lapis -idis* stone]

lapilli /ləˈpɪlaɪ/ *n.pl.* stone fragments ejected from volcanoes. [It. f. L, pl. dimin. of *lapis* stone]

lapis lazuli /ˌlæpɪs ˈlæzjʊlɪ, -laɪ/ *n.* **1** a blue mineral containing sodium aluminium silicate and sulphur, used as a gemstone. **2** a bright blue pigment formerly made from this. **3** its colour. [ME f. L *lapis* stone + med.L *lazuli* genit. of *lazulum* f. Pers. (as AZURE)]

Laplander /ˈlæpˌlændə(r)/ *n.* **1** a native or national of Lapland. **2** a person of this descent. [*Lapland* f. Sw. *Lappland* (as LAPP, LAND)]

Lapp /læp/ *n. & adj.* —*n.* **1** a member of a nomadic Mongol people of N. Scandinavia. **2** the language of this people. —*adj.* of or relating to the Lapps or their language. [Sw. *Lapp*, perh. orig. a term of contempt: cf. MHG *lappe* simpleton]

lappet /ˈlæpɪt/ *n.* **1** a small flap or fold of a garment etc. **2** a hanging or loose piece of flesh, such as a lobe or wattle. □□**lappeted** *adj.* [LAP[1] + -ET[1]]

Lappish /ˈlæpɪʃ/ *adj. & n.* —*adj.* = LAPP *adj.* —*n.* the Lapp language.

lapse /læps/ n. & v. —n. 1 a a slight error; a slip of memory etc. 2 a weak or careless decline into an inferior state. 3 (foll. by *of*) an interval or passage of time (*after a lapse of three years*). 4 *Law* the termination of a right or privilege through disuse or failure to follow appropriate procedures. —*v.intr.* 1 fail to maintain a position or standard. 2 (foll. by *into*) fall back into an inferior or previous state. 3 (of a right or privilege etc.) become invalid because it is not used or claimed or renewed. 4 (as **lapsed** *adj.*) (of a person or thing) that has lapsed. □**lapse rate** *Meteorol.* the rate at which the temperature falls with increasing altitude. □**lapser** n. [L *lapsus* f. *labi laps-* glide, slip, fall]

lapstone /ˈlæpstəʊn/ n. a shoemaker's stone held in the lap and used to beat leather on.

lapsus calami /ˌlæpsəs ˈkæləˌmaɪ/ n. (*pl.* same) a slip of the pen. [L: see LAPSE]

lapsus linguae /ˌlæpsəs ˈlɪŋgwaɪ/ n. a slip of the tongue. [L: see LAPSE]

laptop /ˈlæptɒp/ n. (*attrib.*) (of a microcomputer) portable and suitable for use while travelling.

lapwing /ˈlæpwɪŋ/ n. a plover, *Vanellus vanellus*, with black and white plumage, crested head, and a shrill cry. [OE *hlēapewince* f. *hlēapan* LEAP + WINK: assim. to LAP¹, WING]

larboard /ˈlɑːbəd/ n. & adj. *Naut. archaic* = PORT³. [ME *lade*, *ladde*, *lathe-* (perh. = LADE + BOARD): later assim. to *starboard*]

larceny /ˈlɑːsənɪ/ n. (*pl.* -ies) the theft of personal property. ¶In 1968 replaced as a statutory crime in English law by *theft*. □**larcener** n. **larcenist** n. **larcenous** adj. [OF *larcin* f. L *latrocinium* f. *latro* robber, mercenary f. Gk *latreus*]

larch /lɑːtʃ/ n. 1 a deciduous coniferous tree of the genus *Larix*, with bright foliage and producing tough

---

lap² /læp/ n. & v. —n. 1 a one circuit of a racetrack etc. b a section of a journey etc. (*finally we were on the last lap*). 2 a an amount of overlapping. b an overlapping or projecting part. 3 a a layer or sheet (of cotton etc. being made) wound on a roller. b a single turn of rope, silk, thread, etc., round a drum or reel. 4 a rotating disk for polishing a gem or metal. —v. (**lapped**, **lapping**) 1 tr. lead or overtake (a competitor in a race) by one or more laps. 2 tr. (often foll. by *about*, *round*) coil, fold, or wrap (a garment etc.) round esp. a person. 3 tr. (usu. foll. by *in*) enfold or swathe (a person) in wraps etc. 4 tr. (as **lapped** *adj.*) (usu. foll. by *in*) protectively encircled; enfolded caressingly. 5 tr. surround (a person) with an influence etc. 6 intr. (usu. foll. by *over*) project; overlap. 7 tr. cause to overlap. 8 tr. polish (a gem etc.) with a lap. □**half-lap** = *lap joint*. **lap joint** the joining of rails, shafts, etc., by halving the thickness of each at the joint and fitting them together. **lap of honour** a ceremonial circuit of a football pitch, track, etc., by a winner or winners. **lap-strake** n. a clinker-built boat. —*adj.* clinker-built. **lap-weld** *v.tr.* weld with overlapping edges. —n. such a weld. [ME, prob. f. LAP¹]

lap³ /læp/ v. & n. —v. (**lapped**, **lapping**) 1 tr. a (also *absol.*) (usu. of an animal) drink (liquid) with the tongue. b (usu. foll. by *up*, *down*) consume (liquid) greedily. c (usu. foll. by *up*) consume (gossip, praise, etc.) greedily. 2 a tr. (of water) move or beat upon (a shore) with a rippling sound as of lapping. b intr. (of waves etc.) move in ripples; make a lapping sound. —n. 1 a the process or an act of lapping. b the amount of liquid taken up. 2 the sound of wavelets

æ cat ɑː arm e bed ɜː her ɪ sit iː see ɒ hot ɔː saw ʌ run ʊ put uː too ə ago aɪ my

---

Figure 12.1 A page from the *Concise Oxford Dictionary*, 8th Edition (courtesy of Oxford University Press)

tives and adverbs change from positive to comparative or superlative. The changes are given in brackets after the part of speech (see 'larceny' in Figure 12.1, where the plural is shown). Similarly, with the word 'lapsus' the dictionary tells us the plural is the same. The inflections given are those normally found in British English; if the United States versions are different, these are given with the letters (US). Inflections in verbs, adjectives or adverbs are given similarly.

Definitions

The definitions are listed in a numbered sequence, with the most common use of the word explained first and other uses following in the sequence of their comparative familiarity. With the word 'lap' in Figure 12.1 not only do we have 'lap^1', 'lap^2' and 'lap^3', but there are three definitions of 'lap^1', eight definitions of 'lap^2' and four definitions of 'lap^3', and some of these are also given in two parts, (a) and (b).

Illustrative examples

To help the student understand the use of a word, a number of illustrative expressions may be given in italic. Again see Figure 12.1, where there are several in the sections on 'lap'.

Grammatical information

The definitions are often accompanied by grammatical hints, which explain some of the more common uses of the word. Thus, the word 'lap^3', which is the use of the word 'to drink a liquid', we are told it is usually followed by 'up' or 'down'. Asked whether a class liked a talk by a visiting speaker a teacher might reply — 'Oh, they lapped it up'.

Usage

Sometimes the use of a word is restricted in some way, and this will be indicated by an abbreviated indication (often geographical). Thus (*Austral., NZ, S. Afr.*) restrict uses to the area named. *Colloq.* indicates that the use is restricted to informal everyday speech rather than formal correspondence. *Archaic* indicates a word that is restricted to a special field, usually of historical importance and perhaps to religious or legal use.

Phrases and idioms

Some words are particularly important in forming phrases and idiomatic expressions. They are given in bold after the main definitions, with an explanation of each. Thus the word 'make' has numerous expressions, such as 'make do, make out, make friends, make fun', etc. each of which is explained.

Compounds

Where a compound term makes one word — as with 'bathroom' or 'newspaper' — it is given as the headword. Where they make two or more words, or a hyphenated word, they appear under the first element. Thus 'ant-eater' is found under 'ant', and 'chain-gang' under 'chain'.

Derivatives

Where words are formed from other words by adding a suffix, they are shown under the headword, usually without any definition, because they can be understood from the sense of the main word. Thus 'saint' might be followed by 'saintlike' and 'sainthood'.

Etymology

Etymology is the study of the formation of words, and of how they came to have their present meaning. Although such knowledge is not essential, it is interesting, and Figure 12.1 shows how many languages have contributed to the language that today we call English.

Prefixes and suffixes

Most prefixes have a headword entry of their own in the form ex-, re- and most suffixes have a similar entry in the form -ness, -ly.

Cross-references

These are shown in a number of ways, e.g. *see* ..., *see also* ..., *cf* (which is latin for 'compare') and *opp* ... for a word that is opposite in meaning to the present word being considered.

Abbreviations

A full list of the abbreviations used in the dictionary is given at the end of the prelims.

12.3   Some examples of dictionary entries

In Figure 12.1 a page of the *Concise Oxford Dictionary* has been reproduced. If we take one or two of these entries and explain them in detail, we shall see how the dictionary deals with them.

Example 1 − 'lanthanum'

The word is defined as follows:

lanthanum |lænθənəm| *n. Chem.* a silvery metallic element of the lanthanide series which occurs naturally and is used in the manufacture of alloys. Symb.: **La.** [Gk *lanthanō* escape notice, from having remained undetected in cerium oxide].

The way the word is repeated in phonetic form after the bold headword enables us to work out its pronunciation. The consonants have their ordinary English sound. The symbol æ is the sound of 'a' as in 'cat', θ is the 'th' sound as in 'thin', while the symbol ə is the sound of 'a' as in 'ago'.

The abbreviation 'n'. means it is a noun. We could have 'adj.' adjective; 'v' verb, 'adv.' adverb, etc. The abbreviation *Chem.* tells us the word is a chemical word, and the definition goes on to tell us that it is a metallic element (one of the 92 naturally occurring elements). The abbreviation *Symb.* tells us that its chemical symbol is **La.** (just as hydrogen is H and copper is Cu). Finally, the etymological section tells us where the name was derived from − the Greek word for 'escape notice' because it was one of the elements that did not come to the attention of the chemists until quite recently.

Clearly this is a brief but comprehensive account of the word 'lanthanum'.

Example 2 − lapidary
The word is given as follows:

lapidary|læpidəri| *adj. & n. − adj.* **1** concerned with stone or stones. **2** engraved upon stone. **3** (of writing style) dignified and concise, suitable for inscriptions. − *n.* (*pl.*ies) a cutter, polisher, or engraver of gems. [ME f.L *lapidarius* f. lapis -*idis* stone]

As to the pronunciation, the first 'a' is as in 'fat', the 'i' is as in 'bit', the second 'a' is as in 'ago' and the 'y' is as in 'duty'. The word can be an adjective or a noun.

We then get to first use 1 as an adjective. This gives us three uses of the word as an adjective. They are:

1 'concerned with stone or stones' – as in 'The lapidary examination of the rocks proved traces of garnets were present'.
2 'engraved upon stone' – as in 'The lapidary inscription reads "Death comes as a friend, not an enemy"'.
3 When used to refer to the style of the work, it means suitable for inscriptions, dignified and concise. Thus we might say of the phrase 'Prepare to meet thy God' that it was a lapidary sentiment (dignified and concise enough for a tombstone).

We then get to its use as a noun. Here it refers to a craftsman – a cutter, or polisher or engraver of gems. Its etymology is that it is a Middle English word, from the Latin L. *lapidarius* from *lapis -idis* stone.

Clearly, we now know as much about the word as we shall ever need to know and we can add it to our vocabularies.

12.4 Exercise on the use of the dictionary

Exercise 12a

1 Write down the following words. Then look them up in the dictionary and write their meaning against the word.

bergamot	cephalopod
buffoon	celluloid
characteristic	clientele
colander	cognoscente
contrition	cruciform

2 Write down the following ten words. Then look them up in a dictionary and write down against each word the meaning given.

Heath Robinson	Heaviside
hermaphrodite	hierarchy
hydrometer	hybrid
isinglass	joiner
lanceolate	*laisser-faire*

3 Write down the following ten words and then explain their etymology as given in the dictionary.

maisonette   malady
mocha   nicotine
nightingale   nominate
pertinent   portmanteau
renegade   remuneration

12.5   More about pronouns

We know that a pronoun is a word that can be used instead of a noun (it actually means 'for a noun', the Latin word *pro* meaning 'for'). Whereas a noun designates the person, place or thing being considered (London, France, rabbit, aeroplane, etc.), a pronoun is less specific (he, she, it, etc.).

Consider 'Miss Jones types correspondence. She uses a word processor'. The pronoun 'she' designates who it is that uses the word processor but is less clear than the actual name 'Miss Jones'. We know who it is that uses the word processor because the pronoun refers back to the noun that has already been mentioned. This noun is called the antecedent noun.

Consider 'Arthur Blake is the management accountant. He is well-qualified and knowledgeable about manufacturing processes'. The pronoun 'he' refers back to the noun 'Arthur Blake', who is the subject of the first sentence.

There are several kinds of pronoun. Here we will deal with five types − personal pronouns, demonstrative pronouns, interrogative pronouns, relative pronouns and indefinite pronouns.

Personal pronouns

There are the pronouns used in declining a verb − I, thou (obsolete) he, she, it, we, you, they. They can take different forms according to how they are used in a sentence. Thus each has a possessive form (used to show that something is a possession), or an objective form, where a transitive verb leads on to the pronoun concerned. Listing these we have:

Nominative	Possessive	Objective
I	my (or mine)	me
you	your (or yours)	your (or yours)
he	his	him
she	her (or hers)	her
it	its	it
we	our (or ours)	us
you	your (or yours)	you
they	their (or theirs)	them

Some examples of these are:

(a) I have taken an order.
(b) My order is in the file.
(c) That order is mine. It needs to be credited to me.

Demonstrative pronouns

These are pronouns that point out or indicate the person or thing referred to. 'This, that, these and those' are the demonstrative pronouns:

(a) *This* is the machine you were told about in the video presentation.
(b) *That* is the effect of cash-flow problems on a business.
(c) *Those* are the components which are needed on the production line at 11 am.
(d) *These* are the records of attendance in the machine shop over the last 3 months.

If you look up these words in the dictionary, you will find that they are designated as adjectives as well as pronouns. For example, if they are followed by a noun to which they refer they cannot really be pronouns, and are demonstrative adjectives. '*This* machine needs 250 volts, but we also sell *that* model, which will operate on 110 volts.'

Interrogative pronouns

These are pronouns that ask questions. 'Who, which and what' are the interrogative pronouns:

(a) *Who* is available to help with the demonstration?
(b) *Which* of you will be available to act as hostess for the seminar?
(c) *What* is your name?

The word 'who' changes to show the possessive and objective relationships, i.e. nominative 'who', possessive 'whose' and objective 'whom'.

Relative pronouns

A relative pronoun is one that relates a subordinate clause to an antecedent main clause. In doing so it does two jobs. It acts as the subject or object of the subordinate clause and it acts as a connector between the two clauses it relates with one another. The relative pronouns are 'who, which, that and what'. For example, 'This is the soprano who sang in the concert last night'. Note that 'who' is the subject of the subordinate clause 'who sang in the concert last night' and it also connects this subordinate clause to the main clause by relating back to the antecedent noun 'soprano'.

Who always refers to a male or female antecedent.

'This is the machine which (or that) has developed a fault.' 'Which' refers to a thing or an animal rather than a human antecedent.

'This is the best that I can do for you.' Note that the relative pronoun 'that' is often omitted in everyday speech. 'This is the best I can do for you.'

'The death of the President is what I mean.' In this way the word 'what' replaces and has the same meaning as 'that which'.

There are a number of other compound relative pronouns, e.g.

whoever	whosoever
whatever	whatsoever
whichever	whichsoever

Indefinite pronouns

Indefinite pronouns are pronouns that refer to persons or things in a general way, but not specifically, although the noun they stand for may be understood: Suppose a teacher finds an apple on her desk and says 'Someone is being very kind'. The class may know who donated the apple but the pronoun gives no clue.

There are many such pronouns. For example:

all	everybody	nothing
any	everything	somebody
anybody	everyone	someone
anyone	nobody	something
anything	no one	many
		few

Exercise 12b

1   Here are ten sentences with pronouns printed in italics. In each case write down the pronoun, and then say which type of pronoun it is.

(a)   *I* went to the opera last night.
(b)   The green suitcase is *mine*.
(c)   *Our* reservation has been cancelled.

(d)   Peter gave the documentation to *them*.
(e)   Under the 'just-in-time' system *those* components must arrive by noon.
(f)   *Who* will finance the project?
(g)   *These* are the most precious orchids in the collection.
(h)   Allow me to introduce the engineer *who* built the prototype 10 years ago.
(i)   The accommodation is the best *that* we can offer today.
(j)   *Everybody* is now present, so we can begin.

2   Here are five further sentences containing pronouns. Copy them out, underline any pronouns in the sentence, and in brackets at the end write which kind of pronoun each is.

(a)   I ate my dinner but Mary left hers.
(b)   There was somebody in the factory, I am sure.
(c)   Whoever gave the order, certainly someone fired.
(d)   This is the student who designed the princess's wardrobe.
(e)   Which one of you is writing the text for the brochure.

3   Here are five further sentences containing pronouns. Copy them out, underline any pronouns in the sentence, and in brackets at the end write which kind of pronoun each is.

(a)   What is your rank in the armed forces?
(b)   That is the archaeological site.
(c)   Here is the budget, which is quite unacceptably extravagant.
(d)   I think everyone is agreed that is the best design.
(e)   They regained their freedom.

12.6   More spellings

Here are some more spellings. Ask a fellow student to test you on the first set of words and then reciprocate by testing him/her on the second set.

Secretarial practice		*Business administration*	
shorthand	type	proprietor	decide
transcribe	typist	partner	decision
transcription	typewriter	director	indecision
refer	duplicator	orient	acoustics
referred	duplication	orientation	lighting
references	duplicating	market-orientated	air-conditioning

letterhead	dictate	object	plan
compliments	dictation	objective	planning
slip	executive	objectives	year planner
brochure	administrator	management	span of
catalogue		by objectives	control

12.7   Vocabulary and slang

Slang is vocabulary that is used colloquially. It may come from a particular locality, like Cockney rhyming slang, in which words with a similar ending replace the proper words. 'Get your plates of meat up the apples and pears' is rhyming slang for 'go to bed' (get your feet upstairs). The trouble with slang is that it may not be understood outside the area where it is spoken or the group who use it. A northerner, told by a Cockney that he suspects a friend of being a 'tea leaf', may not realize he means the man is a thief. The person who knows nothing about computers may wonder who is being kicked when someone is described as a 'hacker'.

In business English we avoid slang, and use formal, standard English. Standard English is the type of English used by the average well-educated person. It does permit use of local variations, and it can always employ words known only to the specialist audience to whom a speech or a report is addressed. What it avoids is expressions that might not be understood by the target audience, or are not really suitable to the purpose for which the speech or written work is intended.

Exercise 12c   Here are three sets of colloquial expressions. Write them down one at a time and then give a similar phrase in standard English. For example, 'Off his chump = a crazy, foolish person'.

1   (a)   stuck up   (b)   lion-hearted
    (c)   good for nothing   (d)   all ears
    (e)   mud-slinging   (f)   smell a rat
    (g)   come a cropper   (h)   draw the line
    (i)   sit on the fence   (j)   play the game

2   (a)   a cock and bull story   (b)   bats in the belfry
    (c)   a storm in a teacup   (d)   shanks' pony
    (e)   keep your powder dry   (f)   took French leave
    (g)   blaze a trail   (h)   has a bee in his bonnet
    (i)   a red letter day   (j)   to throw cold water on

3   (a)   keep the pot boiling   (b)   the man in the street
    (c)   a rough diamond   (d)   a bird's eye view
    (e)   a worm's eye view   (f)   to get into hot water

(g)   a feather in your cap   (h)   to throw in the towel
(i)   to show the white feather   (j)   tell it to the marines

12.8   Figures of speech 3: euphemisms

A euphemism is an expression that is used as a substitute for a harsh
or shocking phrase, to lessen its impact and make it more acceptable.
It will generally be a milder, vaguer or more roundabout way of
speaking. Thus the American expression 'I must let you go' is a
euphemism for 'you are dismissed', and appears to suggest that the
employee is just dying to leave, and the employer is positively
helping him/her to go. The term 'intimacy' is a euphemism for
'sexual intercourse' and 'inebriation' is a euphemism for 'drunken-
ness'. A euphemism may be a single word or more often a phrase.

There will be occasions when we use euphemisms in business
English, e.g. when we are complaining about a supplier's behaviour
or a customer's failure to pay. We may, in the initial stages, remon-
strate mildly, since we wish to do what we can to preserve a relation
that up to that time has proved mutually beneficial. Later it may be
necessary to talk more forthrightly.

Exercise 12d   Here are some sets of words which are 'hard' or
'shocking'. Using your dictionary or a thesaurus, find a euphemism
for each.

1   (a)   died,
    (b)   fraudulent,
    (c)   bankrupt,
    (d)   crippled,
    (e)   arsonist.
2   (a)   murder,
    (b)   dismiss,
    (c)   arrest,
    (d)   gullible,
    (e)   ignorant.

12.9   Designing forms for business use

In business we meet many situations where the best solution to a
problem is to develop a form with all the necessary details. We have
already mentioned such things as invoices, credit notes and similar
documents, but there are countless situations where forms are useful.
What we need to do is turn a specialist activity (such as taking an
order from a 'bespoke' customer) into a routine activity − where

anyone on the staff can take the order, whether they have specialist knowledge or not, simply because it is only a matter of filling out a form the specialist has devised. It is true there are situations where we do need to fit in with other firms and international bodies, such as the United Nations or the International Chamber of Commerce. For ordinary in-house forms anyone with a reasonable knowledge of what is required can draw up a form.

The essential features of a form

These are:

- The form must be clear, and unambiguous.
- There must be a box for every piece of information required.
- The layout should be in logical sequence, and preferably such that the applicant can fill it in himself/herself.
- If the final form is to become a card index, e.g. an enrolment form at a college, the name and address of the individual should be on the top of the card where it can be seen as we flick through the cards.
- Sometimes a form has legal implications, e.g. it may make a contract, or give insurance cover, etc. If so, make sure the form states clearly what the legal implications are.
- If the design is to be computer generated, e.g. the computer will be programmed to print out an order form whenever stocks fall to the reorder point, the form must be in the correct style so that the computer can handle it.
- If the form is to be run off in a plain paper copying machine, we must choose an appropriate size, e.g. most copiers produce A4. If we choose A4 size we get one copy per print. If we choose A5 we will get two copies per print.
- If the form is to be run off by a printer, we should liase with the printer on style, size, choice of print, etc.
- If the form is to be returned to you, make sure your own name and address are clear. Do you want to use a freepost address? If you want to use the Post Office reply-paid system consult the *Post Office Guide* about the format and get it approved.
- Some forms have a special section to analyse and collect together the information supplied. (See Figure 12.2 – the cost summary.)

It is always advisable to test out a form carefully – preferably by inviting others to comment on it – before it is put into its final format. Nothing is more irritating than to print 1,000 copies of a form and then find there are serious omissions of information we need to know. For this reason it is always helpful to use the form in real life, in a prototype format run off cheaply on a plain paper

Cost sheet serial number:			Customer's name and address:											
Telephone number:			Job number:			Job description:								

Materials used	F	£	p	Components used	F	£	p	Foundry charges	F	£	p	Machine shop charges	F	£	p	Cost summary	£	p
																Materials		
																Components		
																Foundry		
																Machine shop		
																Drawing Office		
																Packing Dept.		
																Transport Dept.		
Total				Total				Total				Total				Other charges		
Add oncost at 50%				Add oncost at 50%				Add oncost at 200%				Add oncost at 150%				Total costs		
Total to summary				Total to summary				Total to summary				Total to summary				Add profit		
																Invoice total		

Drawing office	F	£	p	Packing dept.	F	£	p	Transport dept.	F	£	p	Other charges	F	£	p	
																Final Report: Note here any problems connected with this order.
Total				Total				Total				Total				
Add oncost at 100%				Add oncost at 75%				Add oncost at 100%				Add oncost at 200%				
Total to summary				Total to summary				Total to summary				Total to summary				

Figure 12.2 A simple cost sheet

copier, before getting the final version (now corrected, we hope) run off by a printer. Some of the exercises given below enable students to try out the cost form of Figure 12.2, just to get the feel of how the form would be used in real life by a cost clerk.

Exercise 12e   Make a number of copies of the cost sheet in Figure 12.2 and use them to record the costs for the following jobs performed by Prefabricators PLC for the customers named. What was the total charge to the customer in each case?

1   Serial number 0001, Job number 284, Light Engineering PLC, 24 Somers Way, London E5 2TS. Telephone 01-008 3124. Job description: spiral staircases. Materials: steel rod, £38.50; brass rod, £72.85; bolts, etc., £8.54. Foundry charges: spiral assemblies 84 at £5.80 each. Drawing Office: plans, £45.80. Transport charges: £39.50. Other charges: quality control, £23.50; painting shop, £38.50. Profit to be based on 40% of total costs.

2   Serial number 0002, Job number 285, Rail Enthusiasts Club, Glen Railway Station, Aberdovey. Telephone 0436−012. Job description: admission turnstiles. Materials used: steel bars, £38.50; steel sheet, £42.50; sand and cement, £15.80. Foundry charges: £31.64. Machine shop charges: drilling, £12.85; shaping, £7.56; turning, £14.25. Drawing office: plans, £35.80. Transport Dept.: delivery, £28.50. Other charges: paint shop, £28.50; inspection and testing, £18.50. Profit to be based on 45% of total costs.

3   Serial number 0003, Job number 286, Interior Fitting Co., 2401 High Street, Southampton. Telephone 0703−01245. Job description: staircases and safety rails. Materials: timber, £62.50; brackets and bolts, £8.84; safety rails, £48.50. Components: Lewis balustrades, 4 sets at £18.50. Machine shop charges: £17.55, drilling. Packing Dept.: crates, etc., £15.80. Other charges: painting shop £25.80. Profit to be based on 25% of total costs.

4   Serial number 0004, Job number 287, Luminex Ltd, 2734 High Street, Great Tenby, Derbyshire. Job description: exhibition stands. Materials used: steel framework, £84.50; light alloy sheet, £164.85; nuts, bolts, etc., £17.20. Components: Zorro lighting units, £34.50; Visi-shelf units, 12 at £15.80 each. Drawing office: plans, £138.50. Transport Department, £34.90. Other charges: electrician, £34.50. Profit to be based on 28% of total costs.

Exercise 12f

1   Your firm is doing a piece of market research for the State of Florida. The State's Tourism Bureau wishes to ask all holiday-

makers leaving the State (a) how long they stayed, (b) where they stayed, (c) what sort of accommodation they used, (d) how much they paid for it, (e) how much other spending money they spent, (f) what activities they engaged in, (g) whether they had any complaints.

For each of these questions you should provide a choice of answers.

For example:

How much did you pay for your accommodation? (Please tick)
Under $10 per day .... $10–$19.99 ....
$20 to $29.99 .... $30–$39.99 ....
$40–$49.99 ....   More than $50 ....

Design a suitable form.

2 Your firm is starting a suggestion box scheme in which cash prizes will be given to those who make suggestions that save the firm materials, labour costs or overheads, or which promote the sale of the firm's products. Design a form that can be left in the reception area near the suggestion box so that all those interested may contribute their ideas. A large part of the form will simply be ruled lines for them to write about their suggestions.

3 Design a form to be printed as part of an advertisement in fashion magazines that invites people to send in two first-class postage stamps for a sample bottle of either *Femme fatale*, a perfume for ladies, or *Parfum masculin*, a perfume for men. You need the full name and address of the applicant, the name of the magazine where they saw the advertisement and the name of the shop where they would normally buy perfume.

12.10   Answer section

Exercise 12a The answers to these questions will be obvious from the dictionary entries.

Exercise 12b (a) personal (nominative); (b) personal (possessive); (c) personal (possessive); (d) personal (objective); (e) demonstrative; (f) interrogative; (g) demonstrative; (h) relative; (i) relative; (j) indefinite. 2(a) *I* (personal nominative); *hers* (personal possessive); (b) *somebody* (indefinite); *I* (personal nominative; (c) *whoever* (indefinite); *someone* (indefinite); (d) *This* (demonstrative); *who* (relative); (e) *Which* (interrogative); *you* (personal nominative). 3(a) *What* (interrogative); (b) *That* (demonstrative); (c) *which* (relative); (d) *I* (personal nominative); *everyone* (indefinite); *that* (demonstrative); (e) *They* (personal nominative); their (personal possessive).

Exercise 12c　1(a) conceited; (b) brave; (c) useless; (d) paying close attention to; (e) making derogatory insinuations; (f) become suspicious of; (g) fail totally or have a heavy fall; (h) set a limit on; (i) refuse to take sides in a dispute; (j) behave fairly. 2(a) a complete invention; (b) crazy; (c) a great fuss about nothing; (d) walking; (e) be prepared; (f) went away without saying goodbye or asking permission; (g) lead the way for others to follow; (h) is obsessed with a crazy idea; (i) a day of special significance; (j) to discourage. 3(a) keep the activity going; (b) the average person; (c) a good, reliable person, but lacking polished manners; (d) a view from above, which sees the whole subject; (e) seen from below (especially from the point of view of a poorer member of society); (f) get into trouble; (g) something to be proud of; (h) to give in, or surrender; (i) to be cowardly; (j) I don't believe a word of it.

Exercise 12d　1(a) passed away; (b) deceitful; (c) insolvent; (d) handicapped; (e) firebug. 2(a) foul play; (b) make redundant; (c) apprehend; (d) easily imposed upon; (e) inexperienced.

Exercise 12e　1　£2797.25; 2　£864.74; 3　£549.61; 4　£1518.43.

Exercise 12f　No numerical answers required.

13
Report writing 1: Gathering information

13.1 The importance of report writing

Countless problems arise across the whole range of business activities. They may be routine problems on such matters as marketing trends or quality control. They may be one-off problems, which require particular attention – such as investigations into an accident, or a labour turnover problem in one particular area related to the appointment of a particular manager or supervisor. We have already said that such problems are handled in many cases by a small committee. An **ad hoc committee** is a committee appointed for a particular purpose, which collects evidence bearing on the problem, analyses it and reports back with recommendations. A **standing committee** is more permanent, and holds a watching brief over the problem area e.g. quality control. It collects its evidence as a routine matter from hourly, daily or weekly reports, and reports regularly to the board or an appropriate director. In such a system it will be the exceptional statistics that become significant, for example a batch of poor quality raw material might produce a 'blip' in the statistics showing a higher rate of failure than usual in test pieces extracted from a production line. This would lead to a report, suitable corrective measures and perhaps legal action against the supplier concerned.

The effective point of control is in all cases the report and the recommendations it makes. The writing of reports is therefore a very important role for middle management and senior staff, and it is essential to be able to write clearly and lucidly about the matter in hand. We may distinguish the following aspects of report writing, which form the subject matter of this chapter and the next two chapters. They must, of necessity, cover some aspects of statistics, which form the basis of many reports. The reader will forgive these diversions away from business English but they are essential to the writing of good reports. Those who feel that they would like to learn more about statistics might like to study a companion volume, *Statistics for Business Made Simple*, by R. Ingram and K. Hoyle.

The chief aspects of report writing are:

(a) The statement of the problem.
(b) The appointment of a team leader and a team to investigate
     the matter. This confers upon them the right to collect infor-
     mation, etc., and to report back their conclusions.
(c) The gathering of information.
(d) The planning of the report, including the analysis of the infor-
     mation, the presentation of any data in suitable form and the
     marshalling of the evidence in good order.
(e) The conclusions to be drawn from the analysed information.
(f) The recommendations to solve the problem.
(g) Publication of the report.

13.2 Stating the problem and appointing the team

Problems arise for all sorts of reasons on all sorts of matters. It is
the function of the managing director to be aware of all the problems
that do arise, and the problem will move rapidly up the chain of
command to managing director level. Usually some middle manager
or supervisor will become aware of the problem and will raise it with
his/her supervisor, who will raise it with a director, who will in turn
raise it with the managing director. Emergency situations will of
course be dealt with at once, but problems concerning company
policy will usually begin by becoming an agenda item, at the next
board meeting.

The chairman will call for an account of the problem from the
most appropriate director; some discussion will take place and a
resolution will be passed requiring either an existing committee, or
an *ad hoc* committee set up for the purpose, to investigate the
matter and report back. This resolution will be minuted by the
minuting secretary and becomes the legal authority for the activities
of the team leader and his team. Such a resolution might read:

> **22 May 19. .**   It is resolved that Mr P. Garrett, Personnel Officer,
> shall choose three members of staff, one from his own department
> and two others, to examine the company's policy on race relations,
> establish what proportion of staff should be of various ethnic
> origins and report back on their findings in due course. Until the
> final report is available interim reports of progress should be
> made at each board meeting.

This resolution is said to set the *terms of reference* of the team, and
the final report always begins by referring to the terms of reference
and recapitulating why the team was appointed, what it was required
to do, to whom it was to report and whether any time limit was set.

13.3 Methods of gathering information

Once the team has been selected and appropriate working arrangements established, the next step is to make a plan for collecting and collating all the relevant information. This may call for a wide variety of activities, depending on the problem. We may have to establish an exact pattern of events, which may require interviewing all those who witnessed the event, or were participants in it or affected by it. We may need to research past events of a similar nature. We may need to visit sites to carry out on-site inspections, or to visit depots and plants. We may need to examine records, such as vehicle movements, or dismissals and redundancies.

The result of these activities is a collection of information, some of which is relevant to the investigation and some of it irrelevant. Much of this information will be in statistical form. It is at this point that we need to consider some aspects of statistics.

The word 'statistics' was originally applied to the collection of numerical facts by the state. Such areas as population, tax revenue, government expenditure and agricultural output were initially covered with a view to finding out how the economy could be influenced and what trends were developing. The facts collected were called 'data', a word which means 'starting points'. Today we use this word frequently because so many of our activities use the 'data processing' made possible by computers. We start with the 'data' we have collected, and process it in various ways to give us totals, averages, future projections, etc. The meaning of statistics has broadened to include not only a set of numerical data, but also the processes used in the collection, presentation, analysis, and interpretation of these data.

It is convenient to divide statistics into two parts:

(a) Descriptive statistics.
(b) Analytical statistics.

Descriptive statistics

This term is applied to any statistics that are collected and arranged in some suitable order so that they can be presented in tabular or diagrammatic form to throw light upon the state of affairs in the field under consideration. In dealing with most human, economic or scientific problems it is helpful to know the true situation. How many people are involved? What expenditure is being envisaged? What is the likely cost of present proposals? Who is most affected by the problem? Such matters call for a clear description in statistical form. Hence, a table showing the number of registered unemployed from 1971 to 1990 falls within the field of descriptive statistics (see Table 13.1).

Analytical statistics

These attempt to reach conclusions and make pronouncements on the basis of the information made available by descriptive statistics. It may be possible to make statements about why the totals of registered unemployed were as they appeared in the 1971–90 table. Measures taken during the decade might be linked to the changes in unemployment in subsequent periods and their effectiveness assessed. The cost of the measures might be set against the benefits to reveal the most cost-effective policies for the future. Such analysis makes use of techniques to be discussed later, such as averages and trends.

Collecting data – census forms and questionnaires

Statistics used by investigators are of two types: **primary** and **secondary**. Primary statistics are collected by the investigator when he/she searches out new information. Secondary statistics are those which an investigator obtains from other sources. Most of these will be published statistics and the government is an active supplier of information in this form.

Of course, at some stage all statistics have to be collected from original sources. Such collection faces the investigator with a number of decisions. The following points have to be considered when about to embark upon an inquiry:

Table 13.1   UK Registered unemployed, 1971–90

1971	806,800	1981	2,520,400
1972	875,600	1982	2,916,900
1973	618,800	1983	3,086,500
1974	614,900	1984	3,159,900
1975	977,600	1985	3,271,300
1976	1,358,800	1986	3,289,100
1977	1,483,600	1987	2,953,400
1978	1,475,000	1988	2,370,400
1979	1,390,500	1989	1,798,700
1980	1,816,900	1990	1,664,500

Source: Monthly Digest of Statistics.
Monthly averages to nearest 100.

(a)   What is the precise purpose of the inquiry?
(b)   What definitions must we lay down if the investigators are to be clear about the classification of the responses they receive?
(c)   How is the inquiry to be conducted and how can we make it as foolproof as possible? This usually requires the preparation of a questionnaire or a census form.

As an illustration of such a series of decisions, consider Figure 13.1, which was designed to conduct a traffic survey on a road going through a particular housing estate. Such an inquiry is called a **census**, since every vehicle passing through will be included in the data collected. In other inquiries, called **sample surveys**, only a selection of the relevant data will be obtained. In this census the answers to questions (a)–(c) above might be:

(a)   The precise purpose of the inquiry is to find out exactly what traffic uses the road through the estate. Residents complain about the volume of heavy goods traffic and the public service through-traffic run by tour operators and excursion organizers. Is there real cause for complaint, or not?

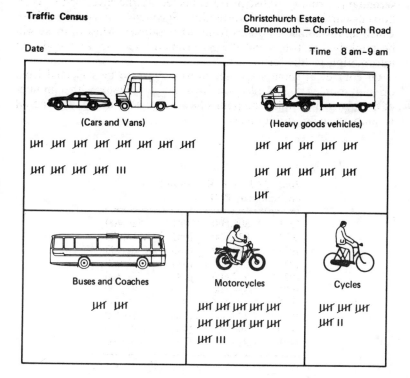

Figure 13.1   A traffic census

(b)   We decide to define heavy goods vehicles as 'large goods vehicles carrying containers, or enclosed vehicles such as removal vans or large distribution vans destined for depots and warehouses'. Small vans and hire-drive vans, caravanettes, etc., will all be treated as 'cars and vans'.

Buses and coaches are to be recorded as such only if they have thirteen seats or more. Minibuses with twelve seats only are to be classed as 'cars and vans'.

The term 'motorcycles' includes scooters and mopeds.

(c)   It seems best to conduct the survey over a full working day, from 6 am to midnight. An hour at a time is considered enough for a stint as 'census-taker'. A rota is prepared to cover each census period, and staff are trained to use the 'five-barred gate' system shown in Figure 13.1. This system records the first four vehicles by upright lines, and the fifth vehicle as a cross bar, as on a five-barred gate. The resulting records are easy to count up in fives.

The Consumers' Association is an official body which conducts investigations into matters of interest to consumers. Its publications are issued under the general title *Which?*, since their aim is to help consumers select the best buy in a particular range of goods or services. Every school and college should receive these publications, and readers are urged to consult *Which?* to discover the range and variety of statistics available.

The Association collects data from volunteers who have actually used the type of equipment or service being investigated, and from this mass of information draws helpful conclusions for the general body of consumers. A recent enquiry about 'Holidays in France' required volunteers to complete a ten-page **questionnaire**, one page of which is reproduced in Figure 13.2. Note the design of the questionnaire, to permit easy response by the holidaymaker.

13.4   Exercises on inquiry forms

Exercise 13a   You are proposing to conduct an inquiry among your classmates about their use of 'out of school/college time'. You particularly wish to know whether they have a part-time job or work in the home in an equivalent way because, perhaps, both parents are working. What hobbies do they pursue and for how many hours a week? What recreational activities do they indulge in and how much time is given to each activity per week? Design a form to carry out such an inquiry.

HAVE YOU BEEN TO ANY OTHER PARTS OF FRANCE?

WE WOULD LIKE TO GET A FULL PICTURE OF WHAT YOU LIKE AND DON'T LIKE ABOUT FRANCE. TO HELP
US WITH THIS WE WOULD BE GRATEFUL TO GET BRIEF DETAILS ABOUT ANY OTHER AREAS WHICH YOU
HAVE VISITED IN THE LAST 3-4 YEARS. EACH OF THE FOUR COLUMNS ON THIS QUESTIONNAIRE CAN
GIVE US BASIC INFORMATION ABOUT YOUR VIEWS ON ANOTHER AREA. PLEASE FILL IN ONE OR MORE
COLUMNS TO TELL US ABOUT OTHER PLACES YOU HAVE BEEN TO IN FRANCE.

CARD 4
(1)(2)(3)(4)
8 5 4 6
(5)-(12) AS CARD 1

AREA/REGION 1

Q1. Which region of France did you visit? SEE Q5 (13)
OF THE WHITE QUESTIONNAIRE. PLEASE WRITE IN.

_____ (14)

Q2. When did you make this visit?
PLEASE WRITE IN YEAR, AND MONTH HOLIDAY BEGAN.
(15) (16) (17)
Year: 19 [ ] Month: _____

Q3. What did you particularly enjoy or like about
your stay in this area? PLEASE WRITE IN DETAILS.

(18)

(19)

(20)

Q4. And what did you dislike about your stay in
this area? PLEASE WRITE IN DETAILS.

(21)

(22)

(23)

Q5. On the whole, how much did you enjoy your (24)
holiday in this area?
PLEASE   Very much .... □ 1
TICK   Quite a lot .... □ 2
ONE   Not very much ...... □ 3
BOX   Not at all .... □ 4

Q6. And summing up, how would you rate it as a (25)
place for a holiday?
PLEASE   Excellent .... □ 1
TICK   Good .... □ 2
ONE   Fair .... □ 3
BOX   Poor .... □ 4
            Bad .... □ 5

Q7. And overall, do you think this area is good (26)
value for money?
            Yes .... □ 1
            No .... □ 2

AREA/REGION 2

Q1. Which region of France did you visit? SEE Q5 (27)
OF THE WHITE QUESTIONNAIRE. PLEASE WRITE IN.

_____ (28)

Q2. When did you make this visit?
PLEASE WRITE IN YEAR, AND MONTH HOLIDAY BEGAN.
(29) (30) (31)
Year: 19 [ ] Month: _____

Q3. What did you particularly enjoy or like about
your stay in this area? PLEASE WRITE IN DETAILS

(32)

(33)

(34)

Q4. And what did you dislike about your stay in
this area? PLEASE WRITE IN DETAILS.

(35)

(36)

(37)

Q5. On the whole, how much did you enjoy your (38)
holiday in this area?
PLEASE   Very much .... □ 1
TICK   Quite a lot .... □ 2
ONE   Not very much ...... □ 3
BOX   Not at all .... □ 4

Q6. And summing up, how would you rate it as a (39)
place for a holiday?
PLEASE   Excellent .... □ 1
TICK   Good .... □ 2
ONE   Fair .... □ 3
BOX   Poor .... □ 4
            Bad .... □ 5

Q7. And overall, do you think this area is good (40)
value for money?
            Yes .... □ 1
            No .... □ 2

Figure 13.2   A questionnaire (*reproduced by courtesy of* Which? *magazine*)

Exercise 13b   You propose to do a census at your local car park to
assess the popularity of British cars compared with foreign rivals.
You wish to record separately British, German, Italian, French and
Japanese cars. All other cars will be classed as 'Other foreign'.
Draw up a census form to be used in the inquiry.

Exercise 13c   Draw up a questionnaire to be used in an inquiry
about student incomes. The inquiry proposes to discover how much

the average student has to live on each week, and what this income is spent on.

Exercise 13d   A fashion magazine proposes to do a census at a local youth centre about the colours preferred by young people. All members will be asked questions as follows:

(a)   If you could buy a completely new rigout for yourself, what colour would you choose?
(b)   If you were dating a member of the opposite sex for a day out next weekend, what colour would you like them to wear?

A note will also be made of the colour of the clothing the member is wearing at the time of the inquiry. Design a form which could be used to record the answers on the five-barred gate system.

13.5   Rounding data after collection

In statistics we are trying to present a picture of the matter under investigation which will be clear, simple to understand and as accurate as we can get it. From these points of view consider the following statistic: 'There are at present 17,265,171 drivers in the United Kingdom'.

What can we say about this statistic? Is it clear, and simple to understand? No, for the mind cannot really envisage it. Once you have 17 million drivers in your mind, it is not very easy to imagine another 265,171. Is it accurate? Here again we must reply 'No', for in fact every minute of the day someone dies, and others pass their driving tests and become 'drivers'. The figure of 17,265,171 is an example of what statisticians call 'spurious accuracy', we just cannot know if it is right.

For this reason, in statistics it is usual to 'round' numbers off to a stated degree of accuracy. In rounding we use the same rules we have already learned for rounding off decimal fractions. Anything over half-way rounds up to the next highest number; anything less than half rounds down to the lowest number. Thus

17,265,171 rounds down to 17 million
17,825,382 rounds up to 18 million
17,500,000, being exactly half way, is rounded to
make the next figure an even number,
i.e. 18 million

So a figure of 16,500,000 will be rounded down to 16 million, not rounded up to 17 million because 17 is an odd number.

Comprehension exercise on rounding

Round off the following figures to the nearest million pounds and rewrite the table in its new form.

Gross value of production in the United Kingdom, 19—

	£
Primary industries	12,766,654,264
Manufacturing	41,744,285,961
Building and construction	17,802,631,419
Service trades	39,185,423,367
Public services	38,354,500,000
Total	149,853,495,011

The numbers are to be rounded off to the nearest million. This means that the last six figures will be left out of the final table, but they may help us to decide whether we need to round 'up' or round 'down'.

Consider 'Primary industries'. The last six figures are 654,264, which is more than half a million − round up to £12,767 million.

Manufacturing: the last six figures are less than half a million − round down to £41,744 million.

Building and construction: 631,419 is more than half a million − round up to £17,803 million.

Service trades: 423,367 is less than half a million − round down to £39,185 million.

Public services: 500,000 is exactly half a million − round to make an *even number of millions* − so we round down to £38,354 million.

The new table will therefore read as follows:

Gross value of production in the United Kingdom, 19—

	£ millions
Primary industries	12,767
Manufacturing	41,744
Building and construction	17,803
Service trades	39,185
Public services	38,354
Total	149,853

Whenever we round numbers to a given degree of accuracy, we must introduce slight errors into the rounded figures. For example, compare the following addition sums:

Actual numbers	Rounded to nearest 10
31	30
37	40
45	40
113	110

Actual numbers	Rounded to nearest 10
31	30
37	40
46	50
114	120

In the second set of figures 114, when rounded to the nearest 10, comes to 110, but the sum of the rounded figures 30 + 40 + 50 = 120. This sort of total often finishes up with a small error, and we frequently find in statistical publications the phrase 'Totals do not agree because of rounding'.

13.6 Exercises on rounding

Exercise 13e An investigation into the enrolment at various secondary schools shows the following number of pupils enrolled:

School A	942	School B	886	School C	837	School D	1,142
School E	1,050	School F	1,829	School G	1,750	School H	1,632
School I	721	School J	882	School K	636	School L	1,945

Round the numbers off to the nearest 100 in each case and present the result in a table, in alphabetical order, i.e.

> *Pupils in Secondary Schools*
> School A =
> School B =
> etc.

Total the rounded figures at the end of the table.

Exercise 13f Output of a particular component by 10 trainee engineers is given as follows in units:

Mr A	27	Mr B	36	Miss C	45	Mr D	83

| Mr E | 13 | Miss F | 67 | Mr G | 59 | Mr H | 47 |
| Mr I | 32 | Mr J | 18 | | | | |

Round the outputs off to the nearest 10 units and present in a table in descending order in the form:

> Output per Trainee
> Mr D   80
> Miss F   ?
> etc.

Where two trainees have the same rounded output, place the one with the higher real output first.

Exercise 13g   Unofficial calculations for the population of the United Kingdom in three census years were as follows:

	Total	Males	Females
1961	52,809,231	25,525,760	27,283,471
1971	55,566,269	26,983,329	28,582,940
1981	55,930,088	27,201,326	28,728,762

It is decided to present these figures in millions, rounded off correct to one decimal place (e.g. 52.8 millions). Round the figures accordingly and present in a new table headed:

> *Population of the United Kingdom (millions)*

Exercise 13h   Tonnages of iron ore shipped from a port in Western Australia to Japan are given in the following monthly table:

	Tonnes		Tonnes		Tonnes
January	582,606	February	536,856	March	724,085
April	498,364	May	724,720	June	667,500
July	648,795	August	721,505	September	495,721
October	565,990	November	638,428	December	720,500

Round these off to the nearest 1,000 tonnes, and present them in a single-column table, totalled to give the shipments for the year. Head the table:

> *Iron Ore Shipments to Japan ('000 tonnes)*

Exercise 13i   Add the following numbers to find the total, then round the total off to the nearest thousand: 7,256 + 11,271 + 13,898 + 14,252 + 16,500 + 8,694.

Exercise 13j Subtract 275,840 from 385,279 and round the answer to the nearest hundred.

13.7 Classification of data

The problem with a statistical inquiry is that we finish up with a mass of data in a very disorganized form − files of completed census forms or questionnaires that have been answered. To present this data in a simple form we must first sort it out into a number of classes. This is called 'classification' of data.

Imagine an inquiry into the fishing industry that collects figures about the fish caught every day for every boat, from every port involved in fishing. There would soon be so many sheets of statistics, that rather than clarify the situation they would only confuse it. To reduce the huge amount of detail available, we must classify the catches into groups of similar or related items. For example, we might find that, of the fish landed, some were haddock, some cod, some mackerel, some herring, etc. It is useful to know how much of each type of fish has been caught. Therefore it would be in order to classify, i.e. group together, the species of fish caught. This also reduces the number of classes. Instead of each fish being an individual, there are only half-a-dozen or so classes for all the millions of fish caught. This makes the handling of the information much easier.

There are a few rules for classifying data, so that we know easily which class to put a particular item into. These are:

(a) *Classes should be few in number*. It is a mistake to have too many classes, for we have to compare them with one another, and this becomes difficult if there are too many of them.
(b) *There must be enough classes to include every item in the data*. Our fishing inquiry may prove that haddock, cod, mackerel and herring are the four chief classes but there will be hundreds of other fish caught, from tiny dabs to huge sharks. Usually we need a class called 'Other varieties' or some similar heading, so that the unusual items can be collected together.
(c) *Classes should not overlap*. If we classify fish by weight, and have classes 0−1 kg, 1−2 kg, 2−3 kg, etc., we shall not know where to classify a fish of exactly 1 kg. Does it go in Class 1, or Class 2? Does a fish of exactly 2 kg go in Class 2 or Class 3? To prevent this sort of overlapping, the classes should have been called

Class 1   Under 1 kg
Class 2   1 kg but under 2 kg
Class 3   2 kg but under 3 kg

Clearly now a 1 kg fish goes in Class 2, and a 2 kg fish goes in Class 3.

Comprehension exercise on data classification

A fishing port has five ships fishing one particular day in July. The catches were as follows:

Ship A   227 plaice, 346 herring, 2 skate, 4 conger eels, 27 soles.
Ship B   386 herring, 474 mackerel, 3 skate, 1 shark, 152 soles, 168 plaice.
Ship C   324 plaice, 486 herring, 286 mackerel, 3 crabs, 2 lobsters, 1 skate.
Ship D   284 herring, 362 mackerel, 42 soles, 4 skate.
Ship E   386 plaice, 998 mackerel, 4,284 herring, 2 skate, 48 soles.

Arrange these catches in classes.

Notes: Clearly we must have classes for plaice, herring, mackerel and soles. We might have a class for skate, since all ships caught some skate, but in view of the small numbers it seems hardly worthwhile. If we put these in a general class of 'Other fish and crustacea' we can put the crabs and lobsters in this class too.

Rough classification

Plaice	227 + 168 + 324 + 386	= 1,105
Herring	346 + 386 + 486 + 284 + 4,284	= 5,786
Mackerel	474 + 286 + 362 + 998	= 2,120
Soles	27 + 152 + 42 + 48	= 269
Other fish and crustacea	2 + 4 + 3 + 1 +	
	3 + 2 + 1 + 4 + 2	= 22
		9,302

Final classification
   Fish Caught by Westport Vessels: Friday 27 July

Herring	5,786
Mackerel	2,120
Plaice	1,105

Soles	269
Other fish and crustacea	22
	9,302

Placing them in this order is not necessary, but it clarifies which was the most common variety, etc.

13.8   Exercises in classification

Exercise 13k   A quality control department in an electric light-bulb factory tests every thousandth bulb to see how long it lasts. Twenty bulbs burn for the following lengths of time:

```
41 hours; 475 hours;  38 hours;   276 hours;  11 hours
139   „ ; 438   „ ; 786   „ ; 1,726   „ ; 274   „
286   „ ;  72   „ ; 149   „ ;   325   „ ; 721   „
 17   „ ; 5 minutes; 285   „ ;   486   „ ;  49   „
```

It is decided to classify these into five groups: (a) under 100 hours; (b) 100−249 hours; (c) 250−499 hours; (d) 500−749 hours; (e) 750 hours and over.

Using the five-barred gate system record the data in the groups and then write out the five classes showing how many in each class. What does the data tell you about the quality of these light bulbs?

Exercise 13l   Recruits to the armed forces are weighed on joining the service. The weights in kg are as follows for 30 recruits:

70 kg	68 kg	81 kg	72 kg	71 kg
64 kg	71 kg	65 kg	69 kg	60 kg
78 kg	78 kg	76 kg	71 kg	66 kg
74 kg	75 kg	70 kg	72 kg	59 kg
59 kg	64 kg	72 kg	76 kg	73 kg
68 kg	67 kg	69 kg	85 kg	71 kg

Group them into classes as follows: (a) under 60 kg; (b) 60 kg but under 65 kg; (c) 65 kg but under 70 kg; (d) 70 kg but under 75 kg; (e) 75 kg but under 80 kg; (f) 80 kg and over.

Use the five-barred gate system to allocate the recruits to classes and then write out the list of classes showing the numbers in each class. What does this tell you about the weight of recruits?

Exercise 13m The wages paid to 30 hotel staff in a year are given as follows in £ sterling:

11,785	12,250	23,860	12,540	13,275
13,060	12,036	8,570	8,250	8,500
4,600	6,285	13,160	3,850	12,900
4,050	13,850	12,350	11,985	13,760
13,658	12,950	4,175	13,125	24,250
7,250	4,850	4,145	12,360	14,350

Arrange them in six classes: (a) under £5,000; (b) £5,000−£7,499; (c) £7,500−£9,999; (d) £10,000−£12,499; (e) £12,500−£14,999; (f) £15,000 and over, using the five-barred gate system. Then write out a table showing the numbers in each class.

Exercise 13n The ages in completed years of blood donors at a blood transfusion centre on a particular morning were as follows:

21	27	36	23	42	56	64
22	20	25	26	31	25	36
63	27	22	56	24	47	64
30	64	29	21	43	36	40
28	37	42	43	33	49	38
54	36	63	48	22	27	24
28	29	30	55	52	23	46

One further donor was aged 62. Classify these donors into age groups, 5 years to a group, starting with the group aged 20− 24 years.

13.9 Tabulation

After data has been classified, the results must usually be made available to those interested in some suitable presentation. One of the simplest methods of presentation is in tabular form; the data are presented in a table that sets out clearly the results of the inquiry. Countless tables are published in official publications such as the *United Kingdom Monthly Digest of Statistics*, the *Annual Abstract of Statistics*, the *Balance of Payments Pink Book* and the *National Income and Expenditure Blue Book*.

When presenting tables, it is usual to follow the lay-out given in Figure 13.3 and described in the notes below it. Table 13.2 then shows a typical table.

1 TITLE

2 Class Description	3 Column Headings
4 Row Headings	5 Data
	6 Totals

7 Footnotes

8 Source notes

Figure 13.3   A general plan for tabular presentation

Notes

(i)   A table should always have a clear title, which states exactly what the information within the table sets out to show.

(ii)   Unless it is obvious, the left-hand column heading will describe what is listed in the column below. For example, a table of industrial production might indicate at the top 'Type of Industry', and below this heading the various industries would be listed.

(iii)   The columns of statistics under scrutiny should have clear column headings indicating what the columns represent.

(iv)   Row headings for the collected data should be listed in the left-hand column.

(v)   The data themselves should appear at (5), ordered according to the information which it is desired to extract.

(vi)   Any totals necessary should be presented.

(vii)   Footnotes, which explain variations or points of importance, should be given immediately below the table.

(viii) Sources should be given where the origin of the table is some other set of published statistics, and acknowledgements should be made if necessary.

Table 13.2 Membership of
working-men's clubs

Membership	Number of clubs
Under 200	68
200−499	185
500−999	1,027
1,000−1,499	130
1,500−1,999	27
Over 2,000	10
Total	1,447

Footnote: Working-men's clubs are
those excluding variety clubs.
Source Note: Workers' Gazette,
Issue 2079.

13.10 Simple tables

The rules of tabulation outlined in Section 13.9 above are easily
applied to some sets of data, since by their nature they are uncom-
plicated and easy to handle. For example, the tabulation of the
following catches of fish in a United Kingdom port for 1−7 October
does not present any difficulties: Sunday, 187 kg; Monday, 2,008 kg;
Tuesday, 2,775 kg; Wednesday, 1,090 kg; Thursday, 2,050 kg; Friday,
1,720 kg; Saturday, 1,928 kg. Table 13.3 is a simple way of presenting
this information more effectively (see page 258).

13.11 Exercises: simple tabulation

Exercise 13o Gas consumption in millions of therms is given as
follows in a report of a nationalized body: 1st quarter, 6,197; 2nd
quarter, 4,611; 3rd quarter, 3,882; 4th quarter, 9,639. Present this
information in tabular form to bring out the total annual consumption.

Exercise 13p The following information from an agricultural research
project refers to: (a) cows and heifers in milk; (b) cows in calf but
not in milk; (c) heifers in calf with first calf; (d) bulls; (e) all other
cattle and calves. Present the data, given in thousands, to show the
information in tabular form, and the total of this type of livestock.
The figures are:
  (a) 8,756; (b) 1,218; (c) 889; (d) 48; (e) 12,726.

Table 13.3 Catches of fish,
1–7 October

Day	Weight caught (kg)
Sunday	187
Monday	2,008
Tuesday	2,775
Wednesday	1,090
Thursday	2,050
Friday	1,720
Saturday	1,928
Total	11,758

Exercise 13q A trade journal gives the following figures for sales of floor coverings: (a) refers to carpets and rugs and (b) to linoleum and plastics. You are asked to round off the figures in each case to thousands of square metres, and present them in a table showing the sales of each type, the total quarterly sales and the total annual sales. The figures are: 1st quarter, (a) 38,474,353 square metres, (b) 19,284,852 square metres; 2nd quarter, (a) 37,891,453 square metres, (b) 16,658,391 square metres; 3rd quarter, (a) 41,884,723 square metres, (b) 14,686,948 square metres; 4th quarter, (a) 38,816,849 square metres, (b) 24,326,824 square metres.

Exercise 13r Exports are listed in five categories. These are (a) foods, beverages and tobacco; (b) fuels; (c) industrial materials; (d) finished manufactures; (e) Other transactions. You are asked to round the figures off to the nearest £m and present them in tabular form for Year 1 and Year 2 to bring out the annual totals. The figures are: (a) Year 1 £3,094,276,153, Year 2 £4,993,463,218; (b) Year 1 £1,724,858,300, Year 2 £5,652,721,494; (c) Year 1 £6,239,434,721, Year 2 £8,738,346,829; (d) Year 1 £4,174,059,628, Year 2 £6,386,995,240; (e) Year 1 £424,736,284, Year 2 £595,106,396.

13.12 More complex tables

Simple tables of the type described above appear every day in newspapers and magazines. A more advanced type of table presents the simple material in tabular form, but then adds further statistics calculated from the simple statistics. These are called **derived statistics** because they are derived from the original data. They often take the form of averages, or percentages. Consider the following example.

Comprehension exercise on more complex tables

The 400 candidates in a particular examination were awarded marks as follows: 17 achieved more than 90 per cent, 24 were given marks between 81 per cent and 90 per cent; 42 were in the group 71−80, 108 in the 61−70 group and 18 in the 51−60 group; 128 scored marks between 41 and 50, 38 had marks in the 31−40 group and 25 scored 30 or less marks. Show these marks in tabular form, and also the percentage of candidates in each group of marks. See Table 13.4.

Note: Since there are 400 candidates the percentage of each group is found as follows, using the 'over 90' group as an example: 17 students out of 400 were in this group. As a percentage this is:

$$\frac{17}{400} \times 100$$

$$= \frac{17}{4} \times 1 \qquad \text{(cancelling by 100)}$$

$$= 4.25\%$$

In fact, each of the numbers of candidates, when divided by 4, gives us the percentage of candidates, in this simple example.

Table 13.4 Examination results

Marks out of 100	Number of candidates	Percentage of candidates
Over 90	17	4.25
81−90	24	6.0
71−80	42	10.5
61−70	108	27.0
51−60	18	4.5
41−50	128	32.0
31−40	38	9.5
30 or less	25	6.25
Total	400	100.0

13.13 Cumulative frequency tables

Table 13.4 exemplifies what is sometimes called a 'frequency distribution', because it shows how frequently an item of a particular size appears in the statistics. It is sometimes helpful to have a 'cumulative frequency' column, as shown in the comprehension exercise below.

Comprehension exercise on cumulative frequency tables

Here the examining body may have a policy which says that only half the candidates at most can be allowed to pass the examinations and become fully qualified. Where does this point occur? Rewriting the table, with extra columns, to give both the cumulative frequency and the cumulative percentages, we have Table 13.5.

Since only half the candidates (200) or 50 per cent are to be allowed to qualify the pass mark must be somewhere in the 51−60 mark range: 9 out of the 18 candidates in this range are to be allowed to pass, so the pass mark will be decided by looking at the distribution of marks in this group.

13.14   Exercises on more complex tables

Exercise 13s   A professional organization has 10,000 candidates sitting for its final examinations. Of these 3 scored 100 per cent, 195 scored 90−99 per cent, 286 scored 80−89 per cent, 894 scored 70−79 per cent, 1,859 scored 60−69 per cent, 1,956 scored 50−59 per cent, 2,553 scored 40−49 per cent and 2,250 scored less than 40 per cent. Four candidates were taken ill and their cases will be reviewed separately. Arrange these figures in a table showing the

Table 13.5   Examination results

Marks out of 100	Frequency	Cumulative frequency	Percentage of candidates	Cumulative percentage
over 90	17	17	4.25	4.25
81−90	24	41	6.0	10.25
71−80	42	83	10.5	20.75
61−70	108	191	27.0	47.75
51−60	18	209	4.5	52.25
41−50	128	337	32.0	84.25
31−40	38	375	9.5	93.75
30 or less	25	400	6.25	100.0
Total	400	400	100.0	100.0

numbers of students in each group, and the percentage of candidates in each group (correct to one decimal place).

Exercise 13t Weekly turnover for 40 shops in a pedestrian precinct is found to be as below. Arrange these in a table using classes of under £2,500, £2,500−4,999, £5,000−7,499, £7,500−9,999 and £10,000 or over. Also show in your table the percentage of shops in each group (correct to one decimal place). Turnover (£):

240	346	7,215	6,584	989	2,100
1,370	1,475	4,800	17,250	5,500	4,975
2,650	3,800	2,980	7,500	15,900	2,950
1,880	4,860	13,500	3,350	1,925	3,290
3,450	4,940	8,500	1,820	4,375	17,000
1,224	25,000	4,950	1,840	32,000	1,775
2,960	1,700	1,416	7,790		

Exercise 13u The wages (in £s) paid to 50 women in a factory in a particular week are given as follows:

65	70	185	108	215
150	78	84	190	105
175	130	136	72	95
210	112	210	200	145
220	160	90	100	142
90	170	155	195	165
80	220	224	65	182
145	120	170	172	149
170	200	175	220	175
195	195	82	170	85

Group the data into seven classes starting with the £50−£74 group, and rising in bands of £25. Then present the results in tabular form, including the percentage of women in each wage group. Why would it be wrong to specify classes as £50−£75, £75−£100, etc.?

Exercise 13v An earnings survey reveals that earnings (in £s) per hour in a certain works were as shown below. You are asked to present the information as a table grouped into eight classes, starting with the £51−£75 class and rising in £25 steps. Include in your table a cumulative frequency column.

| 55 | 76 | 170 | 140 | 128 |
| 100 | 140 | 250 | 130 | 155 |

180	110	165	80	165
195	145	195	190	85
120	125	172	70	150
115	170	95	160	125
145	210	110	174	190
170	90	185	185	230
205	115	200	172	105
105	240	235	110	215

13.15   Planning the report

We shall need more statistical work later when we come to writing the report. First, a word about planning the report. As the data and information about the problem become available, we begin to think about the eventual presentation of this data, the conclusions to which it is leading, and the recommendations we shall need to make.

The analysis of the data is a process of selecting appropriate material for the report and bringing it into correct sequence for presentation. Team discussions will gradually lead to firm conclusions about the matter in hand, but the word 'gradually' is important. It is necessary for someone to play 'devil's advocate' and delay the decision process by arguing against the line of the argument that is in favour of a particular conclusion, so that the case in favour has to be fully justified and the possibility of error reduced. The balance of the evidence has to be clearly in favour of the conclusion arrived at, especially if someone's reputation is at stake.

Circumstantial evidence is evidence which tends to support a particular conclusion because the train of known facts is difficult to explain in any other way. At the same time it is not clear proof, and it is always possible that later evidence will provide an alternative explanation. The report may need to give both sides of the argument, and any attempt to report without revealing the doubts that do exist in the matter is a form of bias, and wholly undesirable.

Arrangement of the evidence in a logical order for presentation is vital if the report is to be effective. The sequence might follow the outline given below:

(a)   The terms of reference of the investigating team, and its composition.
(b)   An outline of the problem.
(c)   A detailed account of the way the problem was handled. What lines of inquiry were pursued; who took charge of each and what was the *modus operandi* in each case.

(d) The conclusions arrived at from each line of inquiry and the bearing they had on the whole problem.

(e) The general conclusions drawn, and the reasons why they were arrived at. The reasons why possible alternative conclusions were rejected.

(f) The recommendations made.

(g) The systematic arrangement of all the evidence in the form of appendices so that it is available for inspection and analysis by any interested parties.

All this requires quite careful planning, and leads on to the actual writing of the report, which is dealt with in Chapter 14 after a further section on statistical presentation of data.

13.16   More spellings

Here are two further lists of words. Ask a fellow student to test you on the first set and then reciprocate by testing him/her on the second set.

Secretarial practice		*Business administration*	
consult	confer	depart	receive
consultant	conference	department	reception
consultancy	conferring	departmental	foyer
organize	prior	caretaking	telephone
organizer	priority	maintain	intercom
organization	*a priori*	maintenance	paging
modem	collate	canteen	merge
transceiver	collator	refreshments	amalgamation
fibre-optics	salutation	chauffeurs	takeover
network	subscription	messengers	absorption

13.17   Figures of speech: personification

Personification is a figure of speech in which an inanimate object or an emotion or powerful force is given human form, either male or female. Often the humanity is emphasized by giving the thing personified a capital letter. Examples are:

(a) Death lays his icy hand on kings.

(b) Comes the blind Fury, with the abhorred shears and slits the thin-spun life.

(c)   Be England what she will
      With all her faults, she is my country still.

Personification is not much used perhaps in business English, and where it might be used, it would just as well be avoided. To write, as journalists often do, 'the blockade is bringing the people to Famine's verge' is excessively literary, when what the journalist means is that 'the people are being reduced to the verge of famine'.

13.18   Answer section

Exercises 13a to 13d   No numerical answers required.

Exercise 13e   140 hundreds.

Exercise 13f   The correct order is D, F, G, H, C, B, I, A, J, E.

Exercise 13g   52.8, 25.5, 27.3; 55.6, 27.0, 28.6; 55.9, 27.2, 28.7.

Exercise 13h   7,526,000 tonnes.

Exercise 13i   72,000.

Exercise 13j   109,400.

Exercise 13k   (a) 7, (b) 2, (c) 8, (d) 1, (e) 2; the data tell us the quality is rather erratic, and even then tend to be biased towards a short life for the light bulbs.

Exercise 13l   (a) 2, (b) 3, (c) 7, (d) 11, (e) 5, (f) 2; this tells us the weights of recruits are chiefly clustered around the 65−75 range, with a slight bias to heavier weights than light weights.

Exercise 13m   The numbers in the groups are (a) 6; (b) 2; (c) 3; (d) 6; (e) 11; (f) 2.

Exercise 13n   The numbers in the groups are (a) 10; (b) 10; (c) 4; (d) 6; (e) 5; (f) 4; (g) 2; (h) 3; (i) 6.

Exercise 13o   24,329 million therms.

Exercise 13p   23,637 thousand animals.

Exercise 13q   Grand total 232,024 thousand square metres.

Exercise 13r   Year 1 £15,657 m, Year 2 £26,366 m.

Exercise 13s   Percentages after correction are as follows: 0; 2.0; 2.9; 8.9; 18.6; 19.6; 25.5; 22.5; 0.

Exercise 13t   Groups total 14, 14, 3, 3, 6 respectively. Percentages 35; 35; 7.5; 7.5; 15.

Exercise 13u   Percentages = 8; 16; 10; 12; 18; 18 and 18 respectively. It would be incorrect to specify classes as £50−£75, £75−£100 etc., because uncertainty creeps in about which group certain items should be entered in, i.e. £75 might be in either of the groups named above.

Exercise 13v   Cumulative table reads 2, 8, 18, 25, 35, 43, 46, 50.

14
Report writing 2: The body of the report

14.1 Analysing the evidence

Having conducted the investigation, we come to the important task of analysing the evidence. As we consider the various sections of the report, and as we summarize the conclusions at the end of each section, we begin to develop what will eventually be our conclusions and recommendations. Certain pieces of the evidence will be found to have major importance. It is usual to collate these significant contributions, leaving other less essential parts to remain as part of the background material. The major items will eventually be presented at the very least as a file of important data. In important investigations they might be bound as a reference book to accompany the published report.

It is important to find the right balance of evidence, so that you can point clearly to it as the reason for your conclusions and recommendations. If there is any doubt in the matter, the adverse evidence should not be suppressed but highlighted. What your recommendations are based on in such a case is a balance of probabilities, in which you reject the evidence pointing the other way as being less likely than your preferred conclusions.

The next stage is to arrange the information in its most logical sequence, so that your report is well-constructed. The reader wants a simple account of a complex matter, one which brings out the important points in correct order and reaches a set of logical conclusions.

This planning stage enables the actual report to be written convincingly and without hesitation. It has all been thought through and discussed in detail among the team to ensure that nothing has been overlooked. Someone has played 'devil's advocate' and presented arguments of a 'what if' sort — to enable the whole team to participate in discussing the evidence, and hammer out a common set of conclusions. If a report is steam-rollered through by a team leader who has a strong personality, it is highly likely it will eventually arouse controversy and may be accused of being a 'whitewash'.

14.2 The structure of the report

The usual structure of a report is as follows:

(a) The title page.
(b) The table of contents.
(c) The summary.
(d) The introduction.
(e) The body of the report.
(f) The conclusions.
(g) The recommendations.
(h) The appendices (if any).
(i) Acknowledgements.
(j) References and bibliography.
(k) An index.

Although this is the final structure, it cannot be written in this order. The title page, the table of contents and the summary are usually written at the end, because the main thing is to write the report – these other items are only part of the general presentation. It may seem strange to have a summary at the front of the report, but it is a fact that many people will not want to read the whole report. They will want a quick breakdown of the subject matter, the conclusions drawn and the recommendations made. The body of the report can be read by those (usually lower level) staff who have to implement the recommendations. The board of a company, for example, will only want to know the bare bones of the matter, on which decisions have to be made.

14.3 The style and tone of the report

By the word 'style' we mean the type of language we use to convey to the reader the information we are imparting. As with all business correspondence, a report is a permanent, tangible record of a business relationship. It almost certainly has legal implications, by which we mean that it can be produced in a court of law if necessary as evidence that we have acted in a proper manner, after careful consideration of all aspects of the matter that is the subject of dispute.

The vocabulary will be appropriate to the subject matter, and couched in clear, relatively simple sentences. We shall not use a long word if a short word will do, or an abstruse expression if there is a simple one available. In one of his books Charles Dickens describes the Circumlocution Office – a government department that never used a simple word if it could find a difficult one or a straightforward procedure if a roundabout method could be developed. Good style requires us to avoid circumlocution like the plague.

Good style requires us to use a nice variety of sentence structures. Too many simple sentences give a staccato effect, but at the same time long and intricate compound–complex sentences, with many subordinate clauses, are undesirable. The tone of the report should be impersonal and formal. It is usual to use the passive voice, which places the emphasis on the activities that have been carried out rather than on the persons who performed the activities. Thus, we might say 'The fire was brought under control' rather than 'We extinguished the fire'. This is particularly true of scientific reports, where the research conducted is always described impersonally – an account of what was done. It is considered bad form to adopt a more personal style, with its implications of inordinate cleverness on the part of the researcher.

14.4   The introduction to the report

A report should always be formal in its approach, as befits any matter that is to be circulated to interested parties and become a matter of private, or even public, record. Many reports are made available to the press, and as such are liable to be commented upon by journalists, editors and the general public. It is easy enough for them to be misunderstood, or misinterpreted, or even misrepresented deliberately, as those who read the daily papers regularly will soon discover. The best way to avoid such problems is to be formal in one's approach, to write carefully, choosing one's words and proving the content of the report, stage by stage, to establish its authenticity.

The introductory stages are as follows:

(a)   The report should have a clear title, which is self-explanatory.
(b)   It should be addressed to the person or the body that commissioned the report, and if necessary say by what authority they appointed the panel giving the report.
(c)   It should bear the name of the individual submitting the report or the chairperson of the committee responsible for its production. The names of other members of the committee should be listed and any special capacities shown.
(d)   Unless it is a routine report, the terms of reference should be given. This is sometimes done as part of the salutation, as shown in the specimen introduction in Figure 14.1.
(e)   It would be usual to date the report to fix its publication clearly at a particular point in time, since it will almost certainly be archived eventually, and referred to, possibly many years later.

Figure 14.1   A typical introduction to a report (*see opposite*)

Accident at the Leigh Bridge Road
Depot on 1 February 19..

Publication date
12 March 19..

To Charles Ratcliffe Esq
The Chairman
Leigh Bridge Petroleum PLC
City Offices
Threadneedle St
London
EC2 8PR

From Peter Marshall Personnel Officer on behalf of the
ad hoc committee appointed by the Board of Directors.

Members of the Committee, besides the Personnel Office.

Terence Banks — Co. Secretary
Mary Larkin — Trade Union Representative
Frank Larch — Transport Manager
Joan Thirkettle — Head of Secretarial Department

Sir,
We were appointed on 13 March 19.. to
investigate the fire at the Leigh Bridge Road Depot, in the
plastics division, with the following terms of reference:

1 To determine the course of events which led to the
   fire.
2 To investigate the actions taken at the time to limit
   the outbreak and to ensure the safety of personnel.
3 To determine to what extent these efforts were, or
   were not, adequate and
4 To make recommendations which would prevent any
   repetition.

The committee began by interviewing all those
who should have been on-site at the time of the fire, and
considering what they normally did on the site, and what
they actually did on that particular day. We questioned
them closely about any non-normal circumstances.
Much of this evidence is referred to in the report, and
appears as signed statements in the various appendices.
We went to considerable trouble to consult with
the various public services about the incident as seen
from their points of view, and these discussions assisted
us greatly in arriving at our conclusions and making our
recommendations.
We have to report as follows:

A typical introduction might look something like the introduction given in Figure 14.1.

Exercise 14a   Getting started on a report

1   You have been appointed chairperson of an *ad hoc* committee to consider the proposals for the use of a piece of waste land owned by your company. The possible uses are (a) as an extension to the car park, (b) as a site for a creche for nursery age children of employees, (c) as a leisure recreation centre for employees and (d) for a new pumping house.

   Draw up the title page and introduction to this report, inventing such names or other information as seem necessary.

2   You are a security guard in charge of industrial premises. Last night you detained an intruder aged 14, who was leaving the premises through a broken window carrying one of the company's microcomputers. The 'boy', who proved to be a girl, was actually detained by your guard dog, who nipped her slightly. She had to have one stitch and some injections at the local hospital. Write an account of the incident, making up such details as you need.

3   You are a senior judge of the High Court who has been appointed to hold a public inquiry into parental charges of abuse of their rights by social workers acting on reports of child abuse by non-interested parties, i.e. neighbours, etc. Draw up a list of aspects of the problem about which you might feel it was necessary to collect evidence.

14.5   The body of the report

We now come to the main body of the report. It depends upon the subject matter of the investigation, but we may envisage the following possible components of the report:

(a)   A description of the situation at the time the investigation began. Without going into enormous detail, we must set the scene by mentioning the most important features of the events. In the circumstances described in the introduction (Figure 14.1) we need a brief account of the fire, how serious it was, who was affected, how long it took to bring it under control and what was the impact upon production, distribution, etc.

(b)   We then move on to deal with the matters raised in our terms of reference and to give a factual account of the events leading to the fire. It may be that a combination of circumstances had led to an excessive concentration of hazardous materials at the site. It could have been a spillage of some material, or an accident. For example, one big fire recently was caused by a forklift truck driver who had a heart attack, and the forks of his runaway vehicle pierced a drum of inflammable solvent. In all such incidents there is the possibility of a cover-up, not only to protect individuals but possibly for the sake of public relations generally. Yet if the true circumstances are not discovered and reported properly, a similar incident may occur at a later date (not necessarily at the same site). Investigations do not just result in changes on-site but in improved practices nationally and internationally. The redesign of equipment, for example, may result.

(c)   If a report is the result of an investigation requiring the collection of statistical data, as outlined in Chapter 13, it may be necessary to use some form of pictorial representation. This lightens the report and makes it easier to follow. It is convenient at this point to look at some methods of pictorial representation.

14.6   Pictorial representation of statistical data

It is generally accepted that pictures, diagrams and graphs are convenient methods of conveying simple ideas of a statistical nature, even to those who are largely uninterested in statistics as a science. Frequent use of pictures, diagrams and graphs is made on television, in the press and in magazines to pass on information relating to the cost of living, the level of unemployment, the cost of building society mortgages, etc. Many reports call for this kind of illustration.

This section deals with some of the more regularly used pictures and diagrams, while the slightly more complicated matter of graphs forms the subject of Section 14.7.

Pictograms

Pictograms are the simplest pictorial representations. Simple outline figures are used to represent quantities or values. For example, if the statistics relate to the changing level of unemployment over 10 years, the pictogram could be drawn as a number of human outlines, each one representing a given level of registered unemployed. Similarly, Figure 14.2 illustrates the population of developing countries by income groups, with each human figure representing 100 million people.

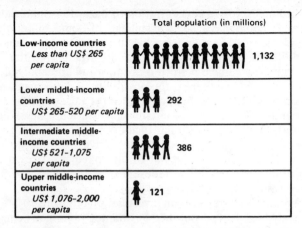

Figure 14.2   Developing countries: population by income groups (*reproduced by courtesy of Finance and Development*)

Exercise 14b   Pictograms

1   The following data have to be displayed in pictorial form. Choose an appropriate symbol and draw a pictogram.

	Colour television sets in use in United Kingdom (thousands)
1966	0
1971	500
1976	9,500
1981	14,000
1986	16,500
1991	18,100

2   The volume of traffic can be measured by discovering the number of vehicles per mile of roads. A comparison of traffic densities in a number of countries produced the following results:

Country	Number of vehicles per road-mile
United Kingdom	61
West Germany	51
Netherlands	51
Italy	49
Belgium	36
France	26
Sweden	20

Using a motor vehicle as a symbol to represent every 10 cars, draw a pictogram to illustrate the set of statistics.

3 The profits of a famous bank are used as follows:

How the profits were used.	£m
Taxation payable	133
Dividends to shareholders	23
Minority shareholders	12
Kept in reserves	100
	£m268

Using piles of pennies as your symbol, illustrate how many pence in each £1 are used for each of these purposes.

4 Using a road sign directing traffic to the M1 motorway as your symbol, with each road sign standing for 500 kilometres of motorway, draw a pictogram to illustrate the growth of motorways as shown in table below.

Motorway growth in the United Kingdom (kilometres)

1965	600
1970	1,200
1975	2,100
1980	2,500
1985	2,900
1990	3,200

(*Source: Annual Abstract of Statistics*)

Bar charts

Bar charts seek to relate information to the horizontal or vertical length of a bar or thick line. They are of two main types: those which compare statistics for a given period of time and those which compare them over a succession of periods.

For example, in Figure 14.3 an ice-cream firm has investigated the popularity of different flavours of ice-cream by collecting statistics about the value of sales in a given week in one particular seaside resort. The statistics collected and presented in a bar chart in this way might lead to a decision to reduce the variety of flavours offered, or to an advertising campaign to promote less popular flavours. The preparation of such a chart presents a few problems, including:

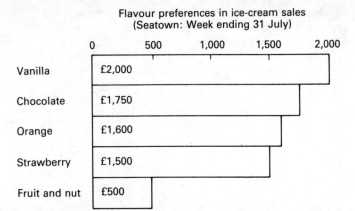

Figure 14.3 A bar chart

(a) *Scale.* Choose a scale that enables the graphics designer to represent the data clearly on the size of paper to be used.
(b) *Length of bar.* The length of bar in each case must be calculated to represent the correct fraction of the full scale chosen. Thus the £1,750 bar in Figure 14.3 must be $\dfrac{1,750}{2,000} = \dfrac{7}{8}$ of the length of the longest bar.
(c) *Shading, colour, etc.* In some bar charts it might be desirable to pick out the bars in particular cross-hatchings or colours to present a clearer picture.
(d) *Title, source details, etc.* A suitable title, explanation of source material and date or dates (if required) should be added to the diagram, and the lettering and layout should be stylish and well-presented.

In Figure 14.4 the vertical bar chart shown gives a clear indication of the number of vehicles in use in Great Britain over the given time range.

Percentage bar charts

A percentage bar chart is one in which the total body of statistics collected (100 per cent) is divided up into its component parts to show each part *as a percentage of the whole*. This is most useful where the total set of statistics has some special significance. This special method of presentation is often used in profit statements to show how the profits made have been allocated. For example, of

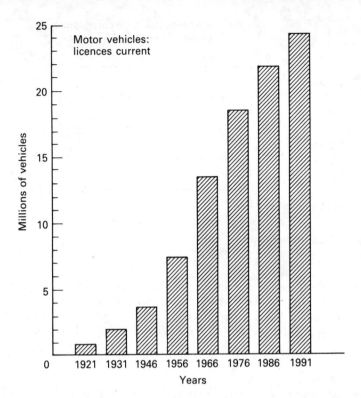

Figure 14.4 A vertical bar chart: vehicles in use in Great Britain 1921–91

each £1 of profit it might be that 33 p. went in corporation tax, 18 p. to ordinary shareholders, 8 p. to preference shareholders, 5 p. to minority shareholders, and 36 p. into general reserves. Such a set of statistics could easily be displayed on a percentage bar chart.

In Figure 14.5 the annual expenditure of an average household is broken down into its percentage component elements of expenditure.

Exercise 14c   *Bar charts*

1   In 4 years the investment funds used by United Kingdom companies were obtained from the following sources:

	Profits ploughed back (£m)	Bank borrowing (£m)	Overseas borrowing (£m)	Other (£m)
Year 1	4,000	1,000	1,000	500
Year 2	5,000	3,000	2,000	500

Item	£	% (to nearest 0.5%)
Food	3,675	41
Housing	1,125	12.5
Heat and light	900	10
Transport	900	10
Entertainment	450	5
Clothes	450	5
Other	1,500	16.5
Total	9,000	100

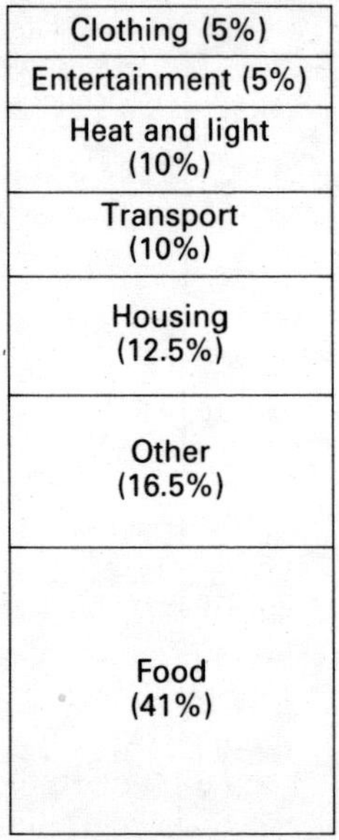

Clothing (5%)
Entertainment (5%)
Heat and light (10%)
Transport (10%)
Housing (12.5%)
Other (16.5%)
Food (41%)

Figure 14.5 A percentage bar chart: annual expenditure of an average household in the UK

| Year 3 | 7,000 | 5,000 | 3,000 | 1,000 |
| Year 4 | 8,000 | 4,000 | 3,500 | 2,000 |

Draw a vertical bar diagram to illustrate the figures, and show the total invested in each of the 4 years.

2 Figures for a year's world fibre output in millions of tonnes were as follows:

Country or bloc	Natural fibre	Man-made fibre
United Kingdom	0.5	1.0
Other West Europe	1.5	2.0
USA	1.5	3.5
Former Communist bloc	2.0	5.0
Third World	3.5	4.5

Draw a bar chart to illustrate these outputs. Use shading or colours to distinguish natural and man-made fibres.

3 Reductions in pupil−teacher ratios are shown in the following table. Draw a bar chart to illustrate the changes.

Pupils per teacher in primary schools
(England and Wales only)

Year	Number of pupils per teacher
1921	48
1931	43.5
1951	39
1961	36
1971	31.5
1981	27

(*Note*: In 1941 wartime disruption prevented the collection of statistics.)

4   A multinational company selling soft drinks made 'profits' of £350 million last year. Of this £175 million was used to pay its employees; £43.75 million was taken by the government as taxation; £77 million was paid in interest and dividends to those who provided the company's capital; and the rest was reinvested in new plant, etc. Calculate those parts as a percentage of the total and draw a percentage bar chart to illustrate the statistics.

Histograms

These are diagrams that display frequency distributions. Here a vertical block is drawn to represent each class interval. Provided the horizontal scales are equal, i.e. the blocks are of equal width, the height of each of the blocks is able to represent the frequency.

The greater the frequency of the group, the higher the block. Where class intervals are equal, as in Figure 14.6, the width of the block is immaterial so long as all are the same width and may be chosen to suit the space available. The rules for drawing a histogram with uniform class intervals are as follows:

(a)   Select a width of class interval that is appropriate for the size of paper to be used and the number of rectangles (class intervals) to be drawn. The class intervals will be marked along the horizontal axis and the frequency per class interval up the vertical axis.

(b)   At the midpoint of each class interval mark in a height above the horizontal axis which is proportional to the frequency of that particular class interval. Draw a horizontal line at this height equal to the width of the class interval.

(c)   Now draw in the sides of the rectangles by joining up the ends of these lines to the horizontal axis. The result is a series of

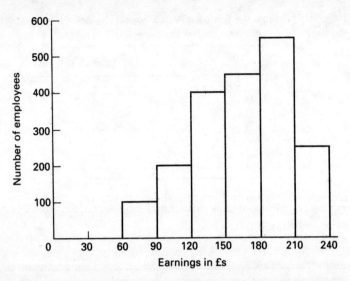

Figure 14.6   A histogram: weekly earnings of engineering apprentices and craftsmen

adjacent rectangles. The areas of the rectangles are proportional to the frequencies of their respective classes. In this particular case we can see that the total earnings are represented by the total area of the histogram.

Exercise 14d   Histograms

1   Employees' wages in the New Town area are shown below for the first week in June. Draw a histogram to illustrate the data.

Class range	Percentage of population with earnings in the group
£80 and under £120	4.5
£120 and under £160	7.5
£160 and under £200	15.5
£200 and under £240	20.0
£240 and under £280	34.0
£280 and under £320	12.0
£320 and under £360	5.0
£360 and under £400	1.5
	100.0

2 Property values in Seatown were found to be as follows in a survey:

Price range	Number in class
£20,000 and under £40,000	250
£40,000 and under £60,000	3,500
£60,000 and under £80,000	4,500
£80,000 and under £100,000	3,500
£100,000 and under £120,000	1,750
£120,000 and under £140,000	125

Draw a histogram to illustrate these statistics.

3 The price of motor vehicles sold by a distributor in one year were as follows:

Price	Number in class
£4,000 and under £6,000	360
£6,000 and under £8,000	400
£8,000 and under £10,000	440
£10,000 and under £12,000	160
£12,000 and under £14,000	120
£14,000 and under £16,000	80
£16,000 and under £18,000	60

Draw a histogram to illustrate the data.

4 Cattle auctioned in a country market fetched the following prices:

Price range	Number in class
£80–£99.99	120
£100–£119.99	150
£120–£139.99	75
£140–£159.99	250
£160–£179.99	130
£180–£199.99	35

Draw a histogram to illustrate this data.

Pie charts

One of the simplest methods to represent the way in which a whole statistical collection breaks down into its component parts is to use the 'pie' diagram. A pie is a circular culinary delicacy, and we are familiar from childhood with the advantages to be enjoyed by securing a larger slice of pie than other members of the family. The pie chart depicts the component parts of any set of statistical data as slices of pie.

The complete circle represents the whole set of data. Any subdivisions within the set are then shown by subdividing the circle in proportion. Consider Figure 14.7.

The keys to the pie chart show the wealth and the liabilities of the UK personal sector, in percentage terms. The actual figures are:

Wealth   £1,126,900,000,000
Liabilities   £440,300,000,000

To turn these figures into a pie chart, we have to decide how much

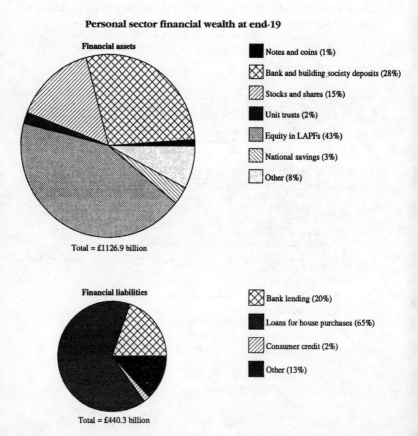

Personal sector financial wealth at end-19

Financial assets

- Notes and coins (1%)
- Bank and building society deposits (28%)
- Stocks and shares (15%)
- Unit trusts (2%)
- Equity in LAPFs (43%)
- National savings (3%)
- Other (8%)

Total = £1126.9 billion

Financial liabilities

- Bank lending (20%)
- Loans for house purchases (65%)
- Consumer credit (2%)
- Other (13%)

Total = £440.3 billion

Figure 14.7 The wealth and liabilities of UK persons (not firms) (*courtesy of HM Treasury Bulletin*)

of the circle (360°) should be allocated to each type of wealth (or liability). For example:

Notes and coins = 1 per cent = $\frac{1}{100} \times 360°$

$$= \underline{3.6°}$$

Bank and building-society deposits = 28 per cent

$$= \frac{28}{100} \times 360°$$

$$= \underline{\underline{100.8°}}$$

In Figure 14.7 therefore the slices have been drawn with 3.6° for 'Notes and coins' and 100.8° for 'Bank and building-society deposits'.
You should now try one or two of the exercises below.

Exercise 14e   Pie charts

1   Draw a pie chart to illustrate the following set of statistics, which is taken from *Social Trends*.

Families in Great Britain, 19..

All families	100
Families with no dependent children	51.9
1 child	20.5
2 children	16.5
3 children	6.9
4 or more children	4.2

2   Consumers' expenditure in 19.. is given as follows, in £ million:

Food	12,500
Drink and tobacco	7,500
Housing, fuel and light	8,300
Clothing	5,100
Cars and motor cycles	6,500
Durable household goods	3,600
Other goods	4,500
Other services	3,000
	51,000

Draw a pie diagram to illustrate the figures provided.

3   The following information relates to the number of people expected to listen to local radio in a 12-month period. Draw a pie diagram to illustrate the relative attractiveness to listeners of the programmes from the four stations.

Expected radio audiences (millions)

Station 1	125
Station 2	120
Station 3	140
Station 4	15
	400

4   The average student's income is found to be £50 per week, of which £30 is spent on lodgings, £3.50 on books, £8.50 on food, £2.20 on liquid refreshment, £3.20 on materials, stationery, etc. The rest is unclassified, covering a huge range of items required by individual students. Draw a pie chart to illustrate this expenditure.

14.7   Using graphs in reports

Pictograms, bar charts and histograms are all ways of presenting data in a form which can be easily understood. A graph is another way of presenting data. It displays the relation between two sets of data, one of which is varying with the other.

Suppose we think of sales of a certain product during the year: the months will be changing − January, February, March, etc. − in the usual way, but the sales will be changing month by month. The changes may be seasonal. Thus we shall sell more umbrellas and raincoats in January than in June in the United Kingdom, while in Australia the situation will be reversed. One of the variables, months, is independent of the other, but the sales is a dependent variable, it depends upon which month we are talking about what the sales will be.

Graphs are widely used in the press, in business life and on television to illustrate a huge range of data.

Constructing a graph

Graphs are drawn on squared paper, since this makes it very easy to '*plot*' the points on the paper that are to be used to illustrate the observed data. To plot these points, we need some starting places, and these are called **axes**. They are lines drawn on the graph paper at right angles to one another. The horizontal axis is called the '*x* axis' and the vertical axis is called the '*y* axis'. The point where they cut one another is called the **origin** O. They are drawn in a little way from the edge of the paper so that we can label the axes with some simple explanation that will assist understanding. We might for example, label the *x* axis 'Months' and the *y* axis 'Sales of umbrellas (thousands)'. Each axis is also labelled with the units being used, and a scale is chosen to enable the full range of data to be shown, as large as possible. In Figure 14.8 we have 12 months in the year, so we have to choose a scale that will enable us to show the 12 months across the *x* axis. The sales of umbrellas are shown up to 100,000. If

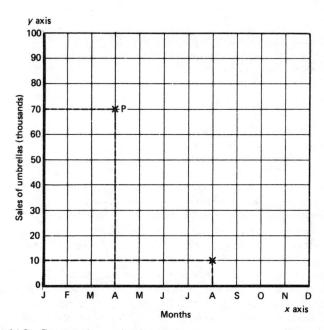

Figure 14.8   Constructing a simple graph

Notes

(i)   The axes are drawn at right-angles to one another, meeting at O, the origin of the graph. (In this graph it is the same as J for January.)

(ii)   The axes are labelled with the name of the variables ('Months' and 'Sales of umbrellas') and the units being used (thousands on Y axis).

(iii)   The points are plotted on the graph by using the values given in the table supplied or found in the statistical enquiry that is being carried out. Each pair of related facts, such as the fact that in August 10,000 umbrellas were sold, give a unique point on the graph. The point may be marked by a tiny dot, but preferably by a small cross made by two short lines intersecting at the exact spot. In such graphs the points are clearly picked out, and the curves joining up the points may be discontinuous to give greater emphasis.

sales had been 1 million umbrellas, we should have needed a different scale (or a piece of paper ten times as big).

Every point on a graph can be identified as different from all other points by referring it to the two axes. Thus the point labelled P in Figure 14.8 can only mean that in April (a notoriously showery month) sales of umbrellas were 70,000.

Simple graphs

The simplest form of graph merely presents the data in pictorial form, rather like the bar charts and pictograms referred to earlier. A **time series**, such as a temperature chart showing a record of a patient's temperature over a period of time, or a sales chart such as the one shown in Figure 14.9 presents a simple picture of the changes as they occur. We can tell how sales change from month to month, by a glance at the chart.

Exercise 14f   Simple graphs

1   The following information relates to the total sales (value) of a supermarket chain over a 12-month period. Using a suitable scale, record the information in the form of a graph.

Month	Sales (£)
1	270,000
2	200,000
3	240,000
4	300,000
5	320,000
6	400,000
7	410,000
8	400,000
9	420,000
10	440,000
11	410,000
12	500,000

2   The following sales for the year were achieved by the two departments of a town-centre store. Plot these on a graph, using a suitable scale.

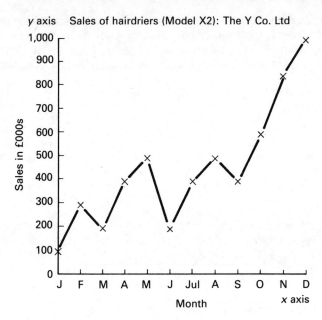

y axis   Sales of hairdriers (Model X2): The Y Co. Ltd

Figure 14.9 'A simple time series graph

Notes
The use of a discontinuous line in this sort of chart pinpoints the actual sales figures for each month, and clearly shows the rise and fall of sales.

Sales of Supertraders PLC

	Groceries (£)	Greengroceries (£)
Jan.	28,250	12,750
Feb.	24,250	11,500
Mar.	36,500	16,500
Apr.	33,750	14,750
May	34,500	15,500
Jun.	37,250	18,000
Jul.	25,000	13,250
Aug.	28,750	14,500
Sep.	34,000	18,500
Oct.	42,500	20,250
Nov.	43,500	21,000
Dec.	56,000	23,500

3 Mechanical Parts Ltd makes two models of a particular machine, the 'Junior' model and the 'Senior' model. Sales during the year are given below. You are asked to record these figures, *and total sales*, on a graph, labelling all parts of the graph as necessary.

Mechanical Parts Ltd: sales during year 19___

	Jan. (£)	Feb. (£)	Mar. (£)	Apr. (£)	May (£)	Jun. (£)
Junior	5,000	5,500	7,000	8,000	8,500	9,000
Senior	14,000	13,500	12,000	13,000	11,000	8,000

	Jul. (£)	Aug. (£)	Sept. (£)	Oct. (£)	Nov. (£)	Dec. (£)
Junior	8,500	7,000	9,500	10,000	10,500	12,000
Senior	8,500	3,500	4,000	4,500	4,000	5,000

Straight-line graphs

The simple graph of sales in Figure 14.8 rose and fell in line with quantity sold – it was a zigzag line. However, some graphs, where the data are in a special relation, consist of straight lines. Such graphs arise where one set of data varies directly with changes in the other set of data.

For example, in Figure 14.10(a) the cost of a particular product is plotted against the number of units required, up to a total of 10. Each unit is £3.50, and there is a direct relation between the cost of a particular order and the number of units ordered. The result is a straight-line graph passing through the origin (since when no units are ordered there is nothing to pay).

Such a straight-line graph can be drawn by plotting a single point, e.g. 8 units cost £28. The point thus plotted, when joined to the origin of the graph O, goes through all the points where other costs can be found, e.g. 3 units cost £10.50. If the straight line is extended, it will continue to pass through all the points where numbers of units and costs are matched, for example, 10 units cost £35.

A straight-line graph of this sort can be used very easily as a ready reckoner. This particular straight-line graph can be used to read off the total cost of any number of units from 1 to 10. To do this, we draw a horizontal line across from the number of units required (say 4 units) until it intercepts the graph. We then drop a perpendicular from that point on to the price axis, where we find that 4 units cost £14 altogether.

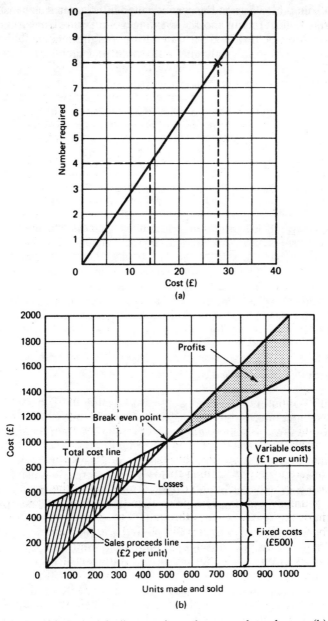

Figure 14.10 (a) A straight-line graph used as a ready reckoner. (b) A break-even chart

Reading off values in this way is called **interpolation** − finding the intermediate terms in the known range of a series from the values already known. If we were to extend the straight line and find values outside the range already given, it would be called **extrapolation**.

Many straight-line graphs pass through the origin, where both variables are zero. For example, in Figure 14.9(a) there is no charge if no units are purchased. *This is not always the case*, and a straight-line graph may intercept one of the axes at some point. In the break-even chart in Figure 14.9(b) certain fixed costs of an output of a certain product are incurred before any output can be produced at all. This might include costs of jigs and tools to be used in manufacture, or design costs incurred before even a prototype product is produced. The cost of manufacture will therefore start with these fixed costs (£500 in the graph) and the other variable costs which vary directly with output must be borne in addition as output commences. The cost line therefore does not pass through the origin but intercepts the price axis at the £500 mark. By contrast, the proceeds from the sale of the output do start at the origin. Since selling price is fixed at a sufficiently high level to achieve a profit eventually, the 'sales proceeds' line is steeper than the cost line. The two lines therefore intersect at the break-even point. At this point the total costs incurred are covered by the sales proceeds and every unit sold after this point will yield a profit.

Exercise 14g   Straight-line graphs

1   (a) Labourers on a road gang earn £3 an hour. Draw a graph of the amounts earned using 15 hours, 30 hours and 45 hours worked as plotting points. (b) Now read off from the graph how much will be earned for 42 hours' work.

2   (a) A farm worker earns £1.50 an hour. Draw a graph of earnings using 18,36 and 54 hours worked as plotting points. (b) Now calculate: (i) the amount earned for 37 hours worked; (ii) find out how many hours have been worked when his earnings are £67.50.

3   (a) A salesman receives 35p commission on every item he sells. Draw a graph to show his earnings up to maximum sales of 2,000 items. (b) Calculate what commission he receives when he sells 1,750 units.

4   A pizza manufacturer has fixed costs of £4,000 and each pizza costs him 50p for materials, labour, etc. He sells them for £1.50 each. Plot the costs and the sales for outputs of 1,000, 2,000, etc. up to 10,000 pizzas. (a) Where is the break-even point? (b) How much profit will he make on 8,000 pizzas?

The Z chart

A Z chart is so-called because when completed it looks like a capital Z. The chart is designed to show up three aspects on the same diagram:

(a) Current figures, e.g. current sales or current output.
(b) Cumulative figures, e.g. total sales or output to date this year.
(c) A moving annual total − which shows the total for the previous year.

Each month the annual total is increased by the current month's sales and reduced by deducting the sales of the same month a year ago. A typical set of figures is shown below, and the Z chart is drawn in Figure 14.11. (*Note*: The moving annual output shown in January is the total for February−December of the previous year and the January figure of the current year.)

Output of refrigerator units: X Co. Ltd

Month	Output in units Last year	This year	Cumulative output	Moving annual output
Jan.	110	120	120	1,655
Feb.	110	115	235	1,660
Mar.	120	135	370	1,675
Apr.	160	180	550	1,695
May	150	145	695	1,690
Jun.	115	140	835	1,715
Jul.	125	125	960	1,715
Aug.	140	135	1,095	1,710
Sep.	140	165	1,260	1,735
Oct.	155	185	1,445	1,765
Nov.	165	200	1,645	1,800
Dec.	155	190	1,835	1,835

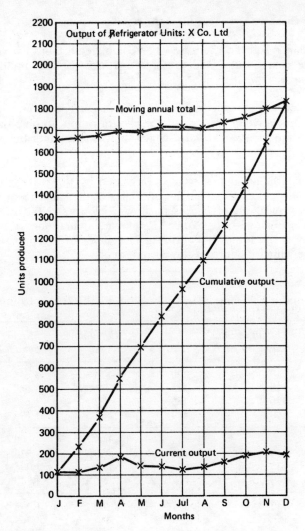

Figure 14.11   The Z chart

Exercise 14h   *Z charts*

1   From the following information prepare a Z chart of the sales performance of Alpha Ltd for the present year and comment on the year's results as revealed by the diagram.

Sales (£000)

	Last year	This year
Jan.	56	75
Feb.	54	78
Mar.	58	82
Apr.	62	85
May	66	91
Jun.	66	93
Jul.	71	96
Aug.	73	98
Sep.	75	105
Oct.	78	108
Nov.	80	112
Dec.	81	115

2 From the following figures for output by the Heavy Components Co. Ltd draw up a Z chart showing the present year's production achievements, and comment on the diagram.

Output in units

	Last year	This year
Jan.	27	45
Feb.	24	43
Mar.	28	27
Apr.	40	15
May	42	0
Jun.	44	0
Jul.	33	0
Aug.	35	38
Sep.	46	58
Oct.	48	64
Nov.	50	72
Dec.	51	74

3. From the following information prepare a Z chart of the sales of Gargantua (Royston) PLC for the present year and comment on the company's sales performance.

Sales (£m)

	Last year	This year
Jan.	26	38
Feb.	30	40
Mar.	32	42
Apr.	38	40
May	52	60
Jun.	58	66
Jul.	51	70
Aug.	60	81
Sep.	62	75
Oct.	38	39
Nov.	39	40
Dec.	32	38

14.8   Continuing the body of the report

Before we began the statistical section about pictorial representation
of data we were dealing with the body of the report. This is written
after the introduction to the report, but in the final published report
it will be preceded by the summary, even though in actual fact the
summary will be one of the last sections to be written. Continuing
with the body of the report, we know that this will be in several
sections, the first of which will deal with the actual situation at the
time the incident or event occurred. If the report is about some
change of policy, we must explain what the situation was when it
became clear that a change of policy was becoming necessary. Each
of these sections may be quite long – in a detailed report each may
be two or three pages long. A long and detailed report, however
absorbing, may leave the reader lost in a welter of detail. It is often
best to give conclusions about a particular section of the investigation
at the end of the section, so that those skimming through the report
can follow the committee's work stage by stage. The use of bullets –
bold round dots – to pinpoint these conclusions is often helpful. For
example:

Conclusions
- We found that an important cause of the fire was the accumu-
  lation of combustible material in the corridors leading to the
  assembly plant. These access routes had been reduced from 6
  feet wide to 4 feet wide by the storage of the extra material.
- The reason for this was the strike on the main production line

the previous day, which had prevented the use of the material. The two 'safety' officials were themselves part of this strike.

- There was only one member of the safety staff unaffected by the strike, Peter Harris. It is only fair to report that, although only an apprentice, he took measures to increase fire precautions, positioning extra fire extinguishers in these corridors. He also asked for extra storage from the No. 2 warehouse manager. The response was uncooperative, especially in the light of Peter Harris's youth and inexperience. Had this material been stored temporarily in No. 2 warehouse, which was undamaged, the fire would have been much less severe.

- The fire actually began when a crate being manoeuvred by a turret-truck from a high shelf in the store room fell to the floor, crushing a small 5-gallon drum of thinners. The spillage ignited and ran under the door into the access corridor to ignite the stored material there.

Such a set of conclusions at the end of a section already begins to show which way the report is tending, e.g. the fact that safety staff were able to be part of a strike is something that is likely to be commented on in the final conclusions and recommendations. It is well-known that even militant labour forces such as mineworkers cooperate with management to the extent that they always keep mine safety staff at work during a strike and may even reinforce them to ensure that the pits on which their livelihood depends do not suffer damage. Where hazardous materials are in use, perhaps the same rules should apply.

Working through the terms of reference

As we deal with each item in the terms of reference, we move on to the next, building up a clear account of each aspect. There may be some difficulty in phrasing particular sections of the report because it may be necessary to allocate blame or pinpoint some dereliction of duty. It is usual to express such conclusions in as moderate a way as possible, because one does not wish to be accused of libellous statements. Libel is the making of defamatory statements in a permanent form, i.e. in writing or in print, or perhaps in artwork or in the form of a statue.

Slander is the same sort of thing in non-permanent form, e.g. spoken defamation or a gesture. It is a less serious defamation than libel. However, if the spoken word is on radio or television it is held to be libel, not slander, because of the bigger audience. Thus, the report should be toned down to do no more than refer to the regrettable lapse – whatever it was – leaving the party that commissioned the report to phrase more serious complaints or charges at some internal inquiry. Of course with a matter of public concern the Crown Prosecution Service may eventually pursue charges.

Where a report is not about a contentious matter at all, but is just investigating the best way for a particular activity to be pursued, e.g. the merger of two companies or a choice between various policies, then such considerations do not enter into the problem. At the same time every problem affects someone – a decision one way will affect some people adversely, and an alternative solution will adversely affect others. One can only do one's best, stating the *pros* and *cons* in each case. The *pros* are the points in favour of a particular case while the *cons* are the points against it.

Remember though that we do have to come to a decision. Those who state both sides but refuse to make a decision do no service to anyone and defeat the whole point of a committee to examine a problem. If the committee cannot come to a decision because its members cannot agree, then the report gives the majority opinion, and those who disagree may hand in a **minority report** explaining why they take a contrary view.

The conclusions

The conclusions (disregarding the possibility of a minority report) restate the conclusions arrived at in each sub-section, though perhaps in slightly less detail. They must be quite specific, if that is possible, relating the conclusions to each aspect of the terms of reference and giving the committee's clear view of the matter. If absolute proof of a particular point is not possible, the wording should state this, but give the committee's view of the balance of probabilities in the matter.

Figure 14.12 gives a set of conclusions for the imaginary scenario described in Figure 14.1. The reader will appreciate that it is difficult to write a report except on the basis of an actual investigation. Study these conclusions now.

The recommendations

The recommendations are the most important part of a report, because they suggest what should actually be done. It depends of course upon the subject matter of the report what they will be, but the essential point is that the individual or the committee carrying out the investigation is now more knowledgeable about the matters than anyone else. He, she or it has become the expert – knowledgeable about the matter and able to see the way ahead. The recommendations should follow directly from the conclusions reached, and should command respect. In the vast majority of cases in ordinary

Conclusions
The committee's conclusions are as follows:

1   That the fire began with a simple accident in which a non-hazardous crate stored on a high shelf, from which it had to be removed by a turret-truck operator, was dislodged and fell upon a small drum of thinners temporarily stored at floor level.

2   As to possible negligence on the part of the turret-truck operator, we do feel that this operation is known to be tricky, and the operator was relatively new to this manoeuvre. We therefore feel that no particular blame can be attached to him.

3   The thinners should not have been stored at floor level in this warehouse, since thinners are known to be hazardous and were marked as such. Their abandonment at that point, however temporarily, was a breach of safety regulations. Unfortunately the person moving them was not aware of the safety regulation and (apart from his induction training) had received no specific training in safety.

4   As regards the action taken to limit the outbreak, the only person at work in the warehouse was the turret-truck operator. He decided to sound the fire alarm to alert staff before tackling the blaze. This involved running some 40 yards to sound the alarm and returning with extinguishers stored close to the alarm point. The fire had already gained some hold in the warehouse, but even more in the corridor outside. It was this outside fire that gained the main hold and let to the destruction of the building.

5   It is our belief that both the turret-truck operator and the apprentice safety officer acted with considerable courage and energy, but their efforts were overtaken by the force of the fire.

Figure 14.12   The 'Conclusions' section of a report

business activity they will be put into effect after discussion at senior management level. It is a sad fact that many reports at government level do in fact gather dust on ministry shelves, usually for financial reasons or because they are politically inexpedient.

The recommendations in our imaginary scenario outlined in Figures 14.1 and 14.12 might be as shown in Figure 14.13.

Recommendations
We recommend as follows

1   That an immediate debate be opened with the trade
    unions to ensure that safety staff are not to take part
    in strike action or other industrial disputes, in the
    general interests of all staff. Further that at times of
    industrial unrest it is agreed that the 'safety' aspect
    will be reinforced by the presence of a Joint Safety
    Committee to be set up at once and convened
    regularly – but especially when any dispute occurs.
2   That consideration be given to the installation in all
    warehouses and workshops of a sprinkler system of
    approved design, in consultation with the local fire
    prevention officer.
3   That more attention be given to safety training,
    especially for new members of staff. It would appear
    that an extra 1-day programme could usefully be
    added to the induction programme to cover various
    aspects of safety. In addition, when promotions or
    sideways-steps bring an employee into a new
    department, a programme of safety training for the
    new work area should be a compulsory requirement.
4   The particular aspect of this fire that causes the
    greatest concern is the storage of materials in the
    corridors. All managers should be made responsible
    for ensuring that corridors are not obstructed in any
    way. They should also be required to ensure that they
    give complete priority to safety matters drawn to
    their attention, however inconvenient it may be.
    Safety staff are entitled to everyone's cooperation at
    all times.
5   Finally, we feel that the two staff who did their very
    best to deal with the fire should be congratulated and
    rewarded.

Figure 14.13   The 'Recommendations' section of a report

14.9   The appendices

An appendix is an addition to a document, report or book that gives
additional information of use to the reader. There are several reasons
for having an appendix.

First, an appendix is useful as an **update to the document** itself.

Many long reports take several months to write, and there will be a time interval between the decision to consider the investigation complete and the date of publication. During this time interval further data of interest may come in or perhaps some social or economic or political change may occur. An appendix would be an appropriate place to give the new information, or to refer to the impact of changes on the views expressed in the report.

Second, an appendix is a useful place to **keep information that is difficult to include in the main text**. For instance, the reader will have noticed that the statistical work in this chapter and the previous chapter is bulky and interferes with the reading of that text. This was quite deliberate of course, since we wanted students who dislike mathematics to be confronted with the fact that this kind of presentation can be helpful in many reports. At the same time there will be many reports where the charts and diagrams can usefully be placed in an appendix. They would be referred to in the main text, and the reader would be urged to peruse them, but they would be a separate section. The reader might like to look now at Section 14.17 below, which is a further statistical section that has been placed at the end of the chapter as an appendix.

Third, an appendix may also be used to **segregate off some useful background material**. For example, a legal report might include a glossary of Latin terms, or a book about computers might include a glossary of computer terms. The *Concise Oxford Dictionary* has appendices of weights and measures, monetary units, and Greek and Russian alphabets.

14.10 Acknowledgements

A report usually includes a list of acknowledgements, which mentions the help given by various people in the preparation of the report. Since this is usually a gesture of thanks from the person writing the report, it can appear at the front of the report following the table of contents.

14.11 References and bibliography

In many reports it is quite common to explain a point that is referred to in the body of a text in a note given in a reference section at the back of the book. For example, the reference in the Recommendations (see Figure 14.3) to the adoption of a sprinkler system might have been followed by (see Note 5). In that case there would be a number of notes listed at the back of the report, and Note 5 would contain details of the various sprinkler systems available.

Similarly, if books or magazine articles are referred to, the name of the book should be given, with its author, publisher, etc. in the form:

> Iman Wilkens, *Where Troy Once Stood*, 1st Edn., Rider Books, 1991, p. 49.

Two terms often used in bibliographies are *ibid.* and *op. cit.* The former is an abbreviation for *ibidem*, which is Latin for 'in the same book'. So '*ibid.*, p. 62' means 'in the same book as the one just mentioned, on page 62'.

Op. cit. is an abbreviation for the Latin *opere citate* and means 'in the work already quoted'. So '*op. cit.*, p. 279 refers to page 279' in the book already quoted.

The mention of books and articles in a bibliography serves two purposes. It enables the readers to obtain the work for themselves and read the opinions and ideas of the author. Secondly, it acknowledges that the author of the report did not think of the point made by himself/herself, but found it in the publication cited. The credit for the idea should not therefore be given to the author of the report, but to the original author.

14.12   Completion of the report

Usually at this stage it is desirable to have a report typed up if it is in handwritten form. The typed copy may be described as a first draft, and it may be subject to a certain amount of rewriting and improvement. If the first draft can be done on a word processor, which stores the first draft in its memory, it will save a considerable amount of retyping later − a tedious chore for the typist. The draft stored in the computer's memory can be recalled to the screen of the visual display unit (VDU) and corrected on the screen. Whole paragraphs can be repositioned if necessary, while correct passages need not be retyped. The exact arrangements depend upon the software used, but the handbook of instructions will make clear exactly what is possible to revise and improve a draft.

Correcting a report

The mistakes to be looked for are the following:

(a) Errors of grammar, syntax, expression, spelling and punctuation.
(b) Incorrect sequence, or a poorly developed argument. It is not unknown to leave out a vital point, or to fail to provide promised back-up material. All such-cross references should

be checked to see that you have provided what you promised to provide.

(c) Unnecessary repetition, or the inclusion of irrelevant material.

(d) Ambiguity of any sort. An ambiguous statement is one that can be taken two ways. For example, to say that 'those who write reports rarely make a fortune' is ambiguous. Does the word 'rarely' refer to the verb 'write' or the verb 'make'. Similarly, to say 'When the supervisor arrived at the managing director's office he was taken ill' leaves us in a little doubt as to who was taken ill.

14.13   The index

Every report, if it is more than a page or two long, needs an index. Those who read a report do not usually make notes about it, but rely upon the index to help them locate a particular point which, at a later date, they wish to re-read. We all know how frustrating it can be to turn to the index at the back of a book and find that it does not list the point we wish to revise.

The best person to draw up an index to a report is its author. An outsider who does not know the subject and is not immersed in the subject matter can rarely make a good index. The starting point is to take thirteen sheets of A4 paper and punch a hole in the top left-hand corner so that they can be secured with a 'treasury tag'. Then cut an index down the right hand side as shown in Figure 14.14 and label each page with two letters, A−B, C−D, etc. We then have a full page for each two letters of the alphabet. As we make the index, chapter by chapter, we can write the index entries down in roughly the right spot. Of course towards the end some pages get very crammed, but with very small writing we can usually get everything in, before writing out a fair copy for the typist.

Suppose the chapter is about 'marketing'. We turn to the M page and fairly near the top (because marketing begins with 'Ma') we make a list of all the marketing matters. For example, the rough index for this book had:

Marketing, 138−59
    acknowledgment of orders, 155
    contracts and, 138−40
    credit control, 152−5
    estimates, 147
    fax inquiries, 145
    Formfill, 158−9
    fulfilment of orders, 156−7
    inquiries, 142−5
    quotations, 147

Abbreviations 　　*dictionary and, 237*	A–B
Acceptance, law of, 139 *Acknowledgement of orders, 155*	C–D
Acronyms, 8, 174 *Active listening, 173* ———— *Active participation, 194* *Ad hoc committees, 254*	E–F
Adjectives, 12–13, 42–4	G–H
Adverbs, 12–13, 133–5	I–J
Advertising copy, 109–10 　　*display material 110–11*	K–L
Agendae, 167, 168–71	M–N
Board of directors, 　　*chart of, 166*	O–P
	Q–R
Aphorisms, 104　　　*Briefings, 127, 186*	S
Apostrophes, 66, 69 *Arithmetic mean, 306–8*	T–U
Attention line, 57　*Business meetings, (see meetings)*	V–W
Averages, 305–12	X–Y
	Z

Figure 14.14　First draft of the index.

responses to inquiries, 146–7
sequence of activities in, 138
standard terms and conditions, 149–52
voluntary offers, 140–41

　　This is only the start of the work. We cannot expect our readers
to know that if they want to find out about 'voluntary offers' they
must look it up in the 'marketing' section. We must go through each
of these entries and decide whether there should be a further entry
in the index. If we decide that there should be a further entry, which
would be the best place.

For example let us take

'acknowledgment of orders, 155'

The best place for this would be under

'Orders, acknowledgment of, 155'

We turn to the 'O' index and record this entry.
Again:

'Contracts and, 138–40'

The best place for this would be in the 'C' index under 'contracts' but it would now have to read:

'Contracts, marketing and, 138–40'

In this way we build up a really comprehensive index.

One final point. If you turn to the index of this book and look under 'marketing', you will find most of these entries but the page numbers are different. This is because the first draft of your index is made from the typed copy, but the final published report will be typeset and typesetting takes less pages. This means that, although your rough copy is written out neatly so that it can be typed, you will not put the page numbers on this neat copy because the eventual page numbers will not be the same.

Some work on indexes

In each of these exercises take a sheet of A4 paper and divide it down the middle. Turn to the chapter referred to in *this* book and pretend you are drawing up the index for it. This will involve a main heading in the index and a number of subsidiary entries. Then you have to make up any alternative entries necessary elsewhere for the subsidiary items in your list, as well as for any entries in the chapter that are not under the main heading.

You can always check your entries with those in the real index, but don't forget that your answer cannot be the same as the main index, because that will have extra entries from all the other chapters in the book.

Exercise 14i

1   Chapter 3 needs an index. Draw it up.

2   Chapter 9 needs an index. Draw it up.
3   Chapter 16 needs an index. Draw it up.

14.14   The presentation of the report

The presentation of a report is important. The content of a report is not obvious until we read it, but the appearance of the report is clear from the start. It may be entirely erroneous, but when we look at a neat, clean, well-presented report, we expect the contents to be equally good, whereas a dishevelled, poorly presented report may deter the reader altogether.

Double-line spacing makes a report more readable (and leaves enough space for the odd correction of a typing slip or minor last-minute alteration.

Reasonably wide margins lighten the appearance of a page and also leave the reader a space for writing the odd comment. For example, where a report is being duplicated and supplied to all members of the board, or a committee, there are bound to be some who will want to make a comment or two in the margin of their copy. To use the full width of the page to save a sheet or two of paper is false economy if it irritates the reader.

Clear headings and subheadings help break the material down. In many cases reports can be prepared with a variety of headings and type styles, e.g. if the right kind of typewriter is available with interchangeable print-heads. Desk-top publishing systems usually have this facility too. The numbering of headings helps the reader to follow the points made in the report. For example, a main heading might be numbered 1 and printed in block capitals:

1   ADVANTAGES OF RELOCATION

Then sub-divisions of this section might be labelled:

1.1   Congestion at the present site

This has a mixture of capital and 'lower case' letters.
    Further sub-divisions might be as follows:

1.1.1   The access from Twyford Street

Here we have an initial capital letter but all the rest are in lower case (except that Twyford Street is a proper noun and needs capital letters). We have also used italic print.
    Many people are erratic in the use of capital letters and type styles, and this is very undesirable. You are free to use whatever style you choose but, having chosen it, be consistent. Some firms lay

down a house style and insist upon its use. The rule in such
to comply with the house style, whatever your personal prefe

14.15 More spellings

Two groups of words that do confuse students are those that end in
'ise' and 'ice', e.g. practise, practice; devise, device; advise, advice;
license, licence. The rule is that if the word is a verb it ends in -ise
but if it is a noun it ends in -ice:

(a)   The solicitor's practice was in the Northern town of Wallsend.
(b)   I practise osteopathy in the town, and am contracted to assist
      the local football club with injuries to playing staff.

Now test a fellow student on the first list of words below, and
then ask him/her to reciprocate by testing you on the second set.

Transport		*Freight forwarding*	
controls	dangerous	solid	reefer
licence	corrosive	solidify	refrigerated
licensing	explosive	consolidate	insulated
distribute	tachograph	terminal	load line
distributor	tachometer	terminate	load factor
distribution	milometer	break-bulk	loading bank
harmony	coordinate	Warsaw rules	convey
harmonization	coordination	Hague−Visby rules	conveyor
regulate	integrate	York-Antwerp rules	pallet
regulation	integration	COTIF rules	unitization
		(railways)	

14.16   Figures of speech 4: hyperbole

Hyperbole is a figure of speech in which we make exaggerated
statements for the sake of effect, without really meaning them to be
taken seriously. Thus, when we are selling our secondhand car, we
might say 'It's the finest Ford Escort in the world', but we don't
really mean it nor do we expect anyone to believe it. It is what is
called in law a 'puff', and the law recognizes that a puff does not
give anyone a right of action for misrepresentation.

The essential thing about a statement that is hyperbolical is that it
is not made to deceive anyone, but to emphazise a point.

Much used in poetry and by those in love − 'She is an angel of
delight' − hyperbole is not perhaps so important in business correspondence. However, it is perfectly permissible in all sorts of situations

where we are making new business friends, and playfully asserting our own beliefs in the merit of our goods and services. Just remember, to say that the Simplex System (see p. 143) is an excellent system of book-keeping for small businesses is a contractual representation, but to say that it is the finest accounting system in the world is hyperbole. There may be, probably is, a better system.

14.17 Appendix on averages

Many reports that require the analysis of data collected during an investigation also require us to describe the data as clearly as possible. One way to begin to describe a set of data is to find an average figure. There are several possible averages, or, to give them their statistical name − measures of central tendency.

Measures of central tendency

Any statistical inquiry results in a mass of data. While each piece of information is of interest, its relation to the whole set of data is more important. Thus, in examining electric light bulbs to see how long they last, the fact that one out of 3,000 went 'pop' the moment it was put into the lampholder is interesting, but is it very significant? If the other 2,999 each burnt for more than 500 hours it would seem that this particular bulb was not typical of the whole group. A particular statistic therefore may prove to be of no significance. Similarly, the presentations of data using pictograms, bar charts, etc., while they display the statistics well, do not summarize the statistics in any way, or indicate which are more significant than the rest. To summarize data, we need to average them in some way, and see how the actual data vary from the average figure.

Because these operations tend to reduce the significance of extreme values and stress the 'middle' ones, the processes are often referred to as **measures of central tendency**. In everyday life phrases like 'average attendance' or 'average score' are commonly used, and they do give a quick, clear impression of a particular situation. Thus the information that a batsman scored 1, 94, 72, 13, 8, 5, 7, 149, 186, 22 and 145 runs in matches played in the first 2 months of the cricket season is of great interest, but rather confusing. To say that his average score over 2 months was 63.8 gives a clearer picture of his ability.

Treating data in this fashion can be extremely useful. Where comparison has to be made between different sets of figures, it is more convenient to take a single (representative) figure from each set as the basis of comparison than to utilize every figure available. For example, a comparison of wage rates amongst the four largest

United Kingdom car manufacturers would be exceptionally difficult if each worker's wage was included in the presentation. Instead, for comparison, a figure representative of each plant, trade or firm is taken.

The three most commonly used measures of central tendency are:

(a)   The arithmetic mean.
(b)   The median.
(c)   The mode.

Let us consider each of these in turn.

The arithmetic mean

This is the simple average most commonly used in everyday life. It is what most people would understand when the word 'average' is mentioned. It is found by adding up the values of the variable (the scores in the cricketing example mentioned earlier) and dividing by the number of items (the innings played). A further instance is given below. It refers to the earnings of an insurance broker for the first 10 weeks of the financial year. The arithmetic mean is found by adding the set of earnings and dividing by the number in the set:

	19— Week ending	£
April	7	220
	14	200
	21	190
	28	260
May	5	240
	12	200
	19	210
	26	230
June	2	260
	9	210
Number of weeks	10	Total 2,220

Clearly the mean earnings are £2,220 ÷ 10 = £222 per week.

Information of this sort is called 'ungrouped data', to distinguish it from information that has been sorted out into a slightly more coherent form, in groups. Had this information, for example, been sorted out into groups in which the salary earned was recorded in groups of £50 each, we should have had: £100−£149 (none); £150−£199 (1); £200−£249 (7); £250−£299 (2).

This would have presented different problems in finding the arithmetic mean.

In business statistics, as the data is only a part (sample) of all such data, we use the sign $\bar{x}$ to represent the arithmetic mean of the sample.

For ungrouped data a formula for the arithmetic mean would be

$$\bar{x} = \frac{\Sigma x}{n}$$

where $\bar{x}$ is the arithmetic mean, x is each of the measurements or values, n is the number of measurements or values, and Σ (sigma) means 'the sum of'.

(*Note*: by using Σ the notation $\dfrac{x_1 + x_2 + x_3 + x_4}{n}$ is avoided.)

Using this notation for the insurance booker's earnings, we have

$$\bar{x} = \frac{\Sigma x}{n}$$
$$= \frac{£2,220}{10}$$
$$= \underline{\underline{£222}}$$

Exercise 14j   Arithmetic means of simple series

Using the formula given above, find the arithmetic mean of the following sets of statistics:

1   Electricity consumed during the quarter in a certain factory was as follows:

    Jan.   27,284 units
    Feb.   35,266 units
    Mar.   41,928 units

    Find the mean monthly consumption.

2   The ages of students attending an evening course, to the nearest year, are as follows: 17, 18, 18, 18, 19, 19, 22, 24, 25, 27, 27, 28, 38, 54 and 63. What is the mean age?

3   A library issues books as follows: Monday 742 books, Tuesday 1,529 books, Wednesday 2,472 books, Thursday 495 books and Friday 1,246 books. Only 237 books were issued on Saturday. What is the mean issue per working day? (Answer correct to one decimal place.)

4   Five mills produce the following outputs of cloth in a particular
week: 72,856 metres; 49,263 metres; 17,256 metres; 29,254 metres
and 86,276 metres. What is the mean output?
5   An experimental crop of wheat from seven plots of land produces
the following outputs:

(a)   224 kg   (e)   495 kg
(b)   330 kg   (f)   532 kg
(c)   75 kg   (g)   184 kg
(d)   176 kg

What was the mean output?

The arithmetic mean from a frequency distribution

In a simple series the individual items may occur only once, and
their frequency is therefore one. In a mass production world many
business statistics deal with frequencies greater than one. Thus, a
garage might sell 7 'Apollo' cars, 15 'Hermes' traveller models and
23 'St Christopher' touring vehicles. With such a frequency distribution the arithmetic mean must take into account not only the
value of an item, but also the number of times that item occurs.
   The formula must now become

$$\bar{x} = \frac{\Sigma fx}{n}$$

where $\bar{x}$ is the arithmetic mean, x the values of the individual items,
f the frequency (i.e. the number of cases of each value), n the total
number of items (i.e. the sum of the frequencies ($n = \Sigma f$)), and Σ
'the sum of'. This is illustrated in the example below:

What is the mean value of the policies sold by the XYZ agency,
whose sales are given in the frequency distribution below (answer to
nearest penny)?

Value of policy (£) (x)	Number of policies sold (f)	Product (f × x)
100	165	16,500
200	290	58,000
300	105	31,500
400	92	36,800
$n = \Sigma f =$ 652		$\Sigma fx = 142,800$

$$\bar{x} = \frac{\Sigma fx}{n}$$

$$= \frac{£142,800}{652}$$

$$= £219.02$$

Exercise 14k   *The arithmetic mean from a frequency distribution*

1   A fish farm has 120 ponds. Find the mean surface area of the ponds from the following frequency distribution (answer correct to one decimal place).

Surface area (square metres)	Number of ponds
65	25
70	40
75	28
80	14
85	13

2   The following table illustrates the annual bonus to be paid by a firm to a number of its employees. What is the mean value of the bonus paid?

Bonus (£)	Number of employees
900	7
800	15
600	8

3   The weight of timber taken from 48 trees is as shown below. Arrange the information in a frequency distribution and calculate the mean weight of timber (answer to the nearest kg).

Weight of timber (kg)

1,000	1,200	1,000	1,100	1,400	1,300
1,200	1,200	1,000	1,100	1,100	1,000
1,100	1,200	1,100	1,400	1,300	1,100
1,200	1,300	1,400	1,500	1,000	1,400

1,400	1,100	1,200	1,300	1,400	1,200
1,300	1,200	1,400	1,300	1,100	1,100
1,200	1,300	1,200	1,200	1,100	1,200
1,100	1,200	1,200	1,300	1,300	1,000

4   Below are listed the sums taken at a box office for tickets sold
    one morning. From the information draw up a frequency distri-
    bution and from it find the mean price per ticket sold (correct to
    the nearest penny).

£1.60	£2.50	£2.50	£3.50
£2.50	£1.60	£3.50	£3.50
£3.50	£2.50	£1.60	£1.00
£5.00	£5.00	£3.50	£3.50
£1.60	£3.50	£3.50	£2.50

The Median

*The median is defined as the value of the middle item of a distribution,
when the items are arranged in ascending order of size.*

For ungrouped data the method of calculation of the median is
very simple. The procedure is:

(a)   Arrange the data in order of size, i.e. so that they run from the
      smallest to the largest. Such an arrangement is called an **array**.
(b)   Find the middle item. The formula for finding the middle
      item is

$$\frac{n + 1}{2}$$

where n is the number of items. Hence where there are seven
items,

$$\frac{n + 1}{2} = \frac{7 + 1}{2} = 4$$

the fourth item would give us the medium value. We know this
to be the case, since in an array of seven there are three items
on either side of the fourth one − it is therefore in the middle.
    Where the number of items is even, it is not possible to
isolate an actual item which is the middle one. Thus where
there are eight items in an array

$$\frac{n + 1}{2} = \frac{8 + 1}{2} = 4\frac{1}{2}$$

the middle item is now the $4\frac{1}{2}$th item, and it is necessary to find
the average of the fourth and fifth items to find the median
value.
(c)   Find the value of the middle item.

Note: Statisticians sometimes refer to the 'median' item. Strictly speaking, this is not correct. The median is, by definition, the *value* of the middle item in an array. In an array with an odd number of items the median value will coincide with the middle item in the array. In an array with an even number of items it will be the average of the two middle items. The danger is that a student may say that in an array of 27 numbers, 14 is the median. It is of course the *value* of the fourteenth number in that array that is the median.

Consider the following examples:

First, the salaries after tax of seven bank employees (per month) are £478, £620, £530, £350, £880, £975, £570. Find the median salary.

(a)   Arrange the data in order of value:

1	2	3	4	5	6	7
£350	478	530	570	620	880	975

(b)   Find the middle item. With seven items this is the fourth

$$\frac{n + 1}{2} = \frac{7 + 1}{2} = 4$$

(c)   Find the median value. The value of the fourth item is £570.

$$\therefore \text{ median value} = \underline{\underline{£570}}$$

If an extra salary of £690 was added, there would be no single median item. It would then be necessary to find the average value of items 4 and 5.

Second, the monthly salaries after tax of eight bank employees are given as £478, £620, £530, £350, £880, £975, £570, £690; find the median salary.

(a)   Arrange the data in order of size:

1	2	3	4	5	6	7	8
£350	478	530	570	620	690	880	975

(b)   Find the middle item:

$$\frac{n + 1}{2} = \frac{9}{2} = 4\frac{1}{2}$$

There is no single item: 4 and 5 are 'in the middle'.

(c)   The median value will be the average of these items

$$= \frac{£570 + £620}{2}$$

$$= \frac{£1,190}{2}$$

$$= \underline{\underline{£595}}$$

Exercise 141   The median

1   Calculate the median life of an electric light bulb based on the following nine examples: (a) 236 hours, (b) 11 hours, (c) 248 hours, (d) 25 hours, (e) 1,294 hours, (f) 728 hours, (g) 5 hours, (h) 1 hour, (i) 483 hours.

2   Farmer Brown's hens laid as follows in one year: Lucy 236 eggs; Speckly 320 eggs; Mary 156 eggs; Crooked Leg 184 eggs; Dainty 156 eggs; Brownie 84 eggs; Polynesia 203 eggs; Margaret 225 eggs. Calculate the median output.

3   The orders received from the representatives of Cosmetics Ltd are as follows for the month of July:

	£		£
Mr A	8,540	Mr F	15,230
Mr B	12,720	Miss G	27,460
Mr C	16,230	Mr H	14,250
Mrs D	18,710	Mrs Y	1,850
Miss E	5,950		

Calculate the median value.

4   The orders received from the representatives of Icepack Ltd are as follows for the month of June:

	£		£
Mr A	18,540	Mr F	8,417
Mr B	12,760	Miss G	19,325
Mr C	29,250	Mr H	28,612
Mrs D	13,286	Mrs Y	14,713
Miss E	48,716	Mrs J	8,450

Calculate the median value.

The Mode

The mode is defined as that value in a set of figures which occurs most often. To arrive at the mode, then, one needs only to find the item having the greatest frequency.

When working with ungrouped data this merely necessitates

counting the frequencies to discover which one predominates. For example:

Weekly contributions to pension fund of employees:

Contribution (£)	Number of employees
1	11
2	18
3	29
4	16
5	10
6	3

The most common payment — made by 29 employees — is £3; therefore this is the modal contribution.

Sometimes it is possible to have bimodal statistics. Had there been 29 people paying £5 per week also, it would have been a bimodal series.

Exercise 14m   The mode

1   In the following cricket scores which is the modal score for each batsman?

Batsman A: 27, 0, 14, 162, 27, 5, 27, 16, 17.
Batsman B: 5, 15, 38, 5, 72, 91, 106, 4, 3, 0, 5.
Batsman C: 27, 14, 36, 7, 21, 9, 19, 36.

2   In the following lists of bowling performances which is the modal performance for each bowler?

Bowler A: Wickets taken 4, 3, 1, 4, 4, 5, 3, 1, 2, 4, 5.
Bowler B: Wickets taken 2, 2, 2, 0, 1, 7, 3, 2, 2, 1, 5.
Bowler C: Wickets taken 5, 1, 4, 7, 1, 1, 3, 2, 3, 3, 4.

3   Houses in Newtown have the following number of bedrooms. Which is the modal-sized house?

Number of rooms	1	2	3	4	5	6
Frequencies	27	272	1,954	825	430	36

4   Containers moving through a certain port are found to weigh as follows:

Weight in tonnes	Number of containers	Weight in tonnes	Number of containers	Weight in tonnes	Number of containers
12	114	19	206	26	136
13	127	20	138	27	127
14	163	21	139	28	142
15	165	22	187	29	156
16	234	23	165	30	165
17	217	24	234	31	139
18	219	35	144	32	234

What is the modal weight for containers passing through the port?

Which is the best 'average' to use?

The arithmetic mean is the main average used, because it is readily understood, fairly easy to calculate, takes into account all the data, and is capable of algebraic manipulation. However, there are certain sets of data for which the arithmetic mean does not fulfil its function of adequate representation. Consider the following illustrations:

(a) Imagine there is an enquiry into the average age of students at a college, classified according to whether they are day-release or evening. The following results might occur: arithmetic average age of day-release students 20 years; arithmetic average age of evening-class students, 20 years. Obviously the mean age is identical but the day-release average may have been computed from a class of 150 students each one aged 20 years, and the evening-class average from a class of 100 students of which 90 were each aged 17 years and 10 each aged 47 years. Clearly, the mean age of 20 is not representative of the evening class but is representative of the day-release group. Therefore if data contain extreme items, the arithmetic mean will tend to distort and incorrectly describe the situation.

(b) The arithmetic average number of children per household might easily be calculated at 2.2 for Great Britain. Many students might find such a figure unrealistic, since obviously no family actually has 2.2 children. The mean number of legs per dog in the United Kingdom may be approximately 3.99, but this conjures up a strange picture of a dog. Clearly the mode conveys the best impression of a dog, and in that enquiry would be the best average to choose.

In the two cases above, to a greater or less extent, the arithmetic mean would appear to be unsatisfactory as a means of description and the median would probably be a better choice since:

(a)   In the case of data with extreme items the median will not be affected by them and will possibly be more representative. Returning to our two classes of students, the median ages would be 20 for the day-release group and 17 for the evening group − a more accurate picture of the situation.

(b)   The median number of children per household in Great Britain is 2, which is a more realistic indication of the average family than 2.2.

Unfortunately, one of the characteristics of the median which is particularly useful in some circumstances, that of concentrating on the middle item, is a disadvantage in the majority of cases, because, in the main, all data relevant to the problem should be taken into account. In addition, the median is unsuitable for further mathematical calculation.

The mode is of limited use, because although it has some of the advantages and all of the disadvantages associated with the median, there is, in addition, the difficulty of distributions that have no mode or two modes (bimodal). For example, the data 2, 3, 8, 9, 12 and 13 have no mode; the data 2, 3, 3, 3, 5, 7, 8, 8, 8, 9 and 10 have two modes, 3 and 8.

In summary, it is a good rule-of-thumb guide to use the arithmetic mean in all those cases where it adequately represents the data. Where this is not the case, the median is usually the best alternative.

14.18   Answer section

Exercise 14(a)   No answers given for these questions.

Exercise 14b−14f   No numerical answers required.

Exercise 14g   1(b)   £126; 2(b) (i)   £55.50, (ii) 45 hours; 3   £612.50; 4(a)   4,000 units, (b) £4,000. *Note*: For the answers given above read off from the graphs, a small error can be excused, and counted as correct.

Exercise 14h   No numerical answers required.

Exercise 14i   Compare your answer with the main index of this book.

Exercise 14j   1   34.826 units;   2   27.8 years;   3   1,120.2 books; 4   50,981 m; 5   288 kg.

Exercise 14k   1   72.9 m^2; 2   £770; 3   1,206 kg; 4   £2.90.

Exercise   14l   1   236   hours;   2   193.5   eggs;   3   £14,250; 4   £16,626.50.

Exercise 14m   1   A, 27; B, 5; C, 36. 2   A, 4; B, 2: C, 1 and 3. 3   3-bedroomed. 4   16 tonnes, 24 tonnes and 32 tonnes.

15
Correspondence about employment

15.1 The Personnel Department

There is a popular misconception that the Personnel Department is a department that looks after the well-being of employees, arranges their holidays and handles any welfare problems that arise. It may do these things of course as an incidental activity, but its true function is to obtain for the firm or company such human resources as it needs, with a nice mixture of the skills and abilities required in all the various departments. Students of economics will know that business activity depends on three classes of resource: land, labour and capital. Land means not only geographical land (every business has to be sited somewhere) but also all the other materials nature has provided — metals, timber, agricultural crops, etc. Labour means the human resources required — everyone from the junior clerk to the managing director. Capital means not only the money to finance the working of the business but also the money to purchase the many other capital assets needed — plant, machinery, tools etc. All these requirements are important, but as far as the human resources are concerned, it is the personnel department that is charged with the responsibility of 'finding such staff as are required, in such numbers as are necessary, with such skills as are needed'.

Good staff are hard to find, and if unskilled staff are taken on, it costs a fortune to train them. Then, if they decide to move elsewhere, all that money is wasted. The personnel officer will always be keen to retain skilled staff, and stop them going elsewhere by offering attractive salaries, conditions of work, etc.

The chief stages of personnel work are:

(a)   Recruitment of staff.
(b)   Induction of staff.
(c)   Training and retraining as required.
(d)   Dismissal in certain circumstances.
(e)   Redundancy, if necessary.
(f)   Retirement eventually.

Some considerations about personnel work are the following:

Costs of recruitment

When we recruit people, it costs money. Even a small advertisement in a local paper or a specialist trade magazine costs between £60 and £300. We must respond to enquiries with letters inviting applicants to fill out an application form, and giving fuller details of the post offered than could be included in an advertisement. The average letter costs about £4 to type and send off. Several letters may pass to and fro − and we may have 100 applicants. All these costs add up to a very considerable sum.

Racial and sexual bias

It is important in our modern society to keep both a racial and a sexual balance in our workforces. Any hint of bias will be a source of complaint. That is why an appeal to staff to bring along any friends they know who may need a job will result in the present balance in the work force being perpetuated, possibly to the exclusion of more worthy unemployed people. If this method of recruitment is used, it is important to watch adverse trends in the mix of employees, and keep the balance fair between the sexes and the ethnic groups.

'Grow your own' may be best

We have said many different skills are needed, but all skill has to be acquired. Firms can, with very little extra expense, 'grow' the staff they require if they plant the right sort of ideas in the minds of young employees. Thus, if a young employee is getting on well in some subordinate position, it may be helpful to say to him/her, 'We feel you are doing well in this field. Why don't you study for full professional qualifications in this type of work'. In this way the young person learns both the theory and the practical side of his/her work, and gradually moves up through the organization to a top-level position. This kind of suggestion is best made at an annual pay review, where the young person is considered for a merit award, a possible promotion or a sideways step (to broaden his/her experience).

15.2   Advertisements for recruiting staff

Recruitment begins with a personnel requisition being completed by some head of department who requires staff. This is sent to the personnel officer. It contains details of the type of staff required, the skills they must have, etc. To comply with this requisition, the personnel officer will first consider 'home-grown' staff looking for a promotion or a change. If none is available, he/she will eventually draw up an advertisement, but if the post is a new one, it may first of all be necessary to draw up a **job description** and decide the level of work and the rate of pay. The job description will, when agreed, be typed out and a number of copies run off, so that one can be sent out to each applicant. The following headings might appear on the job description:

(a)   Job title.
(b)   Purpose of the job.
(c)   Job location.
(d)   Responsibilities of the post.
(e)   Duties to be performed.
(f)   Authority of the position and discretion to be exercised.
(g)   Targets to be met.
(h)   Conditions to be met, e.g. age, qualifications, ability to drive a vehicle, etc.
(i)   Salary scale and other features, e.g. holidays, superannuation schemes, etc.

The job description will also be useful when drawing up an advertisement for publication in the local or trade press. Consider the advertisement shown in Figure 15.1 and the notes below it. Then try some of the questions in Exercise 15a.

Exercise 15a   The four exercises below require you to draft an advertisement for a trade magazine, inviting applications for the positions described.

1   Newbold and Partners, solicitors, of 2174 High St, Lowport, LD7 2HB, require a school-leaver to train for general office duties and legal work concerned with local court procedures. They require a good general educational level, with examination passes in Mathematics and English. Secretarial or keyboard skills will be a recommendation. The salary is negotiable, depending on age and qualifications. Help with travel expenses is possible, or to someone prepared to move to the locality, help with lodgings may be possible. Applications to K. Newbold, or telephone Lowport 217656.

2   Engineering PLC seeks a trainee management accountant, preferably someone with experience of the engineering industry and a basic knowledge of book-keeping. Computer experience would

Mowbray Car Hire Services

PART TIME
MD's SECRETARY

We are a rapidly growing National Car Hire Company. Our MD is in his office about 3 days a week and needs a secretary on these days. The successful applicant will be a competent typist, able to take shorthand and to use (or willing to learn) word processing using Word Star Software.

We are shortly moving from our offices in Blewbury to purpose-built premises in Reading, and the successful applicant will be expected to move with us. Hours by arrangement but to cover periods 9.30am–4pm on 3 days a week.

Applications in writing to: Mrs P. Grant, Dept OT, Mowbray Car Hire Services Ltd, Main Road, Blewbury, Oxon OX11 9QD or ring for informal discussion on (0235) 000 000.

Figure 15.1   An advertisement to recruit staff

Notes
(i)   The advertisement uses a variety of print sizes and styles to give prominence to the post offered, and sufficient detail to prevent the wrong sort of applicant wasting the time of the Personnel Officer.
(ii)   The fact that a move is contemplated in the near future will deter anyone who just wants a local job.
(iii)   A clear name and address are given for applications.
        The telephone number is helpful, because a lot of applicants may be uncertain whether to apply or not. A quick telephone call may save a lot of trouble – either encouraging a good applicant or ruling out a weaker applicant.

be a recommendation. The applicant would have the chance to begin a career in the Costing Department, with student membership of the Chartered Institute of Management Accountants. The entry requirements of the Institute must be met before this can be arranged. Salary negotiable according to age, qualifications, etc. Applications to the Personnel Officer, at The Blackberry Industrial Site, Coventry, CV2 7SP.
3   Imagine you are the proprietor of a small business in some field about which you are knowledgeable. Devise an advertisement

for an assistant in this field, giving the skills and qualifications you would expect from an applicant and all the details necessary to enable him/her to apply.

4   The college you attend or the firm you work for requires to recruit staff for a particular series of posts. Draw up a suitable advertisement, giving a set of details which would enable suitable applicants to offer their services.

15.3   Job applications (the applicant's approach)

If we view job applications first from the applicant's point of view, it is clear that the purpose of the exercise is to secure the job, and it is essential to show some degree of enthusiasm to be successful. At times of business depression this is not always easy, because it may be necessary to make several dozen applications. Every application goes through a number of stages, which may be listed as follows:

1   A brief letter requesting an application form for a post you have seen advertised.
2   The drawing up of a *curriculum vitae* (cv) to be sent with the application form when it arrives.
3   A covering letter, to cover the return of the application form.
4   A letter acknowledging the receipt of an invitation to an interview and confirming your intention to attend.
5   Preparatory work for the interview, including a serious attempt to anticipate the questions that may be asked and to plan the responses you will make.
6   A letter acknowledging the receipt of a letter of appointment, and confirming your intention to start work as requested.
7   Alternatively, a letter expressing your disappointment at not being selected, and asking that your name be borne in mind should a further vacancy occur, or should the person actually selected not take up the appointment.

As an alternative to 1 and 2 above, we could have a letter written to a firm whose activities we are interested in and which we should like to work for, although so far as we are aware no vacancy exists at present. This is a slightly more adventurous activity than the routine application, but it does have the advantage that it is probably the only application the firm will be receiving, and the person who deals with staffing will therefore give it undivided attention.

This group of letters seems a fairly daunting prospect, but once you have written a rough draft for each, they will soon become routine, and will present few problems, except the rather tedious chore of writing or typing them out each time they are required. Don't get depressed about this. You have to keep at it with cheerful enthusiasm. A draft is a rough guide both to the layout and the content of a letter, which you will then adapt to suit the particular letter you are writing.

15.4   The materials for regular letter writing

Sadly, you have to speculate before you can accumulate, and setting yourself up to write regularly for jobs requires a basic organization and the expenditure of a few pounds. You need the following things:

1   Some plain white A4 bond paper − which you can buy from any stationer. If you are hopeless at writing on plain paper and keeping the lines neat, some firms do sell a pad with the first page ruled with thick black lines. You place this *under* the first sheet and the lines show through well enough for you to see them as you write your letters. If you don't find this in a shop, use a ruler and a black ballpoint pen to rule up one page in this way and use it every time you write a letter.
2   Two sizes of envelopes − A5 and A4. You may prefer to get white ones, but brown ones are cheaper and will probably be adequate. Buy about fifty A5 envelopes (210 × 148 mm) and about ten A4 envelopes (297 × 210 mm). These are best for sending in application forms, which are usually A4 size.
3   A couple of black ballpoint pens. 'Medium' pens are better than fine point pens, and black is essential. Many firms copy letters and application forms so that each member of an interviewing panel can have a copy, and black on white paper gives the best copies. Lots of copying machines cannot 'see' blue − so writing job applications in blue ballpoint pen is a positive disadvantage. Don't do it!
4   A supply of first-class stamps. Never send anything second class. With a first-class stamp you are practically guaranteed next day delivery.
5   You need to keep a record of all job applications, and this is best done in a lever arch file. They cost about £1.50 at any good stationers.
6   A box of treasury tags is extremely helpful, and only costs about 50 p. at any good stationers. They are invaluable for keeping papers together, but you do need a tiny punch to punch a hole in the corner of the paper. Two-hole punches can also be obtained very cheaply.
7   Finally, writing your own name and address is one of the really boring things about job applications, especially if you enclose stamped addressed envelopes for replies. You may like to spend the very small sum required to get 1,000 addressed labels printed by a specialist firm. The usual cost is about £2−£3 for the

smallest labels and £10 for large ones. They are a great time saver and well worth the money if you can afford it. There are many firms offering these address labels, but one such firm is Able-label Department, Steepleprint Ltd, Earls Barton, Northampton NN6 OLS. The price is at present £3.25 for 1,000 labels, but this is subject to small increases in line with inflation.

15.5 Making applications

A typical letter of application appears in Figure 15.2. Study it carefully now, and the notes below it.

Addressing the envelope

If an envelope is typed, it is usually done in fully blocked style. This is convenient for the typist and saves time. If an envelope is written freehand, it is usual for each line to be written slightly to the right of the line above. Many people print the delivery town in block capitals, and also the postcode. These styles are illustrated in Figures 15.3 and 15.4.

Returning the application form

Application forms vary, but are usually fairly detailed and give you an opportunity to list the qualifications you have already acquired and the previous posts you have held (if any). There is a document called a CV (*curriculum vitae*) which we can all draw up; it gives an

Notes
(i)   We are already familiar with the writing of business letters so we can see that this is not in fully blocked style but in semi-blocked style. This means that the date, the references and the subscription are on the right-hand side of the page. This is more easy for filing purposes than the fully blocked style – because as you open the file to find any filed letter the references, etc., are more easily seen.
(ii)   Note the salutation: 'Dear Sir/Madam'. This is a permissible salutation if you don't know the personnel officer's name. If you wish to avoid it you should telephone the firm and ask the telephone operator for the correct name of the personnel officer.
(iii) The first paragraph, though short, is the vital one.
(iv)   The second paragraph is to convince the personnel officer that you are a genuine prospect for the post on offer. Whatever job you are applying for, it is always advisable to highlight the qualifications that are most appropriate for the post.
(v)   Offering a stamped addressed envelope (SAE) for a reply is expensive but worth the effort. It shows that you appreciate the costs of recruiting staff. Make sure the envelope is a suitable size – A4 is best but A5 will do at a pinch.

account of our qualifications and experience. The words *curriculum vitae* mean 'course of my life'. This is dealt with below (see Section 15.6), and is chiefly used when an application form is not supplied by the employer.

Since we only have one application form and it is easy to make a slip or two on it, there is much to be said for writing our answers on a sheet of plain paper first, before we complete any line on the form. Alternatively, photo-copy the form at a local copy shop, and

---

The Personnel Officer,
Tamarisk Electrical Ltd,
3475 Queensway,
Suburbtown,
Beds,
ST2 1PQ

Mary E Webster,
27 Canary Walk,
Wildflower Way,
Milton,
Beds,
BD7 3TU
23 July 19..
My Ref. Job application No. 7

Dear Sir/Madam,

Trainee Accountant — Bedford News 23 July 19..

Would you kindly send me the application form and job description for the post referred to in today's advertisement in the *Bedford News.*

I am an 18-year-old college leaver who has just completed a course for National Vocational Qualifications Levels I and II. The subjects covered included Economics, Accountancy, Statistics, Business English, British Constitution, Secretarial Studies and Computer Appreciation — all at Level II standard. I also have nine passes at GCSE level, including Mathematics, Physics, Chemistry, Domestic Science and Needlework. The other subjects are covered by these already mentioned.

I enclose a SAE for reply and thank you for your help.

Yours faithfully,

Mary E. Webster

Enclosure:
1 SAE for reply.

Figure 15.2 A draft letter requesting an application form

The Personnel Officer,

Tamarisk Electrical Ltd,

3475 Queensway,

Suburbtown,

Beds,

ST2 1PQ

Figure 15.3   An envelope typed in fully blocked style

The Personnel Officer,
Tamarisk Electrical Ltd,
3475 Queensway,
SUBURBTOWN,
Beds,
ST2 1PQ

Figure 15.4   An envelope in handwritten style

fill up this copy first in pencil. When you are satisfied with your effort, copy it out on to the original form and post it off with a covering letter. A draft of this covering letter is given in Figure 15.5.

Speculative applications

Sometimes there is a strong case for writing to a firm or company in which we are interested even though no advertisement of a vacancy has appeared to our knowledge. All firms have labour turnover problems, and may have a vacancy, or be prepared to take on a willing applicant who has shown initiative by writing in. Of course such an applicant runs the risk of being rejected out of hand, but there are two advantages to this approach:

(a) Since the application will be the only one arriving, it will be given more attention than an ordinary response to an advertisement.

(b) Since you are initiating the approach, you have the opportunity to find out something about the firm beforehand, e.g. its products or services, its importance in the town or district, etc. This gives you the chance to write a more interesting letter than a routine application in response to an advertisement.

In almost all such applications it is usual to save a lot of explanations by enclosing a CV (*curriculum vitae*). As explained earlier, the phrase means 'story of my life'.

15.6   Curriculum vitae (CV)

It is well worth while drawing up a CV to cover you own qualifications and experience, and having it typed so that it is really presentable (see Figure 15.6). Run off a dozen copies of it at the local copy shop so that you always have a copy available. From time to time it is useful to update it as you gain further qualifications and experience.

15.7   Interviews

From the applicant's viewpoint an interview is a face-to-face opportunity to influence an organization in his/her favour, with a view to appointment. After perhaps years of hard work in acquiring a basic education, and some specialist skills, the opportunity so keenly desired may be thrown away by a shrug of the shoulders or a momentary sign of disapproval e.g. of a firm's products. The approach to an interview should be as careful as the revision period before an examination. One should prepare for the interview thoughtfully, trying to anticipate what the employer is looking for in an applicant, and anticipating the questions that might be asked.

The whole process starts with the arrival of the interview letter,

The Personnel Officer,
Tamarisk Electrical Ltd,
3475 Queensway,
Suburbtown,
Beds,
ST2 IPQ

Mary E. Webster BD7 3TU
27 Canary Walk,
Wildflower Way,
Milton
Beds,
BD7 3TU
27 July 19..
My Ref. Job application No.7

Dear Sir,

Completed Application Form – Trainee Accountant

   My completed application form for this post is enclosed. It is exactly the opportunity I am hoping for, so I hope you will find my application satisfactory and will feel able to grant me an interview.

   Would you please acknowledge the application's safe receipt by returning the slip at the bottom of this letter in the enclosed SAE.

   Thank you for your courtesy and I hope to hear from you in due course.

                    Yours faithfully

                    Mary E. Webster

Enclosures:
1   Completed application form
2   SAE for acknowledgment
- -

                    Personnel Dept,
                    Tamarisk Electrical Ltd,
Date . . . .   3475 Queensway
                    Suburbtown,
                    Beds,
                    ST2 1PQ

   We acknowledge receipt of your completed application form, which is receiving attention.

                    Signed . . . .

Figure 15.5   Returning an application form

which gives date and time of the interview. Unless it has been arranged in a hurry, with a very short interval between the arrival of the letter and the interview, it is best to acknowledge the letter in writing. If the time period is shorter, phone and confirm that you will be attending the interview. Firms like to know what is happening. There are often three or four senior people on an interview panel, all of whom have set their ordinary work aside to deal adequately with applicants. If you intend to be there, at least let them know. Even more important, if you have already accepted another post, or have changed your mind about this particular application, let them know of this decision. There may be someone else they can invite along instead. Firms that are not informed tend to blame the college or school for failing to tell students how to behave in such matters.

A typical letter of acceptance is shown in Figure 15.7.

Exercise 15b   In the following exercises you are asked to do certain things connected with job applications. It depends upon your circumstances how you can best arrange to deal with these questions. Ideally you should attempt them all.

1   You want to get an application form for a job advertised at Crow Ltd for a junior accounts assistant. As the time is short, you decide to telephone for an application form. With a fellow student, act out the part of the applicant at one end of the call, and the receptionist (and anyone else) at the other end of the call.

   Your fellow students might like to comment on your performance. Perhaps someone else could do it better.

2   Write an application form to Richmont PLC at St Peter's Place, Crosby Court, London, EC2 1DP, asking for the application form for the post of Trainee Sales Agent (Computer Databases). Give the company details of your own educational background, emphasizing any that appear to relate particularly to this type of post.

3   Write a letter to the Countryshire County Council, asking for details of a post advertised in your local newspaper for a trainee social worker. Give some details of your qualifications to date to persuade them that you are a worthwhile applicant for the post.

Notes
(i)   There is much to be said for the slip at the foot of the letter asking them to acknowledge the form's safe arrival. It is always frustrating to wait several weeks not even knowing whether your form has arrived – let alone whether it is being considered.
(ii)   Such an inclusion also alerts them to the fact that you are well-organized and businesslike. It may impress them enough to put you on the short-list for interview.

Curriculum Vitae
Name: Mary Elizabeth Webster
Address: 27 Canary Walk, Wildflower Way, Milton, Beds, BD7 3TU
Telephone No: (0000) 412956
Marital Status: Single
Date of birth: 17 March 19..

| **Education**: | (i) | Milton Comprehensive School |
| | (ii) | Bedford Technical College |

Qualifications:	GCSE	Maths (C), English (B), Physics (D), Chemistry (C), Economics (A), Principles of Accounting (A), Domestic Science (B), Needlework (D), Computer Appreciation (C)
	NVQ	Level II Economics, Accountancy, Statistics, Business English, Secretarial Studies, Computer Appreciation
	NVQ	Level I British Constitution
Employment experience		Part-time posts in shops, restaurants and travel agents. Six-week secondment to Industry course in keyboarding – Helpful Bank PLC Bedford (classified 'Superior')
Non-vocational interests		Travel, rock-climbing (Happy Venturers' Rock-Climbing Club). Amateur dramatics (Bedford Playmakers)
Posts of responsibility		Member of Bedford College Road Safety Committee Member of St John's Ambulance Student Section

Figure 15.6   A curriculum vitae (CV)

4   Make a telephone call to John Brown, the Personnel Officer at Countryshire County Council, to say that the form you have been sent (see question 3 above) refers to residential posts only. Explain that as you have family responsibilities (caring for an

```
The Personnel Officer,          Mary E Webster,
Tamarisk Electrical Ltd,        27 Canary Walk,
3475 Queensway,                 Wildflower Way,
Suburbtown,                     Milton
Beds,                           Beds,
ST2 1PQ                         BD7 3TU
                                1 August 19..
                                My ref: Job application No. 7

Dear Sir,

              Interview 8 August 19.. 11.00 a.m.

                      Queen Offices

      Thank you very much for inviting me to this
interview. I confirm that I shall attend as requested, and
will bring with me the original certificates for the
qualifications mentioned in my application form.


                      Yours faithfully,


                      Mary E. Webster
```

Figure 15.7   Accepting an interview

Notes
(i)   The letter is quite brief, and simply confirms the date, time and venue of the interview.
(ii) It is a good idea to mention in the letter anything they have asked you to do before the interview. This focuses the points in your own mind and ensures that you arrive for the interview with anything they have asked to see.

invalid sister), you cannot take up residential work, and ask whether there is any point in filling out the form. (Let us imagine in fact that the CCC has sent the wrong form.) One person should play the applicant, and another the receptionist and other people at the county council end. Other students present should appraise the speakers' abilities to communicate by telephone.

5   Write a letter to accompany your completed application form for the post of Transport Clerk at XYZ Freight Forwarding Ltd, Oxford Way, Ely, Cambs, CB19 3DP. In your letter refer to the fact that you have not enclosed your original certificates as you are uneasy about losing them, but say you have sent photo-copies of them instead, and will produce the originals at any interview to which you should be called.

6   Write a letter of thanks to Mastercare-Services Ltd for the

interview offered you on Friday 28 May 19.. at the Old School House, Chelderbury, Oxon., OX10 9QE. The interview is at 9.30 am. Confirm that you will attend and will present, at the interview, the certificates the company requires to see.

7   Phone Peter Thompson, the Personnel Officer at the Superior Press Ltd, on 0000 429510, to thank him for the appointment at 2.30 pm on Friday 22 June 19.. Explain that you will be unable to attend that interview as you have an appointment with another employer at that time. Can he offer you an alternative appointment please? One person should play the applicant and another the receptionist (and other people) at Superior Press Ltd. Other students present should appraise the speaker's abilities to communicate by telephone.

8   Phone Emma Wright, the Personnel Officer at Heighly Engineering Ltd, to express your regrets that you will not be attending the interview at 10.30 am on Friday 17 May 19.. as you have already accepted an offer of employment elsewhere. At the same time tell her you do have a friend with very similar qualifications to your own who would really like to be interviewed. Is there any chance that he could take your place? Give the friend's name and address, and tell Ms Wright that you will arrange for him to send a CV by recorded delivery today addressed to her personally. (In the meantime she will send him an interview letter.) Don't forget to thank her for her courtesy. One person should play the part of the applicant, and one the parts of the receptionist and the personnel officer. Other students should appraise and criticize their efforts.

Preparing for the interview

Having acknowledged receipt of the interview letter, you must prepare for the interview. Firms usually take a good deal of trouble over interviews, and there may be three or more people present, which can be a little intimidating. Very often the personnel officer will begin by some words of welcome and an invitation to you to tell them a little about yourself. This is really inviting you to repeat the information you have already supplied on the application form, and which they have already read, but it does have some point. It will put you at your ease, because at least you know all about your own level of achievement and can speak about it confidently. It helps them assess your ability to communicate and your self-esteem. Some people have too high an opinion of themselves, some take an unduly pessimistic view of their achievements, while others have a nicely balanced assessment of their own abilities.

These preliminaries also enable them to test you out to a small extent. Thus, if you have weak grades in mathematics, and mathematics is important to them, they may try to find out a little more about you. Do you really dislike mathematics? What is the real reason for the low grades? Try to anticipate what you could be asked about your qualifications. Tell them the facts (not some covered-up version of the facts). Tell them clearly what you are enthusiastic about, what you are hesitant about and any real weak spots. Then if they say that they are really disappointed about your weak spot in one subject, tell them you'll work hard at it to raise your standard. Don't sink into despair, but say you'll do your very best to solve the problem.

They may then ask you one or two general questions, which gives you a chance to show a bit more than mere qualifications. Anticipate these questions before you go to the interview. Take a sheet of paper and write out a possible question and the answer you might make to it. Suppose they say 'You're applying to work for us here at Symonds Electronics. What do you know about the sort of things we do here?' This might be quite a problem, if you know very little about the firm. Find out what you can about the firm – if it is local, go down and have a look at it. Perhaps a receptionist or a security doorman might give you a little help.

Another popular question is 'In what way do you think your services could be of use to us here?' Most young people are so anxious to find a job and solve their own problems that they don't realize that the firm or company is interested in solving its problems, not theirs. They will look more kindly upon your application if you seem to be more interested in them than in yourself. At the very least you can reply that you are hard-working, cheerful, enthusiastic, punctual in attendance and unlikely to be absent.

You should also stress the level of attainment you have reached in certain subjects and that you hope these will prove to be of use to them. Emphasize that you expect some degree of in-house training will be necessary, and you hope to repay this by hard work and conscientious effort. Speak positively, not negatively. Assess your good characteristics and mention them modestly. Don't dwell on your weaknesses, but if they mention them, let them know that you are aware of them, and are doing what you can to overcome them.

It is usual to ask the applicant whether he/she has anything to ask the panel, and although there are some obvious things you do want to know (if they haven't already covered the points), such as the wages or salary payable, the hours of work and perhaps the holiday arrangements, there are other things that make a better impression. For example, almost every business activity leads on to some sort of professional qualification. There is a list of the main professional bodies in the Appendix (p. 385), but there are many very specialized ones that are not listed. If you phrase a question like the one below it may open up a useful train of thought:

I am just a little bit in the dark as to where this post that I'm applying for could eventually lead me. I'd like to carry my education on in my own time once I've started work, and I wonder if you do give any sort of career guidance to employees. Is there a professional qualification that I should aim for, or anything like that?

They won't be able to give you a very clear answer unless you are applying for a position that leads clearly into a particular profession. So many people start off in one direction but eventually find their niche in another area of work. For example, you might start off as a cost clerk but move into the buying department and end up qualifying in the Institute of Purchasing and Supply. Commerce and industry today have dozens of specialist areas, each of which is a lifetime's study in its own right. The point is that asking such a question switches their minds entirely away from your inexperience and naivety. Instead they are already thinking of you as a serious prospect for eventual promotion.

Exercise 15c   With each of these questions write down what you would say in replying to a member of an interview panel:

1   You seem to have done quite well in a range of different subjects. Which subjects do you think are your best subjects? And which subjects would you say are your worst?
2   To some extent we like all new employees to start at the bottom, even though they may be quite well qualified, as you are. How do you think you would react if a certain amount of quite routine, humdrum work was allocated to you in the first few months?
3   We have had cases in the past where well-qualified people have adopted a superior tone when dealing with lower level staff, such as receptionists, porters, shopfloor staff, car-park attendants, etc. What is your own attitude to such staff? Do you think you would be likely to have any difficulties of that sort?
4   We have a no-smoking policy at all times, except in the car parking areas. Is that likely to be a problem to you?
5   The post you are being offered is one where you may, on the firm's behalf, develop devices and systems that will be patented and be a source of major revenue for the firm. The legal position is that what is developed in the firm's time, using the firm's facilities, belongs to the firm and not the employee. Naturally an employee who is particularly successful in such matters gets well rewarded − but do you have any problem with the underlying principle?
6   If you come to work for us, we shall spend, over the course of the years, a great deal of money on training you and teaching

you many things. If you leave us as soon as you are trained and go to some other employer, we have of course wasted a great deal of money. How loyal do you think you are likely to be to the company if we offer you a position?

7　Forgive me for asking this question, but we do have to ask it. Have you at any time been the subject of investigation by the police, or charged with any offence?

8　You are applying for a post that requires you to handle finances. It is usual for employers to ask such people to take out an insurance policy called a fidelity bond. This requires you to fill up a proposal form, which you must answer honestly, and one of the questions asks whether you have ever been charged with an offense about financial matters. It also asks whether you have been made bankrupt in any country. Would you have any objection to completing such a proposal form? I should explain that what this policy means is that if you should at any time abscond with funds, we could claim for the loss, provided the theft had been notified to the police.

9　This does not apply to the post you are applying for at present, but if you gain promotion, it is sometimes helpful if you can drive a car. Do you drive at present? Are you likely to learn to drive a car in the near future?

10　You say you drive a car. Do you have a clean licence?

11　Do you have any family circumstances you wish to reveal to us?

12　Are you disabled in any way? (This does not necessarily affect our ability to offer you employment, but we are obliged by law to employ a certain quota of disabled people and if you do have a registered disability you should reveal it to us for inclusion in our returns to the disablement officer.)

13　Who is your next of kin? (In case of sudden illness, etc., we need to know whom to contact.)

14　It is sometimes necessary to move staff around the country and even to destinations abroad, though we try to limit this to those aged 21 and over. What is your view of such a requirement, given that help with accommodation, moving expenses, etc., would be given?

15　If we offer you employment, do you think you will accept the appointment?

16　If we find we cannot offer you a post at present, we might like to keep you as a reserve candidate. This is because we sometimes get let down by our first choice, and then we might be able to offer the position to you. Would you like to be kept as a reserve candidate or not?

15.8 Acknowledging the letter of appointment (or writing a letter of regret)

A letter of appointment is often couched in terms that constitute an offer of employment, and as such it is always desirable to accept the offer by acknowledging the letter and confirming that you will in fact take up the appointment on the date suggested. In any case it is only courtesy to reply to the letter and express your thanks at this successful conclusion to the application you made, no doubt some time ago. Accepting the offer does of course make a binding contract, but in the United Kingdom a formal contract of employment is not issued at once — a little time is allowed to elapse so that if the employee should terminate the employment fairly quickly, having decided that the work was not what he/she had hoped for, the expense and effort of making out a contract would be saved. Fig.15.8 shows a typical letter acknowledging a letter of appointment, and accepting the appointment.

While it is always good to be offered an appointment, for every

---

T.J. Brown Esq.,   Mary E. Webster
The Personnel Officer,   27 Canary Walk,
Tamarisk Electrical Ltd,   Wildflower Way,
3475 Queensway,   Milton,
Suburbtown,   Beds,
Beds,   BD7 3TU
ST2 1PQ

12 August 19..
My ref: Job application No. 7
Your ref: TJB/DL 10 August 19..

Dear Mr Brown,

<u>Letter of appointment</u>

Thank you very much indeed for this letter of appointment. I confirm that I shall attend on 1 September to take up the appointment as requested. I am most grateful for this opportunity and look forward to working in the Accounts Department very much.

Yours sincerely

Mary E. Webster

Figure 15.8   Acknowledging a letter of appointment

successful applicant there will usually be five disappointed job-seekers, for most 'short-lists' consist of six people. It is possible that you will feel fairly indifferent if you are not accepted, because, on thinking it over, for example, you may have realized that the job wasn't really the one for you. If you do feel very disappointed, it does absolutely no harm (and it only costs a stamp) to tell people how you feel. All sorts of situations arise where the selected applicant gets a better offer, or is prevented from taking up the appointment for some other reason. If you write a dignified letter telling them of your disappointment, they make take you on anyway, and if there is any difficulty over the selected applicant, you will almost certainly get the position. Someone who really wants to work in that situation is worth ten applicants who are indifferent about the job (see Figure 15.9).

15.9 Direct speech and reported speech

Direct speech is a record of what someone actually said, using the exact words he/she used. For example, "The total applications numbered ninety-three", said the Personnel Officer, "of which about eleven were from well-qualified applicants."

Note that the actual words spoken are given in inverted commas, or quotation marks. Sometimes called 'speech marks', the double (" ") or single (' ') forms of quotation mark are used around the words actually spoken. If the actual speech is divided into two parts, as in the above example, the words inserted to show who is speaking are placed between commas, the inverted commas being opened and closed around each part.

In books, inverted commas may be single or double − it depends on the publisher's house style. You are as free as the publisher to adopt your own style. Business firms may lay down a 'house style'.

Reported speech is a report of what was said, but not using the actual words spoken. There are no inverted commas and it is usual for the wording to be changed slightly, e.g. from first person to third person, and from present tense to past tense. Thus the direct speech given as an example above would probably, when changed to indirect speech, (i.e. reported speech) become:

The Personnel Officer said that the number of applicants was ninety-three, of whom about eleven were well-qualified.

Reported speech is important in business English. Supervisors and heads of departments use it when conveying the views of senior staff to lower level staff in their departments. Equally, in reporting the views of shopfloor staff to management reported speech is less personal and of more general impact − less likely to be viewed as

T.J. Brown Esq.,
The Personnel Officer,
Tamarisk Electrical Ltd,
3475 Queensway,
Suburbtown,
Beds,
ST2 1PQ

Mary E. Webster,
27 Canary Walk,
Wildflower Way,
Milton,
Beds,
BD7 3TU

12 August 19..
My ref: Job application No. 7
Your ref: TJB/DL 10 August 19..

Dear Mr Brown,

Post as Trainee Accountant

I cannot tell you how very sad I feel that you are unable to offer me the post as Trainee Accountant. I had such a good interview, and have done so well in my examinations, that I did feel I had every chance of success.

While I appreciate that you must have had a better applicant than me, I wonder if you would keep me on your books as someone who really does want to work for your firm. There is always the chance that the applicant you did select will have other offers and may eventually not accept the appointment. Alternatively, some other vacancy which you could offer me may occur. I really felt at the interview that I could work well in your firm and prove to be a very useful member of your staff.

With apologies for troubling you further.

Mary E Webster

Figure 15.9   A letter that refuses to give up hope.

the complaint of an individual. Reported speech is widely used in passing on messages, such as telephone messages. The important point is to convey what was said accurately, without distortion. The words to be used are to some extent at the choice of the person reporting. For example we might use phrases like:

She requested that ...
He pointed out that ...
He insisted that ...
She very much hoped that ...

Changes when turning direct speech into recorded speech

The following changes may take place.

Changes in nouns and pronouns
Since the person who says the sentence is no longer speaking directly, the pronoun or noun may change from first person to third person. For example: The customer Mrs Jones said, "I should like to be informed of any price changes, please". This piece of direct speech when turned into report speech becomes: The customer said that she would like to be kept informed of any price changes. The pronoun 'I' has turned into 'she'.

"Will you please call in at the bank and bring me a statement of our balance at 5.30 last night?" asked the accountant. This becomes in reported speech: The accountant asked me to call in at the bank and get him a statement of the firm's balance at 5.30 last night. The pronoun 'you' has become 'me' and the pronoun 'me' has become 'him'.

Changes in the tense of verbs
If the original statement is in the present tense, the verb can remain in the present tense when reported. For example, "'I am bringing the cases up now", said the porter' becomes 'The porter says that he is bringing the cases up now'.

However, if the report is changed to any of the past tenses, the verbs in the direct speech must be changed to past tense. "'I checked the dispatch of all loads from the loading bay, and saw that they complied with the documentation", said the foreman' becomes 'The foreman said that he checked the dispatch of all loads from the loading bay and saw that they complied with the documentation'.

Other changes
Often words that denote 'place' and 'time' have to be changed.

- "Do it now", said the transport manager.
- The transport manager told me to do it there and then.

'Now' has turned into 'there and then'.

When questions are reported they turn into statements instead of questions and no longer need a question mark. For example:

- "Do you have your ticket?" his mother asked.
- She asked whether he had his ticket.

Exercise 15d Change the following sentences in direct speech into reported speech:

1   "Not everyone can go", said the director, "because the delivery from Hong Kong is certain to arrive tomorrow."
2   "Do you need some bus fare?" asked the petty cashier.
3   "Our company has always honoured its obligations to the local community", said the Managing Director, "and this footbridge is simply an extension of our concern for local road safety."
4   "Its a fair cop, officer", said the burglar. "I couldn't resist such an easy crib."

Exercise 15e   Change the following sentences in direct speech into indirect speech:

1   "When Her Royal Highness's car approaches the building, please alert Mr Kenningham at once", said the Administration Officer.
2   "Where is the crate for the courier to India?" asked the dispatch clerk.
3   "It was, at the very least, conduct unbecoming a gentleman", said the barrister.
4   "A document in electronic form in the memory of our computer is still a document, in law", said the computer programmer.
5   "Yes", replied the exporter, "but it must be possible for any party who needs the document to access it through EDI."
6   "What's EDI?" whispered the new export clerk.
7   "Electronic data interchange", said the lady supervisor. "Keep your questions until later; this is important."

15.10   More spellings

There are a number of pairs of words that are easily confused, and although there are no spelling rules to help you with them particularly, it is useful to mention them and give their meanings.

assent	=	to agree to
ascent	=	movement upwards
coarse	=	common or inferior
course	=	onward movement, or a series of lectures
desert	=	an arid region of land, or to leave a person or service that has a claim upon you.
dessert	=	the sweet course of a meal.
stationery	=	writing materials
stationary	=	to remain in one place
council	=	an advisory or deliberative assembly.
counsel	=	advice, or a legal adviser (a barrister)
weather	=	atmosphere, conditions prevailing at a particular time

whether	=	a conjunction introducing a statement expressing doubt about the choice of two alternatives.
quite	=	completely or entirely
quiet	=	of a gentle disposition, or undisturbed
their	=	possessive pronoun − belonging to them
they're	=	an abbreviation for 'they are'
there	=	an adverb indicating position.

Now here are some more spellings. Ask a fellow student to test you on the first set and then reciprocate by testing him/her on the second set.

Accountancy		*Production*	
petty	vary	factory	operator
petty cash	variance	manufacture	operation
vouch	variances	manufacturing	cooperate
reconcile	balance	innovation	design
reconciliation	balancing item	invention	designer
conciliation	balance sheet	prototype	designate
cost	budget	search	engine
oncost	budgeted	research	engineer
variable cost	budget officer	develop	engineering
fixed cost	budgetary control	development	engineered

15.11   A summary

Summarize the following article on 'The Marketing of Banking Services', reducing it to about 250 words, which is about one quarter of its present length.

The Marketing of Banking Services

Until quite recently marketing was not a serious concern of the banking community, for it was popularly believed by bankers that the customer would always seek out the banker. This may well be true of the more traditional activities of deposit-taking and lending. Traditionally banks have been reluctant to sell themselves and bankers have often stated that they are not salesmen. In the United Kingdom up to the start of World War II, when it has been estimated that 60 per cent of the population had incomes of less than £100 per year, there was perhaps little market for bankers' services among the mass of the population. The other 40 per cent with 85 per cent of the national income to spend were well able to approach their bankers for whatever services they required.

The gradual change to a more egalitarian society which began about 1850 and reached its high point by 1965 was not noted at first by the banking community. It was the fringe areas of banking, particularly the finance houses which operated in the consumer durables field and in motor finance, that began to market financial services in a new way. The absence of legislation on contractual matters, apart from the Sale of Goods Act 1893, meant that the law still considered the parties to a contract to be of equal strength in negotiation. The use of fine print clauses in standard form contracts meant that hire purchase was a stern business for those determined to use this method of finance to 'buy now, pay later'. Despite this, most people purchased the basic domestic equipment − gas stoves, electric ovens, heating appliances and furniture − by hire purchase. The credit age had dawned.

The situation changed dramatically in the mid-1960s and the pace of bank marketing has accelerated since that time. Some of the factors that led to the changes may be listed as follows:

(a)   The competition from non-bank financial institutions such as the national savings movement and the building societies became more intense as the earnings of lower income groups began to rise. In 1962 the dockers were getting £12 per week; by 1967 it was £33.50. The push to greater equality of incomes broke through the flood barrier.

(b)   The introduction of a giro bank (now National Girobank) in imitation of European girobanks catered for the underbanked sector of the community. This group had formerly scarcely needed banking services, but was now rich enough and sophisticated enough to demand them. A rush to recruit them began.

(c)   Bankers have never been able to compete on price, because any bank offering cheaper loans than other banks soon gets into financial difficulties. This is called 'the need to keep in step', an essential rule for bank lending. The banks had to look for other ways of competing, and the marketing of such services as credit cards was an obvious way to proceed, and had great appeal to the newly banked sector of the community.

(d)   The higher wages and other costs within the banking community itself forced a reappraisal of bank asset utilization. The banks realized that in their enormous branch network they had a huge series of outlets which could and must be exploited if banking costs per cheque cleared were to be kept reasonable.

(e)   The reduction in restrictions on banking activities enabled more competition to be developed, especially as banks moved into non-traditional areas such as mortgage lending, estate agency activities, finance house activities, insurance and pension planning, etc.

(f) Wider publication of financial results and the prohibition of 'hidden reserves' laid banks themselves more open to public comparison on results. It became necessary to do better in financial terms and to be seen to be doing better, and this was a further spur to competition.

(g) Finally the biggest spur of all to greater marketing activities was the growth of other financial intermediaries. In 1955 'banking' meant the clearing banks and the Scottish banks and not much else. Thirty years later there was a heavily government-promoted sector of national savings and National Girobank facilities available; the building societies had grown out of all recognition and were moving into the provision of a wider range of services; the trustee savings banks had been privatized and become very much more like ordinary commercial banks; a plethora of fringe banking institutions was available to broaden the whole area of domestic banking; and a host of foreign and international banks had moved into the City of London and were even competing for ordinary current and deposit accounts.

The banks were faced with an enlarged market place, and needed an enlarged range of banking services (courtesy of *Elements of Banking Made Simple*).

15.12   Figures of speech 4: litotes and meiosis

Litotes and meiosis are two terms that are the opposite of hyperbole (see p. 303). They are understatements for the sake of effect. We might say of a batsman in cricket who scored a double century that he 'had a useful knock'. This is **meiosis**. The schoolboy will be heard declaring a splendid victory at rugby to be 'not bad'. 'I didn't half swear' means 'I swore horribly, I can tell you'; and the soldier sweating profusely under a full pack will describe the day as 'warmish'. They are often described as rhetorical expressions, meaning expressions used to persuade or impress the listener, but with an element of insincerity (in this case understatement) in them.

The special feature of **litotes** is that it uses the negative of an opposite to make an affirmative statement. For example, 'Jones, you are no small liar' means 'Jones, you are a great liar'.

Exercise 5f Identify the figure of speech in each of the following sentences:

1   Despite the heat from the burning warehouse, the maintenance man kept as cool as a cucumber.
2   'Not bad', said the parent, hearing of the boy's gold medal at the Games.
3   'Mathematics may be called the Queen of the Sciences', said the astronomer.
4   A glass fibre cable is the Messenger of the Gods – much faster than Hermes.
5   Then Fury, with flushed cheeks, strikes fiercely, to the detriment of all.
6   'My father, sir, is laid to rest', she sighed.

15.13   Answer section

With *Exercises 15a – 15e* no attempt has been made to give model answers.

Exercise 15f 1   simile; 2   meiosis; 3   hyperbole; 4   metaphor; 5   personification; 6   euphemism.

16
Conferences and functions

16.1　The importance of conferences and functions

As firms grow larger, it becomes more and more difficult to maintain close links with all their various departments. Management must rely more and more on mass communication to motivate the workforce and convey a sense of purpose. With multi-national companies it is necessary to bring in staff from time to time to review procedures, discuss new products, build bridges between multi-ethnic and multi-lingual groups and explain changes of policy and improved methods of work.

A further influence at work is the increasing system of controls that all enterprises face from national and international bodies. Unless staff fully understand the changing environment in which businesses operate, huge fines and even imprisonment of senior managers may result. The fierce penalties being imposed for adverse environmental effects, for misuse of packaging, for spillages of dangerous chemicals, etc., can place a firm's future existence in doubt.

These situations call for a variety of seminars, lectures, conferences and public relations functions aimed at promoting understanding of the law's requirements, the regulations imposed by central and local authorities, and the attitude of the company on many matters relating to the general public and its perception of the firm. Such functions as launching ceremonies for products, books, plays, films and sponsoring activities are pleasant for all concerned. Less enjoyable, but often more essential, are functions held to rebut allegations of malpractice or improper motive in some development, or to forestall criticism of a potential development. Perhaps the biggest functions of all are international conventions held at the very highest level on matters of the greatest significance – such as the laws of the sea, the laws of the air, the global environment, the control of nuclear power, etc.

All such activities take a great deal of organizing and call for communications at all sorts of levels.

16.2 Staffing the conference or function

The success of such an activity depends very largely upon the team appointed to organize it and the backing given to them by top management. It is frequently the case that there are 'too many chiefs and too few Indians'. Many people like to appear on such occasions and be present for the photo-calls. They are less willing to tidy up at the end of the day and stack the chairs. The staffing requirements may be listed as follows:

(a) A conference organizer, at a high level, with the authority to order the seconding to the team of an adequate number of people with the requisite skills, and preferably also with willing, cooperative spirits.

(b) These people then form the conference team, which will sit down and 'think through' everything that is to happen, so that nothing is overlooked; all facilities are booked, purchased or assembled; and the organization is set in train.

(c) Further staff will then be seconded for the actual days of the function. They should not be 'pressed men' (who have been press-ganged into service) but willing, cooperative people who appreciate that it is the work at grass-roots level that is the most important, and who are prepared to arrive early and stay late to see that all goes well.

(d) Certain low-level staff (caretakers, cleaners, canteen staff, etc.) are always needed at such functions, and the success of the event often depends upon their willing cooperation. It is important to keep them cheerfully cooperative by a proper appreciation of their efforts, a reasonably generous overtime allowance and, where necessary, a suitable honorarium. (An honorarium is a payment made to a person who voluntarily does many things that are not actually called for in his/her job description, and a slight increase in the budget to show appreciation of this is justified.)

The conference organizer and his/her personal secretary will be occupied with a wide range of business correspondence and business communication if the event is to be a success. The whole programme must be planned in detail: the right speakers and panels of experts must be found; premises must be booked and facilities ordered; transport, travel, catering and entertainments arranged; and innumerable minor details attended to well before the actual day.

The general pattern of arrangements is for some major speaker to address the whole conference, for the first session of the day, on some vital topic of universal interest. Allowing an hour for this lecture and half an hour for discussion, the conference then usually has a coffee break. The rest of the day may then be spent with people attending a variety of activities according to their specialist interests. Some might be attending lectures, others participating in seminars (small intensive instruction periods on a particular topic) or discussions. Some might be touring exhibitions and talking to exhibitors.

Consider the following subject areas, which the conference organizer and his/her team might discuss at their first meeting.

(a)   The purpose of the conference.
(b)   The possible speakers.
(c)   The topics to be raised at main and subsidiary meetings.
(d)   The possible support staff for speakers. (Every meeting needs a chairperson, and someone else to pass a vote of thanks. A third person will probably be needed at the entrance to each centre of activity to direct people to seats and solve problems − missing equipment, dud light bulbs, etc.)
(e)   The venue, and the dates, and the detailed timing of the activities. Choosing a venue is always a problem. Figure 16.1 tells us about the facilities available at one world-famous university, which is always keen to act as host to conferences and seminars for all manner of professional organizations, learned bodies, etc.
(f)   The charges to be made, the publicity for the event, the enrolment of delegates, etc.
(g)   Hotel arrangements.
(h)   Travel arrangements.
(i)   Canteen facilities.
(j)   Security arrangements.

The list is endless. The reader should now try answering three or four of the following questions. Of course dozens more such exercises would be possible.

Exercise 16a   In all the questions below you are invited to write a letter on the topic concerned to the named individuals (all of whom are entirely imaginary) at an address you have yourself invented. Pretend that you are writing on behalf of your own firm or company, but if you are at an educational establishment, pretend you are writing on behalf of that institution. Just in case, to prevent anyone thinking that the letter was a genuine letter, make the top of your page read 'Educational Exercise Only'.

1   Write to Sir Roland Proudfoot, the Managing Director of Chemeng Products (Wickford) PLC, asking if he would be available to speak on the specialist topic 'Hydrocarbons and the Global Environment'. Give him the date and time and the

UNIVERSITY CENTRE

Granta Place, Mill Lane, Cambridge CB2 1RU. Tel: (0223) 337766
Facsimile (0223) 337745   University network 7766

GWH/ema
22nd April 19..

Mrs G A W Newton
2154 London Road
Asham Peter
York YO27 2DP

Dear Mrs Newton.

Thank you for your recent enquiry regarding the facilities of the University Centre. Since you point out that you are unaware of the Centre itself, I have gone to slightly greater length to give you plenty of details.

The University Centre is situated in the middle of the city, in touch with the quaint charm of the Colleges and the academic centre of the University. The Centre has beautiful riverside views overlooking the river Cam, a feature which has been used to great effect in all the conference rooms. We have available a range of different rooms which would suit your needs, including three large rooms which can accommodate numbers up to 120 in comfort. We can then offer a range of ten meeting rooms for numbers from 10 to 30. Of special interest to you may also be our recently refurbished Mill Lane rooms. Some of these rooms date back to the 16th Century, they have character and many of their original architectural features still remain, yet all the rooms have been designed with the needs of today's modern business in mind.

But rooms are only half the story, to add to these we can offer a range of catering to suit you and your delegates' needs. For lunch or dinner we can accommodate up to 500 people, dependent on your personal requirements. Coupled with this we have a professional conference organiser and staff who will ensure that all your delegates are looked after during your conference, even down to their special dietary needs.

The Centre is a unique venue within the United Kingdom and would be an ideal place to hold a successful conference. The best way to find out more would for you to visit us in the near future so that we can discuss your requirements further.

Yours sincerely

Geoffrey W Hall

Geoffrey W. Hall. M.A. F.H.C.I.M.A. F.B.I.M. F.R.S.H. General Manager & University Catering Adviser.
Telephone (0223) 337768 (direct line).

Figure 16.1 Response to an inquiry about a conference venue (*courtesy of the University Centre, Cambridge, England*)

venue. Ask him what sort of fee would be appropriate, but emphasize that the event hopes to be self-financing and you hope therefore that he will name a reasonable fee. Mention that expenses will be paid as well. Invent such pleasantries as you like to dispose him to view the event favourably.

2   Write to the sales manager of your firm, which wholesales oils and greases, asking him to take the chair at Sir Roland Proudfoot's lecture (see question 1). Ask him to research Sir Roland's background in *Who's Who* and to prepare a 5-minute speech of introduction. In addition, ask him to choose a senior person from his department to give a vote of thanks at the end of the discussion that will follow Sir Roland's talk, and to have at least one other member of his staff ready to ask a question at the start of the discussion if it is slow to get under way. Both these people to be in attendance for the whole of the lecture.

3   Write to the manager of Grand Hotels PLC, asking him for full details of the company's facilities as conference centres. You are chiefly interested in centres in seaside locations, with leisure—pleasure facilities for after-hours use. Your conferences usually have up to 300 delegates, all of whom would need hotel accommodation. Facilities for films, video presentations and overhead projector transparancies would be needed. An evening reception would be necessary at the start of the conference and there would be a banquet on the night before the final session. The conference would close at noon on Friday.

4   Write to the manager of Evening Events Ltd, asking for details of the company's charges for functions. The function you have in mind is the annual dinner of the Happy Wanderers Club — an organization of employees who enjoy rambles and hill-walking. Facilities for music and dancing would be needed. The numbers to be catered for would be between sixty and seventy-five, aged between 25 and 45 years.

5   The managing director feels that the annual representatives' meeting should be made particularly attractive this year by choosing a more exotic location than the usual seaside resort. He therefore proposes that you investigate the possibility of taking the 100 representatives, with spouses, to Sorrento in Italy. Write letters to:

(a)   British Airways to investigate the costs of chartering an aircraft to Naples (and return) for the first week of June.

(b)   To the Royal Hotel at Sorrento asking for details of accommodation, conference facilities and charges for a party of approximately 240 persons in the first week in June. Ask also for the name of a reliable coach company to transport guests from the airport in Naples to Sorrento on arrival, and back again on departure.

6   You are put in charge of the reception area at the start of a convention and the pre-departure farewell arrangements. The former requires the preparation of 'arrival wallets' for each delegate, to be given out on arrival. The wallets are to contain all the things a delegate will need to follow and enjoy all the events, lectures, etc. in the 3-day convention. The latter requires the completion of a questionnaire asking the delegates their opinion of the convention, and the gift to each delegate of a farewell package – and a lot of advertising material. You are asked:

(a)   To sit down and draw up a list of the items that might be needed in the arrival wallets.

(b)   To write to Business Gifts Ltd, which specializes in providing nice gifts for such functions, asking for suggestions – with price lists. Mention that both male and female delegates will be in attendance, and that the price limit dictated by your budget is £15 per delegate.

7   You have been appointed to supervise the provision of hardware required by the lecturers and speakers at a convention. There will be two main lectures a day for 4 days, and eight minor seminars, each half-day, for the first 7 half-days. There are no seminars on the afternoon of the departure day, which closes with a final lecture and a 'round-table' discussion. Draw up a questionnaire to be sent to the many speakers and lecturers, asking them to specify any particular needs they have for their part of the activities, and give them a deadline well before the event to give you a chance to buy, hire or borrow the necessary equipment. Invent such details as you need to make the questionnaire sensible.

16.3   Activities during the event

Imagine you are playing a major part in the organization of a conference – at a relatively low level. Other people of senior grade will be welcoming the chief guests, etc. – you are in the slightly lower but equally worrying position of being the general factotum to whom these senior people will turn when anything goes wrong, or some article or key member of staff is missing. You may even have to step in and play a host or hostess role in case some senior person is taken ill or prevented from playing his/her full part.

It is essential to be well-dressed and well-groomed, with the necessary fund of polite greetings and interesting conversational remarks. The very start of the event is a difficult time, when an information desk needs to be fully manned by a team that is knowledgeable about the event. Many enquiries can be saved by adequate notices showing the disposition of various parts of the function, room numbers, etc. Such notices must be at a height which enables them to be seen above the heads of the crowd standing around in the foyer. Portable direction signposts, which can be labelled to suit the function, can be purchased relatively cheaply and form a permanent asset. Lists of accommodation, groupings for seminars, etc., must be placed at eye level, but the notice indicating their presence (of the 'Which study-group are you in? Please see below!' variety) should be visible above the heads of those studying the lists.

Sets of preparatory notes for staff manning the desk are helpful, especially if they have been gone through beforehand in the run-up to the conference. Insist that subordinates keep you informed of their whereabouts, and equally keep your own superior advised if you have to go off anywhere.

Genuine difficulties may have to be dealt with during the function. Notes should be made of these once they have been resolved, and the record preserved for reference on future occasions, so that they can be anticipated and avoided.

Each part of the programme each day has its own particular arrangements to be made and its succession of deadlines to be met. The provision of 'orders of the day' for each group of employees will facilitate the smooth running of the conference, and you need to be thinking ahead to ensure that all the deadlines are met. Such matters as transport for key personnel; collection of completed documents if orders – or enquiry opportunities – are being received; arrangements for coffee breaks, luncheons, etc., are usually carefully timetabled. Equipment is sometimes moved from room to room during coffee breaks to meet the programme requirements; it must always be checked for efficient operation after such transfers.

Frequently a conference ends with all the delegates meeting for a final session in the main assembly hall. This often takes the form of an 'any questions' session or 'brains trust' of all the major speakers still in attendance. It is a useful way to round off the conference, gives an opportunity for the presentation of bouquets or other gifts to guests, and for passing votes of thanks to groups of people behind the scenes. To prevent such a conclusion falling flat, it is a good idea to prime one or two delegates with appropriate discussion points, designed to remind other delegates of some of the major contributions to the conference made by the main speakers. A request for a clarification or reiteration of some major point gives the speaker concerned an opportunity to summarize his main contribution, and warm up the discussion.

Finally, at the end of the day or days, a great deal of clearing up must take place to leave the premises in a reasonably neat condition. Two tendencies may be observed at such times: the tendency of staff to slope off without playing their fair part in closure procedures and the tendency for valuable equipment to vanish. With regard to the former, a gentle reminder to those concerned with the dismantling operation that they have duties to perform and must not leave until the dismantling operation is completed will save recriminations later. It is a good idea to record these reminders on a pad, so that staff concerned know you have given explicit instructions and there is no excuse for not pulling their fair weight.

The disappearance of property is something that should be prevented at all costs. Nothing is easier when clearing up at exhibitions, etc., than for valuable equipment to be 'collected' by porters, put into vans and whisked away. Such items as display stands, tools, notice-boards, floodlights, chairs, typewriters, etc., are highly pilferable and at risk. All such equipment should be supervised at a central point on the stand, where a deliberate invasion of the firm's territory will be needed if anyone is to make away with it. It should if possible be marked clearly to make it identifiable at a glance, and the serial numbers of machines sent to the exhibition should be taken, so that they are available to the police if required.

Help in the dismantling operations is a great factor in ensuring goodwill and cooperation on future occasions. Since a great deal of the credit for a successful operation quite rightly accrues to the junior management staff, it is nice if these lower down the ladder believe such accolades to be genuinely deserved. It is worthwhile being one of the last to leave, if only to preserve this goodwill, and a quick word of thanks to those still clearing up the residue of equipment is even then desirable.

Exercise 16b   These exercises relate to the organization of a conference that is to be held very shortly:

1   You have been asked to take care of a speaker of the same sex as yourself and to stay with him/her until the time the lecture starts, when your last duty will be to introduce the speaker to the chairperson designated to chair the meeting.

  (a)   Make a list of all the points you think you might need to take care of to ensure that your guest is properly received, etc.
  (b)   Think of ten topics of interest that you might use to cover an awkward moment. Five of them should be to do with your own firm and three more should be about his/her own firm.

2   Write a letter to Conventions Ltd, which sells equipment of use to those organizing a conference, and ask for illustrations and prices of any signposting or labelling equipment for sale or hire. In addition, ask the company whether it can build and

man a small exhibition of books about the conference subject — 'Architecture in the modern world'. The books are to be supplied by three publishers, and you wish the company to handle the arrangements with regard to collection and return of the books.

3 You have a conference area of a main lecture hall and eight seminar rooms. There is also a foyer area to be supervised. You have to make arrangements to cover these areas, using twelve members of staff (six male and six female) other than yourself. Calling your staff Mr A, Mr B, etc. and Miss N, Miss O etc., draw up a plan that will cover the arrangements from 8.30 am to 5.00 pm. Those in charge of seminar rooms should be responsible for all equipment and arrangements in that room, and should keep an eye on adjacent corridors. The foyer should be allocated spare staff, particularly on arrival and during breaks, lunches and at closure. Three of the staff are very young and should not be given major responsibilities but only a supporting role.

4 Draw up a questionnaire to be completed by delegates at the end of a conference on 'Safety in Ports'. The six main speakers are:

(a) The Minister of Transport for the UK.
(b) The Chief Safety Officer, Port of Rotterdam.
(c) The Managing Director, Aberdeen Safety Services Ltd.
(d) The Safety Officer, Port of Galveston, USA.
(e) Officer i/c Port Approaches, Hong Kong.
(f) Chief of Channel Ports, Dunquerque Area.

You want to know: (i) who the delegates are; (ii) whom they represent; (iii) their view of the six main talks; (iv) which seminars they attended; (v) their views of (a) the organizational arrangements, (b) hotel arrangements, (c) catering, (d) travel arrangements; (vi) whether anything that they would have expected to see aired was omitted; and (vii) what they thought of the conference. Was it helpful? Was it value for money? Was it weak in any way?

5 Try this little experiment. Print the words 'To the lecture' with an arrowhead, in lettering 2 centimetres high, 4 centimetres high and 6 centimetres high. Now pin them up in turn on one wall of the room and see how legible they are from the far side of the room. Decide which size is best. Do you need to print even larger? Now try to find how high you need to put them to ensure they are still visible when the room is crowded. At many conferences, notices are too small, too low and insufficient in number. Always save notices used at one conference to use again at a later date.

16.4   Follow-up operations after the conference

There are a wide variety of follow-up operations that are essential to the complete success of a conference or other event. These include such obvious items as letters of thanks to the various speakers, celebrities and distinguished guests. Less obvious, but just as valuable, are letters of appreciation to members of staff who have participated, and this includes very low level staff who have done the really hard work of the function. Sometimes this can be done through a house magazine article on the conference, and the actual naming of staff who participated is desirable. It is also important to ensure that no one is overlooked.

Equipment used should be returned to the appropriate store and a receipt obtained. Useful materials, notices, etc., should be filed away for possible use on some future occasion. Accounts of contractors, lecturers and other bodies should be passed for payment and the final costs compared with the budget. Copies of the final balance sheet should be supplied to the accounts department, the conference organizer and other interested parties. The sales department should be supplied with any names and addresses of interested parties and any other useful results of the function should be passed to appropriate persons.

A final appraisal for your own use, in the form of a review of the function, the way it was organized, the snags that arose, the names and addresses and telephone numbers of firms found to be efficient and helpful, the obstruction met with, etc., is well worthwhile to close the whole procedure. It will prove invaluable next time if this review is read through at the start of the proceedings and a flood of memories, both pleasurable and painful, is recalled to mind.

Exercise 16c

1   Write a letter to Sir Roland Proudfoot (see **Exercise 16a, qu.1**), thanking him for his splendid speech on 'Hydrocarbons and the Global Environment'. Say that the conference was generally agreed to be a great success and much of this was undoubtedly due to the very favourable reaction to his opening lecture. Thank him for waiving any fee, but refer to the cheque enclosed to cover expenses.

2   Write a letter to the members of the team that organized the recent seminar on export documentation and thank them for their efforts. Mention the fact that the sponsors had expressed their pleasure at the smoothness of the arrangements made and HM. Customs had also expressed their belief that it was one of the most useful presentations about the new EC arrangements

they had attended. List the names of all ten members in the 'Copies to ...' section at the end of the letter.

3   Write a short speech to be made to your team at the party given at the end of a week of extremely hard work organizing a Convention. Mention the following items:

(a)   The commendation bestowed by the President of the International Trade Society in his farewell speech to delegates on the organizing committee's work.

(b)   The fact that Mary Bowen, who was slightly injured in an accident when meeting delegates from overseas, is now out of hospital and recuperating.

(c)   The stalwart work done by Harry Smith and his team of porters and messengers in moving the equipment around from room to room.

(d)   Your personal appreciation of everyone's efforts, particulary for the way the final clearing up was done and the orderly way everything was moved back to head office.

Use your imagination to invent such details as seem appropriate.

4   Draft a form to be used as a remittance advice note to be sent to all individuals who are owed sums of money for lectures, expenses or services rendered at a recent function. The form should thank them for their help and refer to the cheque enclosed. It should also list the amounts paid for fees, expenses, other services and equipment hire. It should then give a total. There would be no mention of value added tax.

16.5   Faulty diction

Diction is the wording or phrasing that we use, and therefore 'faulty diction' is incorrect use of words or phrases. In Sheridan's play *The Rivals* a character called Mrs Malaprop shows a great aptitude for misapplying words. At one point she describes her ward as 'as headstrong as an allegory on the banks of the Nile'. It seems her geography was as weak as her diction, for alligators come from the Americas. In another scene she refers to 'a nice derangement of epitaphs' instead of 'a nice arrangement of epithets'. Such errors are called 'solecisms', a word that simply means 'speaking incorrectly'. Her name has moved into the language as a 'malapropism' − the use of one word where another was really intended.

There are many examples of words that are misused, though not all would be outrageous enough to be called malapropisms. Some common examples of misused words are listed below, with short explanations. Some words in the list do have other meanings, but the most common confusions are the ones listed.

'Accept' and 'except'

To accept is 'to take what is offered'. To except is 'to exclude from consideration'.

'Affect' and 'effect'

To affect is to 'produce some material change in', e.g. 'How did your mother's death affect you?' Effect may be a noun, in which case it is the result of the influence that was at work. 'Her death had the most profound effect upon me: my studies suffered and I could not concentrate.' Effect can also be a verb, in which case it means to bring about, or accomplish. 'I shall do my best to effect a real improvement in his work.'

'All right' and 'alright'

The word 'alright' has not yet become acceptable English, although it is frequently used. It is rather similar to 'always' and 'already' in its spelling, and there seems no good reason for rejecting it.

Consider the following two sentences. 'He is the man I saw at the scene of the robbery all right.' 'Is everything all right.' There seems to be a case for saying that the spelling 'alright' would be quite appropriate for the second sentence. However, we'd better not use it just yet.

Some words are called homophones — they have the same sound but different spellings and meanings. Sometimes the sound is not exactly the same, but very close, e.g. 'lose' and 'loose'.

The following are common examples:

'aloud' and 'allowed'
'bought' and 'brought'
'whose' and 'who's'
'formerly' and 'formally'
'know' and 'no'
'has' and 'as'
'his' and 'is'
'wear' and 'where'
'pear' and 'pair'
'sun' and 'son'

16.6   Comprehension exercise

Study the following passage:

The Law Merchant

Trade is older than nationality. For thousands of years ships have plied the oceans and kings have welcomed merchants, and accorded them rights of passage and exemption from local taxes. From the earliest times a sophisticated cosmopolitan crowd of merchants moved around the known world, dealing with one another in ways that were not fettered by legal concepts imposed upon them. Their commercial principles such as 'my word is my bond', 'bethink you of my poor honesty' and 'goodwill' had evolved commercial practices of the greatest importance today: freedom of contract; freedom to transfer property; assignability and negotiability; the seal; stoppage in transit; the bill of exchange; the charterparty; general average — these are almost as old as time.

The law's delay was anathema to the early merchants, who settled cases in their own courts quickly. These were often based in ports, like Lubeck in the Baltic:

What can you want more
Than the old Lubeck law

goes an old German saying. In ports cases were often settled 'between the tides', while in the 'Piepowder courts' at the inland fairs disputes were settled on the last day of the fair. The origin of this name has been suggested as 'dusty feet' — *pieds poudreux*. The judges were senior members of the merchant community, and since disputes were frequently between local people and the foreign merchants, it was usual to have equal numbers of each in the panel who settled cases.

Merchant law was cosmopolitan and uniform wherever trade was conducted. Its privileged system was bound to conflict with the newer concept of a 'nation state' ruled by an autocratic king imposing law from above upon the citizens of his state. The problem was to reconcile the 'law merchant' with the 'common law' of the country, and thus bring the merchants under control without killing the goose that laid the golden eggs.

In England the solution was found in the principle that 'the courts will always uphold the reasonable expectations of business-men'. This principle is sound because it not only supports the existing practices of merchants, but also covers any sensible developments which may be devised. Thus, in the City of London, over the years, new markets have been established in all sorts of commodities and monetary instruments, without any legislative activity. If a market is needed in Sterling Certificates of Deposit, or palm oil, or crude oil, etc., it is only necessary for a body of interested persons to come together, lay down agreed guidelines and start to quote prices, for the market to be established and have the full backing of the law. To the extent that it is reasonable the law will uphold the commercial practices of the merchants.

The law merchant, which during the Middle Ages had become the basis for an expanding commerce throughout the Mediterranean, the Atlantic seaboard and the Baltic, became in the next 300 years an integral part of the law of the separate great trading nations – the English, the French, the Dutch, the Spanish and the Portuguese. In England, for example, by the mid-eighteenth century the Common Law Courts had absorbed almost all the jurisdiction of the local courts merchant, with the exception of maritime law and prize law which was applied in the Maritime Courts. Eventually the whole area of law relating to merchants and traders was absorbed into the common law of England. In the process of absorption by national laws the law merchant lost to some extent its cosmopolitan nature, but in the fields where a conflict of laws between national legal systems was inevitable – in carriage by sea, in international trade, in marine insurance, etc. – there were sufficient threads remaining to settle disputes in peace time, and preserve reasonable behaviour in times of war. Nations had still to behave reasonably if trade was to prosper (courtesy of Business and Commercial Law Made Simple).

Now answer the following questions:

1 Why does the author say that trade is older than nationality?
2 What is the meaning of 'cosmopolitan'?
3 What do you think is the meaning of 'My word is my bond'?
4 Why were the courts at inland fairs called 'piepowder courts'?
5 Why was it necessary to settle cases 'between the tides'?
6 How did English law bring the merchants under its control?
7 You and ten similar businessmen want to set up a market to trade in emeralds. Would it be legal to do so in the United Kingdom?
8 What would you need to do to set up a market in emeralds?
9 Why might there be a 'conflict of laws' in international trade (say between the United Kingdom and Malaysia)?
10 How could such a dispute be settled?

Answers   1   Because trade had been carried on for thousands of years before the new concept of 'the nation state' emerged at the end of the Middle Ages. 2   'Coming from many cities in the world'. 3   It means 'my word is as good as a binding signature on a legal agreement'. 4   Because the people listening to the trials had dusty feet (*pieds poudreux* – French). 5   To miss the tide meant that a delay of 12 hours must occur before the next high tide would float the ship away. 6   It adopted the principle that its judges would always uphold the reasonable expectations of businessmen. This meant that the merchants could not really object to having to come into court. 7 Yes. Anything is legal that is reasonable. 8 Get together with one another, draw up a set of rules and start to quote prices for the different categories and qualities of emeralds. 9 Because the United Kingdom trader might want the case decided under English law, but the Malaysian trader might want the case settled under Malaysian law. 10 Only by the judges of the two countries behaving reasonably, and getting at the truth of what was done.

16.7   Changing to reported speech

The following sentences are in direct speech, exactly as they were made. Turn each sentence into reported speech.

1 "My husband", said Mrs Malaprop, "was the very best oysterman that ever walked the streets of Belfast."
2 "I am arresting you", said PC Thomas to the erratic driver, "and you will be cautioned at the police station."
3 "Management", said the Director General of Fair Trading, "must be as solicitous of the well-being of its customers as it is of its own well-being."
4 "I expect all my drivers to bring me back a clean signature on the delivery note", said the transport manager.
5 "Those of us who travel frequently by air", said His Royal Highness, "know the very great services the airlines provide to commerce and industry."

16.8   More spellings

Here are some words that end in 'our', but when a suffix 'ous' is added, they drop the 'u' in the second syllable:
humour − humorous
valour − valorous
labour − laborious
glamour − glamorous
clamour − clamorous
flavour − flavorous

Now here are some more spelling lists. Ask a fellow student to test you on the first set and then reciprocate by testing him/her on the second set.

Commerce		*Insurance*	
commerce	agent	fire	claim
commercial	broker	life	average
commercialization	factor	accident	premium
trade	capital	actuary	insurable interest
trader	capitalist	loss adjuster	utmost good faith
tradesman	capitalism	underwriter	fidelity bond
wholesale	transport	indemnity	cargo policy
retail	banking	contribution	floating policy
import	insurance	subrogation	open cover
export	communication	proximate cause	proposal form

16.9   Figures of speech 5: synecdoche

Synecdoche is a figure of speech where only a part of a thing is named but the whole of it is understood. Alternatively, the whole of a thing is named, but only a part of it is really meant.

(a)   Fifty Spanish sails heaved themselves over the horizon. (Only the sails were mentioned but the Elizabethan sailors took it there were ships attached to them.)

(b)   Germany defeated England at soccer last night. (Actually − by the rules of the game − there were only eleven representatives of each nation on the field.)

(c)   At the factory gate − 'Hands Wanted'.

A poetic example concerns soldiers on their way to fight in the Boer War:

Fifty thousand horse and foot
Going to Table Bay

16.10   Answer section

No attempt has been made to answer *Exercises 16a, 16b and 16c*, which are mostly in letter form.

17
Technical aids to business communication

17.1 Information technology

To use the term 'information technology' in its widest sense, we would have to start with the humble typewriter and proceed through to the most advanced electronic systems available. These systems can, for example, link a retailer in the United Kingdom with a databank of stolen credit cards in the USA, check that the credit card being tendered by an American tourist has not been stolen and authorize its use for the customer's transaction, and only take six seconds for the whole procedure at a cost of about 5 pence. As 'business English' becomes 'business communication', we need to have some idea of all these services, but a full understanding is difficult to acquire without practical experience. This chapter consists of a number of short accounts of devices available at the time of writing. When setting up in business, it is false economy not to adopt the latest communication systems available. Services are improved and updated regularly, and a call at your local British Telecom or other centre will provide you with demonstrations of all the systems on offer.

17.2 How the telephone system works

When Alexander Graham Bell, a teacher of the deaf, patented the telephone in 1876, he surely could not have dreamed of the revolution he was making in communications, and the effect it would have on the business world in particular. The whole quality of our lives has been transformed by this facility to speak personally and instantaneously to almost anyone else in the world.

It helps our understanding if we know the basic principles on which Bell's telephone worked, and what improvements have recently made an equally dramatic impact on business communication.

Traditional telephone systems are called analogue systems. They work from the waveform created by human speech at one end, which is turned into an electric current with a similar wave pattern. This is transmitted along a wire to the receiver's telephone, where the wave pattern is turned back again into a sound wave that can be picked up by the receiver's ear. The word 'analogue' means 'parallel system very similar to one another'? This is illustrated in Figure 17.1 and explained in the notes below it.

The trouble with the traditional system is that the wave pattern of speech produced at the caller's end becomes weaker and weaker the farther it travels, and distortions in the cables make it difficult to pick out the signal easily, because of background noise. The more

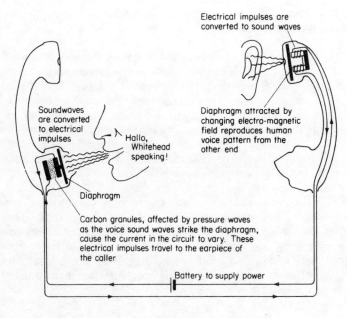

Figure 17.1   The principle of the traditional telephone

Notes
(i)   The human voice makes sound waves that strike the diaphragm of the microphone in the telephone handset.
(ii)   The pressure waves cause the diaphragm alternately to compress and release the carbon granules behind it. This alternately increases and decreases the flow of current in the circuit passing through the telephone network to the earpiece of the receiver's handset.
(iii)   In the earpiece the current is led around an electro-magnet that becomes more or less magnetized as the current varies. The strong current attracts the earpiece diaphragm strongly − the weaker current releases the diaphragm.
(iv)   This movement of the diaphragm imitates the movement of the human voice box miles away, which is causing the current to vary, and we hear the same sounds the speaker is making.

modern system is to send the message in digital form, i.e. as a series of numbers. The two parts of Figure 17.2 show what happens.

17.3   The present telephone system

There is a huge range of equipment now available for telecommunications and it is impossible to describe it all. Most telephone networks are still based on telephone lines with metal conductors, but the big development is to glass-fibre cables. Only one country in the world has a 100 per cent glass-fibre network (Iceland). The advantages are the enormous speed at which messages travel and the clarity of the conversation they make possible. The calls are connected as soon as you dial the last digit, and, for example, a nuisance call can be detected instantaneously.

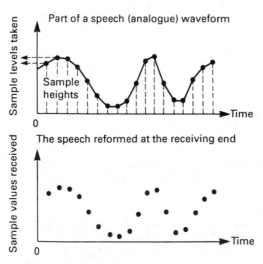

Figure 17.2   Turning an analogue wave into a digital stream of information

Notes
(i)   The original voice pattern can be seen as a wave in the top half of the diagram.
(ii)   The size of the wave can be measured at any given moment by measuring how far it is from the two axes that meet at O. Thus, the position of any part of the wave can be stated by measuring its height above the horizontal axis and its distance from the vertical axis.
(iii) This is actually done every 125 millionths of a second, in other words, 8,000 times every second.
(iv)   If these millions of measurements are then sent over a first-class quality line as a 'bitstream', i.e. a stream of data in computerized form, they can be used to reassemble the wave at its destination so accurately that the speech produced in the earpiece is clear and free of background noise. It is possible to have 'dedicated' phonelines to give top quality reception.

Telephone systems can be as simple or as complex as the user requires. Generally speaking, it is helpful to have a reasonably sophisticated system. Even the sole trader can have one of the latest 'Inphones' − with a number of useful facilities that are 'in' at the time of writing. For example, you may have:

(a) *Last number redial* So often when we call a number, and most numbers have at least nine digits, these days, we find it is engaged. A telephone that remembers the last number dialled, and will redial it on touching a single key, is a great help.

(b) *Number memories* Some phones have four, and some ten memories, where you can record the numbers you most frequently call. They can then be dialled automatically by pressing just two keys to select the number you require.

(c) *Notepad memory* These record a number as you are given it by directory enquiries or some outside caller. When you replace the receiver, the number is ready to dial, and on lifting the receiver and pressing a single key the numbers on the 'notepad' will be dialled automatically.

(d) *Number display* Some phones show a number display of the number dialled. Any mis-dial will be obvious to the sender who can break off the call and start again.

More sophisticated systems

Many firms and companies need a full network of internal and external facilities and a system can be tailormade to fit anyone's needs exactly. Some of the common facilities in use are as follows:

1 *Multi-extension and multi-line systems* We can have as many extensions as we like, and as many lines as we like. A line is an outside link to the general telephone system. Suppose a company has ten outside lines but fifty extensions. Any one of the fifty extensions can obtain an outside line (usually by dialling 9). Of course if all the ten lines were busy, the engaged tone would be heard, but usually one of the lines will be clear. The lines are interconnected so that if one is busy, the call is switched to the next or the next if necessary.

2 *Multi-operator systems* Some systems avoid the need for a telephone operator by switching calls through to any extension. The person who answers the extension can redirect a call from his/her extension to any other extension. In this way everyone is a telephone operator and calls are only one step away from the desired point of contact.

3 *'Follow-me-anywhere' calls* An extension-user is about to leave his/her own desk and go to see a colleague. By keying in the

colleague's number, one can divert an incoming call. Similarly, if the extension-user is leaving the building, calls can be diverted to a secretary or a colleague who has agreed to handle them.

4   *'Hold' keys*   If a caller phones in with a query, it may be helpful to discuss a point with a colleague before answering the query. If the telephone has a 'hold' button, the outside caller will be held on a security line (unable to hear the second conversation taking place). When the point has been resolved, the extension-user can go back to the outside caller and answer the query. This is cheaper than having to ring the caller back, for it is the caller who pays for the call.

5   *'Trunk-call barring'*   Some extensions can be barred from making outside calls altogether, or they may be barred from anything but local calls. This prevents mis-use of the telephone system.

6   *'Call logging'*   Abuse of the telephone system can be prevented by logging all calls, i.e. keeping a written log of all calls made. The general administration officer will then check the print-out to see whether the numbers are business or private numbers, and will instruct the petty cashier to collect the charges from staff who made private calls.

7   *The touch-tone phone*   This electronic telephone offers a wide range of facilities (see Figure 17.3).

8   *The call diversion service* enables you to direct all your calls to another phone number – from home to the office, or to a friend's house. When someone calls they are diverted at once to the revised destination.

9   *The three-way call service* enables you to talk to two callers at the same time, holding one on the line while you check a point with the other, and then enabling you to confirm the point with the first caller straight away.

10   *The call waiting service* lets you know by a discreet bleep on the line when you are talking to a caller that someone else is trying to reach you. By putting the first call on 'hold', you can find out who is trying to reach you and then answer the more important call first. In this way you never miss a call by being engaged.

11   *The charge advice service* enables you to find the charge for a call within a few seconds. Tapping in two digits before you start to dial the call alerts the exchange, and at the end of the call when you put the phone down, the exchange will dial you to tell you the exact charge.

12   *Reminder calls*   Such calls can wake you up in time to catch a flight at the airport.

13   *Code calling*   This gives you a memory at the exchange for all the calls you dial regularly. The touching of two keys only will wake-up the memory, and it will dial the number for you.

Figure 17.3   A Touch-tone phone (*courtesy of British Telecom*)

The videophone

The latest breakthrough in telephone technology is the videophone, equipped with its own camera and 3 inch screen mounted on a fold-up flap. The telephone camera films the caller as he/she makes a call, and relays it to the destination, where the caller appears on the screen. At the same time the person answering at the other end is being videoed and appears on the screen at the caller's end. Naturally, to produce such pictures, a huge stream of data has to be fed down the lines. Figure 17.4 shows an early version of the videophone system.

Telephone answering machines

Telephone answering machines (Figure 17.5) are now relatively cheap (less than £100) and can be purchased from a wide variety of outlets. They do need a special device called a jack to be fitted by telephone engineers, but this is relatively inexpensive. Most machines can now be accessed remotely −, i.e. you can call them from

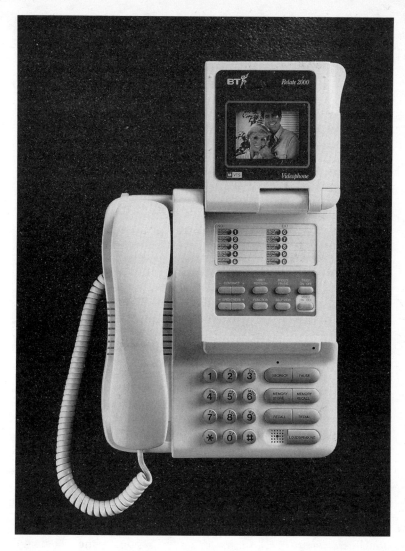

Figure 17.4   The videophone system (*courtesy of British Telecom*)

anywhere in the world and get them to play your messages back to you, though with some models the playback wipes the machine clear and you get one chance to listen to the message. The playback can be voice-activated, i.e. the machine will not play back for other people, only if your voice matches the silence-speech pattern the machine recognizes.

Many people misunderstand the telephone answering machine. 'I

Figure 17.5 A Kingfisher II telephone answering machine (*courtesy of British Telecom*)

won't have one', they say, 'because I don't often get important messages.' This overlooks the fact that what you need to know, usually, is that no one has been trying to get you. If the machine has no message on it, that too is information. You can get down to work straight away, knowing that no one is pressuring you for anything.

One amusing sideline to telephone answering machines is that you need to leave a message on the tape. Of course most people just leave a utilitarian message – 'Sorry, I'm not in at the moment.

Please leave your name and number after the tone and I'll contact you as soon as possible'. Other more inventive souls make up little poems. Here is one for Julius Caesar:

> I came, saw and conquered
> But now I've gone home.
> If you wish, you can reach me
> By contacting Rome;
> Or please leave a message,
> They'll page me 'en route'
> And if I can do so,
> Your troubles I'll shoot.

Readers might like to try (a) composing a tape message for themselves, (b) composing a tape message for some favourite top personality.

Paging devices

A paging device takes its name from the pageboy in nineteenth century hotels who would go through the lobbies calling 'Message for Mr Jones please; Message for Mr Jones'. Today the radio paging device will find anyone within a designated area. There is a **tone page** in which you hear an audible tone to attract your attention. A **silent page**, which is worn on the wrist vibrates to attract your attention. This is useful in hospitals at night, or in noisy situations where the tone page might not be heard. The **display page** and the **message master** give written messages that can be read from a screen, which can be illuminated if lighting is poor. Many small businesses find a paging device a great help. For example, a sole trader (say a plumber) who is out on a job can be kept in touch with a display page or a message master and can go on to an emergency job as soon as possible − rather than ringing back to the office to find out if anyone has phoned in with an emergency request. A message master will take up to ten different messages of thirty characters each. Thus 'Bailey; 10 King St.; pipe burst' would be all that was needed. Figure 17.6 illustrates a Message Master radio pager.

Cordless phones

These are radio-telephones with a very limited range − about 100 metres. They enable a sole trader who is working away from the phone, perhaps in a workshop down the garden or on a smallholding, to take the portable handset away to the workplace. Any incoming call will be transmitted to the portable part, and any number dialled

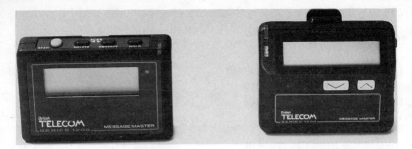

Figure 17.6   A Message Master radio pager (*courtesy of British Telecom*)

Notes
The messages, which are not shown in these illustrations, appear in the rectangular blocks shown white in the photographs.

by the sole trader on the portable part will be transmitted in the opposite direction. There is a paging system so that someone in the house or shop requiring the trader can press a button that will buzz the handset. The handset has a 'last-number-redial' facility and a secrecy button that prevents the caller hearing private discussions. Figure 17.7 illustrates the cordless phone.

Fax machines

A fax machine is a device that scans documents, correspondence, diagrams and photographs, turning them into electronic data that can be sent over the telephone lines to any destination around the world. The term 'fax' is a corruption of 'facsimile', which means exact copy. It takes about 20 seconds to send an A4 page. There are some 12 million fax users around the world. The cost is the same as a phone call, and for those who prefer to wait for the cheap rates an automatic timer enables you to send the message – which is stored in the machine as 'page memory'. One of the problems in export trade is the non-arrival of documents, which prevents goods that have arrived being cleared through customs at destination. When documents are faxed, they are at the destination end in less than a minute, before the goods have even left the port or airport.

Fax can be linked to the 0800 service, which enables a customer to send you an order or enquiry by Fax at your expense. The overseas customer who doesn't like paying for long-distance calls is encouraged by your generosity to do business with you. Figure 17.8 shows the CF50 Compact Fax.

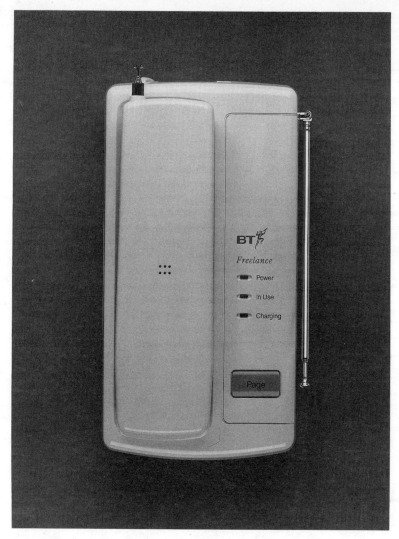

Figure 17.7 A Freeway cordless phone (*courtesy of British Telecom*)

17.4 Comprehension exercise

Here is an account of the early history of the computer. Read it carefully and then answer the questions below it.

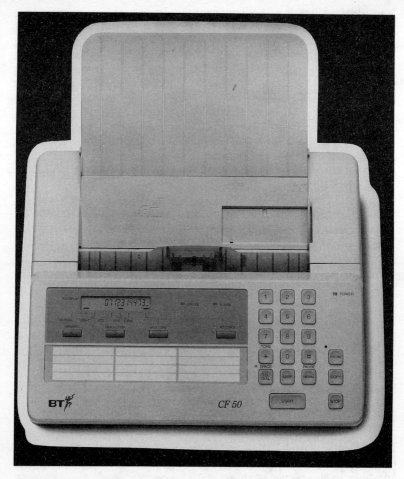

Figure 17.8   A CF50 Compact Fax (*courtesy of British Telecom*)

The early history of computers

The father of modern computing is generally agreed to be the Englishman Charles Babbage, who drew up the concept of an analytical engine in 1833. He conceived the engine as having an *input device* to feed numbers into the machine, a *store* to hold them while they were in it, a *program* of instructions to manipulate them in various ways, a *control unit* to keep the sequence of operations correct, a *mill* to do the actual calculations and *output devices* to put the answers arrived at out to the end-user. He envisaged punched cards and printed outputs as possible methods of making the results available.

Most of the words given in italics above are in common use today, but over a hundred years were to pass before the full implementation of Babbage's ideas. In the meantime a mechanical 'engine' of sorts, the Hollerith Tabulator, had been produced in America to analyse election results, using punched cards and magnetic forces to attract iron rods through the holes to make and break an electrical circuit.

The first generation of real computers was produced in the years leading up to 1950. An essential element in the idea of a computer is that current must be able to flow, or not flow, according to the information which is being processed, because the whole system works using binary arithmetic, which has only two numbers, namely 1 and 0.

We can represent all the numbers in the decimal system and all the characters in the alphabet, using only 1 and 0, by their place value. Just as the number 365 represents 3 hundreds, 6 tens and 5 units in the decimal system, any number can be represented by a place value using 2 instead of 10 as the required figure for moving to a higher position in the system. Thus:

$0 = 0$
$1 = 1$
$2 = 10$ (one two and nothing else)
$3 = 11$ (one two and one more)
$4 = 100$ (one 2^2 and nothing else)
$5 = 101$ (one 2^2 and one more)
$6 = 110$ (one 2^2, one 2 and nothing else)
$7 = 111$ (one 2^2, one 2 and one more)
$8 = 1000$ (one 2^3 and nothing else)

Instead of hundreds, tens and units we have 2^3, 2^2, 2^1 and 2^0 (units). (Those who remember their algebra will remember that anything to the power nothing = 1 (a unit).)

Clearly some numbers in binary form are going to be very long but as the computer works so fast — several hundred million processes in a second — even the largest number can be readily distinguished in a fraction of a second. What an input device does is turn the information supplied in words and figures into binary data which the machine can 'read'. The data are said to be in machine-readable form. The machine obeys the program it has been fed with in order to process the data in binary form. It then delivers the revised data to an output device capable of turning it back into ordinary alphabetical, numerical or graphical form and printing it out, or making it available in some other way, such as on a screen or a film.

The basic elements in the binary system are 1 and 0. One number can be indicated when current is flowing, and the other when current is not able to flow. The original semi-conductor designed to control the flow was the thermonic valve, used in first generation computers. As these required to heat up before current could flow at all, and since thousands of them were needed, computers required special premises, with air conditioning and other devices.

Within twenty years the development was:

(a)   first generation computers with thermionic valves;
(b)   second generation computers with transistors − very small semi-conducting devices the size of a peanut and more efficient than the thermionic valve;
(c)   third generation computers with the semi-conductor activity performed by a silicon chip − a natural product which possessed the semi-conductor property;
(d)   fourth generation computers with VLSI technology (very large scale integration). Integration is a procedure for putting more than one circuit on a silicon chip, and by 1971 the first complete computer on a silicon chip − a microprocessor − had been developed. Fourth generation computers have many silicon chips, each with a microprocessor on it.

As yet there is no fifth generation of computers, though research into robotics (machines which are almost human in their ability to think) may eventually prove to be so distinctive as to merit the name. What we do have at present is a massive expansion of power (more and more capacity packed into the same space) and a huge extension of the use of computers into every field of business activity. The change to user-friendly software, so that everyone can use the computer and the subject is no longer one of mystique for specialist staff, is also an important development. Networking, the interlinking of computers to form a network of data-processing and information facilities accessible on a multi-user basis, is another important feature.

Today the variety of computers is enormous, with lap-top computers that can be used on a journey and are as powerful as the original computers which needed their own air-conditioned premises. The three main classifications are:

(i)   **Mainframe computers**   These are large, sophisticated computers with enormous capacities, able to handle the work of a major government department or public company. Often those who possess such computers act as bureaux for other firms that need data processing, and (for a fee) the mainframe owner will sub-contract to do the work for hundreds of other firms.

(ii)   **Mini-computers**   These are smaller than mainframes, but able to do all the data processing required by most medium-sized firms. Costing between £15,000 and £50,000, these machines are relatively small, robust, easily housed and able to do an enormous amount of work.

Even the biggest organization may find it more flexible and convenient to use two or three mini-computers controlling various sections of its work, rather than a single mainframe.

(iii) **Microcomputers**   These small, relatively inexpensive computers are able to handle all the work required by many small firms, and are also available as personal computers (PCs) for individual clubs, societies and people.

The essential point of computers is that they can carry out their simple functions – reading input data, reading a program of instructions, carrying out the calculations required and putting out the answers in readable form – at simply fantastic speeds, so that the results appear to be instantaneous. In fact they are carried out in logical sequence just like any human calculation; but at a speed of about 700 million calculations a second. Even a complicated calculation, with several hundred different processes, does not take long at such speeds. (Courtesy of John Murray (Publishers) Ltd, from *Success in Management Accounting: An introduction.*)

Exercise 17a   Questions on the passage

1   Who was the father of modern computing?
2   In what year did he lay down the specifications for an 'analytical engine'?
3   How long was it before a successful machine was developed?
4   Explain the part he envisaged that would be played by the following devices:

  (a)   The input device.
  (b)   The program.
  (c)   The mill.
5   (a)   Why does binary arithmetic lend itself to computerization?
  (b)   What would be the binary version of the decimal number 15?
6   What was it that changed with each 'generation' of computers?
7   At what speed does a computer operate?
8   What is meant by the term 'user-friendly' software
9   What is 'networking'?
10   How would the decimal number 13 be represented in binary arithmetic?

17.5 A network of computers

Although a computer has many uses for a business as a stand-alone facility for such records as accounting, stock-keeping, payrolls, etc., it can of course be developed into a more sophisticated communication network. The essential features of a network are illustrated in Figure 17.9. The essential points are the following.

First, the host computer is the central computer, which may be at head office or at a main access point somewhere in the system. For example, an airline which has a computer that may be accessed by many travel agents to book seats on planes will probably base the host computer at the hub airport (the one from which its services radiate).

Second, this host computer has all the main files in computerized form. These may be accessed by any number of remote terminals, all of which are given access (seemingly instantaneous). In fact the human operators keying in a booking, or asking a question, go so slowly compared with the computers' 700 million actions a second that it has time to take them all separately one after the other and yet appear to be instantaneous.

Third, each remote terminal can access the computer for a number of different purposes, e.g. to make an inquiry of some sort, to place an order, to notify a payment received, or for any other purpose for which a program has been written.

Fourth, all data input is validated (checked for corrections so far as the computer can tell). For example, if an account no. was given and the computer did not have an account with that number, it could not accept the entry, which would be returned to the terminal for immediate correction. Perhaps the operator miskeyed. Perhaps the account number on the document was incorrect. Perhaps the whole thing was fraudulent.

Fifth, valid data will be accepted and will be used to update the master file. With some records (said to be on-line) the update can be made at once. For example, with airline or hotel bookings we must update the records at once to reserve the seats and show them as not being available any longer — otherwise we shall have double bookings. On-line communication is instantaneous. With less urgent records — say an order for raw materials — the orders can be queued in an orderly sequence on a memory file (usually a magnetic disc) for off-peak booking when the computer has a spare moment.

Sixth, the updating of master files may simply leave them in a better state for the next day's work, but it may also generate all sorts of records. For example, we might generate orders (for those raw materials, or anything else that has reached its re-order point, as notified to the computer). It may alert people to particular problems (aircraft No. 2704 is due for a major overhaul and must be withdrawn from service). It may generate any number of management

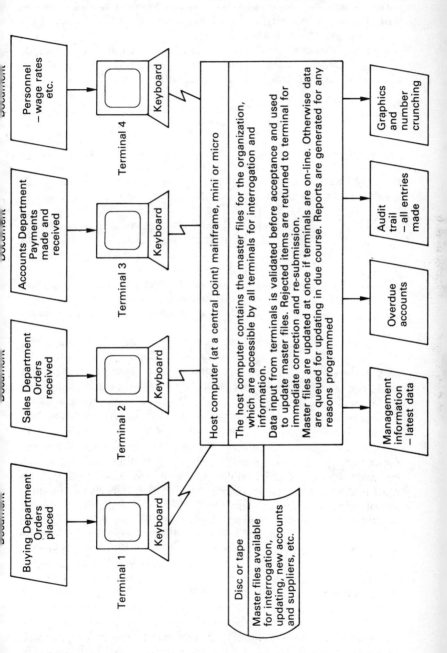

The diagram contains the following labels and text:

Buying Department — Orders placed

Sales Department — Orders received

Accounts Department — Payments made and received

Personnel — wage rates etc.

Terminal 1   Terminal 2   Terminal 3   Terminal 4

Keyboard   Keyboard   Keyboard   Keyboard

Host computer (at a central point) mainframe, mini or micro

The host computer contains the master files for the organization, which are accessible by all terminals for interrogation and information.

Data input from terminals is validated before acceptance and used to update master files. Rejected items are returned to terminal for immediate correction and re-submission.

Master files are updated at once if terminals are on-line. Otherwise data are queued for updating in due course. Reports are generated for any reasons programmed

Disc or tape

Master files available for interrogation, updating, new accounts and suppliers, etc.

Management information – latest data

Overdue accounts

Audit trail – all entries made

Graphics and number crunching

Figure 17.9 A network of terminals around a host computer

reports – sales by volume and value, overdue accounts, etc. It will certainly generate an audit trail – which keeps a record of every entry made – which terminal made the entry, at what time, on which date, and exactly what the entry was.

This is a different kind of business communication from the sort of correspondence mentioned in earlier chapters, but it is a very efficient use of electronic media in all sorts of useful situations.

17.6   A glossary of computer terms

The computer terms listed in the left-hand column are explained (in jumbled order) in the right-hand column. Write down the numbers 1–12 and against each write the letters that give the correct explanation. The answers are given at the end of the exercise.

1	MICR	(a)	A data highway consisting of a number of transmission lines along which data can be moved like passengers seeking to reach a destination.
2	Data processing	(b)	Common Business-orientated Language; a programming language designed to solve a number of business-based problems.
3	Bus	(c)	The location of an item in a computer's memory, so we know where to find it.
4	ROM disc	(d)	Electronic Funds Transfer at the Point of Sale: a system that permits customers to pay for goods at a till, using a bankcard. The till checks that the customer has the necessary funds, which will in due course be transferred from the customer to the retailer.
5	EFTPOS	(e)	Magnetic Ink Character Recognition. A system for machine reading of cheques, paying in slips, etc., at speeds of 2,500 documents per minute. The details are printed on the cheques with magnetic ink, which the cheque-reader can sense to deduct the amount from a debtor's account.
6	Bug	(f)	The automatic performance of operations on data. A program of instructions tells the computer what process to perform: for example, 'Compare T with 300. If T is more than 300 deduct 10% for pension payment'.

7	Key-to-disc	(g)	A storage device to hold programs and data 'off-line' until called for. The backing store is always in machine-readable form, and hence is ready for transfer into the central processor at any time.
8	COBOL	(h)	A typewriter keyboard used by a computer operator to interrogate the computer, or feed in further instructions. It will have a VDU attached to give a visual display of inputs and reponses.
9	Bit	(i)	A system for converting input into machine-readable form. The data are keyed into the disc file by any number of VDU operators, and when complete the data on the disc can be input into the computer very rapidly.
10	Address	(j)	An error in coding, which causes a program to fail. Test runs of programs are essential to eliminate any bugs.
11	Backing storage	(k)	An abbreviation for *binary digit*. Each position (i.e. each place value) is a bit. So 15 (which is 1111 in binary) has 4 bits; 1 unit, 1 two (the second place is a 2), 1 four (the third place is $2^2 = 4$) and 1 eight (the fourth place is $2^3 = 8$).
12	Console	(l)	A read-only-memory disc. Such a disc can be read by the computer user, e.g. it might contain all the drugs for doctors' prescriptions, but it cannot be written to (because the physician would not know the facts to change it in any way).

Answers 1 (e); 2 (f); 3 (a); 4 (l); 5 (d); 6 (j); 7 (i); 8 (b); 9 (k); 10 (c); 11 (g); 12 (h).

17.7 More punctuation

Exercise 17b In the following sets of sentences the only punctuation given is the opening capital letter. Rewrite the sentences giving the full punctuation.

1 (a) You'll be surprised how beautiful venice is
  (b) Its some time since the fax machine interrupted sir george with its clatter

(c)   Are you visiting tokyos royal gardens on your visit she asked

(d)   An outstanding commander he was at one time CIGS field marshal montgomery never lost the common touch which endeared him to the rank and file

(e)   She can declared the prime minister give support to any cause which satisfies Parliaments criteria that the cause is in the interest of a substantial number of her majestys citizens and is not catered for by other legislation

2   (a)   You must be joking

(b)   If you want this further order he said send us a bankers draft by monday and well dispatch it by our tuesday delivery

(c)   Rubbish

(d)   The trouble with that garden centre exclaimed the accountant is that its owner specializes in forget me nots unpaid bills

(e)   Those studying economics can take consolation from this fact that whatever happens in other disciplines economics is king for music literature art and even science cannot flourish without it and neither can education welfare or any other socially desirable policies

17.8   Organization of a business correspondence department

Business is a complex affair. It comprises a multitude of different organizations. They vary in size, and in function, and many solutions to the problems of organizing a business correspondence department are possible. If we call those who initiate the correspondence the 'authors' and those who eventually receive it the 'addressees', we have in between a group who actually arrange the typing of the correspondence. Let us call these the 'word processors'. Sometimes the 'word processors' may be short-circuited, e.g. when e-mail (electronic mail) messages are sent, the 'authors' initiate the messages on their keyboards and the electronic infrastructure ensures that the message reaches the 'addressees'. There is no 'word processor' acting as intermediary, though there may be a technician available if anything goes wrong with the network.

Apart from e-mail, the problem in organizing business correspondence is to ensure that each 'author' has an efficient 'word processor' available at reasonable economic cost. If we consider the problem as size increases, we go through the following stages:

(a)   The sole trader may simply handle everything personally, writing letters, invoices, credit notes, etc., freehand.

(b)   The sole trader may take on a typist/secretary, who (according to qualifications) represents the intermediary 'word processor' between the author and his/her addressees. This link will almost always be better than the sole trader operating unaided. Frequently the secretary is better educated than the 'author' as far as business English is concerned, and consequently the quality of the correspondence, filing, etc., is improved.

(c) As the business grows and other administrators need 'word processors', the cost of secretarial services has to be more carefully considered. Personal secretarial services can rarely be provided for all 'authors', and some system of 'shared' services has to be devised. Questions of priority ratings for some executives or for some classes of work then arise. The departmental secretary can be at a disadvantage if he/she is being pressured for correspondence by too large a number of 'authors'. The alternative to a departmental organization is a central typing pool: perhaps a multi-bank system of tape recorders, with a supervisor allocating the work on a priority basis. Priority may mean not only on timing but also on quality − the work of top executives being done by the best secretaries, while lower priority staff will have to be content with the best efforts of trainee staff.

(d) From time to time a review of secretarial services may become necessary. Such a review may start with the collection from all staff of an extra copy of all material typed during a given period − say 2 weeks. This provides a mass of correspondence, memos, etc., which is in effect the 'raw data' of our investigation. The investigation then requires the following procedures:

(i) Identifying the authors and the nature of the communications they initiate.

(ii) Identifying the addressees, and whether they are internal or external. To which types of correspondence do these addressees respond most favourably? Is an alternative method of approach desirable?

(iii) Finding out what types of equipment are necessary to produce the memos, correspondence and other forms of communication. There needs to be a full evaluation of both the equipment and the methods of making it available to the authors, so that it is effective and yet economic.

(iv) Finding out what numbers, types and quality of staff we need to operate the selected system.

Other aspects of a business correspondence organization

It is usual for senior management to take the view that all correspondence is written on behalf of the firm or company, and that it should therefore show a degree of uniformity in style and layout. To this end, it is usual to proceed as follows:

(a)   Specify a house style – usually in consultation with senior secretaries and supervisory staff in the correspondence field.

(b)   To train (and periodically retrain) all staff who reach 'author' level, so that they know the prescribed style and learn to abide by it. Not all staff who reach 'author' level have mastered correct English usage – they may be good technicians or good salesmen but have a poor command of the written language.

(c)   To reserve the right to change a letter if it is manifestly poorly written, or flouts the agreed house style. While this would only be done at supervisory level, so that an executive who complains is complaining about someone at a responsible level, managements can justly claim that it is their letter really, not the executive's, and they have a perfect right to change it.

Managements usually specify the right to open all correspondence that arrives at the firm or company, irrespective of whether it is marked 'personal' or 'confidential'. This rule will not be strictly observed, it usually being the case that an envelope marked 'personal' would be passed on unopened. However, it does enable a senior manager to say, when passing on the letter, that the management would prefer not to have such letters delivered to the firm unless there are special reasons that have been explained to them. An employee with difficult home circumstances might thus be helped with a problem.

Most advisers to those setting up in business include in their advice 'Open all your letters yourself'. All sorts of criminal activities go on under cover of a firm's name and address. One has only to read the daily press to notice such cases. The sole trader or senior partner who gets in early or collects the mail personally from the local sorting office and opens it all will know everything that is going on. While this cannot be done in a large firm, it is the usual practice to have senior staff from the various departments, armed with date stamps of a different colour, to sit around the table opening the mail – date-stamping both the envelope and the correspondence before putting it into the tray of the member of staff most likely to deal with it. Such matters as the arrival of cheques, registered letters or recorded delivery letters would of course be given particular attention.

One final point is that security routines play a part in this procedure. Before opening mail it is important to scrutinize it for possible letter bombs. Regrettably we live in violent times, when instruments of danger are all too readily available to the political activist, the extremist, the criminal and the mentally unstable. The executive secretary is in the front line of such engagements, for it is precisely the top executive who is usually selected as a target. In the light of their experience in this field the Metropolitan Police of London have issued advice to office staff concerned. The advice is printed in the form of a hang-up card which reads:

Bombs in the Post − Be Alert

Look for the unusual:

Shape	Wrapping	Writing
Size	Grease Marks	Spelling
Thickness	Signs of wires or batteries	Wrong name, title or address
Sealing	Postmark	Unsolicited mail

If you are suspicious:

DON'T
1 Don't try to open it.
2 Don't press, squeeze or prod it.
3 Don't put it in sand or water.
4 Don't put it in a container.
5 Don't let anyone else do any of these.

DO
1 Keep calm.
2 Look for sender's name on back.
3 Check with the sender.
4 Check with the addressee.

STILL THINK YOU'VE GOT ONE?
● Leave it where found.
● Evacuate the room.
● Lock the door and keep the key.
● Send for the Security Officer.
● Phone the police − Dial 999.

This advice is self-explanatory and covers the points which have come to the attention of the Metropolitan Police after dealing with several hundred cases in the last few years.

Exercise 17c   The organization of a correspondence department

1 Draw up a memo from the business administration officer to all staff, asking them to take a copy of all memos, letters and reports produced in the two weeks commencing 15 Feb. These copies are to be coded with the following codes. A = Author's name; WP = the word processor's name; D = Date if not already on the document. All copies are to be enclosed in a file folder and delivered to Mary Haley, the statistician, before

departure each day. A special table will be placed outside her door for the folders. Make a special point of saying that all rejected work is to be enclosed in the folders to give a true picture of the output of individuals. Notes on the reasons for rejection may be marked on the rejected letters if the word processor wishes, but please use red biro for such remarks.

2   Argue the case for the personal secretary as the best system for business correspondence in a medium-sized firm.

3   The head of sales believes a departmental secretarial system is the best for his department. The head of business administration is in favour of a centralized dictation system. What arguments might each submit in support of his/her point of view, and against the other system. Write your answer as a conversation between the two.

4   'This word processor system not only provides the operator with an excellent system for producing top quality correspondence, but it also counts up the number of pieces of work performed by the operator.' Give reasons why an operator might, or might not, be happy at the introduction of the new word processor.

5   List the points about correspondence that might be made in a document specifying a 'house style' for a growing limited company.

17.9   More spellings

Sometimes it helps our spelling if we group together words which have similar beginnings, or similar endings, even if they have little similarity of meaning. For example, magnify, identify, horrify, falsify, justify, pacify, satisfy, sanctify, solidify.

The suffix 'fy' usually takes an 'i' in front of it and means 'to make' − so 'identify' means 'to make out the identity of' and 'sanctify' means 'to make saintly', etc.

Similarly there are many words ending in 'ness', such as keenness, greenness, goodness, suddenness, bitterness. In each case the suffix 'ness' makes a noun out of an adjective − to give a name to a condition. Thus a bitter drink shows the quality of bitterness, and a keen worker shows the quality of keenness. Notice that if the adjective ends in 'n' we have a double letter in the noun, e.g. 'green' becomes 'greenness'.

Now, here are two more sets of spellings. Ask a fellow student to test you on the first set and then reciprocate by testing him/her on the second set.

Purchasing		*Commerce*	
materials	stocks	markets	ring trading
consumables	inventory	futures	open outcry
assets	stores	hedges	private treaty

supplies	acquisition	charter	actuals
supppliers	delivery	charterer	contango
supply	inspection	charterparty	backwardation

investigation	physical	tramps	option
analysis	distribution	liners	margin
approval	management	tankers	deposit
negotiation	logistics	bulk-carriers	premium

Here are two final sets of spellings. Ask a fellow student to test you on the first set and then reciprocate by testing him/her on the second set.

Management		*Premises*	
manage	function	offices	design
manager	functional	factories	construction
management	functionary	warehouses	layout

director	object	finance	conservation
executive	objection	mortgages	insulation
official	objective	grants	conversion

delegate	techniques	survey	foreclose
delegation	principles	surveyor	foreclosure
command	theory	structure	repossession
hierarchy	practice	structural	eviction

17.10 Answer section

Exercise 17a   1   Charles Babbage. 2   1833. 3   120 years approximately. 4(a)   The input device would feed numbers into the machine; (b) the program would instruct the machine how to manipulate the inputs, (c) the mill would do the actual calculations. 5(a)   It reduces all numbers and letters to a pattern of numbers based on 1 and 0; (b) 15 would become 1 1 1 1. 6   The type of semi-conductor used. 7   About 700 million operations per second. 8   Software that keeps the user informed about what is happening and invites him/her to carry out the next activity required. It may also prevent the user from making mistakes, e.g. by asking 'Are you sure?' questions. 9   Networking is the linking of terminals and other computers to a central (host) computer, and to shared facilities such as printers. 10   13 would become 1101.

Exercise 17b

1 (a) You'll be surprised how beautiful Venice is.
   (b) It's some time since the fax machine interrupted Sir George with its clatter.
   (c) "Are you visiting Tokyo's Royal Gardens on your visit?" she asked.
   (d) An outstanding commander − he was at one time the CIGS − Field-Marshal Montgomery never lost the common touch which endeared him to the rank-and-file.
   (e) "She can", declared the Prime Minister, "give support to any cause which satisfies Parliament's criteria − that the cause is in the interest of a substantial number of Her Majesty's citizens and is not catered for by other legislation."

2 (a) "You must be joking!"
   (b) "If you want this further order", he said, "send us a banker's draft by Monday and we'll dispatch it by our Tuesday delivery."
   (c) "Rubbish!"
   (d) "The trouble with that garden centre", exclaimed the accountant, "is that its owner specializes in forget-me-nots; unpaid bills!"
   (e)
       Those studying Economics can take consolation from this fact; that whatever happens in other disciplines Economics is king; for music, literature, art and even science cannot flourish without it, and neither can education, welfare or any other socially desirable policies.

Exercise 17c   No answers provided for these essay-type questions.

Appendix: Professional bodies

Those studying business English should know that in many vocations the fullest recognition is only accorded to those who have gone through various levels of education and then become members of the professional organization representing the industry or profession in which they actually put their skills and expertise to work. It is essential to enrol at the appropriate point as a student of whichever professional body is best for you, and to 'qualify' with them. The word 'qualify' is quoted because it means not only that you must pass the necessary examinations, but you must acquire the necessary practical experience by working in the industry or profession. Thus, it is possible to acquire academic qualifications that bear upon transport and distribution, for example, but still to be hopelessly lost when faced with a practical freight-forwarding problem. Only membership of the Institute of Freight Forwarders or the Chartered Institute of Transport, or some similar professional body, will give the necessary knowledge and status in the industry or profession of your choice.

Let us assume that some readers of this book are aged 16, some are in the 16−19 age group, some are undergraduates expecting to get their degrees shortly, and others are mature middle management staff brushing up their English to improve their ability to cope with increased workloads in the administrative field. All these groups can apply to join their professional bodies, but they will join at different levels, taking exemption for any subjects they have already studied and pursuing the rest to achieve full qualification. They will also be registering with the institute what degree of practical experience they already have, and building on that from the date of enrolment as the years pass.

It is hoped that the following list will help readers locate the professional body most appropriate to their field of activity. The list is up to date at the time of going to press, but addresses and telephone numbers of course may change.

Your aim should be to obtain full qualifications in the professional body of your choice, after concluding any academic course you are presently embarked on. For those in employment already, and not possessing the necessary qualifications for entry to a professional body, guidance will usually be given about subjects to study. The **Made Simple** series contains most of the books you will need, and 6–12 months' study is usually enough to qualify for student entry. Write well in advance to educational bodies whose examinations you wish to sit, so as not to miss vital deadlines for entry.

A businesslike approach to such studies is essential. Buy the books, and enrol on courses in your own locality if you can; if not, study hard on your own and work systematically.

Professional bodies whose names and addresses are not included in the list are invited to submit details for inclusion at the next edition. The author apologizes in advance for any such omissions. Mention of this textbook as a set book for students, or as a 'recommended-reading' book, would be appreciated.

Professional bodies

Acronym	Name of institution	Address and telephone number
AAT	Association of Accounting Technicians	154 Clerkenwell Road, London, EC1R 5AD. (071) 837 8600
ABE	Association of Business Executives	William House, Worple Rd, London, SW19 4DD. (081) 879 1973
ACCA	Chartered Association of Certified Accountants	29 Lincoln's Inn Fields, London, WC2A 3EE. (071) 242 6855
CA	Institute of Chartered Accountants in England and Wales	Moorgate Place, London, EC2P 2BJ. (071) 628 7060
CAM	Communications, Advertising and Marketing Educational Foundation	Abford House, 15 Wilton Road, London, SW1 1NJ. (071) 828 7506
CBSI	Chartered Building Society Institute	19 Baldock Street, Ware, Herts, SG12 9DH. (0920) 465051

CIB	Chartered Institute of Bankers	Emmanuel House, Burgate Lane, Canterbury, Kent, CT1 2XJ. (0227) 762600
CII	Chartered Insurance Institute	31 Hillcrest Road, London, E18 2JP. (081) 530 6242
CIMA	Chartered Institute of Management Accountants	63 Portland Place, London, W1N 4AB. (071) 637 2311
CIM	Chartered Institute of Marketing	Moor Hall, Cookham, Maidenhead, Berkshire, SL6 9QH. (06285) 24922
CIPFA	Chartered Institute of Public Finance and Accountancy	3 Robert Street, London, WC2N 6BH. (071) 895 8823
CIT	Chartered Institute of Transport	80 Portland Place, London, W1N 4DP. (071) 636 9952
CLE	Council of Legal Education	Inns of Court School of Law, 4 Gray's Inn Road, London, WC1R 4AJ. (071) 404 5787
FOA	Faculty of Actuaries	23 St Andrews Square, Edinburgh, EH2 1AQ. (031) 557 1575
HCIMA	Hotel, Catering and Institutional Management Association	191 Trinity Road, London, SW17 7HN. (071) 627 4251
IAM	Institute of Administrative Management	40 Chatsworth Parade, Petts Wood, Orpington, Kent. (0689) 875555
IAS	Institute of Agricultural Secretaries	NAC Stoneleigh, Kenilworth, Warwickshire, CV8 2LZ. (0203) 696592

Acronym	Name of institution	Address and telephone number
ICM	Institute of Commercial Management	PO Box 125, Bournemouth, Dorset, BH2 6JH. (0202) 290999
ICOMA	The Institute of Company Accountants	40 Tyndalls Park Road, Bristol, BS8 1PL. (0272) 738 261
ICS	Institute of Chartered Shipbrokers	3 Gracechurch Street, London, EC3V 0AT. (071) 283 1361
ICSA	Institute of Chartered Secretaries and Administrators	16 Park Crescent, London, W1N 4AH. (071) 580 4741
BIFA and IFF	British International Freight Association and Institute of Freight Forwarders,	Redfern House, Browells Lane, Feltham, Middlesex, TW13 7EP. (081) 844 2266
IHSM	Institute of Health Service Management,	75 Portland Place, London, W1N 4AN. (071) 580 5041
IMS	Institute of Management Services	1 Cecil Court, London Road, Enfield, Middlesex, EN2 6DD. (081) 363 7452
IOA	Institute of Actuaries	Staple Inn Hall, High Holborn, London, WCIV 7QJ. (071) 242 0106
IOTA	Institute of Transport Administration	32 Palmerston Road, Southampton, SO1 1LL. (0703) 631380
IOX	Institute of Export	Export House, 64 Clifton Street, London, EC2A 4HB. (071) 247 9812

IPM	Institute of Personnel Management	IPM House, Camp Road, Wimbledon, London, SW19 4UX. (081) 946 9100
IPS	Institute of Purchasing & Supply	Easton House, Easton on the Hill, Stamford, Lincs, P69 3NZ. (0780) 56777
IQPS	Institute of Qualified Private Secretaries	126 Farnham Road, Slough, Bucks, SL1 4XA. (0753) 522395
IRTE	Institute of Road Transport Engineers	1 Cromwell Place, Kensington, London, SW7 2JF. (071) 589 3744
MRS	Market Research Society	175 Oxford Street, London, W1R 1TA. (071) 439 2585
NEBSM	National Examining Board in Supervisory Management,	76 Portland Place, London, W1N 4AA. (071) 278 2468

Index